Poor and Homeless in the Sunshine State

Poor and Homeless
in the
Sunshine State

Down and Out in Theme Park Nation

James D. Wright
Amy M. Donley

Transaction Publishers
New Brunswick (U.S.A.) and London (U.K.)

Library of Congress Catalog Number: 2010043864
ISBN: 978-1-4128-4221-1
Printed in the United States of America

Library of Congress Cataloging-in-Publication Data

Wright, James D.
    Poor and homeless in the Sunshine State : down and out in theme park nation / James D. Wright and Amy M. Donley.
        p. cm.
    Includes bibliographical references and index.
    ISBN 978-1-4128-4221-1
        1. Poverty--Florida. 2. Homelessness--Florida. 3. Florida--Economic conditions--21st century. 4. Florida--Social conditions--21st century. I. Donley, Amy M. II. Title.

HC107.F63P627 2011
362.509759--dc22

2010043864

Dedication

To our spouses and children:
Alexis, Bryn, Chris, Derek, Jason, and Matthew,
the living, breathing proof that family is shelter for the soul.

Contents

Acknowledgements

Much of the work reported in the following pages involved faculty and student collaborators from the UCF Department of Sociology. Where appropriate, we have acknowledged these collaborations by denoting our fellow travelers as co-authors of the various chapters, both in the table of contents and in the endnotes appended to chapter titles. A special note of gratitude is due Lindsey Singer, whose assistance was invaluable in preparing the index. Most of the research reported here is based on studies we have done through the auspices and in the facilities of the Coalition for the Homeless of Central Florida, and while much of this work has been in the service of the Coalition and its information needs, some of it was made possible by the willingness of the Coalition to let us scratch where we itched. The two Coalition CEOs under which we have done this work, Robert Brown and Brent Trotter, and their respective Directors of Program Services, Jose Irizarry and Daune Brittlebank, have always been gracious and accommodating hosts, even when our projects brought a dozen or more people under foot. The Coalition staff at all levels has also been delightful to work with over the years.

Numerous people have taken the trouble to review earlier versions of these chapters and make innumerable suggestions for improvement, nearly all of which we have followed. We are pleased to extend our thanks for this assistance to David Raymond, Cathy Jackson, Jean Worrall, Jana Jasinski, Ray Nelson, and several anonymous reviewers. Our friends at Transaction Publishing have also been wonderfully encouraging and tough-minded critics. Special thanks to Mary Curtis and Irving Louis Horowitz for everything they have done, not just for us but for the social sciences as a whole.

Our research has been financially supported by a number of local government agencies, non-profit organizations, and public-private entities, among them Workforce Central Florida, the Heart of Florida United Way, Orange County Government, the UCF Metropolitan Center for Regional Studies, Metroplan Orlando, the Coalition for the Homeless of Central

Florida, the Homeless Services Network, the Central Florida Commission on the Homeless, the Orange County Department of Housing and Community Development, the UCF Institute for Social and Behavioral Sciences, and the Miami-Dade County Homeless Trust. It is an honor to acknowledge the support of these organizations and the people who lead them, even as we hasten to absolve them of any responsibility for such errors of omission or commission that the following may still contain.

1

In the Shadow of the Mouse: Central Florida as Myth, Metaphor, and Reality

October 1, 1971, the day Walt Disney World opened, was a signal day in the history of Central Florida. The opening was the culmination of eight years of legal machinations, land acquisition, engineering (or as we now say, "imagineering"), and construction. In those eight years, Disney purchased, mostly through dummy corporations, 27,400 acres of land (about forty-three square miles) in the southwestern part of Orange County, Florida. Once Disney World opened, Orange County and its principal city, Orlando, were transformed, more or less instantly, from a regional backwater economy based largely on citrus, cotton, and cattle into a major national and international tourist destination. Today, nearly fifty million people visit one of the Disney theme parks each year. With total employment near 66,000 employees, Walt Disney World in Orlando is the largest single-site employer in the United States (Koenig 2007; Foglesong 2003).

Disney was soon followed by a succession of other Orlando-area theme parks and tourist attractions ("like bees to honey," as Foglesong [2003: 3] puts it): Sea World, Universal Studios, Busch Gardens (in Tampa), the Kennedy Space Center Visitors Complex, the Holy Land Experience (a Biblically-themed attraction). These are the survivors, the parks and attractions that are still with us. Quite a number of others have come and gone: Circus World (opened 1973, closed 1986); Splendid China (opened 1993, closed 2003); Boardwalk and Baseball (opened 1987, closed 1990); the Guinness World Record Experience (opened 2000, closed 2002); Stars Hall of Fame (opened 1975, closed 1984), and on through quite a list.[1] To all the above, add scores of water parks, miniature golf courses, bowling alleys, wax museums, dinner theaters and related "attractions," plus all the hotels and motels required to house the influx of tourists, plus all the restaurants to feed them once their frolics are over, plus all the rental car agencies so visitors could get from airport to hotel to theme park and back again, plus all the churches where the pious could seek redemption for their theme-park excesses, plus all the roads and highways necessary to connect the dots and you end up with a pretty big chunk of economic activity. A wag once remarked that the entire post-1971 economy of Central Florida seems to have developed solely to provide an answer to the question, "So, what are we going to do the day after we do Disney?" To a significant extent, that remains the major economic driver in the region.

Disney itself has also expanded dramatically since the Magic Kingdom opened in 1971. In the years since, the mega-park has added Epcot Center (1982), Typhoon Lagoon, the first of what are now several on-property water parks (1988), MGM Studios (1989), Pleasure Island and Downtown Disney (1989), the Disney Wide World of Sports complex, complete with baseball diamonds, a track-and-field venue, and tennis facilities, the Richard Petty Driving Experience on Disney's own mile and a half race track (1997), and the fourth complete theme park, Animal Kingdom (1998), along with numerous resort hotels. Between the four theme parks, multiple water parks, assorted miniature golf courses, regular golf courses, movies theaters, restaurants, and countless other activities and attractions, the Disney visitor need never leave "the property," and in fact is encouraged not to do so. One thing you absolutely cannot do at Walt Disney World is rent a car that you could use to get somewhere else.

Disney-related tourism and employment stimulated rapid population growth. In 1950, Orlando was a sleepy little city of 52,000 people. By 1970, just before Disney's opening, it was nearly 100,000 people. Growth thereafter was steady and predictable: 128,000 by 1980, 165,000 in 1990, and almost 230,000 by 2007. Growth in the surrounding county was sharper still: a mere 115,000 in 1950 and well more than a million today. Between 1990 and 2000, the Orange County population grew at a rate of 32.3 percent, the fastest growing county in Florida and one of the fastest growing in the entire nation (data from the U.S. Census Bureau, various years).

Population growth at this rate and scale demands housing and infrastructure—lots of it, in a hurry. Regional developers were quick to respond and very rapidly created a booming secondary economy based on construction—homes to house new arrivals, strip malls to cater to their needs, schools to educate their children, and highways, streets and roads to get everyone from place to place. Tourism and construction soon became the new base of the Orlando regional economy, displacing the orange groves, cotton fields, and cattle ranches that had previously been the region's economic life blood.

Central Florida as Myth

"When people tell the story of Orlando's stunning transformation from swamp and sinkhole to 21st century metropolis, they begin, inevitably, with the man and the mouse. The mouse is Mickey, the man Walt Disney" (Allman 2007: 1). And surely, it is Walt and Mickey and all they created that have given us the *myth* of Central Florida, a myth whose central theme is "The Happiest Place on Earth."

The Happiest Place on Earth (originally a marketing slogan developed for Disneyland in Southern California, but now used to describe all things Disney) is by no means the only slogan to have been used in marketing Disney's brand over the years. At the various Disney installations around the world, for instance, 2006 was the Year of a Million Dreams. (Interestingly, the Year of a Million Dreams promotion began October 1, 2006 and ended December 31, 2008—so it was about twenty-six months of a million dreams, but never mind.) Other park slogans have included Where Dreams Come True, Where Friends Share the Magic, Where the Party Never Ends, and Where the Magic Began, but none of these have the immediate appeal or the staying power of the Happiest Place on Earth.[2]

The Happiest Place on Earth would be a tall order for any community, what with crime, pollution, poverty, homelessness, and all, but in Central Florida, the Happiest Place on Earth is just the beginning. The region's principal city, Orlando, is the City Beautiful and Florida itself is the Sunshine State. Happy people, beautiful city, warm sunshine—Eden on Earth! Add in a big helping of magnificent sprawling homes near verdant rolling golf courses in spectacular gated communities with screened-in swimming pools in every backyard and it is easy to understand why the region has been among the fastest growing in the nation for years. In a focus group we did in Osceola County in 2008 (the southern-most of the counties in the Central Florida region which abuts Disney's property), one local referred to the region's drawing power as "Pixie Dust." When asked to explain, our participant remarked that people come to Central Florida on vacation, become enchanted with their Disney experience to the point where they come to believe that Disney life *is* Central Florida's real life, then uproot themselves and move to the region only to discover that it is all a mirage—a wonderful, upbeat, glorious fantasy enjoyed by children of all ages, but a fantasy nonetheless.

Regional planners and policy-makers, perhaps taking the Central Florida myth a bit too literally, assumed until quite recently that the area's unparalleled growth would continue forever, and with it, presumably, the economic boom times that growth propels. As Andrew Ross (1999) has said, "Keep the World Coming to Florida" has forever been the state's calling card. A much-discussed local planning report, known as the "How Shall We Grow?" report (originally released in 2007), projected a population of 2,162,000 in Orange County by 2030, and a total regional (seven-county) population of just over seven million.[3] The planning problem, basically, was where to house and how to transport all those people and the economic activity they would generate over the next twenty-five years. The thought that the Happy, Beautiful, Sunny Central Florida Growth Machine (Molotch 1976) might grind to a halt seems not to have occurred to anyone until quite recently.

Nearly all the region's movers and shakers, then and now, have been consumed by the Disney-esque vision: "To all who come to this happy place: welcome … . Here age relives fond memories of the past … and here youth may savor the challenge and promise of the future." This is a passage from Walt Disney's dedication speech at Disneyland in Anaheim, CA, July, 1955, but could just as easily stand as Central Florida's regional anthem, something one can easily imagine Orlando's fifth-grade boys and girls solemnly reciting during their morning devotionals.

The apotheosis of the myth of Central Florida is the Disney-inspired, Disney-owned, Disney-built town of Celebration, just south of Walt Disney World and clearly built to give Central Floridians the opportunity "of living, and dying, on Disney land" (Ross 1999: 2). Persons accustomed to conventional urban or even suburban living would describe Celebration as a small town that looks and feels like it was sent up from Central Casting. Built on the principles of the New Urbanism appropriately Imagineered, Celebration consists of about 1100 prim houses and townhomes all neatly arranged on broad boulevards that sweep gracefully to Celebration Place, a hundred-acre "business district" that houses the town's commercial enterprises, all of them within an easy walk of every occupied home—and most of them, frankly, useless to average Celebration homeowners who complain that they have a very convenient monogramming store right downtown (Confetti, "a full service monogramming store"), a Lollipop Cottage (children's designer clothing boutique), numerous galleries and frame shops, and even a gourmet food store, but no Target, no large supermarket, not even a Home Depot, none of these being quite cute enough to warrant space in downtown Celebration. That the place was devised by the guy who originally thought up Never Never Land says a great deal, as does the town's official slogan: "You've got to see this place!" Indeed, you do—as Ross (1999), Frantz and Collings (2000), Mannheim (2003) and many other Celebration commentators make clear.

One story that circulates about Celebration is that when homes there first went up for sale (the original homebuyers were chosen by lottery, incidentally), the developers hired young boys to sit by the central lake (an artificial lake, of course) with fishing poles in hand and lines in the water, just to drive home the Norman Rockwellian serenity and nostalgia that residents could expect to encounter there. Whether this is true or not is hardly the point. It surely could be true, and that says everything that needs to be said. Another story, definitely true, is that there is a restriction in every deed stipulating that the owner must pay a monthly fee to the official landscape maintenance company, Celebration's way of assuring that all adjacent lawns are mowed at the same time and to the same height to prevent any unsightly yard-to-yard variation in grass length. (True!) House colors are chosen from a common palette; landscape plantings must be approved by a central landscape planning committee. It certainly wouldn't do—not in Celebration, anyway—for the roses in front of one house to clash with the gladiolus in front of another.

Census 2000 data on Celebration reveal it to be, as expected, a small homogeneous town of 2700 people living in 1100 housing units, 94 percent of the residents white, 96 percent of them not poor. In 2000, the median value of single-family owner occupied homes was just under $400,000 and the median annual family income was just less than $100,000 (about twice the U.S. average at that time). Happy, beautiful, sunny—*and* well-to-do and white.

Nothing expresses the myth of Central Florida quite so poignantly as the lyrics to the Disney classic, "When You Wish Upon a Star." The song was introduced in the 1940 Disney movie *Pinocchio* and is sung by Jiminy Cricket over the opening credits and in the film's final scene. For those whose recall of Disney trivia is uncertain, the lyrics follow:

When you wish upon a star
Makes no difference who you are

Anything your heart desires
Will come to you

If your heart is in your dream
No request is too extreme
When you wish upon a star
As dreamers do

Fate is kind
She brings to those who love
The sweet fulfillment of
Their secret longing

Like a bolt out of the blue
Fate steps in and sees you through
When you wish upon a star
Your dreams come true

Like Disney World itself and the region now so entirely engulfed in the Disney mythos, the song expresses the boundless optimism that fate (the stars) will be forever kind, that anything you need or want will come to you, that wishes and dreams make everything possible. The happiest place on earth, indeed.

Central Florida as Metaphor

Central Florida has also evolved into a *metaphor* for the twenty-first century post-industrial city: a vast, sprawling, congested, unplanned, overbuilt, environmentally indifferent growth machine that has created a few thousand square miles of metro-area suburbs with practically no urb at the center. The recent National Geographic article on Central Florida, "Beyond Disney" (Allman 2007: 1) describes the metaphor of Central Florida in lyrical terms:

> Everything happening to America today is happening here, and it's far removed from the cookie cutter suburbanization of life a generation ago. The Orlando region has become Exhibit A for the ascendant power of our cities' exurbs: blobby coalescences of look-alike, overnight, amoeba-like concentrations of population far from city centers. These huge, sprawling communities are where more and more Americans choose to be, the place where job growth is fastest, home building is briskest, and malls and mega-churches are multiplying as newcomers keep on coming. Who are all these people? They're you, they're me.

Andrew Ross says that "the damage wrought by thirty [now forty] years of this kind of market-driven development, propelled by short-term profit and asleep-at-the-wheel planning, is painfully evident on all sides" (1999: 7). And so it is. Orlando, the region's "central city," has a current population of 222,000, roughly the eighty-second largest U.S.

city. The Orlando Metropolitan Statistical Area, comprised of Orange, Seminole, Osceola, and Lake Counties, contains a bit more than two million people and ranks twenty-seventh among metro areas. Finally, the Orlando "urbanized area" ranks seventeenth in urban sprawl (according to data recovered at http://www.sprawlcity.org/hbis/index.html), with its two million people sprawled out over hundreds of square miles of urbanized space.

One consequence of sprawl is long commuting times and traffic congestion, especially since there is no public transportation to speak of. (There is a bus system, Lynx, but the universal perception is that the only people who ride it are people who can't afford to own a car.) Survey after survey in the Orlando metro area documents widespread public dissatisfaction with traffic congestion. In a 2001 survey, "traffic congestion" ranked behind only public safety and health care as important regional policy issues, with similar results in numerous other studies. In a 2005 study done in our research institute for Metroplan Orlando (the region's transportation planning agency), 58 percent said that congestion was a problem when travelling to and from work and 55 percent opined likewise when trying to shop. The local interstate, I-4, is often described, especially during rush hours, as Orlando's largest parking lot. A 2002 study of traffic congestion in U.S. cities ranked Orlando fourteenth, with the average metro resident spending about sixty-six hours per year in traffic jams. In most years, we also rank somewhere among the top five most dangerous cities for pedestrians and bicyclists. According to a November 10, 2009, report posted on the MSNBC web page, "The Worst Cities for Walking," Orlando was ranked as the number one "most dangerous city for pedestrians." We break loose from the traffic jams, it seems, just long enough to run down the poor schmucks trying to get around on foot!

The exurban nature of life in and around Orlando is illustrated by some results from a poll done in our research institute in 2004. The poll focused on Orange and Seminole counties, the counties closest to Orlando, and ignored the more rural Osceola and Lake counties. One module attempted to identify why metro area residents tend not to go downtown. One question asked, "Do you and your family live in downtown Orlando, or do you live away from downtown?" Of those responding, 92 percent said they lived away from downtown, indicative of the degree of sprawl. Those 92 percent were asked, "Have you ever thought about going into downtown Orlando, say in the evening or on a weekend, but then decided not to for some reason?" Encouragingly for the central city, 61 percent said, "No, never." (Or maybe not so encouraging, as some of this 61 percent would be people who would never think of going downtown in the first place and would therefore never have reason to reconsider.) But the remainder, four in ten, said yes, this had been their experience at least once. When asked why, the number one response was that the stores where people like to shop are in the suburbs where they live, not downtown where they don't. The next three most frequently cited reasons were all traffic-related: they don't want to fight the traffic; the toll roads are too expensive; parking is hard to find. These four were far more important reasons for not venturing downtown than crime, panhandlers, or homeless people (the latter depicted in the news at the time of the survey as "destroying" downtown and driving away business—when, all the while, it was traffic, parking, and congestion).

> In this place of exurban, post-modern pioneers, the range of choices is vast even when the choices themselves are illusory. Here life is truly a style: You don't want to live in a mass-produced instant community? No problem. Orlando's developers, like the producers of instant coffee, offer you a variety of flavors. ... In Orlando's lively downtown, it's possible to live in a loft just as you would in Chicago or New York. But these lofts are brand-new buildings constructed for those who want the postindustrial lifestyle in a place that was never industrial.

> Orlando's bright lights are not the garish displays of Las Vegas or the proud power logos of New York. Instead, Orlando glimmers with the familiar signage of franchise America: Denny's, Burger King, Quality Inn, Hampton Inn, Hertz. ... This, truly, is a 21st century paradigm [or as we would say, a metaphor]: It is growth built on consumption, not production; a society founded not on natural resources, but upon the dissipation of capital accumulated elsewhere ... a place somehow held together, to the extent it is held together at all, by a shared recognition of highway signs, brand names, TV shows, and personalities, rather than by any shared history. ... Welcome to theme-park nation (Allman 2007: 3).

The "dissipation of capital accumulated elsewhere" is evidently a reference to the third leg of the Central Florida economy: retirement. A 2004 article in the Orlando Business Journal ranked "the region's behind-the-scenes industry: the retirement industry" as the third major source of the then-recent "boomlet" in local employment, just behind construction and tourism. Retirees, the article said, are "coming here ... to spend their retirement checks"—to dissipate capital accumulated elsewhere (Beall 2004).

At times, the Central Florida retirement industry seems every bit as phantasmagorical as the tackiest tourist trap. Case in point: the Villages, a huge retirement community occupying about 3,600 acres in Lake and Marion Counties and marketed as "Florida's Friendliest Retirement

Hometown." All homes in the Villages must be occupied by at least one person fifty-five years of age or older. Persons under the age of nineteen years are allowed to visit for a maximum of thirty days per year. (There are some family dwellings that are exempt from this restriction, but not many.) According to a 2008 report from the U.S. Census, the Villages were (at the time) America's fastest growing "micropolitan" area. In 2000, the Census enumerated 8,333 residents, of whom 98 percent were white, 93 percent were age fifty-five or older, 96 percent had incomes above poverty, and 87 percent were out of the labor force. The Villages are Florida's, and probably America's, quintessential retirement community (Blechman 2008).

The Villages feature central squares and multiple golf courses, some of them spectacular. Golf is by far the leading activity. There are also movie theaters, restaurants, recreation and wellness centers, shopping, churches galore, and lifelong learning colleges where residents can brush up on art appreciation and history, crafts of every description, computers, the culinary arts, dance, personal finances, languages, and on through a large catalogue. There are even lectures by professors from the nearby University of Florida, although it was distressing to learn that the October 2009 lecture on "strategies for successful aging" had been cancelled.

A characteristic Villages feature is Lake Sumter Landing, a shopping and restaurant complex complete with an ersatz lighthouse. (The absurdity of the Lake Sumter lighthouse becomes apparent in realizing that the Villages are about seventy miles from the nearest open water, which is about as close to landlocked as you can be anywhere in Florida.) Marketing materials boast that "Lake Sumter Landing's colorful waterfront setting reminds many folks of quaint seaside villages they frequented during their childhood." The "colorful waterfront" opens onto a man-made lake. In the Lighthouse town square, retired and elderly people can dance, swill beer purchased from open-air beer carts (drinking apparently ranks second only to golf as the favorite leisure time activity), take a boat tour of the fake lake, even visit a fake shipwreck in the middle of the fake lake. Everything is made to look old—the Old Mill Playhouse, Cody's Original Roadhouse, the Rialto movie theater. Each business sports a plaque with a fake founding date and a fake history and the streets are paved in fake cobblestones. Lake Sumter Landing, redolent with nostalgia, evocative of America's simpler small town past, was built in 2005.

Life in the Villages seems to begin and end with golf (or perhaps, to begin with golf and end with a round of cocktails).[4] Driving through, there appear to be many more golf carts than cars, the ubiquitous golf cart being the preferred mode of Village transportation. (Golf carts have the right of way everywhere, their own lanes on Villages roadways, and their own garages—almost every home has one!) The town webpage, TheVillages.com, assures visitors that "Our residents say it's like being a kid again: golf, recreation, shopping, dining, medical and professional services—everything you need to live life to the fullest—just a golf car ride away, in a beautifully designed and gated community. You'll make friends, you'll make memories, and you can ultimately make yourself a happier, healthier person too! These are the good old days, so why not enjoy them right now—each and every day!" This glowing self-promotion is followed by a resident on video who says, "I don't know how much happier I can get than right now."

Surely, Villages residents are happier than, say, Florida's indigenous flora and fauna, because the theme-park nation and the sprawl it has stimulated have been disastrous for the regional environment. During the peak growth years, the state was adding about 120,000 new dwelling units, building 800 miles of new highway, consuming forty million additional gallons of fresh water, and losing 164,000 acres of forest and 150,000 acres of farmland each year, all of it to sustain a seemingly endless proliferation of exurban subdivisions featuring three or four bedroom, two and a half bath suburban homes with two-car garages on large lots four or five miles from the nearest place to buy a loaf of bread and a gallon of milk. (Following the principles of New Urbanism, the newer exurbs all have conveniently located strip malls and shopping areas nearby (Duany, Plater-Zyberk, and Speck 2000; Katz 1993). No wonder Florida was rapidly transformed in a mere three or four decades from a wild, exotic wetland teeming with ecological diversity—swamps, lagoons, birds, insects, alligators, manatees, fish, pristine rivers and creeks—into a pathetic caricature of southern California.

The American journalist and muckraker Lincoln Steffens visited the Soviet Union in 1919 and when he returned to the States in 1921, he famously said, "I have seen the future, and it works." Urban critics who visit Orlando these days might likewise say, "I have seen the future. No thanks!" Central Florida has become a metaphor for all that is wrong with unplanned, free-market, profit-driven, anything-goes growth. It is a place where habitat for storks and ibises and sand hill cranes is gladly sacrificed to build Dolly Parton's Dixie Stampede (opened 2003, closed 2008).

This dramatic transformation from swamp to tourist megalopolis did not "just happen." It was the result of hard-headed, profit-driven business decisions abetted by a local political atmosphere of asleep-at-the-wheel planning and an almost religious devotion to growth at any cost. One result is the kind of social and human devastation described in this book. (As for the environmental devastation, we leave that to other authors.) A place like Orlando obviously does not just "spring up" through Peter Pan flights of fancy, but rather by theme park expansions and correlated growth, and by tough-minded developmental schemes that often exacerbate relations between the wealthy and the poor. Employment opportunities on the scale represented by Disney and all that Disney has entailed have enticed hundreds of thousands of people, many of them economically marginal, into the region to take jobs that do not alleviate and often exacerbate their marginality. The homeless arrive with their own illusions and aspirations, shattered soon enough by a decidedly un-Pixie-like labor economy. Meanwhile, the rest of the population, those neither rich nor poor, makes its peace with the new regional realities: tourism brings jobs, tourists spend money, tourists can be taxed with impunity; and the homeless are reduced to dependence on models of welfare assistance and advocacy that most of the population simply couldn't care less about. Most would be happy if the homeless just "went away." As for the homeless, they are the contemporary version of Ellison's (1952) "invisible men," largely lacking awareness of kind and dependent for their very identities on the bigotries of the larger population, much unlike all the other "minority groups" in the American socio-political landscape. They are not Pan-like addicts to Pixie Dust so much as they are victims of the toxic fallout of unrestrained growth run amuck.

Foglesong (2003: 5) has asked whether Orlando "snared" Disney or the other way around. Growth, he reminds us, has generated immense sums of wealth, but the largesse is very unequally distributed.

> Urban growth both gives and takes away. It transforms cultural life, the natural environment, and the character of the urban economy … It creates public expenditure needs, but not always matching tax resources; it brings new employment, though not always living wages. It is a process … in which some gain while others lose … Disney World has generated traffic congestion, public facility deficits, affordable housing shortages, and a low-wage economy.

Perhaps no one has expressed the Janus-like reality of the Disney-Orlando marriage better than Carl Langford, who was mayor of Orlando when the city "won" Disney World. Early on, Mayor Langford enthused, "Show me a mayor in the United States who wouldn't just love to have Walt Disney sitting on his doorstep as a neighbor." A decade later, Langford had retired to the North Carolina mountains to, as he said, "escape from all the traffic" (Foglesong 2003: 3).

Central Florida as Reality

The *reality* of Central Florida has been created both by its myth and by its metaphor. Lots of Floridians got rich off tourism, construction, and retirement, but the result has been a labor economy dominated by low wage jobs in the service industries and a construction sector comprised in substantial measure of illegal immigrant workers.

> Farther along route 192, Disney was drawing a different kind of migrant to [the region]. Workers from Central America and the Caribbean were arriving to fill minimum wage jobs at the theme parks. The same day families from the suburbs of Detroit and Miami were banking on Disney's guilt-edged name [in the lottery for homes in Celebration], families from San Juan and Guadalajara, with the promise of a thin Disney pay slip in hand, were combing the apartment complexes just off the Kissimmee strip looking for affordable shelter (Ross 1999: 19).

The Central Florida bubble burst at about the same time the national economy tanked. Leading the way was raw demography. The rate of state population growth began to slow in 2007, just when "How Shall We Grow?" was forecasting continued exponential growth through to mid-century. Growth halted entirely in 2008, and in 2009, the state actually lost population for the first time in sixty-three years (Dougherty 2009). According to demographers who monitor these things, even the most optimistic projections forecast growth rates of, at best, a fraction of a percent for the next several years. So everything in the state that lived on continued population growth—and that is just about everything—has now died. That certainly includes the construction industry, which has seen several major developers (e.g., Levitt and Sons, Engle Homes, and numerous others) pull out of Central Florida entirely. Several downtown developments have been halted mid-construction. New home start-ups are at their lowest level in decades.

The recession that beset the national economy in 2008 had a devastating effect on tourism throughout the state. Traffic through the Orlando International Airport dropped off (especially domestic traffic), hotel occupancy rates fell, receipts at the theme parks flattened out (with some recent signs of a modest recovery), and visitors' centers closed their doors. Fewer and fewer families around the nation found that they could afford to drop a couple of grand so that Mickey and Goofy could entertain the kids. (In characteristic fashion, Disney responded to the crisis by raising ticket prices and recently raised them again, even though the latest economic figures do show some recovery in the state's tourist sector.)

As indicated earlier, Disney is, by far, Central Florida's largest employer with a labor force of about 60,000. So any dip in Disney's fortunes reverberates throughout the regional economy. A 2007 report out of Florida International University in Miami analyzed Disney's wage structure and its impact on the Central Florida economy (Nissen, Schultz and Zhang 2007). Because of a two-tiered wage system instituted in 1998 (and allegedly abandoned in 2004—we say "allegedly" because reliable information about Disney pay practices is virtually impossible to obtain), whereby new employees received lower pay increases than older employees, and because of the predominance of part-time hourly wage workers in the Disney labor force, the authors estimated that Disney's annual payroll was about $19 million less than it would have been had the pre-1998 system remained, and that pay levels for new workers were 12.2 percent behind where they would have otherwise been. The effects of these wage "losses" on Orange and Osceola Counties were estimated to amount to some 178 fewer jobs and $23 million fewer goods and services produced annually. Moreover, "these losses will continue to grow in future years as 'old timers' retire or leave ..." (p. 2). Disney's wages also lost ground in the 1998-2006 period to starting wages at both Universal Studios and Sea World. Yet in the era studied, Disney was one of America's most profitable industries (Nissen, Schultz, and Zhang 2007).

Whether Disney has been a "good thing" or a "bad thing" for Central Florida has been debated since Walt Disney World opened in 1971. As the FIU report notes

> Boosters argue that Disney has provided a huge payroll, major investment, massive purchases from local businesses, philanthropic giving in the local community, and net tax savings for other Orlando area taxpayers. Critics charge that Disney has created additional costs and demands for social services not factored in to the above claims. They also fault the company for providing mostly low-wage employment that drags down average living standards, creating traffic gridlock and obstructing creation of a rational mass transit system, being stingy with its philanthropy, and creating extra government burdens that more than nullify any tax savings to local taxpayers (Nissen, Schultz and Zhang 2007; see also Foglesong 2003).

It is not for us to weigh in on this debate, except to note that there is some truth to both positions. Jobs are definitely preferable to no jobs and Disney (and tourism more generally) provides a lot of jobs. Compared to revenues, one could probably argue that Disney is "stingy with its philanthropy," but Walt Disney World has always been generous to the Coalition for the Homeless of Central Florida, has always had company VP-level executives sitting on the Coalition's Board of Directors, supports numerous other local charitable causes both financially and with its Volunt-EARS program, and is year in and year out the largest single contributor to the Heart of Florida United Way. At the same time, a lot of those sixty-plus thousand Disney jobs are part-time jobs with low wages and limited to no benefits (see Mussenden 2004). And that fact unquestionably contributes to the region's sizable poor and near-poor population (see the next chapter).

The impact of the economic recession, falling construction, and flagging tourism on the state's budget was brutal. The deficit for the fiscal year of 2009-2010 was about $2.4 billion, which the state legislature "covered" with severe cuts to education, health services, law enforcement, transportation, and pretty much everything else. 2010-2011 was even worse, with state-wide budget deficits in the $4-6 billion range.

Data from the latest American Community Survey for the City of Orlando show the broad outlines of economy and society in Central Florida. Unemployment was 7.2 percent and has since surpassed 10 percent. The largest industry is "arts, entertainment, recreation, accommodation, and food and other services" (read: tourism) which employs about 24 percent of the labor force, followed by "education, health care and social services" at 15 percent and "professional, scientific, managerial, and administration" also at 15 percent. Then come retail trade at 12 percent and construction at 9 percent. There is practically no manufacturing (4 percent) or agricultural (0.1 percent) employment remaining. By occupation, half the labor force is in sales, office, and service positions. The Orlando poverty rate is 16.6 percent, well ahead of the national average (13.2 percent). Among children under eighteen, the local poverty rate is 23.7 percent. Median family income in Orlando was $48,423 versus the national median family income of $63,211. A quarter of all households reported a 2008 household income of $25,000 or less. African Americans comprise 27 percent of the Orlando population, Hispanics 22 percent. The Census issued a 2009 report showing that Orange County had become a "majority minority" county, one of about 300 such counties nationwide and Florida's seventh. A press report on the new distinction noted that "Until Walt Disney World opened in 1971, Orange County was demographically akin to Huntsville, Ala., Southern in accent and attitude with a strong defense and agricultural presence. But the opening of the theme park resort turned the area into a tourism hub that attracted visitors [and residents] from all over the world." (Schneider 2009).

Not everyone in the region was taken in by the Happy, Beautiful, Sunny Central Florida Growth Machine. In 2008, our institute did a regional survey focused on the question, "Why should we grow?" The survey was intended as an antidote to the "Grow, Grow, Grow!" mentality that has always characterized the region's decision-makers and to the "How Shall We Grow?" report and its tacit assumption that growth is as inevitable as it is desirable. One question asked whether the quality of life had gotten better, worse, or stayed the same in the last five years. Fifty-seven percent of the nearly 1,500 people who were surveyed said that it had gotten worse. When asked about the things that were reducing the quality of life in the region, e.g., traffic congestion, too many tourists, and the like, the most frequently mentioned response was "too much growth," noted by 56 percent, followed by traffic congestion at 53 percent. Just over two fifths (43 percent) said that if they were given the opportunity, they would like to "move out of this community."

A lengthy sequence asked people to talk about the "good things" and the "bad things" about "life here in Central Florida today." The good things (in the minds of the majority) were the climate, environmental amenities (lots of lakes, parks, open space), and arts and cultural opportunities. The bad things, in descending order, were roads and traffic (71 percent rated this as one of the bad things), the availability (or rather, non-availability) of good-paying jobs (67 percent), the way the political system works (56 percent), public education, the health care system, and social services (all seen as "one of the bad things" by just about half).

We also asked a series of forced choice questions about the ideology and reality of growth. One required respondents to choose between "Growth is an important driver of jobs and the economy, and brings us better cultural, sports and educational facilities" or "Growth doesn't really improve my life; it mostly benefits big developers and real estate interests." 48 percent opted for the former pro-growth view, 44 percent for the anti-growth view, with the remainder undecided. Contrary to the pro-growth ideology promulgated, for example, by regional Chambers of Commerce, the tourism and construction industries, local governments, and a very active local pro-growth organization called MyRegion.org (they are for "smart growth," but growth just the same), Central Floridians are pretty evenly divided on the fundamental question of whether growth is basically a good or a bad thing. A large majority, 70 percent, had never heard of the term "smart growth," and once it was explained, only 11 percent agreed that the concept accurately described "most" or "all" of the recent growth in Central Florida. About 90 percent had never heard of the "How Shall We Grow?" report. When asked whether Central Florida would become a better or worse place to live in the next five years, one third expected life to get better, one third thought it would get worse, and the remainder thought it would stay the same.

Half the people in the survey said that it had recently become "more difficult for me and my family to afford to live the kind of life we want." A mere 8 percent thought things had become "easier." More than half (56 percent) thought that "things in Central Florida have pretty seriously gotten off on the wrong track." The happiest place on earth? Not to a lot of the people who live here. Certainly not to the one Orlando child in four, or the one senior citizen in six, who lives in poverty and may or may not be sure that there will be something on the table for dinner tonight. And not to the 10,000 people in the region who will endure an episode of homelessness this year.

Gallup-Healthways has developed a "Well-Being Index" that they use to reveal which states are the happiest. The index captures six important dimensions of well-being: emotional health, physical health, healthy behaviors, job satisfaction, economic well-being, and overall happiness. The most recent survey, released in July 2010, did not show Florida to be the Happiest Place on Earth, not even the happiest place in the United States, in fact, not even in the upper half of the fifty states. The Top Five happiest states were Hawaii, Alaska, North Dakota, Nebraska and Colorado. Florida came in at fortieth place, just behind Indiana and just ahead of Tennessee (Mendes 2010).

There was also a 2008 study ranking the various nations in the world according to aggregate national happiness.[5] In this particular study, the U.S. ranked sixteenth, well behind Denmark, Switzerland, the Netherlands, Canada, and even Puerto Rico and Colombia. (In other similar studies, we've ranked as low as twenty-third or twenty-fourth.) But somehow, "the Fortieth Happiest State in the World's Sixteenth Happiest Country" just does not work very well as a marketing slogan.

The Plan of the Book

As has no doubt been surmised from our tenor and title, this book is about what it is like to be down and out in Central Florida—it is about the poor, the near-poor, the homeless, and the dispossessed in Orlando and its surrounds. The phrase "down and out," used to describe people who are destitute or penniless, appears to be an Americanism dating to the late nineteenth century. TheFreeDictionary.com lists synonyms for the adjectival form: destitute, ruined, impoverished, derelict, penniless, dirt-poor (informal), flat broke (informal), on your uppers (informal), and without two pennies to rub together; noun substitutes include: tramp, bum, beggar, derelict, outcast, pauper, vagrant, vagabond, and bag lady. Here we use the term in a more expansive sense, as synonymous (more or less) with anyone who lives near, at, or over the edge of financial catastrophe. However, the bulk of the book deals with those (to invoke another metaphor) who are at the very bottom of the barrel—Central Florida's substantial homeless population.

We have been doing homeless research in Central Florida and elsewhere in Florida since 2003. In 2003, Wright was appointed to the Board of Directors of the Coalition for the Homeless of Central Florida (the region's largest provider of homeless services) and was asked to create and chair the Board's Research and Evaluation Committee.[7] At the time, Donley was a student in the UCF master's program in applied sociology, volunteered to help out on an early survey of homeless men, and worked on every subsequent homeless study done at the UCF Institute of Social and Behavioral Sciences, both in and out of the Central Florida region. The grist for the book inheres almost entirely in the various studies we have done since the initial shelter survey.

Obviously, the vast majority of the approximately two million people who live in the Orlando Metropolitan Statistical Area (the four county region that will we refer to generically as "Central Florida") are not homeless. According to our Homeless Services Network (2009) annual Point in Time count, however, about 10,000 of them will be homeless at least once this year; about four thousand are homeless *right now*. In addition, somewhere around one in six or seven will be below the official federal poverty line this year and an even greater number are "near poor," i.e., officially "above poverty" but well short of anything we would consider "affluent." In 2008, our institute undertook the first-ever survey of the region's low and moderate income families; results from that survey comprise the following chapter, "Poverty in Central Florida: Work, Wages, and Well-being among the Region's Low and Moderate Income Families."

In Chapter Three, we turn our attention to the truly down-and-out, Central Florida's homeless population. In most respects—though not all—homeless people in Central Florida are much like homeless people everywhere. Some flagrantly confirm every hostile stereotype ever conjured up in the mind of man (or woman) about homeless people. As Stuart Bykofsky (1986) once stereotyped the homeless, these are "the drunk, the addicted, and the just plain shiftless" (a phrase we have co-opted as the title of Chapter Eight, which discusses addiction issues among Central Florida's homeless). But many more contradict those conventional stereotypes. A surprisingly large number are working people, free of addictions and mental illness, struggling to find some path to self-sufficiency in the tangled morass of the Central Florida economy. Many are women with children; some are intact husband-wife families. Quite a number avoid local homeless services altogether and live instead in the woods and other undeveloped parts of the metro area. Many were attracted to Central Florida by a belief that jobs could be found here, or as one young woman living in the woods told us, "We heard Disney was hiring." And it is true: Disney is *always* hiring, but alas, not always at wage rates sufficient to cover the region's high housing costs.

We mentioned above "an early survey of homeless men." Our first foray into local homelessness was a survey we did in 2003 of men who slept at the Pavilion, a large open-air shelter for homeless men located in downtown Orlando and operated by the Coalition for the Homeless. Studies of Coalition patrons comprise the largest share of this book. We initially undertook the Pavilion survey to establish a baseline of data for Pavilion men; we continued building the database until it contained a thousand homeless men, then stopped and prepared the report from which Chapter Three, "One Thousand Homeless Men," is crafted.

A line of research initiated by Dennis Culhane in the 1980s showed that in New York and Philadelphia, at least, a relatively small fraction of chronically homeless people—people who tend to remain homeless for long periods of time—consume a relatively large fraction of the total shelter capacity, or "shelter nights." Most homeless people, that is, are irregular or infrequent shelter utilizers, people whose shelter consumption amounts to a night here, a night there. But some are "frequent flyers," i.e., people who are in the shelters night after night after night. This led to the insight that if the small group of frequent flyers could somehow be permanently housed, the demand for emergency shelter could be drastically reduced. These men have, in any case, long since stopped using the shelters as "emergency housing." The shelters are where they live. Culhane's findings and insights form the basis for an entirely new approach to homeless services called Housing First. Chapter Four, "Transients and Frequent Flyers," presents our data on patterns of shelter utilization among Orlando's homeless men and amounts to an important replication of Culhane's findings in all particulars.

In recent years, women, children, and families have made up more than half the people presenting for services at the Coalition and much the same is true of the Salvation Army, the other large facility in the region that accepts both men and women. A great deal of our research over the years, particularly the qualitative work, has dealt specifically with homeless women, and these studies, plus a large statewide survey we conducted concerning the experience of violence in the lives of homeless women (Jasinski, Wesely, Wright and Mustaine 2010), form the basis for our fifth chapter, "It's Not Who We Are: Realities of Homelessness for Women and Children." The title is taken from the comments of a homeless woman interviewed in Kim Hopper's outstanding ethnography, *Reckoning with Homelessness*: "You have to understand that this is a condition, this homelessness. It's not who we *are*."

Very few people have any realistic idea of what it is like to be homeless and living, however temporarily, in an emergency shelter. A few years back, we were asked to prepare a chapter on "shelter life" for a multi-volume collection of papers on contemporary homelessness. Data for the chapter were from a long series of focus groups we did with both men and women about their experiences living in shelters. The observations and comments of our focus group participants, and our reflections upon them, comprise Chapter Six, "Shelter Life: Risk or Respite?"

Like many cities, Orlando has a large stratum of homeless people who are shelter-resistant and treatment-aversive who find places to live outside the conventional shelter system. In Orlando, many of these people live in camps in the woods—in East Orange County along Highway 50, in south Orange near the I-4/John Young Parkway interchange, and in more suburban Seminole and rural Osceola counties as well. In 2008, the Orange County government took an interest in the "unsheltered homeless" living in the county, outside of the City of Orlando limits, and commissioned us to undertake a study. The result was a series of focus groups with 39 homeless people living in the woods of East Orange County (near the UCF campus), the evidentiary basis for Chapter Seven, "Lovely, Dark and Deep: Orange County's Woods People."

Volumes have been written, literally, on alcoholism and drug addiction among the homeless, and certainly, in Central Florida and everywhere else, addiction issues loom large among the proximal causes of homelessness. Unfortunately, the literature on recovery from addictions among homeless people is largely a literature of failure; the emphasis, in short, has been on how the conditions of homelessness blunt the effectiveness of most intervention strategies. In the Coalition's Men's Pavilion, however, one finds an alcohol and drug recovery program called First Steps, and in that program are a number of homeless, underemployed or unemployed men, most with felony convictions, who have nonetheless managed to accumulate months or even years of sobriety. Just how homeless guys manage to do that is the question we take up in Chapter Eight.

As intimated earlier, many people think of Central Florida as a destination site for the retired and elderly, where old people can spend their days on the golf course and their evenings at the mahjongg table or perhaps the shuffleboard court, or maybe engaged in a frenzied game of pickleball. Those who have travelled through the Villages will recognize that this image of Florida's elderly is not entirely without foundation. At the same time, in Florida and around the nation, many elderly people are not worried as much about their golf handicap as they are about being poor and homeless. Although at present the elderly comprise only a small portion of the total poor and homeless populations, their numbers are growing as the population continues to age. The elderly homeless, often ignored in recent studies of various homeless populations, are the topic of Chapter Nine, "No Place for Sissies."

How Central Floridians, and people in general, *perceive* the homeless is taken up in Chapter Ten. Many people apparently fear the homeless because they believe them to be violent or crazy; others regard them with contempt because they think homeless people are "lazy, shiftless bums" who could do better for themselves if they really wanted to. How widespread are these perceptions? What do people think about the larger issues of homelessness? Do they want local governments to do more, or do less? These and a range of related topics are considered in Chapter Ten, "Mean as a Snake, Crazy as a Shithouse Rat: Public Perceptions of the Homeless."

All agencies that provide services to homeless people rely to a greater or lesser extent (and usually, greater) on volunteers who donate their time, talent, and treasure to making life better for those whom Jesus would have called "the least of mine." What motivates people to dig into their pockets or free up the time to volunteer at a homeless shelter? What kinds of people do such things? Our work at the Coalition and in the community has given us numerous opportunities to gather information about volunteers in homeless facilities, and this information has been gathered up and analyzed in Chapter Eleven, "The Kindness of Strangers."

In 2008, we received a contract to undertake a comprehensive evaluation of the Miami-Dade County continuum of care for homeless people, a project on which we spent the better part of a year. This project has given us the opportunity to reflect on how different cities have approached their homeless problem, and to what effects. We thus wrap up the substantive portion of the book with "A Tale of Two Cities," a comparative analysis of homeless politics and homeless services in Miami and Orlando. A concluding Chapter Thirteen draws out the larger lessons from our Central Florida research and discusses how our findings relate to the national debate over homeless people and what to do for, with, or about them.

As we have already noted, the story of Central Florida over the past three decades is a story about swampland evolving into a major American metropolis, something that only happens with agency, planning, and human volition. Orlando did not become what it is through some inexorable inner logic of urban and suburban development, but because people in positions of authority made decisions to grow this way rather than that. Our book is about the unintended human consequences of those decisions, about the human offal created by growth-at-any-cost, asleep-at-the-wheel planning, and the structural distortions that come with a growth-oriented tourist economy. Our argument is that people come to be poor, and ultimately homeless, as a result of those distortions, not because they have somehow "chosen" to live as they do. Our intention here, however, is mainly descriptive, not prescriptive. Our aim is to describe, sympathetically, but honestly, the various groups of poor and homeless Central Floridians that have come to exist in the post-Disney era, not to assign moral responsibility for the problems of poverty and homelessness nor even to make specific recommendations about how the various structural distortions need to be or even could be repaired.

Some might reasonably wonder why we have written an entire book on poverty and homelessness in Central Florida. What makes Orlando and surrounds the least bit interesting as a venue for homelessness research? Our answer is four-fold. First, as we trust readers will agree once they've plowed through what follows, we've learned quite a bit about homelessness through our Central Florida research that is not commonly reported in the literature. Chapter Four, to illustrate, is a rare but important replication of a set of studies whose generalizability we need to know more about; Chapter Five reports on aspects of fertility among homeless women that have been noted only rarely in prior studies; Chapter Nine reports at length on a subgroup among the homeless, the elderly, that is almost never discussed; Chapter Twelve is one of the few comparative studies of homeless policies and politics available anywhere in the literature. Secondly, with the principal exception of Martha Burt's national survey (Burt et al. 2001), virtually the entire modern social science literature on the homeless is derived from single-city samples, for example, Rossi's (1991) work in Chicago, Culhane's studies in New York and Philadelphia (see Chapters Three and Four), Bassuk's many studies in Boston (e.g., 1986, 1987), the countless homeless studies situated in Los Angeles (e.g., Koegel et al. 1999), Hopper's (2003) work in New York City, etc. There is a notable absence of smaller southern cities in this literature, a shortfall our Orlando research attempts to address. Third, we've been doing this research for seven years, mostly as applied work designed to answer very specific applied questions. Writing this book has given us the opportunity to put our Central Florida work into a larger context and to refract our local studies through the prism of a much larger literature. Finally, we fancy our book as a partial antidote to the Pixie Dust—a small spoonful of reality to offset the effusive fantasies promulgated by Central Florida's very active marketing machine. When people think of Central Florida, the region's poor, near-poor, and homeless populations are usually not what come to mind. But they are very much a part of our regional reality.

Chapter Eleven discusses volunteerism in homeless service agencies and contains quotations from several people who volunteered over the years to help out with the research reported in this book. One of them gave us a passage that eloquently expresses the overriding purpose of our work:

> I think homelessness is one of those social problems that can only truly be appreciated by seeing it. It has the ability to instill a sense of genuine empathy that cannot be achieved in any other way, and also gives participants the opportunity to see how pervasive the problem is (i.e., it is quite shocking to see how many people are at each of the facilities).

Our hope is that the book helps others see the homeless as we have come to see them, as real, honest-to-God human beings each with unique talents, problems, biographies, aspirations, and failings, not as a "social problem," not as a disembodied abstraction, and certainly not as the "invisible men" and women of modern America.

Notes

1. http://lostparks.com/ is a website dedicated to "Florida's lost tourist attractions" and is the source of the above list.
2. There is a blog dedicated "to all things Disney" that documents various Disney marketing slogans over the years: http://disneygene.blogspot.com
3. Available at http://www.myregion.org/Portals/0/HSWG/HSWG_final.pdf
4. Another favorite leisure time activity is pickleball, a form of geriatric tennis played with paddles on a court similar to a badminton court. The game is described at www.pickleball.com as a "combination of Ping-Pong, tennis, and badminton."

The Villages are known as "Pickleball Paradise" and there is an annual Villages Pickleball Championship now in its third year.

5. These results come from the annual World Values survey done at the University of Michigan. See http://www.ns.umich.edu/htdocs/releases/story.php?id=6629
6. These results come from the annual World Values survey done at the University of Michigan. See http://www.ns.umich.edu/htdocs/releases/story.php?id=6629
7. Despite Wright's long and enriching association with the Coalition, nothing stated or implied in this book is intended to speak for the organization or its views.

2

Poverty in Central Florida:
Work, Wages, and Well-being among
Low and Moderate Income Families[1]

A 2005 issue of *Alliance News*, the monthly newsletter of the National Alliance to End Homelessness, contained two separate news items, jarring in their juxtaposition. The first was an item from the Washington-based Center on Budget and Policy Priorities, an entry focused on the effects of U.S. social safety net programs on reducing poverty. The specific programs analyzed included Medicaid, the State Children's Health Insurance Program (SCHIP—in Florida, this is "KidCare"), various food and nutrition programs (Food Stamps, WIC), the Supplemental Security Income (SSI) program, and the Earned Income Tax Credit. Surprisingly, the Center concluded that these "public benefit programs cut the number of poor Americans nearly in half—from fifty-eight million to thirty-one million. And for those who remain poor, these programs reduced the severity of poverty by providing food, health insurance and income assistance."

Later on the same page, however, there was a story about a recent study in Los Angeles that said there were ninety-one thousand homeless people in LA County, a number that, even as it approached a hundred thousand, was described as a "vast undercount." How can we be slashing poverty nearly in half while the numbers of hungry and homeless citizens continue to grow? The apparent paradox cries out for explanation.

Poverty Definitions, Rates, and Trends

Data on trends in the national poverty rate are readily available from the U.S. Census Bureau. We comment briefly on these trends, compare the national poverty situation to the Central Florida situation, then discuss how poverty is defined for these purposes and why the real rates of poverty are *far higher* than the official rates suggest, both regionally and nationally.

The overall national poverty rate—the percentage of people (not families or households) living at or below the federally defined poverty line—has varied over the past forty years in a fairly narrow range, from of a low 11.1 percent in 1973 to a high of 15.2 percent in 1983. In the very first year we gathered poverty data, 1959, the rate was over 22 percent, so definite progress has been made. But the bulk of that progress came in the 1960s during what was called the War on Poverty. Since the early 1970s, the rate has bounced around erratically, increasing in some eras (such as the early 1980s), decreasing in others (e.g., the 1990s), and now on the increase again (Iceland 2006; Devine and Wright 1993).

The late 1990s downward trend in poverty bottomed out in 2000, at 11.3 percent. Since then, the rate has registered successive increases, up to 11.7 percent, then 12.1 percent, then 12.5 percent, and finally to 13.2 percent in the most recent year for which data are available. A one-year uptick might well be a statistical fluke, but a consistent decade-long annual increase is a **trend**. So we are living, once again, in an era of generally increasing poverty rates, even using the official poverty definition.

The Central Florida poverty situation is not much different than the national figures just cited (one reason among several why we are confident that the results reported in this and subsequent chapters generalize well beyond our local region). The 2006-2008 poverty rate for the nation as a whole was 13.2 percent. In the city of Orlando, it was 16.6 percent; in Orange County, 12.1 percent; and statewide, 12.6 percent. The social and demographic composition of our poverty population is likewise about the same as in other cities of comparable size, with women and minorities overrepresented. Table 2.1 gives current poverty data for the five counties included in the survey that forms the basis for this chapter.

Table 2.1
Central Florida Poverty Rates[2]

County	2008 Estimated Population	2006-08 Poverty Rate
Orange	1,063,098	12.1
Osceola	254,622	11.5
Seminole	409,283	9.5
Lake	298,726	9.4
Sumter	71,614	12.5

The Orlando metropolitan area, like all other cities of appreciable size, also has a very sizable population of what have come to be called "the working poor" and the "near-poor," that is, families whose adults work but whose incomes are such that they struggle week to week to get by. Much of this chapter focuses specifically on these families.

In light of the documented recent increases in poverty rates, locally and across the nation, what does the Center on Budget and Policy Priorities mean when it claims that our social safety net has cut the number of poor Americans nearly in half? What this apparently means is that in the absence of the safety net programs they reviewed, there would be almost twice as many poor Americans as there in fact are. In other words, without Medicaid, SCHIP, various food and nutrition programs, SSI, and the ETIC, there might be sixty or seventy million poor people in America instead of about forty million, and the official poverty rate might be closer to 20 percent than somewhere around 13 percent.

But as has been pointed out many times, calculations of this sort are inherently misleading (Blank 2008; Willis 2000; Beeghley 1984). Medicaid does not make poor people less poor, just less sick. And likewise, food stamps do not make poor people any less poor, just less hungry; housing subsidies do not make poor people less poor, just less likely to be homeless; and so on. EITC is different: by letting low income people keep more of the money they earn, Earned Income Tax Credits directly lower the overall poverty rates. But for the most part, Medicaid money goes to health care facilities and professionals; the cash from housing subsidies goes to landlords; and the money from food stamps goes into the coffers of supermarket chains and consequently food suppliers.

How does the government decide what constitutes poverty in the first place? And is the procedure reasonable? Barbara Ehrenreich's widely read book on the working poor, *Nickel and Dimed,* along with many other more scholarly sources (see Weinberg 2006; Fisher 1997; Devine and Wright 1993), points out that "the official poverty level is still calculated by the archaic method of taking the bare-bones cost of food for a family of a given size and multiplying this number by three." Back before the advent of techno-speak, the "bare-bones" food budget to which Ehrenreich refers was called the "emergency, temporary low budget diet," defined as the "minimum nutrient intake required to sustain human life for short periods." This diet consists of so many daily calories, so many grams of protein and carbohydrates, so many vitamins and minerals, and so on. And why times three? Because studies done in the 1950s showed that the average low income family spent about a third of its income on food.

Thus, the original poverty line, first determined at the onset of the War on Poverty in 1964, was calculated by determining the cheapest possible way to purchase the least amount of food a person would need to stay alive for a short period, then multiplying that dietary expenditure by three. *Et voila!*—the official federal poverty line, which was calculated in the manner just indicated in 1964, and which, with annual corrections for inflation, has been used ever since (despite a long string of commissions and blue ribbon panels that have recommended over the years that the standard be changed). (The story of how the poverty line was created has been told many times, see Blank 2008 for details.)

Ehrenreich also notes that the cost of food has been relatively inflation-proof over the years, compared for instance to the cost of housing, which increases every year. Food prices have been kept artificially low by federal agricultural subsidies. Recent data from the U.S. Department of Labor and the Bureau of Labor Statistics (2010) show that in the lower income quintile, food represents about a sixth of annual expenditures, not a third. Should we therefore multiply the minimum food budget by six and thereby double the poverty standard? In the meantime, the average cost of housing for low income families has increased to 37 percent of monthly income (despite the admonition by HUD and mortgage lenders that families cannot afford to spend more than 30 percent of their income on housing).

As many have argued, including a widely publicized report from the National Academy of Sciences in 1995, that is exactly the problem with the official poverty standard (Wright 2010; Citro and Michael 1995). The entire basket of goods and services upon which low-income people and families survive has changed dramatically since the poverty line was first calculated, and so too the relative proportions of income spent on each item in the basket. And yet we continue to use a poverty standard that is, indeed, "archaic."

Alas, if we based the poverty line on a more current basket of goods and services and let the price of minimally acceptable housing or health care, say, rather than the price of a minimally acceptable diet, dictate the calculation, the poverty standard for a family of four would not be just over $20,000 per year, but quite a bit higher than that, and the official federal poverty rate would not be 13.3 percent, but maybe as high as one in five, or possibly higher.

Recently, the Census has published some 2008 poverty data using both the "old" poverty line (and definition of income) and the "new" measure (and definition of income) as suggested in the 1995 NAS report. The "new" poverty measure, to be clear, redefines both what counts as income and how the poverty threshold is established. On the income side, it includes transfer payments and income-in-kind from government assistance programs (the cash value, for example, of food stamps, housing subsidies, free school lunches and the like), all of which is excluded as income in the "old" definitions. The rationale for including these transfers as income is that by excluding them, it is essentially impossible for our anti-poverty measures to bring down the rate of poverty (DeNavas-Walt, Proctor and Smith 2009).

On the threshold side of the equation, however, the "new" poverty definition takes into account the costs of clothing, housing, and out of pocket medical expenses, as well as the costs of food, commutation to work, and other factors. It also adjusts the poverty threshold for regional differences in the overall cost of living. And since the inflation-adjusted cost of food has not increased much over the years because of agricultural price subsidies, adding in these other costs (which *have* increased, in some cases dramatically) causes the poverty thresholds for families of various sizes to go up.

What are the overall effects of the new definitions on the poverty rate? The latest data from the U.S. Bureau of the Census give us an answer. The overall effect on the poverty threshold is to push the new poverty standard up to $24,755 for a standard family of four, versus $21,834 under the "old" definition. And even though more things count as income under the new formula, the overall poverty rate nonetheless increases, from 13.2 percent under the old definition to 15.8 percent under the new. That might not sound like much of a difference, but it amounts to more than seven million poor people who would not be considered poor in light of the old poverty standard.

If nothing else, this example illustrates the hazards of reifying "the poverty line." When the number of the poor can be made to vary by several millions with apparently reasonable changes in how poverty is defined, one begins to sense that the number of the poor is not a real or fixed number and that there can therefore be no precise answer to questions about the "true" extent of poverty in America.

In recognition of these definitional issues, we have abandoned the official federal poverty guidelines altogether for the purposes of this chapter and rely instead on a set of income groupings derived from the

U.S. Department of Housing and Urban Development (2009) (which has also given up on the old poverty standards). In Central Florida, recent escalations in the costs of housing, energy, and health care have undoubtedly impacted families in ways not recognized by the poverty standards utilized in five decades of research on poverty. In the data and results reported later, then, "low income" refers to households earning half or less of the "area median income" (which translates to families earning about $30,000 per year or less), "moderate income" refers to households earning between 50 percent and 120 percent of the area median income (families earning between about $30,000 and $70,000 a year), and "upper income" refers to households earning 120 percent or more of the area median (more than roughly $70,000 per year). (Precise income standards for these various categories depend on family size, of course.) Using percentages of median income to define income groupings puts us in line with most of the rest of the advanced industrial societies, where the near-universal poverty standard is half or less the median income (Blank 2008). In the rest of the Western world, in short, a family is considered poor if it survives on half or less of what the average family has to live on, an elegantly simple, intuitively appealing, and statistically meaningful definition that has been adopted in this chapter.

Welfare Reform

Quoting again from Ehrenreich (p. 196): "In the rhetorical buildup to welfare reform [enacted in 1996], it was uniformly assumed that a job was the ticket out of poverty and that the only thing holding back welfare recipients was their reluctance to go out and get one" (see also Lein et al. 2008; Hays 2004; Lichter and Jayakody 2002 for treatments of this topic). Of course, those who have read the book know that Ehrenreich in fact went out and got several jobs, often two of them at a time, and yet the book is a relentless chronicle of her inability to find housing and keep herself fed, healthy, and happy on the income she was able to earn in low wage work. At one point, she realizes in despair that even the local trailer park is beyond her means.

Despite the "rhetorical buildup," the goal of welfare reform was never to end poverty, but rather to "end welfare as we know it," that is, to get people off the welfare rolls and into the labor force[3] (Berke 1992). In that respect, welfare reform has been quite successful because the overall welfare population has been cut nearly in half since welfare reform was enacted (Lichter and Jayakody 2002). However, as Berg (2007) states: "judging the success of welfare reform solely by how many people leave welfare is a bit like judging the success of a hospital by how many people leave it, without differentiating between how many people leave it cured, ill, or dead." While by all accounts the old AFDC welfare system was awful, it could scarcely be said that the poverty rates have also been halved. To the contrary, they are higher today than they were when welfare reform was enacted. And it is also not at all clear that the millions of women (and their children) who have been taken off welfare and shoved into the labor force are the least bit better off for it.

People, mainly women (and their children), were taken off welfare and placed in the labor force largely through the mechanism of time-limited welfare benefits. Under the old AFDC (Aid to Families with Dependent Children) regime, women with dependent children could stay on welfare as long as they remained eligible. For that reason, it was often argued that welfare bred dependency ("welfare queens") and that dependency deepened and worsened the "cycle of poverty." Thus, the centerpiece of welfare reform was time-limited eligibility for benefits: no more than twenty-four months of welfare benefits in any single stretch, and no more than sixty months of benefits in the lifetime (thus TANF: *Temporary* Assistance for Needy Families).[4] Once the eligibility limit is reached, recipients are in essence forced into labor force participation or left with no income. After sixty months of welfare, in short, it is either work or starve. (This, not coincidentally, is akin to the kinds of coerced decisions homeless people make when they "choose" to be a homeless, a theme that recurs throughout this book.)

It was never stated, only implied, that by leaving welfare for work, former welfare families would experience some improvement in living conditions, i.e., that participation in the paid labor force would lift these women and children out of poverty. But what has happened instead is that the number of the *working poor* has increased (Loprest 1999; Blank and Haskins 2001). The hardships that were consequently visited upon these families have been discussed in detail by Olivia A. Golden, assistant secretary for children and families in the Clinton administration and the government official whose job it was to implement welfare reform. She writes (Orlando *Sentinel*, July 24, 2005):

> Even though their parents are working more, children in low income families are doing just about the same as they were before welfare reform. That means they fare worse on a whole range of measures including physical health, emotional health, family stress, and school engagement. In less than a decade, welfare has faded as a means of support for impoverished families. Many of these families are working long hours despite low wages, shrinking health insurance coverage, and serious tradeoffs

between work and decent care for their children. Neither our politics nor our policy have adjusted to our success at bringing more of these parents into the labor force.

What Golden is saying is that we enacted national policy to get people off welfare without considering what they would do or what tradeoffs they would face as labor force participants. And now, with welfare no longer an option, we are confronted with serious issues of wages, benefits, job security, health coverage, and day care. The net result, according to Golden, is a wide swath of American families living, literally, on "the edge of catastrophe." Why should we worry about these issues, she asks? "One reason is fairness: When parents play by the rules, they ought to be able to provide the basic necessities for their families." More importantly, "the children in struggling families are America's future. If hardworking parents cannot assure their children a stable family life, decent and safe housing, and health care, a large proportion of America's children will continue to fall short of the educational success and economic productivity the nation needs from them."

How wide is the swath of people living "on the edge of catastrophe" in Central Florida? How many families are "struggling?" How many are working in jobs whose wages fail "to provide the basic necessities?" How many are unable to "assure their children a stable family life, decent and safe housing, and health care?" These are not merely academic questions. They strike at the very heart of our regional quality of life and illustrate the downside of an economy dominated by service work in the tourism industry.

The remainder of this chapter is based on a survey of more than 1400 Central Floridians done in the summer and fall of 2007. Counties included in the sampling frame are Orange, Osceola, Seminole, Lake, and Sumter. Households with incomes at or below 120 percent of the area median income were **oversampled** and asked detailed questions about their labor force participation; income, savings and debt; housing costs; medical care; food security; and transportation expenses. More affluent households were also included for comparison purposes but were sampled at a one-in-three rate and were only asked a subset of questions.

The Low and Moderate Income Population of Central Florida

We have become accustomed to thinking of the poor, and the low income population in general, as economically idle, i.e., people who could do better for themselves if they just sobered up, took a shower, and got a job. But as people like Ehrenreich and many others (see Shipler 2005; Newman 1999) keep reminding us, many low income people are in fact working.

Our survey includes data on the labor force status of low income people in the Central Florida region and *half of them are in fact working* (see Table 2.2). An additional one-sixth are retired (elderly) people who are too old to work, another sixth are permanently disabled and incapable of working, and a tenth are students, stay-at-home moms, and miscellaneous others. That leaves the remaining one in ten of the low income population—a mere tenth—who are laid off, unemployed, out of the labor force, or otherwise economically idle.

As an aside of some significance, almost three-quarters of the region's disabled population fall into the low income category. Elderly and retired people, in contrast, are found all across the income spectrum. See the following section, *The Retired and the Disabled.*

The same is generally true of the national poverty population. About ten million poor people work. Half the poor are either children too young to work or elderly who are beyond their working years, so if you remove the young and the old, about half of the poverty population works at least part of the year. Percentaging in the other direction, among all U.S. workers—i.e., persons who work at least part of the year—the poverty rate is ~6 percent (Acs 2009).

At the same time, as is obvious from Table 2.2, the higher one goes in income distribution, the higher the rate of labor force participation. So as a rule of thumb, the admonition to "get a job" is wise advice—most of all if the job pays good wages and offers acceptable benefits. The problem, of course, is that many jobs do not, both in Central Florida and around the nation.

Table 2.2
Labor Force Status of Low, Middle and Upper Income Respondents

Labor Force Status	Low Income	Middle Income	Upper Income
Working	49	68	75
Disabled	16	2	2
Retired	16	15	7
Students, Housewives	9	10	13
Idle	10	5	3
Total =	100%	100%	100%

The Retired and the Disabled

At the onset of the War on Poverty, poverty rates were substantially higher among the elderly than among any other age group; today, using the official poverty definition, children have the highest poverty rate and elders have the lowest (Meyer and Wallace 2009; Wright 2005). The much-improved economic circumstances of the elderly, the exceptionally high cost of our health and income-maintenance programs for them, and the rapidly deteriorating conditions to be found among various non-elderly segments of the population have caused some to question the wisdom of continuing to invest so much in programs for the aged.

Increasingly, these issues are being framed in terms of *intergenerational inequity* (see Binstock 2007; Minkler and Robertson 1991). The basic concept is straight-forward. Through programs such as Social Security and Medicare, elderly persons receive substantial income, health, and other welfare benefits that are paid for mainly by taxes on the working (that is to say, the non-elderly) population. Thus, these programs transfer income from young to old and the question is increasingly asked whether this inter-generational transfer of income is fair. Many recent discussions have concluded that it is remarkably unfair to younger working people.

Having made substantial progress in the struggle against poverty among the elderly, however, is different than eliminating poverty in this group altogether, which is how our progress is sometimes depicted in the inter-generational inequity debate. Our programs for the elderly have *not* eliminated poverty among that group, only *reduced* elderly poverty to a level slightly beneath that of the population as a whole. The long-term trend has left approximately one in ten of the nation's over-65 population below the official poverty line.

The above figures, of course, reflect the age differences in poverty as measured by the old poverty standards. The new standard, as it happens, not only increases the overall rate of poverty but also redistributes poverty across age groups. Under the new poverty and income definitions, the poverty rate for the young declines from 19.0 percent to 17.8 percent (because single mothers and their children are disproportionate recipients of non-cash governmental aid such as food stamps); the poverty rate for the economically active increases from 11.7 percent to 14.2 percent (mostly because of commutation and child care costs born disproportionally by the working population); and the poverty rate for the elderly *doubles* from 9.7 percent to 19.3 percent (due mostly to out of pocket medical expenses, rising Medicare premiums, increased deductibles and co-pays, etc.). Rather than the lowest poverty rate of any age group, the elderly turn out to have the highest (Wright 2010).

Among retired persons in the Central Florida survey data, 30 percent (N = 214) fall into the low-income group, 59 percent in the middle income group, and only 12 percent in the upper income group. So there remains a very sizable pocket of low-income retired persons in the Central Florida population.[5]

Compared to retired people in the middle and upper income categories, low-income seniors:

- Are more likely to rent rather than own
- Are far more likely to live in public housing (13 percent versus 1 percent).
- Are more likely to live in neighborhoods they describe as "fair to poor."
- Are far less likely to be currently married (i.e., are disproportionally widows).
- Are predominantly women (67 percent versus 47 percent of middle and upper income seniors).
- Are far less educated (47 percent high school or less versus 26 percent of middle and upper income seniors).

So our region's low income retired people are mainly less-educated, widowed women living in rental units in shabby neighborhoods. Very few of them will be found in the Villages.

The general financial circumstances of our low-income retired population are best described as "straitened." Compared to retired people in the middle and upper income categories, low income retirees:

- Are much less likely to have any savings account (45 percent to 17 percent).
- Have less in their savings accounts if they even have a savings account.
- Are more likely to say they couldn't pay their bills if they missed a month of income (45 percent to 25 percent)
- Are less satisfied with their present financial situation (35 percent versus 17 percent "not at all satisfied").
- Do not feel that they have enough income to live comfortably (42 percent to 30 percent).
- Are twice as likely to receive Food Stamps (22 percent to 10 percent).
- Are more likely to take meals at free meal programs (8 percent of the low income retired versus none of the retired in the middle and upper income categories).

- Are much more likely to report that "we sometimes need more food than we have" (10 percent to 2 percent).
- Are less likely to own a car (29 percent versus 5 percent).
- Are more likely to be saddled with medical bills they are "trying to pay off" (27 percent to 10 percent).

Most of the retired people in our sample, whether low-income or not, report receiving Social Security pensions and Medicare. Those for whom Social Security is the main or sole source of income are concentrated in the low income category; those with substantial incomes from other sources (private pensions, spouses' earnings, investments, savings, and the like) escape low-income status and the financial anxieties and uncertainties that accompany that status. Thus, contrary to a widespread misperception, receipt of Social Security benefits does not guarantee an income above the poverty level. In fact, about 85 percent of the elderly poor nation-wide receive at least some Social Security income. Low income elderly also receive SSI and other assistance at rates exceeding those in the middle and upper income categories, but the coverage of these programs is even more limited than Social Security coverage. (For an analysis of Social Security and poverty state by state, see Van de Water and Sherman 2010.)

In Central Florida especially, we have come to think of "the retired" as a monolithic, economically comfortable, and rapidly growing segment of our population, with the inhabitants of the Villages serving as the embodiment of this stereotype. In fact, for every well-to-do retiree whiling away his or her years on the Central Florida golf courses, there is another living on a fixed (or nearly fixed) income in a subsidized rental unit, depending on Meals on Wheels for sustenance and Medicare for health care. As our data make abundantly clear, we cannot simply assume that our seniors are in a position to take care of themselves. Many clearly are not.

About 12 percent of the U.S. population is considered disabled (Erickson, Lee and von Schrader 2010). In Orange County, the corresponding percentage is 10 percent, and for the state as a whole, 13 percent (U.S. Census Bureau 2010). As already indicated, in our data the disabled are heavily concentrated in the low-income category (72 percent), with most of the remainder in the middle category (21 percent) and a few (7 percent) in the upper income group. The disabled as a whole are mainly renters (59 percent), especially those in the low income group (65 percent).

The major factor that keeps disabled people out of the lower income category is **marital status** (i.e., a spousal income). Among low-income disabled people, only 21 percent are currently married, versus 68 percent of disabled people in the middle and upper income groups. The majority of low-income disabled people are either divorced (35 percent), widowed (14 percent), or have never been married (29 percent).

Overall, the disabled are about evenly dispersed across gender lines (52 percent male, 48 percent female), but there is a huge difference by income group: the low income disabled are 57 percent female; the middle and upper income disabled are 76 percent male. So among disabled persons, women are grossly overrepresented within the low income group. So too are African Americans: among low income disabled, 32 percent are African American; among middle and upper income disabled, only 12 percent. And likewise, Hispanics, who comprise 21 percent of the low income disabled, only comprise 4 percent of those in the middle and upper income groups. Overall, the low income disabled population of Central Florida, about three-quarters of the entire disabled population, consists disproportionally of unmarried African American and Hispanic women. (Demographic characteristics of the national population of Census-defined disabled persons is available in Center for an Accessible Society 2002.)

The financial circumstances and anxieties of the low-income disabled generally parallel those of the low-income retired (and indeed, of low-income households generally): They tend not to have savings accounts, have low balances when they do have savings accounts, would have a hard time living without a month's pay, are unsatisfied with their financial situations, believe things are getting worse, do not have enough income to live as comfortably as they'd like, and on through a familiar litany. Interestingly, the differences by income group within the category of the disabled are not as sharp (and often not statistically significant) compared to the equivalent differences among the retired, presumably because all disabled people have a relatively tough row to hoe regardless of their relative incomes.

About three-quarters of households containing one or more disabled persons receive SSDI (Social Security Disability Insurance). That this figure is not closer to 100 percent bespeaks issues with SSDI eligibility that have been widely discussed elsewhere; that three quarters of these households fall into the low income category clearly suggests something about the inadequacy of SSDI payment levels. In addition to SSDI, 15 percent of households with one or more disabled persons receive food stamps, 11 percent take at least occasional meals at free meal programs, one in four gets free food from charitable organizations, and yet almost half (45 percent) say they sometimes need more food than they have.

National data on food insecurity show that "in 2008 ... 14.6 percent of households were food insecure at least some time during that year, up from 11.1 percent in 2007. This is the highest recorded prevalence rate of food insecurity since 1995 when the first national food security survey was conducted" (Economic Research Service 2009).

As with seniors supported by Social Security and Medicare, we often find it convenient to believe (or perhaps hope) that the social service programs that support the disabled enable them to live a reasonably decent, secure life free from economic insecurity. This, assuredly, is **not** the case. The disabled comprise another significant pocket of poverty and economic insecurity that is practically invisible to society at large.

The Working Poor

Who, demographically, are the working poor—i.e., people in our low-income category who are, nonetheless, labor force participants? The important demographic factors, it turns out, are age, race, gender, and marital status. Among **working respondents only** in these data, only about a third in the lowest income category are currently married, versus 58 percent in the middle category and 82 percent in the top category. This illustrates the economic advantages to households with multiple adults who can be deployed into the labor force. In general, the more earners in a household, the higher the income (Treas 1987).

The working poor are also disproportionately younger people, at the start of their careers: 37 percent under 30, versus 28 percent of the middle income workers, and only 11 percent of the top earners. Thus, many of the working poor will graduate to better incomes once seniority, promotions, and raises accrue. That circumstances may improve in ten or fifteen years, however, is little comfort to young workers struggling to pay rent and make payments on a six-year-old car, or hoping to buy a home and start a family. As many have pointed out when discussing the problems of today's younger workers, a dream delayed is, increasingly, a dream denied (Edwards and Hertel-Fernandez 2010).

Blacks and Hispanics are overrepresented among the poor in general and among the working poor in particular. Of the total number of low-income working families, 29 percent are African American (versus about 15 percent of middle and upper income families) and about 20 percent are Hispanics (versus less than 10 percent of middle and upper income families). This illustrates the economic penalty of not being white (Rank 2009; Shapiro 2004; Siegel 1965).

And finally, the working poor are disproportionately female: 54 percent versus 49 percent and 38 percent in the middle and upper income categories, respectively. This illustrates the lower wages typically paid to women workers and the feminization of poverty about which many have written (Starrels, Bould and Nicholas 1994; Schaffner, Goldberg and Kremen 1990; Pearce 1978). The economic liberation of women has been underway for some four decades now and yet the wages of full time employed women still average only about three-quarters of the wages of comparable men—a persistent and inadequately addressed wage disparity (this notwithstanding significant improvements and near gender equality in some sectors).

So, in the main, when we speak of the region's working poor, we are talking about relatively young, unmarried, non-white, and predominantly female workers.

Among those classified in our survey as working poor, 44 percent would prefer to work more hours than their employers give them, one in seven works a second job, and over half would be unable to pay their bills if they missed a month's income. Among middle income families, 17 percent want to work more hours; among upper income families, none. Lower income people change jobs more frequently, are less likely to receive benefits, have fluctuating monthly incomes, and are less likely to have received a raise since starting at their current jobs. Also worth noting, however, is that 38 percent of middle income families and even 24 percent of upper income families say they would be unable to pay their bills if they missed a month's pay. Substantially large fractions of all income groups live at the absolute limit of their paychecks.

As would be expected, the type of job greatly impacts household income and there are large differences in occupation by income group. The clear majority of upper income respondents work in professional, technical, or managerial jobs whereas low income respondents are primarily employed in clerical and manual jobs. Among working people in the lower income group (as among working people in all income groups), most respondents work 36-40 hours on average each week.

Low income people recognize that a lack of education and job skills holds them back. One question in the survey asked, "Do you think you could improve your work situation if you got additional education or job training?" The percentages answering yes: 68 percent of low income, 58 percent of middle income, and 47 percent of upper income respondents. Here, clearly, is a leverage point for social policy intervention.

A Note on Marital Status

As the preceding suggests, marital status (and family composition in general) can be decisive influences on a household's overall economic well-being (Smock, Manning and Gupta 1999; Duncan and Hoffman 1985), so it is important to understand the marital status differences among the various income categories we are considering (Table 2.3).

Among low income males, the plurality (45 percent) are men who have never married (or better, men who have yet to marry). The same is true for a quarter of middle-income males, but true for less than a tenth of upper income males. Most men (and women) in the upper income category (82 percent and 80 percent respectively) are married and, as we see shortly, most families in that income category have two working adults and thus two incomes.

The picture for women is slightly more complicated, with a sharp overrepresentation of divorced and separated women in the low income group. (We, of course, are not the first to remark on the deleterious effects of marital dissolution on the economic well being of women.) Among low-income women, 30 percent are divorced or separated, versus only 9 percent of low income men and 19 percent and 11 percent of middle and upper income women. Never married women are also overrepresented in the low income category.

Table 2.4 thus contains two important lessons: One, for both men and women, marriage has a strongly positive effect on economic well-being

Table 2.3
Gender, Marital Status, and Household Income

Income =	Low	Middle	High
Male Respondents			
Married	41	63	82
Separated, Divorced	9	8	8
Widowed	4	3	1
Never Married	45	25	9
Female Respondents			
Married	30	56	80
Separated, Divorced	30	18	11
Widowed	15	7	2
Never Married	25	17	7

(see also Waite and Gallagher 2000; Nock 1998). And two, for women in particular, marital dissolution is often an economic disaster (Smock, Manning and Gupta 1999; Holden and Smock 1991).

The main (but not only) reason that marriage promotes economic well-being is that married couples can enjoy the benefits of dual incomes whereas single, divorced, separated, and widowed persons generally do not. Thus, family financial well-being is often a function of total household labor force involvement (Treas 1987). The contribution of multiple wage earners to overall household affluence is not well-appreciated, but the effect is often decisive. To illustrate, 7 percent of our low-income households but 23 percent of middle income households and 49 percent of upper income households have two or more adults in the paid labor force. Indeed, of all the economic penalties a young, non-white, inner-city single woman suffers, the penalties for being female, black, and young pale in comparison to the penalty of no second wage earner.

Effects of Household Income on Economic Well-Being, Hardship, and Anxiety

It will come as no surprise that low income households suffer the most economic hardship or that they live month-to-month in difficult financial situations. Likewise, it is hardly shocking to learn that Central Floridians at or above 120 percent of the area median income are getting by nicely. The real surprise in our data is how far into the middle income categories financial hardship and anxiety have penetrated. What follows is a sector-by-sector outline of just how tough life has become for those at the bottom of the income distribution and just how precarious the economic well-being of the "middle class" has also become (Mishel, Bernstein and Allegretto 2007).

Housing. 64 percent of low-income families rent (versus a third of middle income and only 13 percent of upper income families), so when low-income households settle up their monthly housing expenses, in the majority, they are not adding to their equity, but rather to the wealth of their landlords. Only two-fifths of low income households live in single-family detached homes (versus 70 percent of middle income and 92 percent of upper income families). Almost half live in neighborhoods of a quality rated as "fair or poor," versus 19 percent of middle income families and zero percent of upper income families. Lower income families also change residences more frequently, either to lower housing costs (40 percent) or to get their kids into better schools (39 percent).

Most low income respondents have lived in their current residence five years or less while those in the middle and upper income groups are more likely to have resided in their current residence for six years or more. Their incomes are also more variable: one in three low and middle income respondents said that their incomes fluctuated monthly (versus one in five upper income respondents).

Certainly, housing costs were an issue for families in this survey, especially those in the low and middle income categories. To capture this issue, we calculated monthly housing costs for each household (rent or mortgage plus utilities) and expressed the result as a percentage of monthly income. This is, in essence, the HUD "housing burden" calculation (see Schwartz and Wilson 2008).[6] An acceptable housing burden is anything at or below 30 percent of income. Housing costs between 30 percent and 50 percent of monthly income are considered a "high housing burden," while anything from 50 percent and higher is considered "severe." Table 2.4 shows the distribution of housing burdens across our three income groups.

Table 2.4
Housing Burdens and Household Income Category

Income Category	Low	Middle	High
Housing Costs as a Percentage of Monthly Income			
Less than 30%	22	50	87
30-50% (high housing burden)	24	37	10
More than 50% (severe housing burden)	54	13	3
Totals	100	100	100

Overall, just 51 percent of the households in the survey have housing costs within the HUD recommended guidelines (30 percent of income or less). Since low and moderate income households were oversampled in this study, this percentage is downwardly biased and not indicative of the regional household population as a whole; still, it is a dramatic illustration of how housing costs have come to dominate family finances, especially outside the highest income categories.

As in the nation at large, high and severe housing burdens impact mainly upon low income (and renter) populations (Rice and Sard 2007). Housing consumes half or more of the monthly incomes of slightly more than half of our lower-income households (and more than 30 percent of the monthly incomes of 78 percent), versus 13 percent of middle income households and a mere 3 percent of upper-income families. At the other end of the distribution, only 22 percent of low income households, exactly half of the middle income households, and almost 90 percent of upper income households having housing burdens within HUD's acceptable range. (Housing burdens are also particularly severe for households containing one or more disabled persons. In these families, one in four spends half or more of their monthly income on housing.)

If we sort households into renters and owners and look at housing burdens as a function of income, we see that high housing burdens are concentrated among low income renters, 60 percent of whom spend half or more of their income on housing. (Among middle income renters, the figure is 13 percent, and among upper income renters, 4 percent). For low-income homeowners (a relatively small group, of course), severe housing burdens fall upon "only" 43 percent (versus 13 percent and 2 percent of middle and upper income homeowners, respectively).

For all the recent concern about housing foreclosures in the middle and upper middle classes, it proves to be the lower income groups, especially renters, who have suffered the most as a result of the run-up in housing costs. Nationally as well as locally, the housing burden is concentrated among renter households; overall, homeowners as a group have extremely low housing burdens, dedicating on average 16 percent of their income to meet their housing costs (nationwide). Renters typically pay over 30 percent. The median (national) income for homeowners in 2003 was $51,061, more than twice the median income of renters ($24,313.) Moreover, 25 percent of renters in 2003 lived below the poverty line, compared to just 7 percent of homeowners. So while there is a definite "affordability" issue on the home ownership side of the housing equation, the true crisis is in affordable rental housing, more and more of which seems to disappear with each passing day (Wright, Donley and Gotham 2008).

What are the real life impacts of excessively high housing burdens? Basically, families that are spending half or more of their income on their housing do not have enough disposable income left over for the rest of life's necessities. In our data, to illustrate, families with severe housing burdens (50 percent or more of income being spent on housing) are significantly less likely to have a savings account (45 percent with no savings compared to 18 percent of those with acceptable housing burdens) and among those with a savings account, more than half (56 percent) have less than $1,000 in that account. Unexpected bills resulting from any type of emergency would have dramatic consequences for these families, more than half of whom (56 percent) say that they would be unable to pay their bills if their monthly incomes were disrupted.

Even more telling are the difficulties these severe-housing-burden families face in meeting everyday needs such as food. Families with severe housing burdens are much more likely to receive food stamps, to rely on free meal programs, and to obtain food from other charitable organizations than families with "acceptable" housing burdens. Even with Food Stamps, meal programs, and charitable food outlets, almost one in four (24 percent) families who are experiencing severe housing burdens say they sometimes need more food than they have. (Among families with "high" but not severe housing burdens, one in five report that they sometimes need more food.) In addition, the more severe the housing burden, the more likely families were to delay or go without medical care because they could not afford it. Thus, families compensate for "overspending" on their housing by underconsuming food, medical care, and, one may safely suppose, all of life's other necessities as well.

The everyday struggle of trying to make ends meet, to provide adequate shelter, food, and medical care in the face of rising costs and inadequate monthly incomes, takes its toll on one's health and psychological well-being as well. Individuals with severe housing burdens were more likely to report poor health, were less happy, and reported more frequent feelings of isolation, depression, and sadness than people with acceptable housing costs.

The ultimate price paid by households suffering high housing burdens is, of course, loss of housing and a descent into homelessness. Severe housing burdens, especially among low income renters, are universally recognized precursors to homelessness (Lee, Tyler and Wright 2010).

Financial Well-Being. Half of low income families, a quarter of middle income families, and even an eighth of upper income families say they have *no savings account.* Among low income households who have a savings account, 60 percent say it contains less than $1,000. In contrast, among the 88 percent of upper income households with savings accounts, over half have savings of more than $10,000 and more than a quarter have savings of more than $50,000. With minimal or non-existent savings, it comes as no surprise that only 14 percent of low income families say their retirement planning is "adequate." Even among middle income families, the figure only rises to 30 percent (but rises to 60 percent in the upper income group).

Our low income respondents are also less likely to have received a raise since starting with their current employer (58 percent) than middle (72 percent) and upper (84 percent) income respondents, in part because they also change jobs frequently. In our data, the percentages of those who worked three or more jobs in the past ten years were 53 percent of low income respondents, 49 percent of middle income respondents, but only 28 percent of upper income respondents.

Life at the economic margin is reflected in people's feelings about their financial situation. In the low income group, more than half (56 percent) are "not satisfied at all" with their present financial situation, 37 percent feel that their financial situation is "getting worse," and 69 percent say they do not have enough income to live as comfortably as they would like. In the middle income group (which, recall, extends up to about $70,000 per year), a third are not satisfied, 28 percent think things are getting worse, and half need more income to be as comfortable as they would like.

One often hears that "all of us" are only "one paycheck away" from destitution, repossession, foreclosure, or even homelessness. We have always felt that this was a useful metaphor for the increasing financial insecurity of the American population, but was probably not *literally* true. We asked a direct question on the point: "If for whatever reason you missed a month's worth of pay, would you still be able to pay your bills?" Fifty-six percent of low income respondents, 38 percent of middle income respondents, and even 24 percent of upper income respondents said no. Perhaps "one paycheck away" is not so metaphorical after all.

In order to make ends meet, about a fifth of low income families take on odd jobs, do laundry or mending, or otherwise find ways to supplement their monthly incomes. More than a quarter also share resources

Table 2.5
Fringe Benefits by Income Category: Working Respondents Only (Percentage Receiving Each Benefit Listed)

	Low	Middle	Upper
Health insurance for you	45.7	67.2	73.2
Health insurance for the rest of your family	38.7	49.2	59.0
A retirement plan that your employer pays into	36.7	58.4	73.2
Paid vacations	53.1	64.7	71.5
Personal time off	58.8	71.0	79.6

with family, neighbors, and friends, a "survival strategy" that has been noted in nearly every study of low income families since Carol Stack's famous *All Our Kin*, first published in 1975. About one low income respondent in seven also works a second job.

Fringe Benefits. Jobs provide not just hours of labor and dollars of income; many also come with an array of fringe benefits that represent additional economic or quasi-economic resources to families. Alas, as it is written in the Gospel according to St. Luke (19:26), "to him that hath shall be given, and from him who hath not shall be taken away." *Every* fringe benefit we asked about is more available to working people in the upper income groupings, i.e., those financially least in need of the benefits in question. (The same was also true of the fringe benefits received by the working spouses of our respondents.)

Food. One in six low income households receives Food Stamps; one in ten participates in WIC; 60 percent of low income households with school age children say their children participate in the free or reduced school breakfast and lunch program. Just under a tenth eats meals at free food programs; one household in seven (in the low income group) receives "free food from food banks, churches, and other charitable organizations." More than one in four (versus about a tenth of the respondents in the middle and upper income groups) say there are times when they feel their families need more food than they have. Food insecurity, while not widespread, is for all practical purposes a near-exclusive experience of those at the bottom of the income distribution.

Transportation. A quarter of low income households have no car (versus almost none of the middle and upper income households without vehicles). Most (62 percent) of the cars owned by low income families are eight or more years old versus about 40 percent of middle income families and 20 percent of upper income families. Low income families therefore rely on public transportation far more regularly than middle and upper income families. And while all groups commute roughly equal distances, it is obvious that commutation expenses as a percentage of monthly income will impact most strongly on the lower income groups.

The Costs of Children. All parents learn early in their careers as parents that children are a gratifying but expensive proposition. Certainly, children increase the need for household space, bedrooms, outdoor play areas, and such; increase the monthly food and utility costs; pose various back-to-school expenses; and require costly day care while the parents are at work (Corcoran, Duncan and Hill 1984). Here, as in all other areas examined, one would expect the costs of children to weigh most heavily on the lower income categories, and indeed they do.

One question posed to parents of school aged children was, "Is the start of the new school year a very serious financial burden, somewhat serious, or not really serious at all?" Nearly half (46 percent) of low income families said this was a very serious burden, as compared to only about a fifth of the middle and upper income groups.

All families with children have to arrange for after-school care for the school-aged kids and daycare for children not yet old enough to attend school. In the majority of cases involving school aged children, the kids were either on their own until the adults got home or their care was handled within the household (by spouses, other siblings, etc.). However, 27 percent of low income households (versus 15 percent and 19 percent of middle and upper income households) made for-pay arrangements for after school care. In most cases (88 percent of low income families), the cost of this care was less than $60 per week. Higher income households can afford to purchase, and therefore do purchase, more expensive after-school care. Also, more than half (55 percent) of low income households with preschool children pay out of pocket for their care as well. In about a third of these cases, the out-of-pocket cost exceeds $100 per week.

Health. 32 percent of low income families, 10 percent of middle income families, and less than 4 percent of upper income families have NO health insurance coverage—not for themselves or for their spouses or children. This, of course, is a national problem that is as serious in Central Florida as anywhere else (DeNavas-Walt, Proctor and Smith 2009). The principal reason why people do not have health insurance, of course, is that their jobs do not include health benefits and private insurance plans are far too expensive. As one consequence of not having health insurance, 28 percent of low income families and even 12 percent of middle income families (but only 2 percent of upper income families) said there was at least one time in the past year when they needed health care but delayed or did not get it because they couldn't afford it.

Complicating matters, the low income group is also in the poorest health (see Hayward, et al. 2000; Evans 1994). The proportions of those who self-rate their health as "fair" or "poor" vary from 32 percent in the low income group to 16 percent in the middle income group and 12 percent in the upper income group. Also, a greater proportion of low income respondents (44 percent) compared to middle (30 percent) and upper (35 percent) income respondents reported that they went to the emergency room within the past year to get health care. Respectively,

18 percent, 9 percent and 5 percent of the children of each group were reported as having some sort of serious chronic health condition.

Debt. Debt is ubiquitous throughout society and is used increasingly by families in all income categories to get through each month (Mishel, Bernstein and Shierholz 2009). Still, the debt burden, as always, falls heaviest on the low income group. To illustrate:

- 42 percent, 24 percent, and 11 percent of the low, middle, and high income groups respectively have "outstanding medical bills" they are trying to pay off.
- Nearly equal proportions in all groups—37 percent, 51 percent, and 43 percent—are currently carrying unpaid credit card balances, but the unpaid balances are larger for the low income group. The percentages carrying $5000 or more in unpaid credit card balances are 38 percent, 29 percent, and 30 percent. If these differences were expressed as a percentage of average monthly income in each group, they would be far more dramatic.
- 25 percent, 14 percent, and 10 percent of low, middle, and high income families respectively are so far in debt they feel "they will never be able to get out."
- 7 percent of low income households and even 6 percent of middle income households, but no upper income households, are "currently behind on rent or mortgage payments" and therefore at some apparent risk of homelessness.
- 29 percent, 21 percent, and 14 percent of low, middle, and upper income households, respectively, have had a debt collection agency trying to get them to settle an unpaid debt.

Quality of Life. In general, there is a statistically significant linear relationship between income group and such things as poor appetite, inability to "shake off the blues," trouble concentrating, feeling depressed, loneliness, sadness, and a sense of failure in life, with the lower income group higher on all of these measures. Lower income families also have fewer family members in the area who could help if they ran into troubles and fewer close friends.

Money Does Buy Happiness After All. The French philosopher Jean-Jacques Rousseau wrote in 1750 that "Money buys everything except morality and citizens." Through a thousand retellings, this has evolved into the knowing adage, "Money can't buy happiness," often uttered by people with plenty of money to those with less than plenty, as a consolation prize for their impecunious means. One question we asked was: "All things considered, would you say you are very happy, happy, not very happy, or not happy at all?" Again, there is a strong linear relationship with income: The more money you have, the happier you are. The percentage "very happy" increases from one fifth of those in the low income category to more than twice that in the upper income category. At the other end of the distribution, those not very happy or not happy at all are *five times* more common in the low income category than in the high.

The Costs of Being Poor

A common response to data such as the above is to acknowledge that we seem to have a lot of low income people around, more perhaps than the overall levels of national affluence would lead one to expect, and even that the overall quality of life for low income people seems to suffer in comparison to the more affluent. But at the same time, we also have any number of programs to improve the lives of low income people: food programs, Medicaid, subsidized housing, various income supplement programs, and on through a long list, such as the programs reviewed by the Center on Budget and Policy Priorities study that was mentioned in the introduction to this chapter. In the end, given all that we spend to ameliorate the conditions of the poor and provide them with life's necessities, does it really matter whether a family is "low income" or not?

We can begin by agreeing that poor people in Haiti or Honduras are definitely much worse off than low income families in the U.S. But is there truly any comfort in knowing that our low income population is better off than poor people in the poorest countries in the Western hemisphere? Our data show that being poor or near-poor—at or below half of the median family income—means living at the edge of financial catastrophe, where an unexpected car repair or unbudgeted medical bill might make the difference between paying and not paying the rent, or the difference between food on the table and nights in the soup kitchen line. Too, in emphasizing the straitened circumstances of the low income population, we should not lose sight of the fact that many moderate and middle income people are also struggling, as our data demonstrate. Surely, constantly hovering at life's precipice must be stressful, and stress, we know too well, is linked to a vast array of unwanted health outcomes ranging from alcoholism to cardiovascular disease and nearly everything else.

A great deal of research (Braveman 2010; Adler and Rehkopf 2008; Lasser, Himmelstein and Woolhandler 2006) has been undertaken in the past decade to determine what are called "health disparities" and to find some means of reducing them. In some versions, the "disparity" in question is the difference between blacks and whites, but in many renditions, it is the difference between poor and non-poor. Everywhere we look, we find these disparities: in rates of various illnesses, in life expectancy and infant mortality, in psychological health and subjective well-being, in short, in practically everything. If you are low income, to borrow a phrase from Thomas Hobbes, life is "nasty, brutish and short."

Many people try to explain away these disparities by citing other variables that might produce them. Low income people drink too much! They eat lousy diets! They don't exercise! No wonder they die at elevated rates. Other analysts cite social differences in the consumption of health care or in health insurance coverage, or differences in social support, or social differences in environmental exposure: lead paint; environmental racism; unsafe and unhealthy workplaces; and the like. All of these points are true, but in most studies, controls for these factors reduce—but almost never eliminate—the effect of social variables such as race or poverty on health. And that fact has led some health scientists and medical sociologists to the conclusion that perhaps economic hierarchy is inherently unhealthy.

Marmor and his colleagues (1994) develop this theme most fully. These authors conclude that stress is the critical intervening variable: hierarchy is inherently stressful, and differential stress produces disparate health outcomes. The women Barbara Ehrenreich wrote about in *Nickel and Dimed* all seemed resigned in varying degrees to the cards life had dealt them, but they didn't seem happy or emotionally healthy. Likewise, low income people are often resilient and incredibly resourceful, but very few actually *like* the hand they've been dealt. As we see, the same is true of the vast majority of the homeless.

A study presented at the 2007 meetings of the American Association for the Advancement of Science explored the effects of poverty on childhood cognitive development. The study found that "many children growing up in very poor families with low social status experience unhealthy levels of stress hormones, which impair their neural development" (Krugman 2008). Poverty, like war, "is not healthy for children and other living things."

Conclusions

The myths and metaphors of Central Florida notwithstanding, the reality is that there are a lot of low income families in our region and they are struggling. This, perhaps, comes as no surprise given prevailing regional wage rates, the predominance of our service sector, and generally high housing costs (which have only recently abated—mainly in the home ownership category, not so much for renters). More surprising by far is just how deeply into the middle classes economic insecurities have penetrated. Consider:

- A quarter of the middle income population has no savings to fall back on.
- Nearly two fifths of middle income families would not be able to pay their bills if they missed a month's pay.
- Half of those in the middle income category are concerned that their retirement planning is inadequate.
- More than one in four feels that their economic situation is getting worse.
- Nearly one in five middle income families are **not** covered by any kind of health insurance plan.
- One in eight went without medical care at least once last year because they could not afford it.

Clearly, many middle income families are struggling too—burdened by debt, medically uninsured, worried about retirement. As a recent MSN news item put it, "The problem is that 'middle' and 'median' incomes no longer seem to provide the kind of comfort and security that Americans have become accustomed to. In most parts of America, a $48,000 annual income [the national median—locally, the figure was about $53,000 while the survey was being conducted] isn't enough to fund a comfortable life—dinner on the table at 6 p.m., the kids watched by a safe and affordable caregiver, a guaranteed summer vacation and a nest egg accruing so that, at age 65, Mom and Dad can look forward to their leisure years worry-free."

Still, the bulk of America's economic woes fall on low and moderate income families, whose real earnings have stagnated or dropped while their housing, energy, food, insurance, health and all other costs have escalated. And this must have surely expanded the pool of persons and families at some risk of homelessness. Just how wide and deep is this pool at risk? How many have already fallen in? These, conveniently, are the very questions we take up next.

Notes

1. This chapter was co-authored by Dr. Jana L. Jasinski, UCF Department of Sociology. It needs to be noted that "Central Florida" means different things to different people. Many local service agencies, e.g., our United Way, define the region as the three counties of Orange, Osceola, and Seminole. The Census includes Lake

County in its definition of the Orlando MSA. This chapter is based on those four counties plus Sumter County (which is part of the Workforce Central Florida definition of its catchment area). Myregion.com considers Central Florida to consist of seven counties; the University of Central Florida sphere of influence is officially designated as eleven counties, etc.

2. All table entries are derived from the 2006-08 American Community Survey estimates available at American Factfinder on the U.S. Census Bureau home page.

3. Then presidential candidate Bill Clinton stated in a campaign ad which first aired in September of 1992: "I have a plan to end welfare as we know it—to break the cycle of welfare dependency. We'll provide education, job training and child care, but then those that are able must go to work, either in the private sector or in public service."

4. Those were the federal TANF standards. States could enact more restrictive time limits, but not less restrictive ones.

5. Note that the low, middle, and high income categories take household size into account. For a four-person household, the low income category ends at about $30,000 per year. For a one-person household, it ends at about $20,000.

6. Since incomes and housing costs were obtained in fairly broad categories, these calculations are by no means precise.

3

One Thousand Homeless Men

One question we asked in the survey of low and moderate income households was, "Are you currently behind on your rent or mortgage payments?" In the total sample, 6.2 percent said yes, a response that varied from 7.4 percent of the low income group to 5.9 percent of the middle income group (no one in the upper income group was in arrears on their housing).

The question is probably not a bad indicator of a household's risk of becoming homeless. Based on the above results, the pool of risk is, say, 6 percent of the bottom half of the household income distribution. In Orange County alone, there are just under 400,000 households; by definition, 200,000 of them are in the bottom half of the income distribution (i.e., below the median income). At 6 percent, the ensuing risk pool is comprised of ~12,000 households. Other counties in the Orlando MSA would approximately double that number. So by these standards, the population at some risk of homelessness in the Central Florida region is on the order of, say, twenty-five thousand households. Years ago, the local Homeless Services Network (HSN) also tried to estimate the population at risk of homelessness, and while the precise methodology of their estimate is lost in the sands of time, passages in the 2004 Mayor's Working Committee on Homelessness report put the figure at a number near 30,000, about the same as the number derived from our survey question.[1]

Current data from HSN's 2009 Point in Time Count (and from previous counts) show that about 10,000 people in Central Florida will suffer at least one episode of homelessness this year. All of the above calculations are obviously imprecise, but the suggestion is that if one's household is "currently behind" on its rent (or mortgage payments), the odds on being homeless before the end of the year might well be on the order of three or four in ten. If one has no savings account, is carrying a significant debt burden, and does not have family in the area who could help if one got into trouble, the risk of becoming homeless would be higher still. Thus, the kinds of social and economic marginality discussed in Chapter Two, which in turn results from the jobs economy described in Chapter One, can and often do lead directly to the topic of this and subsequent chapters, namely, Central Florida's sizable homeless population.

On June 30, 2003, a research team from our institute surveyed every man who sought shelter that evening at the Pavilion, the Coalition's shelter for homeless men. Including persons interviewed later in the evening after the survey team had left, the "Pavilion Survey" initially covered 328 men. In ensuing weeks and months, identifying information on every man who presented for shelter at the Pavilion was screened through a database built from the June 30 survey and new surveys were administered to every client not previously seen, thus enabling an unduplicated count of men seeking shelter at the Pavilion. (This process has continued ever since, now for more than six years, although the questions asked at intake have been modified from time to time.) On the weekend of August 16-17, about six weeks later, the unduplicated count reflected in the spreadsheet exceeded a thousand. This chapter describes what we learned from these one thousand homeless men.

Context

The Coalition for the Homeless of Central Florida (hereafter, simply the Coalition) is the largest provider of homeless services in Central Florida, with a daily client load of about 700-800 people on two campuses: the main campus, consisting of the Men's Pavilion and the Center for Women and Families; and an auxiliary campus in a separate downtown location housing the Women's Residential and Counseling Center, a transitional program for about one hundred homeless women, many with children. A great deal of the research reported in this book is based on data gathered at these Coalition facilities.

The Pavilion itself is a large (13,000 square feet) traditional drop-in shelter that can house 375 men on a given night. (Recently, the nightly count has been around 200.[1]) It is the only low-demand emergency drop-in shelter in Central Florida. Men who stay at the Pavilion are provided with a warm evening meal, a shower if they want one, and a place to sleep for the night. There are also lockers that can be rented to store one's "stuff," although most of the lockers are empty most of the time. Some of the Pavilion's controversial history as Orlando's largest homeless shelter is recounted in Chapter Twelve.

The evening meal is provided through a soup kitchen-type feeding program open to the community. On busy nights, as many as 500 hot meals are served in this program. These meals are usually prepared off-site, brought by van to the Coalition, and served by volunteers, the majority of whom are church-affiliated. (See Chapter Eleven for details.) In March of 2004, we surveyed 285 persons who either ate their evening meal at the Coalition or had lunch earlier in the day at Daily Bread, a feeding program at the Christian Service Center across the street from the Coalition. A key finding was that about more than one in five (22 percent) of the people fed in these two facilities were not literally homeless, but rather were individuals and families from the surrounding community who were using these programs as way to stretch their monthly incomes. In other soup kitchen surveys, the non-homeless proportion is as high as one in three (Burt et al. 2001). (Recall from Chapter Two that about a tenth of the region's low income families eat at least an occasional meal at community feeding programs such as these.)

The sleeping arrangements at the Pavilion consist of thin plastic mats that are unrolled onto the Pavilion's concrete floor, which is marked up into painted rectangles rather like parking spaces, except that these are places to park your body, not your car. The evening meal is eaten in the same large open space, so once the dinner service is completed, the tables and chairs are broken down and stored, trash and litter are picked up, and the area is hosed down. The men then begin signing in for the evening, picking up their mats and claiming a space. Many of the Pavilion "regulars" sleep in the same space night after night for months on end and consider it a form of trespass when others try to infringe upon "their" spot on the floor.

The Pavilion is a "low demand" shelter in that hardly anyone is turned away. Persons who are clearly a threat to self or others are sometimes encouraged to go elsewhere, as are people who are too drunk to stand up or too high to know where they are, but lesser degrees of inebriation and mental incapacitation have traditionally been tolerated. Technically, men must pay one dollar to sleep in the Pavilion for the night, but hardly anyone is denied admission if they don't happen to have a dollar. (There is always some small chore they can do instead.) Also, technically, men presenting for shelter are supposed to produce identification, but no one is turned away if they cannot. (Such, in any case, was the Pavilion policy while our research was underway. Recently, Pavilion policy about the need to produce identification has been toughened up.) Two or three times a week, the Pavilion log is run through the Florida Department of Law Enforcement's online sex-offender registry and men who show up on the registry are required to leave[3]. (The Pavilion is adjacent to the Center for Women and Families, which houses children, so adjudicated sex offenders violate the state residency restrictions by sleeping in the Pavilion.)

Although the Men's Pavilion is the only emergency shelter in downtown Orlando, indeed, in the whole of Central Florida, there are three other fairly large homeless service facilities nearby. Just across the street and up a block or two from the Pavilion is the Christian Service Center mentioned earlier, which feeds homeless people a noon meal, operates a thrift store, and provides residential and rehabilitation services to homeless men in recovery. About equally distant, but in the opposite direction, is the Orlando Union Rescue Mission (OURM), an 80-bed faith-based recovery program for down and out men. (The Mission also operates a facility for women and children.) Unlike the Pavilion, OURM clients must have months of sobriety under their belts before they are eligible for services. A "dormitory fee" of six dollars per night is requested. Also nearby is the Salvation Army's Men's Lodge and Adult Rehabilitation Center, which, like the Mission, demands sobriety of its clients and eleven dollars per night for the stay. There is a general consensus among homeless men in the area that a night at the Mission is better than a night at the Pavilion, and the Salvation Army is better still. Both the Mission and the "Sally" have real beds, for example, not plastic mats on concrete floors. But they also cost quite a bit more for the night's accommodations, there are limits on how long one can stay, one can't show up drunk, high, filthy, or reeking of alcohol, and both are also frequently full. At the Men's Pavilion, in contrast, hardly anyone is turned away (although they do sometimes run out of mats in which case men sleep right on the concrete).

Some indication of the inadequacy of Central Florida's services for its homeless population is that with an estimated nightly homeless population of more than 4,000 persons, the total emergency shelter bed capacity is 1,207 beds (925 of them in downtown Orlando). Perforce, large numbers of the region's homeless are "unsheltered homeless," who are either doubled up with other households, renting cheap motel rooms on an extended-occupancy basis, or are living out-of-doors (Wright 2009; Hopper and Baumohl 1996). Every night, some dozens of homeless men sleep on benches in a small open area just outside the Pavilion.

Dozens more sleep either elsewhere on the Coalition's property (parking lot, basketball court) or on the street adjacent to the main Pavilion entrance, and scores more can be found strewn around the city, sleeping in doorways, alleys, abandoned buildings, under highway overpasses, or in the public parks. No satisfactory count of the "outdoor homeless" in downtown Orlando has ever been produced, but no one would scoff at a guess somewhere in the few hundreds. And there are hundreds, maybe thousands, more in the surrounding metro area.

The Coalition, Christian Service Center, Union Rescue Mission, and Salvation Army are known as the Big Four, and most homeless men in Central Florida have at least some experience with all four of these facilities. This is true equally of homeless men who normally sleep in the shelters and homeless men who normally don't (see Chapter Seven). There are bound to be at least some differences in the client populations of the four facilities, and likewise at least some differences between sheltered and unsheltered homeless men. These points granted, there is no reason to think that what is true of Pavilion men is not true of the region's homeless men in general.

Client Flow

As of the initial baseline survey (June 30, 2004), 328 men were in the Pavilion database. By August 25, the number had grown to 1,077. In the seven days immediately following the original survey effort, 29.2 new clients were enrolled each evening, on average. Most of these "new clients" were actually Pavilion "regulars" who, for one reason or another, had found alternate sleeping arrangements the night of June 30 and off and on during the following week. As the days and weeks progressed, the number of new clients registered each night fell off significantly as more and more "regulars" returned. Still, critically, that number never did drop to zero—not in the months when we monitored it closely and not in the six years since. In the last seven days that we kept close track of (August 19 – 25), the nightly number of new clients averaged 8.1 and that average has been about constant *ever since*. This is an important point to which we return shortly.

Altogether, in the fifty-six days from June 30 to August 24, 749 names were added to the database, an average of 13.4 new names nightly. If this rate were to hold for an entire year, we reasoned, the implication would be that the unduplicated count of men receiving shelter at the Pavilion would top 5,000 ([365 x 13.4 = 4891] + 328 from baseline = 5,219) by the end of the year. In fact, the actual unduplicated count for the fiscal year (FY) of 2003-2004 was 3,477, and has hovered right around 3,500 in most years since. The reason for the discrepancy is that the nightly "newbies" (men being seen for the first time) do not average 13.4, but rather somewhere around eight or ten.

It is thus immediately apparent that the nightly Pavilion population consists of at least two very distinct groups: one group of regulars, many of them chronically homeless men who sleep most nights at the Pavilion (although almost all of them also spend occasional nights elsewhere), and a second group of people who are new to the Pavilion that night and, perhaps, new to the condition of homelessness.[4] The implications of these points are explored in depth in the next chapter.

Since the number of men sheltered nightly at the Pavilion tends to be roughly constant (ranging from 300 to 350 in the early years and averaging about 200 recently), the easy assumption is that these are the same men night after night. In one sense, that easy assumption is correct, but in another important sense, it is profoundly misleading. As a matter of fact, most of the men sleeping at the Pavilion on any given night have, indeed, slept there before and sleep there quite regularly. (In Pavilion surveys we did in 2009, upwards of two-thirds of the men interviewed had spent *every night* of the previous month there and most of the remainder had slept in the Pavilion at least ten out of the previous thirty nights.) At the same time, the number of new clients appearing nightly is sufficient to generate an annual unduplicated count amounting to several thousand men. Thus we see that the nightly shelter count is a misleading indicator of the extent of the homeless problem in the Orlando metropolitan area, a point that becomes even more apparent in the analysis of shelter utilization that appears in the next chapter.

How can a facility shelter nearly the same 200 men night after night yet generate an annual unduplicated count in the thousands? Easy. Consider a nightly shelter population of 200 men, 190 of them regulars who sleep there every night and ten of them new men who have never slept there before (and never do again). The regulars would comprise 95 percent of the men in the shelter *on any given night* (190/200 = 95 percent). However, over an entire year, there would be 190 regulars (the same 190 every night) and 3,650 (10 x 365 = 3,650) one-timers, for a total unduplicated annual count of 190 plus 3,650, which comes to 3,840. Thus, in the *annual count*, the regulars would comprise a mere 5 percent of the total clients served (190 / 3,840 = 5 percent). These facts prove highly consequential for our understanding of the magnitude and nature of the homeless problem both regionally and nationally.

Client Demographics

Table 3.1 presents basic demographic data on the original 1,000-man sample. Consistent with other studies (Burt 1999), Pavilion men are relatively young, with an average age of 43.8 years (standard deviation of 10.4 years). More than half (56.1 percent) are African American, about a sixth (15.5 percent) are Hispanic, and just over a quarter (27.2 percent) are white, with a very small sprinkling of others (1.2 percent). Compared to the Orlando metro population, whites are underrepresented and blacks are strongly overrepresented among these men. The strong overrepresentation of African Americans among homeless men has been widely noted (See, e.g., Orr 2006; Hopper 2003). Also, about one in four is a veteran of the United States Armed Forces, somewhat higher than the percentage registered for American men in general (13 percent) (HUD 2009).

Relatively few Pavilion men are native to Florida. One in ten was born in or around the Orlando area and an additional 14.8 percent were born elsewhere in Florida. Florida natives comprise only about a quarter of the total. Members of the largest group, 59 percent of the total, were born elsewhere in the United States, and nearly one in six (15.7 percent) was born in a foreign country (or Puerto Rico). Of the 155 men born outside the U.S., 72 percent gave their ethnicity as Hispanic, so these are mostly recent immigrants from Puerto Rico with a sprinkling from Mexico, Cuba, and other nations. Another thirty of the foreign-born gave their ethnicity as black and many of these men are also from nations in the Caribbean.

Although the figures on place of birth seem to depict Pavilion men as geographical transients, a common stereotype of the homeless, they turn out to be not much more "transient" than the Orlando metro area population at large. In the 2000 Census, the total Orlando metro area population was 1,645,000. Of these, 18.2 percent (versus 15.7 percent of Pavilion men) were born outside the United States (including those born in U.S. territories such as Puerto Rico), 31.3 percent were native Floridians (versus about 25 percent of Pavilion men), and the remainder, 50.5 percent, were born elsewhere in the U.S. (versus 59 percent of Pavilion men). Obviously, in geographic origins, Pavilion men tend to mirror the larger Orlando population pretty closely. The very rapid population growth of the region discussed in Chapter One implies massive in-migration, and this is clearly as true of the region's homeless as it is of everyone else (Rukmana 2008).[5]

Table 3.1
Client Demographics

Racial Composition		
	Black	56.1
	Hispanic	15.5
	White	27.2
	Other	1.2
	Total	100%
	(N = 1005)	

Where were you born?		
	In, around Orlando	10.4
	Elsewhere in Florida	14.8
	In USA, not Florida	59.0
	Out of U.S.	15.7
	Total	99.9%
	(N = 984)	

If not born in Orlando: How long have you lived in the Orlando area?
  Mean time in Orlando = 80.1 months (6.7 years)
  (N = 891)

Age	Average (Mean) Age =	43.8 years
	Standard Deviation =	10.4 years
	(N = 1001)	

Are you a veteran?		
	No	75.2%
	Yes	24.8%
	(N = 996)	

Where were you living before your current spell of homelessness?		
	Orlando	55.8
	Other place in Florida	17.1
	Some other state	25.2
	Out of U.S.	1.9
	Total	100%
	(N = 904)	

Regardless of origin, most Pavilion men (55.8 percent) were living in the Orlando area before their current spell of homelessness (versus moving to Orlando once they became homeless). About one in six (17.1 percent) were living elsewhere in Florida, a quarter (25.2 percent) were living in other states, and a small handful (1.9 percent) were living outside the U.S.

Among those who were not born in or around Orlando (N = 891), the average length of time they had lived in the Orlando area was 80.1 months, or 6.7 years. Thus, on the whole, it would be erroneous to depict them as recent arrivals to the state. At the same time, about one in five (21.8 percent) had been in Orlando for one month or less when we interviewed them. It is therefore fair to conclude that while some homeless men are recent arrivals to Florida, many are lifetime residents, with still others everywhere in between, again not at all unlike the Orlando population in general.

Experiences with Homelessness

Table 3.2 summarizes data on the sample's prior experiences with homelessness. Although men who sleep at the Pavilion are almost always described as Orlando's "chronically homeless" male population (as, indeed, we have described them), the substantial majority (57.3 percent) are in fact currently experiencing their first episode of homelessness. Another third (32.3 percent) said they had been homeless "a few times." Call them the episodically homeless. The truly chronically homeless, those who have been homeless "many times" or "more times than I can remember," comprise barely a tenth of the total Pavilion population. This, too, is generally true of homeless populations everywhere, with policy implications discussed at length in the next chapter.

In the total sample, the mean duration of the current spell of homelessness is 25.6 months, or just over two years, but this is somewhat misleading because the mean duration varies drastically between first-time, episodic, and chronically homeless men. Among men in the midst of their first spell of homelessness, the mean duration is 17.8 months; and among those who have been homeless "a few times," 23.5 months. Among the chronically homeless, of course, the mean duration is much longer: 63.2 months (or a bit more than five years) for those who have been homeless many times, and an astonishing 132.4 months, or about eleven years, for those who have been homeless more times than they can remember.

Averages depict the central tendency of a distribution but say nothing about the variation around that central tendency. In point of fact,

Table 3.2
Selected Homelessness Experiences

How many times have you ever been homeless in your entire lifetime?

Just this once	57.3
A few times	32.3
Many times/more times than I can remember	10.4
Total	100%
(N = 1000)	

Average length of **current spell** of homelessness

Total sample	25.6 months
First time homeless	17.8 months
Episodically homeless	23.5 months
Homeless "many times"	63.2 months
More times than I remember	132.4 months

Length of current spell in categories

One month or less	35.9
More than a month, less than a year	34.1
More than a year	30.0
Total	100%
(N = 984)	

the current homeless spell is one month or less for about a third (35.9 percent), more than a month but less than a year for another third (34.1 percent), and more than a year for the final third (30.0 percent). The averages shown in the previous paragraph are therefore inflated by the small number of men with exceptionally long homelessness spells (e.g., by the one elderly gentleman we interviewed whose current episode of homelessness—his first, incidentally—has lasted fifty-two years—and counting!)

Pavilion men seem less "chronic" than the single homeless men in Martha Burt's National Survey of Homeless Assistance Providers and Clients, a 1999 survey that is still the closest anyone has yet come to a true nationally representative sample of homeless people (Burt, Aron and Lee 2001). Her Table 3.2 shows that 47 percent of single homeless men have been homeless just once (i.e., are in their first spell of homelessness); the figure for Pavilion men is higher, at 57 percent. Likewise, 54 percent of her single men have accumulated a year or more in their current spell of homelessness; the equivalent figure for Pavilion men is 30 percent. So quite in contrast to the image of Pavilion men as Orlando's most severely chronic homeless male population, men who sleep at the Pavilion are more likely to be experiencing their first episode of homelessness and have accumulated less time homeless during that episode than the single homeless men in Burt's national sample.

Despite the persistent stereotype of chronicity among the homeless, that is, the common view that once people become homeless, they usually stay homeless for long periods, the fact, as research reviewed in the next chapter shows, is that the chronic component is only about 10-20 percent of the total. The large majority of people who ever experience a bout of homelessness get through the episode pretty quickly (in a matter of days, weeks, or at most, a few months) and in many cases are never homeless again. These are what we now know as the *transitionally* homeless (as opposed to the chronically or episodically homeless), and in most studies, they make up ~80 percent of the total (Culhane and Kuhn 1998; Kuhn and Culhane 1998).

Why do we associate homelessness with chronicity? This chapter has already hinted at the answer. The vast bulk of what we know about homeless people is what we have learned through one-shot surveys usually done on one night in large homeless shelters like the Pavilion. And on any given night, the shelter regulars, the chronics, may comprise nineteen out of every twenty clients. And yet of all the people who pass through the shelter in a year, those who are there for just one, or at most a few nights—i.e., people whose homelessness resolves itself quickly—might well outnumber the chronics twenty to one. Unfortunately for research, but fortunately for them, they do not hang around in the shelters long enough to show up in any numbers in the customary one-shot shelter survey.

Panhandling

Of all the behaviors associated with homelessness in the public mind, beggary is evidently the most offensive. Empirical studies report with great consistency that "contrary to common belief, panhandlers and homeless people are not necessarily one and the same. Many studies have found that only a small percentage of homeless people panhandle, and only a small percentage of panhandlers are homeless" (Scott 2002). Estimates of the percentage of homeless people that engage in panhandling have ranged from 5 to 40 percent, i.e., always fewer than half.

Orlando's public perception of Pavilion men is that they are "beggars and bums," and most Central Floridians see a very close linkage between homelessness and panhandling (see Chapter Ten). However, the large majority of Pavilion men say they *never* panhandle and the few who do appear to panhandle irregularly. In the original baseline survey, we asked, "Do you ever panhandle or beg for money or spare change from people to help you get by?" Here are the results:

"Do you ever panhandle…?"

No, never	86.0
Yes, not very often	7.0
Yes, from time to time	5.0
Yes, regularly	2.0
Total	100%
(N = 363)	

A very large majority, 86 percent of the total, responded "No, never," many of them quite emphatically, as if to say, "Yes, I am a homeless man but there are depths to which even I do not stoop." (For the record, many took umbrage at even being asked the question.) An additional 7 percent said "Yes, but not very often" and another 5 percent said "Yes, from time to time." That leaves about 2 percent who panhandle regularly, a mere seven men among the 363 who were asked the question. Although sharply at variance with common stereotypes, these findings are in accord with other studies such as Scott (2002). About one Pavilion man in fifty panhandles regularly, maybe one in six does so from time to time, and members of the 85 percent majority never panhandle and even appear to take some pride in that fact. But none of this has prevented Orlando from trying on several different occasions to criminalize panhandling behavior (see Chapter Twelve).

Empirical studies of panhandlers do not depict the activity as highly profitable. "Most evidence confirms that panhandling is not lucrative, although some panhandlers clearly are able to subsist on a combination of panhandling money, government benefits, private charity, and money from odd jobs such as selling scavenged materials or plasma" (Scott 2002). Credible estimates range from a few dollars a day to perhaps a hundred dollars a day for those who are very skilled at the activity. Most panhandlers combine begging with other income-producing activities to generate a subsistence income, at best. Chapter Seven discusses panhandling among homeless people living in the woods, where the activity seems to be more prevalent than among Pavilion men living downtown, and also confirms that panhandling yields only small sums of money. The idea that panhandlers are not truly needy, that beggary is some sort of scam, and that aggressive panhandlers rake in improbably large sums of money, only to drive home at the end of the day in shiny new Cadillacs, is so widespread in contemporary American society that it has attained the status of an urban myth.

Panhandling has been ruled by the U.S. Supreme Court to be legally protected behavior under the First Amendment. One can no more ban people from asking for spare change than one can ban people from asking for the time of day (free speech), and likewise, the asking for and giving of alms is constitutionally protected religious behavior. Thus, efforts to ban panhandling outright have been stricken down as unconstitutional. But the Court has also ruled that regulations concerning the "place and manner" of panhandling are not unconstitutional. Thus, numerous laws prohibiting "aggressive panhandling" have withstood Court challenges, one of them Orlando's. It turns out that most panhandling is in fact passive, not aggressive (see Lee and Farrell 2003), and the definition of what constitutes "aggressive" panhandling varies wildly from place to place. Scott notes, "Enforcing aggressive-panhandling laws can be difficult, partly because few panhandlers behave aggressively, and partly because many victims of aggressive panhandling do not report the offense to police or are unwilling to file a complaint." Many of these laws require police discretion and therefore invite selective enforcement, which leads to citizen and business owner complaints that the police are letting panhandlers get away with too much.

Because of these and other enforcement issues, many cities have experimented with efforts to control the behavior of givers, not the behavior of panhandlers. This was one of the (unimplemented) recommendations of the 2004 Mayor's Working Committee on Homelessness, whose history is recounted in Chapter Twelve. Implementation of such measures entails public education to discourage giving money directly to individuals and encourage people to donate their spare change to area service providers instead. In Baltimore, the "Make a Change" campaign provides collection boxes inside area hotels and businesses for people to deposit money that would have otherwise gone to panhandlers.

Similarly, in Athens, Georgia, among other places, parking meters have been converted into donation kiosks, where people can deposit spare change that is then given to local homeless service providers. Miami has just enacted a similar program. Many cities (Savannah, Memphis, Baltimore, Evanston, Nashville) post signs asking people not to give to panhandlers, encouraging citizens to report panhandling to the police, or urging people not to feel guilty for saying no.

Labor Force Participation

If homeless guys don't pick up the money they need for shelter fees, cigarettes, and other necessities by panhandling, just how do they support themselves? We asked Pavilion men, "During the day, when the Pavilion is closed, where do you spend your time?" A few men responded that they spent their days hanging out, drinking, trying to score drugs, or, in a very few cases, panhandling, but this was very few indeed. By far, the largest majority said they spent their days working or looking for work. Indeed, the two most common specific answers, by far, were "at work," mentioned by 175 men (16.7 percent), and "looking for work," mentioned by 118 men (11.3 percent). Adding in all other work-related or job-search activities (i.e., "day labor," "get some work," "finding work," "job hunting," and the like), 67.1 percent of the total who were asked the question (N = 929) said they spent their days either at work or trying to find work. In contrast, "panhandling," "begging," and all plausible variations were mentioned by only three men.

More recent Pavilion surveys continue to show the same pattern, except that these days, there are many more men looking for work than actually working. Our recent needs assessment surveys of Pavilion men, done largely to determine the interests of these men in case management and related services, showed again and again that what these men said they need most is a job. As we learned in the first Pavilion survey, "work" for the largest share of these men is temporary work in the day labor outlets. Our annual Point in Time count done in conjunction with the Homeless Services Network always includes the day labor outlets as places where we go to count. For the January 2008 count, we identified just under fifty labor pools in the region. By the time of the January 2009 count, *half* of the day labor outlets had disappeared, institutional victims of the severe downturn in the local construction industry.

We are by no means the first to find that most homeless men work (or at least try to when work is available). Rossi's survey of the homeless in Chicago, undertaken in the mid-1980s, had a very detailed sequence of questions about sources of income (welfare benefits, general relief, begging, financial support from families, etc.) and reported, somewhat surprisingly at the time, that income from work dominated over all other sources combined (Rossi et al. 1987). Since the Chicago survey, the finding has been replicated in any number of studies (Zuvekas and Hill 2000). In Burt's national study, 51 percent of single homeless men had worked for pay in the previous thirty days (a question about looking for work was not asked). Clearly, the majority of homeless men are *not* homeless because they refuse to work, but rather because no work is available or because the prevailing wage rate is inadequate to sustain them in housing.

In addition to the two-thirds that spend their days working or looking for work, there are a number of Pavilion men, then and now, who are obviously disabled and incapable of working. We did not ask about physical disabilities in the 2003 survey, but we did in a 2009 survey, and 27 percent of those surveyed had a self-described physical disability of some sort. (A few respondents may have been exaggerating, but by the observations of our interviewers, the large majority clearly were not.) If we add those who can't work to those who do or are at least trying, we get a total of more than 90 percent. That leaves fewer than a tenth to be described as "lazy, shiftless bums."

The problem, clearly, is not that homeless men won't work, but that they can't work, no work is available, or the wages they earn from work in the day labor outlets is inadequate. A study released in January 2006 by the Center for the Study of Urban Poverty examined the experiences of day laborers in 139 municipalities across the country (Valenzuela et al. 2006). This is the first-ever national study of day laborers. Contrary to stereotype, nearly half (49 percent) of day laborers are hired directly by homeowners or renters, usually to do light construction or yard maintenance work. About 43 percent are hired by construction contractors. Income from day labor represents the sole source of income for 83 percent of those studied. Average annual earnings of day laborers are at or below the poverty threshold, with incomes rising in peak months to as much as $1,400 while falling to $500 or less in the slower months. Incomes to be earned in day labor are also compromised by widespread industry practices such as charging laborers for transportation to and from the work site, for lunch, to cash checks, and related dubious practices. Also contrary to stereotype, day laborers are active members of their communities, not transients or low-lifes. Half, for example, attend church regularly (a much higher attendance percentage than the average sociology department could boast).

A Note on Homeless Veterans and Trends

Altogether, there were 247 U.S. veterans in the Pavilion database, about a quarter of the total. Subsequent surveys conducted in the Pavilion and with other groups of homeless men in Central Florida always show the percentage of veterans to be around 25 percent. The veterans (average age = 48.1 years) are marginally older than the non-vets (42.5 years) and are also more likely to be white (38 percent white versus 23 percent white). About half the veterans (49.0 percent) believe they are eligible for VA benefits, about a third (31.6 percent) know that they are not, and the remainder are uncertain. Homelessness histories of the two groups are very similar (roughly the same number of prior homeless episodes and roughly the same duration of the current episode). In most other variables examined, the veterans were indistinct. These data are currently being used by the Coalition in its efforts to get VA support for an expanded facility for homeless men to be built on the current grounds of the Coalition.

A press release from the U.S. Department of Veterans' Affairs, dated March 6 of 2008 and featured in numerous papers, announced that the "Number of Homeless Vets Drops 21 Percent." The story was that "the number of veterans homeless on a typical night has declined 21 percent in the past year, thanks to the services offered by the Department of Veterans Affairs (VA) and its partners in community- and faith-based organizations." From this one might infer (certainly, this is the explicit implication) that the VA has figured out some method to reduce homelessness among veterans. Alas, not so.

The specific numbers on which this assertion is based are the 195,000 homeless veterans in FY 2006 as opposed to the 154,000 in FY 2007. The release mentions in passing that "improvements in survey techniques" may account for some of the announced difference, but in the main treats the decline as a real result of "significant progress in the fight against homelessness."

Interestingly, as it turns out, neither the 2006 nor the 2007 number is based on an actual count. In both years, VA "points of contact" (POCs), of which there are 138 nationwide, were asked in the annual "Point of Contact Survey" to "estimate the number of homeless veterans in her or his service area." (The VA Points of Contact are usually the local VA homeless program coordinators.) And while it is reasonable to assume that the POCs have a rough general idea of the number of homeless veterans in their service areas, there is no reason to suggest that their rough ideas would be very precise, even to the nearest few hundred.

In FY 2006 and in all previous years that this annual survey was conducted, the POCs were asked specifically to report "the highest estimated number of homeless veterans in your service area for any given day during FY 2006." In the FY 2007 survey, the question was changed in an important way. Rather than estimating the highest number for any given day of the prior year, the FY 2007 respondents were asked "to provide a point-in-time estimate of the homeless veterans in their service area on any day during the last week of January 2007." Since the odds are only seven in 365 that the number on a particular day during the last week of January would also happen to be the "highest estimated number of homeless veterans ... for any given day" of the entire preceding year, all or virtually all of the POCs would have, perforce, reported a lower number in the 2007 survey than they would have reported in 2006. Since the question was altered between the two years, it cannot be said whether the apparent decline from 195,000 to 154,000 homeless veterans is real (and therefore indicative of progress) or a simple artifact of method and therefore substantively meaningless. Instinctively, one presumes the latter, since a real drop of 21 percent in a single year fails the laugh test.

Update 2009

We've referred in several passages to "more recent Pavilion surveys." The reference here is to recent needs assessment surveys of Pavilion men that we did on behalf of the Coalition in order to determine an optimal mix of services in the new Men's Service Center being built in 2010 and 2011 to replace the obsolete and crumbling Pavilion. (The history of the Coalition's efforts to get City approval for the new facility is recounted in Chapter Twelve.) The first of the needs assessment surveys was conducted on June 3, 2009, beginning at 4:00 p.m. and ending at the onset of the evening meal service. Altogether, 110 men completed this first survey. The first survey was conducted in the early afternoon, when some Coalition men are allowed into the Pavilion to shower, watch TV or a movie, catch up on the news, or just socialize. The distinct possibility that these men comprised a self-selected and therefore biased sample, and that the hard-core chronically homeless men do not show up until much later, caused us to do a second survey several weeks later that began during the evening meal service and continued, basically, until everyone had checked in for the night. The second survey, a considerably shortened version of the original, was administered on June 26, 2009 and forty-eight men participated, none of them respondents to the first survey. However, we did recognize a few individuals who had also participated in our survey in 2003.

The major anticipated difference between the new Men's Service Center and the old Pavilion, aside from nicer amenities, is a strong emphasis on case management in the new facility. In the current facility, no case management is available except to men enrolled in the Pavilion's alcohol and drug rehabilitation program (36 men). In offering strongly enhanced case management services, however, Coalition management wants to be certain they do not abandon their more intractable, hardcore clientele, whose interests may be to find a place to crash and be left alone rather than to "sober up, take a shower, and get a job." Knowing how many Pavilion men are actually interested in case management and in making a real effort to move towards self-sufficiency, versus how many are looking mainly for a place to sleep it off, further enhances our understanding of Orlando's homeless men.

Ninety-two percent of the men in the first survey (N = 110) were planning to spend that night at the Coalition and 66 percent had spent every evening in the past month there. We see once again the preponderance of Pavilion regulars in a one-shot survey. Of the few who were not planning to sleep at the Coalition that evening, 80 percent had spent one or more nights at the Coalition in the past.

Respondents were asked about the importance of various amenities that the Coalition is thinking about including in the new facility. The amenity deemed most important (highest percentage of "very important" votes) was new shower facilities. Tied in second place were on-site laundry facilities and access to case managers. Job training and mattresses were also "very important" to more than 80 percent. New lockers and programs for ex-offenders were also highly-rated. In contrast, things like "games and recreation space" were important to fewer than 40 percent.

We asked these men to think about their own personal situations and assess how important it would be for the Men's Service Center to offer a place to "hang out" during the day (i.e., a daytime drop-in facility). The majority (61.8 percent) said this would be very important; another 15.5 percent said it was somewhat important. We asked what they would want to do with their time if this option was available. Rather than watch TV, hang out, or check e-mail, the most frequent responses focused, again, on employment. Most said they would spend their time using Coalition computers to look for work. Others that already have jobs said they would like to sleep during the day, as they work at night. Some of the men, particularly the elderly and disabled, would like a place that is out of the heat. Very few indicated that they intended to spend their days "just hanging out," playing cards, or watching daytime television. Most of the men who said having a place to stay during the day was not important were either currently working or actively looking for work.

The men were then asked if they would be interested in receiving case management if available. 83.5 percent said that they would definitely be interested. Another 8.3 percent said they would probably be interested. Only 7.3 percent said they would not be interested.

Anticipating generally positive responses, we then posed a series of questions explaining in greater detail what case management entailed, fully expecting enthusiasm to fall off very rapidly as additional constraints were imposed. The sequence began by explaining that case management is "not just something that would be done **for** you or **to** you. It requires that you also actively participate in order to achieve your goals." The anticipated fall-off in interest did not materialize. Even with the stipulation that case management would require their active participation, almost everyone (92.5 percent) still said yes, they would be interested. Another question stipulated getting and staying clean and sober as a precondition, and even with that restriction, 91.5 percent of the men said they would still be interested and 93.5 percent were very confident they could do so.

In this connection, it is relevant to mention that 13 percent of the men surveyed said that they were currently in need of alcohol detox, treatment, or rehabilitation, 17 percent said they needed detox, treatment, or rehabilitation for drugs other than alcohol, and 18.9 percent had been in detox at least once in the past few years. Nearly a quarter said that if there were an opening in First Steps (the Coalition's drug rehabilitation program—see Chapter Eight) and they were offered the chance to enroll, they would. We take this number, roughly one in four, as an indicator of the percentage whose case management needs are predominantly for addiction-related issues.

We next proceeded to offer descriptions of various models of the new Men's Service Center to determine which one or ones they liked most. The first model:

> One idea for the new Men's Service Center is to have different sleeping and service arrangements for men with different kinds of needs. For example, one part of the Center might be a residential program where men would sleep in beds rather than mats on the floor, have lockers for their things, eat in their own dining room and enjoy other privileges. Guys in this program would be **required** to work with a case

manager, set goals, and work seriously toward those goals. And there would also be **strict expectations** about behavior, including drug and alcohol abuse.

We then asked, "Are you the kind of guy who would be interested in a program like the one I just described?" 84.5 percent of the men said "Yes, definitely." 8.7 percent were unsure. Only a very few said "Not for me."

The second model:

> Another part of the Center might be more like the current Pavilion. Men who were still drinking or using would be welcome so long as they were not too drunk or high to behave themselves and were not a danger to anyone. There would be a community food line like now. Men in this part of the Center would have a case manager to talk to if they wanted but they would not be required to get clean and sober or work a program in order to stay there.

Just over one in five (21.5 percent) said they were "the kind of guy who would be interested in a program like this." Exactly two-thirds (67.7 percent) said this model was not appropriate given their own situation.

The final model:

> Finally, part of the new Men's Service Center might be set aside as a mini-Pavilion for guys who need a place to sleep it off or just get off the streets for the night but don't want anyone to get in their face about anything.

Only 5 percent of the men said this is what they want. 31.7 percent said the Coalition should not cater to men that want to use the Coalition for this purpose. 42.6 percent said they would want better services offered, while for 20 percent it was difficult to determine their opinion.

To get to the bottom line, we asked: "Would you personally be more interested in a residential program that required you to participate in case management and work a program, or would you rather just sleep on the floor and be left alone to do as you please?" A total of 93.1 percent opted for the first option. So at the outside, nearly everyone who sleeps at the Pavilion is "interested" in case management at some level. The concern that large numbers would just want to be left alone was not confirmed in these results.

The second survey was much more of an "on the run" survey and was considerably shorter than the original. Men who participated in the first survey were excluded (that included the majority of the men in the Pavilion during the night of the second survey). For the second survey, N = 48.

Between the 110 men in the first survey and the forty-eight in the second, we had a total of 158 respondents. In August 2009, the Pavilion provided 5,775 shelter nights to homeless men, an average of 186 men per night. Thus, our two samples combined amount to ~85 percent of the usual Pavilion population. The 15 percent we were unable to interview would include men who refused participation, who were too intoxicated or too mentally ill to complete an interview, or who showed up very late and were let in. Our informed guess is that the rates of behavioral disorders are probably quite a bit higher among non-respondents than among respondents and this has to be kept in mind when we later discuss the implications of the results.

As with the first survey, men in the second survey were predominantly Pavilion regulars. One quarter had spent ten nights or less at the Pavilion in the past thirty days; nearly half had been at the Pavilion every single night of the last thirty. About four-fifths (79.2 percent) of these men were interested in having a place they could hang out during the day, and again, the majority said they would want to spend that time using computers to look for work. Others mentioned recreational pursuits such as working out or relaxing.

These men were also informed as to how case management works. Eighty-three percent said they would be interested. Ninety percent of them said they would like help from a case manager in applying for benefits. Just over one in four (27 percent) said they personally needed help getting into an alcohol or drug treatment program. Of those that said they did not need such help, almost all (93.6 percent) said it was because they were already clean and sober. When asked about specific services they would like to see offered in the new Men's Service Center, the most popular services were help finding a place to live (95 percent) and medical assistance (82.5 percent).

Men in the second survey were told:

> One idea for the new Men's Service Center is a more residential program where men would sleep in beds, have lockers, and eat in their own dining room. But this would **require** people to work with a case manager, set goals, and work toward those goals. And there would also be **strict expectations** about behavior, including drug and alcohol abuse. Would you personally be interested in this kind of program or are you happy enough to just sleep on the floor and be left alone to do as you please?"

Consistent with what we learned in the earlier survey, 92.3 percent said they would prefer the more residential program with case management over being left alone to sleep on the floor.

In assessing what we learn from the results just summarized, two methodological issues leap to mind: social desirability bias in the answers, and self-selection bias in the sample. Concerning the first, it is very easy for a homeless man to tell a pleasant young student interviewer that he is interested in "case management" and in doing everything he can possibly do to improve his life. Actually accepting case management, working a program, and completing an entire case plan are incomparably more difficult. Perhaps a useful parallel is provided by the Homeless Assistance Centers in Miami (see Chapter Twelve), where clients have three days of grace and then are required to accept case management or leave. About two in ten do not last through the 72 hours, and of those that do, only 57.5 percent complete the program.

Concerning sample bias, two points must be made. First, as we have been stressing throughout this chapter (and will stress again in the next), any one-night shelter sample will oversample the regulars and undersample transients, the episodically homeless, and the transitionally homeless. Clearly, the regulars are those to whom case management would be directed, but that fact cannot be allowed to obscure the shelter needs of episodically or transitionally homeless men or the large number of transients who spend a night or two in the Pavilion and are never seen again.

Secondly, our two surveys apparently "cover" about 85 percent of the nightly Pavilion population, but the 15 percent that did not participate are probably very different than those who did, and we suspect that they would be more resistant to case management than those we were able to interview (more addicted, more mentally ill, less rules-compliant, etc.).

If we had to make "best guesses" about the demand for case management in a new and improved facility based on everything we have learned about Pavilion men in five or six years worth of research, our key observations would be these:

- About one in five (21.5 percent) Pavilion men described themselves as "the kind of guy who would be interested" in a program somewhat like the current Pavilion (with improved amenities, of course, and with access to a case manager if desired, but still a place welcome to all as long as they behaved themselves). If we allow for the transient population, factor in the 15 percent we were unable to survey, and take possible social desirability biases into account, a prudent guess would be, say, one Pavilion client in three or four for whom case management would be of passing interest at best.

- This leaves two out of three (or thereabouts) as the predicted percentage with more than a passing interest in case management. (Taking the men strictly at their word, this percentage would be even higher.) In both surveys, roughly one respondent in four admitted a need for alcohol or drug treatment services; in the first survey, nearly a quarter said they would enroll in First Steps if given a chance.
- Also, in the first survey, 27 percent of those surveyed either said they had a physical disability of some sort or were so obviously disabled that it was pointless to ask the question.
- The remainder, i.e., the very large majority who said they were interested in case management but did not face addiction issues and were not physically disabled, were nearly unanimous in describing their principal unmet "need" as employment, jobs, and incomes.

These points make it clear that it is fruitless to think in terms of "case management or not." Rather, we need to ask what kinds of case management homeless men in various situations need. The initial "though the door" sort-out should not be into one pile of guys who need case management and another pile who do not, but rather a five-group "triage" (Would that be a "quintage"?) that identifies the following groups:

- Men not yet ready for case management. These are not men to be warehoused, abandoned, or simply given up on; rather, they are treatment-aversive and will require a lot of attention and handholding before they will accept the assistance they need to become self-sufficient. Mental health and addiction issues figure prominently in this group.
- Men whose principal need is for alcohol and drug rehabilitation, who know this is their principal need, and who are ready and willing to accept placement in a treatment program.
- Men whose principal need is for assistance in applying for disability benefits (or other benefits, such as VA benefits, that, once acquired, might be sufficient to place them in permanent housing).
- Transient men whose principal or only need is for a few nights of shelter from the elements and who will move on of their own accord rather quickly.
- And finally, men whose major issues are finding jobs that pay incomes sufficient to sustain them in independent housing. Here, there is probably as much work to be done with potential employers as there is with the men themselves.

Our surveys over the past decade have indeed identified a group of Pavilion men who just want to be "left alone"—the "lazy shiftless bums"—but they are a gratifyingly small fraction of the total, maybe fewer than one in ten (a conclusion derived from very different surveys done six or seven years apart). Most of the homeless men we've interviewed over the years, both at the Pavilion and elsewhere, either have jobs, know they need help finding jobs, are physically unable to work, or have other issues that make it difficult or impossible for them to find and keep work. Most of the men of this latter description are evidently aware of their problems and would accept assistance if offered on the right terms. In most cases, this implies understanding and treating homeless men as poor people down on their luck and in need of assistance, not as defective or broken human beings who require major repairs before they can be safely turned loose on society at large.

Unfortunately, concluding that what most homeless men need is a decent job makes solving the problem of homelessness more difficult, not less. In an employment economy dominated by relatively low-wage service work, even people working full-time will often struggle to make ends meet, and those whose employment is discontinuous or irregular will rarely escape poverty, and often will fall off the edge and into homelessness.

In 1999, a group of social workers from the University of Central Florida prepared a report for the Florida Institute of Government entitled *Homelessness as a Regional Problem in Central Florida: Analysis and Recommendations*. The findings and recommendations of this report are discussed in detail in Chapter Twelve, but one critical finding is worth mentioning here, a finding with respect to the regional causes of homelessness:

> The single most critical predictor of homelessness is the proportion of the population employed in the service sector. This is particularly relevant in Central Florida, where the largest [job] gains have been—and will continue to be over the next decade—in the service sector. Most of the jobs in this sector involve lower-order services at minimum wages with marginal benefits. People most at risk of homelessness in a service economy are single male adults, persons of color, women and single parent families, and young people with minimal education, especially those living in inner-city neighborhoods (Poole, Chepenik, and Zugazaga 1999).

So even a decade ago, it was easy to see that the regional homeless problem results, at least in a substantial part, from the factors we discussed in Chapter One. Results from this chapter reinforce the "jobs nexus" as a critical issue for the region's homeless men, a point to which we return again and again.

Notes

1.   The Mayor's Working Committee on Homelessness is discussed at length in Chapter Twelve. The figure cited above is in the Committee's *Executive Summary*, p. 8.

2. With a shortage of shelter space relative to the number of homeless people needing shelter, the fact that the Pavilion has operated beneath capacity for several years begs for an explanation. Alas, all we can offer are two speculations: First, Pavilion accommodations are only marginally better than sleeping rough, and so various outdoor locations in downtown Orlando have become viable alternatives. Secondly, there are many "urban legends" about the Pavilion's safety and cleanliness that circulate among homeless men, which may keep many of them away. See Chapters Six and Seven for details.

3. According to Andrew Patterson, the Lead Resident Assistant at the Men's Pavilion, in a typical recent month, four or five men would be denied admission because of these issues. Since January of 2010, Pavilion management requires a state issued ID and Social Security card as an admission requirement, this to allow for background checks.

4. This is of course not unique to Orlando. See Kuhn and Culhane 1998; Donley and Wright 2009 for other examples.

5. The general pattern is that in areas of rapid population growth, where much of the local population originates elsewhere, so likewise do most of the homeless originate elsewhere, as in Miami (Rukmana 2008), Orlando, Las Vegas, Phoenix, etc. And in turn, in areas of low growth or decline (i.e., Rust Belt cities), most homeless people are local (e.g., Culhane, Lee and Wachter 1996). In short, homeless populations tend to mirror the larger populations from which they are drawn.

4

Transients and Frequent Flyers: Patterns of Shelter Utilization and Their Implications for Social Policy

We referred briefly in Chapter One to research by Dennis Culhane and his associates showing that in New York and Philadelphia, at least, a relatively small fraction of chronically homeless people—people who tend to remain homeless for long periods of time—consume a relatively large fraction of the total shelter capacity, or "shelter nights." High-rate shelter users are known in the literature as "frequent flyers," people who are in the shelters night after night after night. Although the frequent flyers make up the large majority of homeless people in the shelters on any given night, in the span of a year, the irregular or infrequent shelter users, people whose shelter consumption amounts to a night here and a night there, come to comprise a far larger share of the annual unduplicated count.

Probably no single line of research in the past thirty years has been so immediately consequential for national, state, and local policy with respect to homelessness as Culhane's studies of shelter utilization. This chapter reviews the original studies, their methodology, findings, and implications; reviews earlier research by numerous scholars that antici-pated the Culhane results but failed to see clearly the policy implications; presents data from our own studies in Central Florida that confirm the original findings in all important particulars; and then comments, al-though briefly, on the homelessness policy that has emanated from this line of research, namely, "Housing First."

Patterns of Shelter Utilization: The Culhane Studies

The "Culhane studies" consist of four very important papers published between 1994 and 1999. All four are based on essentially the same data from the same two cities, or based on subsequent updates (Culhane et al. 1994; Culhane and Kuhn 1997; Kuhn and Culhane 1998; Culhane and Metraux 1999). Sharply in contrast to a long tradition of shelter studies, these are not one-night shelter surveys, or for that matter, surveys of any sort, but are based, rather, on analyses of administrative data focused on patterns of shelter utilization (or admission rates) over time, specifically, over a year. The basic idea behind the research was to follow individual persons over time in the shelter databases, i.e., to determine how many people of which description were in the shelter every night of the year, most nights of the year, just a few nights or, indeed, only one night of the year, and so on.

All of Culhane's research came to the same essential conclusion, namely, that a relatively small fraction of chronically homeless people consume a relatively large fraction of the total shelter capacity, or "shelter nights." Most homeless people, that is, are irregular or infrequent shelter utilizers, people whose shelter consumption amounts to a night here, a night there, however, some are in the shelters night after night after night. This has been explained in detail in the previous chapter.

Based on these findings, Culhane thus came to distinguish among three different kinds of homeless people: the transitionally homeless, the episodically homeless, and the chronically homeless (Kuhn and Culhane 1998), terms we introduced earlier.

The **transitionally homeless** are comprised of persons who enter the shelter system due to some calamitous incident, such as job loss, fire, eviction, divorce, abandonment, or some other transitory misfortune. These people, by definition, are only homeless for a short time before they "transition" back into a stable housing situation, perhaps never to be homeless again. (As these things are measured, the "transitionally homeless" would also include transient homeless men roaming from city to city, rarely spending more than a few weeks in one place before moving on.) Remarkably, in studies where this group of homeless people can be identified, they account for the substantial majority of the homeless population. In the New York and Philadelphia shelter data specifically, the transitionally homeless accounted for 81 percent and 78 percent of the total homeless studied, respectively. The transitionally homeless are generally younger than other groups and have the smallest percentage of non-whites. They are also the least likely to suffer from mental illness and substance abuse.

The **episodically homeless** are people who pop in and out of homeless episodes, typically on short time scales. They have many episodes of shelter use that vary in length. The episodically homeless represented 9.1 percent of the New York clients and 11.7 percent of the Philadelphia clients in the Kuhn and Culhane study. Illustrating the disordered housing dynamics of episodically homeless people, a study by Sosin, Piliavin and Westerfelt (1990) of homeless adults in Minneapolis found that sixty percent went from being homeless to being housed and then back to being homeless again in a single six-month period. The episodically homeless, like the transitionally homeless, are younger than the chronically homeless but similar to the chronics in terms of substance abuse and mental illness.

Lastly, the **chronically homeless** are people who become homeless and stay in that condition for extended periods, often years. They are more likely to be enveloped in the shelter system and to use the shelters as long-term housing rather than emergency shelter. The chronically homeless comprised roughly a tenth of the Kuhn and Culhane samples and yet they consumed about half of the total shelter days. They tend to be older, non-white, and consistent with HUD's definition of "chronically homeless"; they suffer high rates of mental illness and substance abuse.

An essential point, one central to the policy implications that were drawn from this line of research, is that there is a very large disparity between the percentage of homeless people in each of these three groups and the percentage of shelter days consumed by each group. Transitionally homeless people comprise the very large majority of homeless people over any extended time span, but because they are homeless only rarely, and then only for short periods, they consume a very small fraction of the total shelter days. The chronically homeless, in contrast, are but a tenth or so of the total, but because they are homeless for long periods of time and in the shelters night after night, they consume far more than a tenth of the total shelter days, indeed, about half in the Culhane studies.

We consider the implications of these results later but note in passing that two implications have proven especially salient. One, these results have obvious implications for producing an "unduplicated" count of shelter users in any stated time frame since the nightly count and the annual count can differ quite dramatically. In the Orlando data presented below, a nightly Pavilion count of between 300 and 350 men nightly produced an unduplicated annual count of 3,477 persons. So in this one Orlando facility, the ratio of annual to one-night homeless is on the order of ten to one.

Two, more significantly, the implication is that if permanent housing could be found for the small fraction of chronics who consume far more than their fair share of the shelter capacity, the total demand for emergency shelter would drop precipitously. This is the key insight behind the effort to "end chronic homelessness in ten years" through Housing First, and is something we come back to at several points in the remainder of this book.

Prior Studies

Culhane and his associates, of course, were not the first to call attention to the existence of different types of homeless people or to the fact that there was a large transitional component or a great deal of turnover in the homeless population. In the 1986 survey of Chicago homeless, Rossi et al. (1987) reported that "the modal time homeless in these samples was one month (median, 7.6 months), indicating considerable turnover within the literally homeless population. *It therefore follows that many more people are homeless over a year than are homeless on any given evening*" (pg. 1339). Some additional calculations suggested that in Chicago, the ratio of annual to one-night homeless might be on the order of three or four to one (versus the 10:1 ratio noted above).

A few years later, in 1989, Wright published *Address Unknown: The Homeless in America*, which was (so far as we can determine) the first publication to specifically differentiate between chronically and episodically homeless people.

> The popular view of homelessness would certainly include chronicity as an important part of the depiction; the image is of persons who have been "down on their luck" for years. In contrast, recent research shows homeless people to be a mixture of chronic long-term and transitory short term homeless. ... Homelessness, therefore, is not a stable condition in all cases; over any reasonable time span, there is considerable movement into and out of the homeless state. A further implication is that the chronically homeless will not constitute the overwhelming majority of any sample of homeless people (Wright 1989).

Data from the 19-city Health Care for the Homeless program presented in *Address Unknown* suggested that about half the homeless who were served in that program were episodically homeless, perhaps a quarter were chronically homeless, and the remainder were recently homeless for the first time, such that no pattern had yet been established. Comparing these numbers with Culhane's findings shows broad agreement on the percentage of chronics, but Wright's definition of "episodic" seems to have included a large number that we would now recognize as transitionally homeless.

Address Unknown returned to chronic versus episodic homelessness in the discussion of policy implications, but the emphasis was on prevention, not on the implications for housing and the shelter system. Reasons for homelessness among the non-chronically homeless "tended to revolve around housing, jobs, and related economic issues," whereas among the chronics, "alcohol, drug and mental-health problems were far more commonly cited" (Wright 2009, p. 141).

A number of other researchers reported findings in the late 1980s and early 1990s that challenged the adequacy of point prevalence data (night-time counts) for policy and program planning, either by calling attention to the high turnover rates among various homeless populations, by noting the relatively short average lengths of stay in the shelter system, by pointing to the similarities between homeless families versus poor-but-housed families, by calling attention to the vast disparity between the numbers ever-homeless versus those currently homeless, or by otherwise suggesting that not all homelessness was of the chronic variety. These researchers include Martha Burt, Kuhn and Culhane, Ellen Bassuk, Bruce Link, Paul Koegel, Marjorie Robertson, and many, many others. (This literature is summarized thoroughly in Wong 1997.) But while many anticipated the finding that a small fraction of chronically homeless people would consume a large fraction of the shelter capacity, it fell to Dennis Culhane and his associates to nail down this pattern unambiguously and put a sharp point on the policy implications.

Patterns of Shelter Utilization in Orlando

Some have wondered if the patterns observed in very large cities such as New York and Philadelphia would generalize to smaller cities. That Culhane's findings generalize to all homeless populations has surely been assumed more often than it has been demonstrated.[1] Big cities are generally more turbulent and perhaps that is also true of their homeless populations. So it is possible, at least, that the transitional component is smaller in smaller cities. A replication of Culhane's studies in Orlando shows this not to be the case.

Two sources of data were used in the replication: the original (2003) Pavilion Survey data discussed at length in the previous chapter, and information extracted from the nightly Pavilion logs. As discussed, on the evening of June 30, 2003, our team interviewed every man who spent that night at the Pavilion. On each subsequent night since, men presenting for shelter at the Pavilion have been screened through the database, and if no survey on them could be found, a survey would be administered prior to being admitted for shelter. (If, on the other hand, presenting clients already had a survey entered in the database, they were admitted without further ado.) After one year, these data generated an estimated unduplicated annual count of 3,477 homeless persons served. In other words, at the end of one year, 3,477 completed surveys had accumulated.

In addition to the survey data, Pavilion staff also maintains nightly log books that record the name, Social Security number, and other identifying information for each person spending that night at the shelter. To study patterns of shelter utilization among Pavilion men, we took all the nightly logs from June 30-July 1, 2003, the night of the original survey, through the last night of the year, a total of 183 nights worth of data. We then appended 183 dummy variables to the survey spreadsheet, one variable for each night a man might have stayed at the shelter. Each variable took the value 1 if that man was among the clients sleeping in the shelter that night and 0 otherwise. Summing across these 183 variables, we could then identify the number of nights spent at the shelter by each man in the database, of which there were 2,295 over the six month period studied. (We did this for six months rather than a year, or several years, just to reduce the sheer tedium of the project, which was considerable in any case.)

As would be expected, the process of merging logbook data with survey data was not without problems. We discovered duplicate names, misspelled names, and reversed names (i.e., Robert James identified in the record as James Robert). We need also to acknowledge the possibility that some shelter-seekers may have given false names or aliases. Where possible, name problems were resolved by using Social Security numbers, dates of birth, and other demographic information. We found some clients with two or more surveys in the database. In these cases, we simply deleted the redundant entries. We also found a few clients who had surveys but no logbook entry, and likewise clients with logbook entries for whom there were no surveys. Absent any other information, if a man had a survey or a logbook entry, we entered him as having spent one night in the Pavilion and used whatever date appeared on the survey or logbook to identify the appropriate night. All together, approximately 10 percent of the data records analyzed in this chapter had one or another problem. It made very little difference in the results whether this tenth was retained or omitted from the statistical analysis.

It needs also to be mentioned, if only in passing, that the nightly Pavilion check-in process is not such as to promote careful data-gathering.

Usually, there would be three staff members to process, check in, and pat down a line of 300-350 men, all of them anxious to check in and call it a night, many of them in various states of agitation or inebriation. That only about one data record in ten was problematic is near-miraculous under the circumstances.

The research sample consists of 2,295 men who stayed at the Pavilion at least one night in the six month period studied. For reasons that we trust are obvious, this includes all of the one thousand homeless men discussed in Chapter Three. A review of the demographics for the entire sample revealed that 54 percent of the men utilizing the shelter in the six-month period were black, 28 percent were white, and 16 percent were Hispanic, with small sprinklings of Asians and others. The mean age was forty-two years with a mode of forty-seven and a median of forty-two. A little more than 20 percent reported having served in the military. These results are effectively identical to those reported in the previous chapter, which is hardly surprising giving the overlapping samples.

The total number of nights each client stayed at the shelter from July 1 through December 31 was computed. The mean number of nights spent at the shelter was 21.9, or about three weeks worth of shelter consumption in the span of six months. However, the median was just under eight days (about one week) and the mode was only one day, indicating that many men (about one in five) spent only one night at the shelter in the six month period studied. The largest number of nights any man stayed at the shelter was 175, or 96 percent of the available 183 days. Even the heaviest consumers of emergency shelter occasionally find alternate accommodations from time to time!

Table 4.1 shows the distribution of people across shelter nights and the number of shelter nights consumed by the people in each "shelter night" grouping. To illustrate, of the 2,295 men studied, 477 (or 20.8 percent) were determined to have spent *one and only one night* at the Pavilion. By definition, these men consumed 477 shelter nights, or one-tenth of one percent of the total. (In these data, the total shelter nights consumed = 50,190, which implies an average nightly census of 50,190/183 = 274, and an average number of nights in shelter of 50,190/2,295 = 21.9 nights, as reported above.) At the other end of the distribution, exactly 10 percent of the sample spent sixty-five or more nights at the shelter, and this 10 percent consumed 45.4 percent of the total shelter nights. As in other studies, then, the tenth of the homeless population that is comprised of the most frequent shelter users consumes nearly half of the total emergency overnight shelter capacity.

Table 4.1
Total Number of Nights Spent at the Pavilion, June 30 – December 31, 2003.
N = 2,295 Homeless Men

Number of Nights in Shelter	Number of People	Percentage of People	Cumulative percentage of People	Number of Shelter Nights	Cumulative percentage of Shelter Nights
1	477	20.8	20.8	477	0.1
2	192	8.4	29.2	384	
3	117	5.1	34.2	351	
4	102	4.4	38.7	408	
5	80	3.5	42.2	400	
6	76	3.3	45.5	456	
7	54	2.4	47.8	378	
8	51	2.2	50.1	408	6.5
9	47	2.0	52.1	423	
10	39	1.7	53.8	390	
11	38	1.7	55.5	418	
12	34	1.5	56.9	408	
13	30	1.3	58.3	390	
14	35	1.5	59.8	490	11.5
15	36	1.6	61.4	540	
16	31	1.4	62.7	496	
17	31	1.4	64.1	527	
18	27	1.2	65.2	486	
19	24	1.0	66.3	456	
20	25	1.1	67.4	500	
21	23	1.0	68.4	483	
22	29	1.3	69.6	638	19.7
23	23	1.0	70.6	529	
24	24	1.0	71.7	576	
25	24	1.0	72.7	600	

Table 4.1 (cont.)

Number of Nights in Shelter	Number of People	Percentage of People	Cumulative percentage of People	Number of Shelter Nights	Cumulative percentage of Shelter Nights
26	15	0.7	73.4	390	
27	21	0.9	74.3	567	
28	16	0.7	75.0	448	
29	22	1.0	75.9	638	
30	24	1.0	77.0	720	
31	25	1.1	78.1	775	
32	15	0.7	78.7	480	
33	17	0.7	79.5	561	
34	16	0.7	80.2	544	33.3
35	8	0.3	80.5	280	
36	11	0.5	81.0	396	
37	9	0.4	81.4	333	
38	5	0.2	81.6	190	
39	14	0.6	82.2	546	
40	15	0.7	82.9	600	
41	13	0.6	83.4	533	
42	8	0.3	83.8	336	
43	7	0.3	84.1	301	
44	11	0.5	84.6	484	
45	6	0.3	84.8	270	
46	13	0.6	85.4	598	
47	7	0.3	85.7	329	
48	8	0.3	86.1	384	
49	4	0.2	86.2	196	
50	11	0.5	86.7	550	

Table 4.1 (cont.)

Number of Nights in Shelter	Number of People	Percentage of People	Cumulative percentage of People	Number of Shelter Nights	Cumulative percentage of Shelter Nights
51	9	0.4	87.1	459	
52	5	0.2	87.3	260	
53	4	0.2	87.5	212	
54	12	0.5	88.0	648	
55	3	0.1		165	
56	2	0.1		112	49.6
57	6	0.3		342	
58	6	0.3		348	
59	3	0.1		177	
60	4	0.2	89.1	240	
61	6	0.3		366	
62	5	0.2		310	
63	6	0.3		378	
64	5	0.2	90.0	320	54.6
65	9	0.4		585	
66	9	0.4		594	
67	4	0.2	91.0	268	
68	2	0.1		136	
69	4	0.2		276	
70	5	0.2		350	
71	3	0.1		213	
72	4	0.2		288	
73	6	0.3	92.0	438	
74	2	0.1		148	
75	4	0.2		300	
76	0	---	---	---	

Table 4.1 (cont.)

Number of Nights in Shelter	Number of People	Percentage of People	Cumulative percentage of People	Number of Shelter Nights	Cumulative percentage of Shelter Nights
77	4	0.2		308	
78	4	0.2		312	
79	3	0.1		237	
80	3	0.1		240	
81	5	0.2	93.1	405	
82	4	0.2		328	
83	2	0.1		166	
84	6	0.3		504	
85	3	0.1		255	
86	2	0.1		172	
87	5	0.2	94.1	435	
88	6	0.3		528	
89	2	0.1		178	
90	3	0.1		270	
91	4	0.2		364	
92	3	0.1		276	
93	3	0.1	95.0	279	72.2
94	2	0.1		188	
95	3	0.1		285	
96	1	0.0		96	
97	4	0.2		388	
98	2	0.1		196	
99	1	0.0		99	
100	4	0.2		400	
101	3	0.1		303	
102	1	0.0		102	

Table 4.1 (cont.)

Number of Nights in Shelter	Number of People	Percentage of People	Cumulative percentage of People	Number of Shelter Nights	Cumulative percentage of Shelter Nights
103	1	0.0		103	
104	2	0.1	96.0	208	
105	3	0.1		315	
106	0	---	---	---	
107	1	0.0		107	
108	3	0.1		324	
109	3	0.1		327	
110	3	0.1		330	
111	2	0.1		222	
112	1	0.0		112	
113	3	0.1		339	
114	5	0.2	97.1	570	
115	3	0.1		345	
116	3	0.1		348	
117	1	0.0		117	
118	0	---	---	---	
119	1	0.0		119	
120	0	---	---	---	
121	4	0.2		484	
122	2	0.1		244	
123	5	0.2		615	
124	3	0.1	98.0	372	
125	5	0.2		625	
126	5	0.2		630	
127	1	0.0		127	
128	4	0.2		512	

Table 4.1 (cont.)

Number of Nights in Shelter	Number of People	Percentage of People	Cumulative percentage of People	Number of Shelter Nights	Cumulative percentage of Shelter Nights
129	1	0.0		129	
130	1	0.0		130	
131	0	---	---	---	
132	2	0.1		264	
133	0	---	---	---	
134	2	0.1	99.0	268	92.8
135	2	0.1		270	
136	0	---	---	---	
137	3	0.1		411	
138	0	---	---	---	
139	0	---	---	---	
140	0	---	---	---	
141	1	0.0		141	
142	0	---	---	---	
143	0	---	---	---	
144	2	0.1		288	
145	0	---	---	---	
146	2	0.1		292	
147	4	0.2		588	
148	1	0.0		148	
149	1	0.0		149	
150	1	0.0		150	
151	1	0.0		151	
152	0	---	---	---	
153	0	---	---	---	
154	0	---	---	---	

Table 4.1 (cont.)

Number of Nights in Shelter	Number of People	Percentage of People	Cumulative percentage of People	Number of Shelter Nights	Cumulative percentage of Shelter Nights
155	0	---	---	---	
156	0	---	---	---	
157	1	0.0		157	
158	1	0.0		158	
159	0	---	---	---	
160	0	---	---	---	
161	0	---	---	---	
162	0	---	---	---	
163	0	---	---	---	
164	0	---	---	---	
165	0	---	---	---	
166	0	---	---	---	
167	0	---	---	---	
168	0	---	---	---	
169	0	---	---	---	
170	0	---	---	---	
171	1	0.0		171	
172	1	0.0		172	
173	0	---	---	---	
174	0	---	---	---	
175	2	0.1	100.0	350	100
Totals	2,295	100.0%	100.0%	50,190	100%

There are many different ways to express the disproportions shown in Table 4.1. Just over half the sample spent eight or fewer nights in the shelter, so the lowest-consuming half account for a mere 6.5 percent of the total shelter capacity. About 70 percent of the sample spent twenty-two or fewer nights in the shelter and those 70 percent consume just under a fifth (19.7 percent) of the total shelter capacity. Working from the other end of the table, the upper 1 percent of the distribution eats up 7 percent of total capacity; the upper 5 percent eats up 28 percent; the upper 10 percent eats up 45 percent; and the upper 20 percent eats up 67 percent.

To illustrate the possible implications of these disproportions, consider that the 20 percent of heaviest users (men spending thirty-five or more nights in the shelter) amount to 459 men and consume 67 percent of total shelter capacity. If permanent housing could be found for these men, who number fewer than 500, the Pavilion would need only a third of its present capacity. Likewise, if permanent housing could be found for the upper tenth of the distribution, for the 230 men who spent sixty-four or more nights in shelter, the size of the Pavilion could be approximately halved.

Multivariate analyses were run to identify demographic factors associated with the number of nights in shelter. Consistent with other research, the heaviest shelter consumers were older, more likely to be black or Hispanic, and more likely to be veterans than less heavy consumers. Given what is known about chronicity of homelessness among similar samples, we are also safe in assuming that the mentally ill and substance abusive also tend to fall into the heavier-use categories.

Policy Application

The Culhane studies and subsequent replications suggest that most adult homeless (on the order of 80 percent) experience short-term, temporary homelessness and would therefore appear to be candidates for prevention or rapid relocation (rehousing) programs. Most of them appear to exit from homelessness without formal rental assistance or, for that matter, without much in the way of "services" of any kind. Importantly, most do not have significant behavioral health treatment histories or other disabling conditions that complicate their search for jobs and housing.

Men sheltered at the Orlando Pavilion receive a meal, the opportunity to take a shower, and a mat on the floor, and that's it. There are no case managers, social workers, or other "helpers" to assist them in any way. And yet, entirely without assistance, almost half the men who ever sleep at the Pavilion are there for a week or less and are never seen again. Some may "graduate" to other shelters in the area, a researchable proposition that we have yet to look into. Some may abandon shelter completely and sleep in the streets or woods. But surely some, and probably most, of these very short-term men resolve whatever issues placed them in the shelter in the first place and exit because they have solved their crisis and found somewhere to live. In Miami's Homeless Assistance Centers (see Chapter Twelve), about one client in ten or eleven leaves the program before completion because a housing opportunity presented itself. Even more leave to go back to family or friends. The important point is that they find some way to "cure" their homelessness with little or no assistance from anyone.

The implication is obviously that we should figure out some way to prevent homelessness from befalling these people in the first place or discover some way to rapidly rehouse them once they become homeless. That, of course, is precisely the point of President Obama's Homeless Prevention and Rapid Rehousing program (HPRP), which is now implemented in Orlando and in most other cities. In any case, we should do everything we can to remove any barriers that might prevent people from solving their homelessness on their own. They don't need to use, nor should they be allowed to use, the emergency shelters as permanent housing. The other side of the coin is the obvious need to concentrate on finding permanent housing for the remaining 20 percent—the 20 percent who are frequent flyers and consume half the shelter capacity. The result would presumably be large cost savings in the short run (earned by reducing the needed emergency shelter capacity) and an end to chronic homelessness in the long run (as the frequent flyers are taken out of emergency shelter and placed in permanent housing). This is exactly the strategy of "Housing First," a strategy whose appeal derives almost entirely from the Culhane findings and subsequent replications such as the one just reported.

What is "Housing First"?

Housing First is a model for intervening in homelessness that differs dramatically from the traditional "treatment first" approach. The traditional approach avoids placing homeless people in housing prematurely, before they are "ready" to assume the responsibilities that housing placement entails. Often, this means extensive psycho-social assessments, individualized treatment plans, and then months of addiction treatment, mental health counseling, adult education, job readiness and skills training, financial management workshops, housing readiness workshops, and on through a long list. The CEO of a large homeless facility in Florida once explained it this way. "Here, we assume that homelessness per se is never the problem. Homelessness is the result of other problems. And until we identify and address what those other problems are, we cannot effectively address homelessness."

In sharp contrast, most Housing First models entail some combination of the following principles:

- The emphasis is on placing homeless individuals and families in permanent housing as quickly as possible.
- Housing placement is intended to be permanent, not time-limited.
- Services of various sorts are made available primarily after placement in permanent housing, and are intended to promote stability and individual well-being, not to "ready" people for housing.
- Such services may be time-limited but are usually indefinite, depending upon individual need.
- Housing is not contingent on compliance with services—instead, participants must comply with a standard lease agreement and are provided with the services and supports that are necessary to help them do so successfully.

As a leading advocate for Housing First once put it in a private conversation, "We suddenly realized that there was very little we could to make our people unpoor, unaddicted, or uncrazy. So we stopped trying and concentrated all our efforts on making them unhomeless. And that strategy seems to be working!"

Housing First has been described in generally glowing terms, as a "breakthrough strategy," "imaginative," and an "effective anti-crime program." Proponents claim very high success rates, but much of the evidence is anecdotal, not systematic or scientific. As is perhaps obvious from what we have already said, Housing First initiatives are typically targeted to "frequent fliers," chronically homeless people who are heavy users of emergency services. Further, Housing First is grounded in the idea that housing is a fundamental right. Therefore, the model prioritizes housing over treatment. Housing First programming also stresses consumer choice, relying on "harm reduction" with optional treatment for alcohol, drug, or mental health problems (ADM), the traditional "disabilities" of the homeless population. In contrast, traditional "treatment first" models prioritize ADM treatment above housing, embracing the idea that individuals must undergo treatment for substance abuse and mental illness before they can live independently in the community.

Housing First has been a controversial philosophy in part because it reserves the most valuable of all resources, permanent housing, for the most chronic, least sympathy-engendering subgroup within the homeless population. In most cities with active Housing First programs (for example, Miami, Denver, Los Angeles and many others, but not Orlando), the total program capacity is very small relative to the number of eligible homeless people, so long waiting lists are a frequent program element. Thus, as implemented, "Housing First" is a something of a misnomer—it is really Waiting List First, Housing Later (and often, much later—these lists can sometimes be years long.)

In some important respects, Housing First could be considered a "low demand" permanent housing program. Chronically homeless people are placed in decent accommodations with wrap-around "on-demand" social services and are only required (more or less) to behave themselves—they can even drink and do drugs so long as they are reasonably discreet about it. Such arrangements are so vastly preferable to living in the streets that it has proven very easy to recruit chronically homeless men into these programs (hence, the very rapid appearance of long waiting lists.)

Still, not all providers are enthusiasts for Housing First. One Miami provider told us, "We have problems getting these people into a program. It can be difficult to make things work when you take someone right from the street and put them into apartments where they are living on their own." Chronically homeless people with months or years of accumulated street time "do better when there is some stabilization first. You have to get them ready for the transition" to permanent housing. "With Housing First, you take the client right off the street and then you are stuck with them." This informant believed that there needs to be some progression of readiness and entitlement that Housing First simply ignores. "That's not how we prefer to deal with our housing programs. We have rules. You follow the rules. You progress. You get employed, you pay rent, maybe you complete some other kind of intervention. Then—*maybe*—you are 'ready' for a permanent housing placement."

Controversies aside, some evaluations have shown that in some cases, Housing First provides better outcomes at lower costs. For example, Bulcur and associates (Bulcur et al. 2003) compared housing outcomes and community costs of Housing First clients versus clients in traditional treatment first models using a sample of 225 homeless individuals with varying degrees of behavioral disability. Participants were assessed every six months over a period of two years. Results showed that Housing First participants spent less time homeless and in psychiatric hospitals and incurred fewer costs. A similar study compared long-term housing outcomes among ADM homeless people enrolled in Housing First and treatment first programs. Five years after initial service delivery, 88 percent of the participants in the Housing First program were stably housed versus only 47 percent of treatment first participants. Still another study found that homeless participants with psychiatric diagnoses who were enrolled in Housing First spent less time homeless and more time in community housing, demonstrated fewer psychiatric symptoms, reported less difficulty meeting their basic needs and reported greater life satisfaction compared to participants in traditional programs. That notwithstanding, many clinicians and providers continue to insist on "treatment first" programming and believe that placing behaviorally challenged homeless people directly into housing without first treating their addictions and mental health issues is a recipe for disaster (Schutt, Weinstein, and Penk 2005).

In the end, the basic difference between Housing First and Treatment First is that Treatment First is based on the assumption that homeless people are somehow "broken" and need to be fixed before they can be successfully placed in housing. Housing First assumes instead that homeless people are simply people who have lost their residences and who need to be put back into housing at the very first opportunity, and that it is the urban political economy that is broken and needs to be fixed. We venture to surmise that Housing First is so popular because its basic assumptions are more palatable (and for that matter, perhaps more empirically correct). More and more, Treatment First seems to be less a program of intervention to assist the homeless than it is a "jobs program" for MSWs, case managers, and like professions. Some have even argued that in some, and perhaps many, cases, Treatment First promotes dependency more than it encourages self-sufficiency. This is the "shelterization thesis," the thesis that long-term shelter residence encourages passivity and dependence, weakening peoples' drive to escape homelessness as shelter-dwelling peers become the reference group (Grunberg and Eagle 1990). And while the research on this thesis has been mixed, no one who has spent time observing large populations of "frequent flyers" would be inclined to dismiss it out of hand.

Notes

1.   We note in passing some residual regional bias in assumptions made about the generalizability of research. The literature on homelessness is dominated by studies in large Eastern, Midwestern, and Western cities: there are literally hundreds of widely cited studies based on samples of homeless people in Boston, New

York, Philadelphia, Chicago, and Los Angeles. Whether results from such studies generalize to other cities or regions is rarely questioned. But reviewers of earlier versions of the material included in this book have been very quick to point out that what is true of Central Florida may or may not be true elsewhere. A reasonable person would wonder why results from New York or Chicago should be taken as indicative of larger truths when results from Orlando or Atlanta or New Orleans should not be.

5

It's Not Who We Are:
Realities of Homelessness for
Women and Children[1]

Previous chapters have described Central Florida's homeless men, their social and demographic characteristics, and their patterns of shelter utilization. But what about women and children? In the fiscal year of 2008-09, 54 percent of persons who received services from the Coalition for the Homeless of Central Florida were women, children, or members of homeless families. Clearly, these groups are not immune to the larger forces that undergird the homeless problem both regionally and nationally. Indeed, Chapter Two made it obvious that women, children, and families might be at even higher risk of homelessness than single men.

Prior research shows that men and women become homeless for different reasons and experience homelessness in different ways (North and Smith 1993). Compared to men, women are more likely to be homeless for economic reasons and less likely to have complicating behavioral disabilities such as substance abuse or mental illness (although both are problems for homeless women as well as men) (Burt and Cohen 1989). Also, many women become homeless as a result of male abandonment and many are homeless because they are fleeing unacceptable domestic situations (Browne and Bassuk 1997; Richards et al. 2010; Rosenheck et al. 1999). Indeed, about one homeless woman in four is currently homeless because of domestic violence.

The Coalition operates three separate programs for homeless women. At the main campus, the Center for Women and Families (CWF) has separate programs for single women, which is to say, women who are homeless by themselves with no husbands or children in tow; and homeless families, which can be single mothers with children or intact husband-wife couples with or without children, or in some cases, single fathers with children. On a separate campus a few miles away resides the Women's Residential and Counseling Center (WRCC), a transitional program for homeless women (with or without children) who are (in theory) clean, sober, employed, and making the transition back to self-sufficiency. In most ways, the WRCC is a considerable "step up" from the programs on the main campus and a WRCC placement is therefore coveted by many of the women at the CWF. And likewise, being sent back to the CWF from the WRCC is considered punitive by WRCC women.

Our data on homeless women in Central Florida derive in part from client charts for all women seen in the calendar year 2007 at the main campus and from numerous focus groups that we have conducted at both facilities over the years. In 2003-04, we also formally surveyed about 200 homeless women in Orlando (and another 600 in Miami, Jacksonville, and Tampa) about their experiences with violence (see Jasinski, Wesely, Wright and Mustaine 2010). All of the above, plus countless informal conversations with and observations about women at the Coalition, comprise the material for this chapter.

Demographics of Homeless Women and Families

Table 5.1 gives basic demographic data on the 1,137 clients (men, women, and children) seen at the Center for Women and Families in the calendar year 2007. Information in the table is derived from client charts, which are in turn comprised of intake and assessment interviews done at the point of initial contact, and case managers' progress notes that are entered into clients' charts periodically throughout their stay. At the Coalition and most other homeless services organizations, data management practices are less than optimal, so these data must be used with some caution—the connection between paperwork and "helping people" is not always obvious.

Note first that of the 1,137 clients seen at the CWF in 2007, 41 percent, or about 467, are children. These children are about equally divided between boys and girls, with an average age of 6.2 years (standard deviation 4.8 years), and mirror the race and ethnicity of their parents. Unfortunately, the client charts contain very little information on the children; their data are kept in files maintained by the Coalition's Child Development Program. These files contain a great deal of confidential

Table 5.1
Demographic Characteristics of CWF Clients in 2007 (N = 1137)

"Single" Women	34.7
Heads of Household	20.0
Spouses	4.1
Children	41.1
N =	1137
Children per parent	1.7
Children per family	2.1

Gender of Parents (N = 274 parents)

Homeless Mothers	74.8
Homeless Fathers	25.1

Type of Family (N = 228 families)

Homeless Single Mother	58.0
Homeless Single Fathers	8.0
Homeless Dual Parent Families	34.0

Child Separation for All Women with at least One Child (N = 411)

Separated from at least One Child	29.9
Not Separated from any Children	70.1

Race of CWF Adults (N = 658)

Black	49.1
White	47.3
Other	3.6

Ethnicity of CWF Adults (N = 657)

Hispanic/Latino	16.0
Non-Hispanic/Latino	84.0

assessment material that we have never been comfortable asking to see. So other than their numbers and basic demography, we don't know a great deal about these children.

We do know that the Coalition's Child Development Program attempts to screen every child over age four that comes through the CWF and WRCC. In the fiscal year of 2008-09, CDP screened 385 homeless children, of whom 181 (47 percent) were determined to be "in crisis" or "at risk." Thus, approximately half of the children who come through the Coalition have identifiable emotional, psychological, or developmental issues and needs. Interestingly, among children determined to be in crisis or at risk, only about three-fifths remained at the Coalition for two or more months. And of those, somewhat more than half (57 percent in the 08-09 report) showed improved emotional health during their stay. Some of this improvement is no doubt due to the counseling efforts of the Child Development program; some of it is the salutary effect of being in a relatively stable, services-rich living situation.

We also know from many other sources that homelessness and poverty are not healthy for children. Studies show that homeless kids suffer fair or poor health twice as often as domiciled children and have higher rates of asthma, ear infections, nutritional deficiency disorders, gastro-intestinal ailments, and a variety of developmental disorders involving speech, cognition, and related systems (Wright 1990, 1991; McLean et al. 2004). Homeless kids are also at risk for anxiety, depression, anger, and withdrawal. Older homeless kids face other barriers: enrolling in and attending school, transportation to and from school, residency issues, lack of proper clothing and school supplies, and stereotyping by schoolmates and teachers (see Buckner 2008; Rafferty and Shinn 1991; Wright 1990).

Subtracting the children from the total client base leaves 669 adults. Of these, 59 percent are represented in the database as "single women," although as we see later, many of them are in fact mothers who are separated from their children. Single women are sheltered in dormitory style accommodations. The remainder are adult members of homeless families (N = 274) sheltered in family rooms when space is available and in mother-child dormitories otherwise. Of the adult members of homeless families, a quarter (25.1 percent) are adult men and the remainder are adult women. Of the adult men, incidentally, about a third are single men with children; the others are members of intact husband-wife households. Thus, there is a far greater male presence in homeless families than is usually assumed: of all adults with children seen at the CWF in 2007, fully a quarter of them were men.

Case managers' notes yielded data on women's fertility histories including, critically, data on children from whom the women were separated. Among all women who had ever borne a child (N = 411), regardless of whether they had their child(ren) with them, 29.9 percent were currently separated from at least one child. Among the "single women," i.e., women who entered the shelter with no children in tow, exactly one third (33.2 percent) had one or more children from whom they were currently separated. Likewise, among parents (male or female) entering the shelter with at least one child, almost exactly one in four (24.8 percent) had other children from whom they were separated. We return to these points momentarily.

Demographically, almost half the CWF clients (49.1 percent) are African or Caribbean American blacks and most of the remainder are white (47.3 percent). About one in six is Latino or Latina. The Hispanic percentages are about the same for both men and women, but the Coalition's homeless women are much more likely to be white (47 percent) than the men (27 percent—see Table 3.1). Single women are older on average than parents (41 versus 32 years).

Child Separation

Loss of one's children is evidently a common experience for homeless women in Central Florida and presumably elsewhere, although with only a few exceptions, this topic has not been extensively studied. One in four of the homeless women interviewed in New York City by Cowal and associates reported being separated from one or more of their minor children at least once (Cowal et al. 2002). Another study suggested that only 65 percent of mothers and only 7 percent of fathers remain with *any* of their children once they become homeless (Shin, Rog and Culhane 2005).

Why parents would abandon or seek alternative care arrangements for kids once they (the parents) had become homeless is not hard to fathom. First, life on the streets and in the shelters is hard enough when there is just the "you" to worry about. Once it becomes "you and the kids," life is incomparably more difficult and complicated. Relatively few emergency shelters are set up to handle women (or men) with children; if the children are of school age, getting them to and from school may present formidable obstacles; regardless of age, children need food, medical attention, intellectual stimulation, and many other things that the material conditions of the homeless may prevent homeless adults from providing. A further complication is that in many states, including

Florida, the very condition of homelessness itself appears to satisfy the legal definition of child neglect (i.e., inability to provide proper care and housing for one's children). As a result, many children of homeless parents are removed by the State and placed in foster care and many others are clearly at risk of such an outcome. Studies of homeless adults show that one out of four or five came up in the foster care system, with some evidence that the percentage is much higher among younger homeless people than among older (Burt et al. 2001; Bassuk et al. 1997; Piliavin et al. 1993; Susser et al. 1991).

In December 2008, we convened a focus group with ten CWF women who had been identified by program staff as being currently separated from at least one child. The focus of the group was on the whereabouts and well-being of the children, on the circumstances surrounding the separation, and on the women's intentions and plans for reunification. The following account of the focus group results uses pseudonyms throughout.

The ice-breaker discussion question was, "What are some of the reasons you are homeless?" Megan cited poor health; Sandy and Betty cited drug abuse; Jane mentioned her drug use and associated problems with law enforcement (i.e., she was thrown in jail and had no place to go when she got out). Theresa, Samantha, and Jennifer focused on loss of jobs, loss of income, and the downward spiral of the local economy. Amanda became homeless when her husband walked out. Another woman, Cynthia, said she was homeless because of the "falsification of mothers," and when we probed for clarifying information, it became clear that Cynthia suffered profound psychiatric problems that, directly or indirectly, caused her to lose custody of her child. The two final women, Rachel and Leslie, chose not to join in any part of the discussion and should not be considered as group participants.

The bulk of the session focused on how and why these women had become separated from their children. As anticipated, two themes dominated the discussion: voluntary separation by mothers who saw an episode of homelessness headed their way and found some safe haven where they could "park" their kids while the storm passed; and involuntary separation, i.e., state termination of parental rights because of various personal and social problems. Two women fell clearly into the first category and six into the second; again, Rachel and Leslie were silent.

Although clearly painful, voluntary child separations seemed to provide the mothers with a more positive outlook about their children's living situations. Theresa had agreed to joint custody of her child during her divorce from her first husband. When a job loss forced her into homelessness, the ex was more than willing to assume full time parenting duties. This has made it more difficult for Theresa to see her child, but she is quick to acknowledge that the father provides good care and a stable environment. She does not seem happy about the child's living arrangements; rather, she is resigned to them as the best possible alternative at least for now.

Amanda's situation is different, although it still constitutes a voluntary child separation. She and her husband were going through very difficult economic times and saw that they were on the verge of homelessness, so they gave their children to the husband's parents "for safekeeping." Like Theresa, Amanda acknowledges that her children are in a good, safe, stable living arrangement, a source of great comfort to her since both her children, she says, have been diagnosed with attention deficit/hyperactivity disorders and require a great deal of care, care that she and her husband are in no position to provide themselves.

The other women's stories were very different and arguably much more painful, even, than the two just recounted. Betty and Sandy both lost their children to drug use. Sandy's story was the more detailed of the two. She and her husband had been living with cousins and were actively using drugs when an FBI raid caused their children to be taken away and placed in foster care. The husband's parents were eventually designated as the children's custodians[2] and have legal custody of all their children save one, the newborn that Sandy brought with her to the focus group. Betty was more cryptic, stating only that because of her "drug problem," her husband currently has custody of the children. Megan's chronic and severe alcoholism caused her to lose custody of her children, then once she had managed to stop drinking, her health was so poor that she was unable to maintain a stable relationship with her children, much less obtain custody of them. Although she was not explicit about their current whereabouts, our impression is that they were taken by the state and placed in foster care.

True to form, when we asked Cynthia what had become of her children, she stated that they had been stolen by the leader of some religious cult. Her elaborations of the story became progressively more outlandish and paranoid. In superficial interaction, Cynthia seems cognitively intact and well-spoken, but the more she speaks, the more floridly psychotic she becomes. Although it was impossible to get a believable explanation from her about what had happened to her kids, it seemed clear that uncontrolled mental illness must have had something to do with it.

Of all the stories we heard in the focus group, those of Jennifer and Jane were the most disturbing. Jennifer began by relating how her daughter had been molested by her partner (the child's father) while she was working the night shift at a local convenience store. Jennifer professed no knowledge of the molestation, but apparently someone knew what was going on, because at some point the police showed up and took the child away. The child is now in the custody of Jennifer's parents, but this relationship (with the parents) has recently become strained because Jennifer now has a second child, a biracial son who is homeless with her. The parents refuse to accept the other child as "theirs" since he has a black father. Our impression is that Jennifer would prefer to have her young son with the parents along with her other child, but that the parents' hostility towards their biracial grandson makes this impossible.

Jane's story was similarly disturbing. She and a lesbian lover were sharing responsibilities for raising Jane's daughter when Jane went to jail on drug charges. While she was in jail, the partner, who had retained custody of the child, hooked up with a man with whom she was shooting heroin. During their frequent highs, the man would molest Jane's daughter. (It was impossible to determine if this was done with the consent, or even the participation, of the former partner, or done behind her back.) Somehow (again, details were not forthcoming), Jane learned of this while she was still in jail, arranged for her daughter to go into foster care for a few months, and then ceded her parental rights to the child's godparents, where the daughter remained as of the date of the focus group.

A final line of questioning asked these women if they would like to reunite with their children and, if so, whether they had any idea what this would require or how they would go about it. All of them stated a wish to be reunited with their children, and many had a legitimate idea about what this would entail, but few had a clear plan to do so. Reunification was something they seemed to desire in the abstract, not something towards which they were actively working. As noted, several already had "new" children with whom they were coping.

Cynthia and Megan both felt and stated that reunification was "hopeless." Cynthia's profound mental illness made her seem hopeless about almost everything. As for Megan, her health had deteriorated to the point where she did not feel she would be physically capable of caring for a child in any case. All Amanda thought she would need to get her children back is a stable job, but as a former felon, she realizes the deck is stacked against her. Her conviction was ten years ago and, she felt, should not prohibit her from getting a job in the field in which she is trained (medical assistant), much less prevent her from learning another trade. But health care employers, colleges, and vocational schools all do background checks of potential employees and students and each time they run a background check on Amanda, the red flag pops up. This occasioned one of the more poignant statements of the evening: "Look, I don't do drugs or drink. I made my mistake ten years ago and I am still paying for it today. McDonald's just won't do."

When asked about reunification, Theresa spoke of her joint custody agreement, then went off on a rant about the Center for Women and Families not allowing her children to visit. Amanda quickly joined in: "Give us a bus pass or let the kids come here or something. We[3] have kids too and we can't see them. These kids [the children living with their mothers at the CWF] are seeing Santa tonight and we can't get our kids anything." In fact, Coalition policy does allow for child visitation, although not for overnight stays.[4] The few bus passes available are reserved for people who need them to get to work or to doctors' appointments.

Jane, Jennifer, and Sandy all had basic ideas about how to achieve reunification with their children, but were concerned that their legal situations would probably rule it out. Jane and Sandy both have recent drug convictions; it was never made clear just what Jennifer's legal situation was, but something drug-related is a good guess. One of the women was aware that a nearby law school holds regular law clinics at the Coalition and suggested that the others speak with one of the law school's attorneys about their situations.

In light of the gratitude expressed by all the women in being told about legal services that might be available to them, we necessarily wondered why their own case managers never explained that this service was available. Subsequent investigation revealed that the free legal clinic does appear on the list of available services that women are given when they enter the CWF, but when women first show up at the CWF, they are in crisis, often riddled with anxieties, uncertain about their futures, and not always in full possession of their faculties. It is scarcely the time to bombard them with information about available services. And it is also clear that these women and their admission paperwork quickly part ways.[5]

A quantitative analysis of child separation showed that drug-abusing women were more likely to be separated from a child than non-abusing women were, but otherwise there were few differences between the two groups. Neither mental illness, domestic violence, nor any of the usual background variables predicted whether a woman was separated from her child(ren) or not.

Sympathetic as we are to the plight of these women, it is not obvious that reunification with their children would be a sensible goal even if it were somehow possible, nor is it obvious that the children would be better off living with their mothers than they are in their current living situations. The focus group reminded us of a female client in the New Orleans Homeless Substance Abusers Project in the early 1990s (see Wright, Devine and Eddington 1993). This woman—we'll call her Wanda—was a hardcore crack addict who turned tricks to support her drug habit. She had three children, all of them in foster care. She came into the rehabilitation program, got and stayed clean, did well in the Transitional Care program, found a decent job, and with a great deal of effort from program staff and legal aid, had been successfully reunited with two of her three children, who were living with her in NOHSAP's Extended Care/Independent Living program. In all ways, she was the cover girl for the program—until one night when a former boyfriend showed up with a pocketful of crack and an urge to go party. Wanda left her kids alone in the apartment and headed off downtown with the boyfriend. We found her four or five days later, filthy and half-naked in a crack house, high as a kite, and virtually incoherent. "Ain't goin' back to no goddamned program. That's just a bunch of bullshit." "But Wanda," she was asked, "how about your kids?" And she replied: "Fuck 'em. Give 'em back to the state."

Histories of Homelessness

What we can say about the homelessness histories of Orlando's homeless women is what we learned in a 2003-2004 survey of 199 Coalition women who were participating in our statewide survey of the experience of violence in the lives of homeless women. In addition to questions about violence, some results of which we present in the following section, the survey also asked extensive questions about geographical origins, homelessness histories, and other background characteristics. All these surveys, incidentally, were face-to-face interviews conducted by CWF caseworkers who had been trained to do these interviews by our research team.

Concerning origins, 91 percent of the Orlando women in the sample were born in the United States (compared to 84 percent of the men discussed in Chapter Three). Four percent were born in the U.S. territory of Puerto Rico, and the remaining women were from around the world. Of those born in the U.S., 35 percent were born in Florida (versus 25 percent of the men), 16 percent were native to the Orlando area (versus

10 percent of the men), 10 percent were from nearby Southern States (Alabama, Georgia and the Carolinas), 22 percent were born in New York, New Jersey and Pennsylvania, and 10 percent were from Indiana, Illinois and Ohio, with the remainder strewn thinly across the remaining states. Thus, while the majority were born outside of Florida, the Florida natives are somewhat more common among Central Florida's homeless women than among the corresponding men. As with the men, most of the women who migrated to Florida from elsewhere had lived in Florida for quite some time, about six and a half years on the average. So as we concluded with the men, the homeless women of Central Florida are not much more geographically mobile than Central Florida residents in general.

Homeless women in the sample average thirty-seven or thirty-eight years of age. They began living on their own at about age twenty; those with children (73 percent of the sample) first gave birth (on average) at about age twenty-four; and the women first became homeless, on average, at about age thirty-three. The substantial majority (59 percent) have only been homeless just this one time; another quarter have been homeless two or three times; a few (about 3 percent) have been homeless ten or more times. Most (65 percent) have been homeless only for a matter of months; about 12 percent have been homeless for more than two years. So clearly, very few of Orlando's homeless women would be considered chronically or long-time homeless people. Most are in their first homeless episode and have only a few months of accumulated time on the streets.

Three-fifths (61 percent) of the Orlando women are homeless by themselves; 26 percent are homeless with one or more children but no adult partner; 8 percent are homeless with one or more children *and* an adult partner; and 5 percent are homeless with an adult partner but no children. (Almost all the adult partners, incidentally, are men and are also the women's husbands: 14 percent of all Coalition women describe their marital status as "married.") Thus, just over one homeless Orlando woman in three has a child or children with her on the streets; nearly 40 percent qualify as homeless families by the CWF definition.

Immediately prior to the current episode of homelessness, 42 percent of the women were living in their own place (house or apartment), either alone or with spouses or children; 23 percent were living with parents or guardians; 19 percent were doubled up with someone other than parents or guardians; 8 percent were living in motels, hotels, or some other similarly temporary housing arrangement; and the remaining 8 percent were in other housing arrangements (jail, group home, institutional setting, etc.).

To say that many of these women grew up in dysfunctional, abusive, or neglectful homes is something of an understatement (Table 5.2). We need not dwell at length on the specifics, which are laid out in the table for all to see. Three-quarters of the women were spanked as children, 28 percent were beaten up by parents, one in five had parents who threatened to kill them, and so on. Summing across the twenty acts shown in the table, about one respondent in six reported that none of these things had happened to her (as a child), and another one in six reported only one or two of the less serious acts. Charitably, then, we might conclude that about a third of these women grew up in home situations no more abusive than, say, the average American home. But across the entire sample, the mean number of acts experienced was more than six and a tenth of the women had experienced fifteen or more of them.

It would be misleading to describe the early childhood experiences of this sample as a universal vale of tears. At least some of our women

Table 5.2
Childhood Experiences of Orlando's Homeless Women (N = 199)

When you were a child, did any parent, step-parent, guardian, or other adult person:

	Percent Yes
Spank you?	73
Swear at you?	55
Insult you?	54
Threaten to hit you?	54
Humiliate or embarrass you?	53
Push, shove or grab you?	48
Hit you with an object?	46
Slap your face?	38
Pull your hair?	36
Throw something at you that could hurt?	34
Kick or hit you with a fist?	33
Neglect you?	28
Beat you up?	28
Threaten to kill you?	20
Choke you?	16
Threaten you with a knife or gun?	15
Lock you in a closet or tie you up?	12
Burn or scald you on purpose?	7
Use a knife or gun on you?	8
Cut you?	6

were raised in more or less "normal" homes by intact, non-abusive, non-neglectful parents. That important point acknowledged, it is also safe to conclude that the large majority of these women were raised in generally unpleasant home environments; many were raised in neglectful and abusive environments; and some suffered home environments that are best described as gruesome.

Another question in the same "childhood experiences" sequence asked whether the respondent had ever left or run away from her childhood home because of abuse or violence. One in four said yes. Much later in the interview, we asked these women whether they had ever moved out "of a place you were living because of violence," and here, two-fifths (41 percent) said they had. One final question provides the perfect segue between this section and the next: "Are you currently homeless because of violence or abuse committed against you by an adult partner in your last residence?" This was averred to be the main reason for the woman's current homelessness in 16 percent of all cases and one among several reasons in another 9 percent of cases. Thus, as shown in many other studies (Richards et al. 2010; Rosenheck et al. 1999; Browne and Bassuk 1997), one Orlando homeless woman in four is currently homeless in whole or in part because she has left a violent or abusive relationship and has ended up on the streets.

Violence, Domestic and Otherwise

Our focus group participant Amanda became a homeless woman when her husband walked out on her and took his income with him. Male abandonment is a common path to homelessness for women. Indeed, one of the very earliest examinations of women's homelessness determined that marital dissolutions were a—and perhaps *the*—main cause of homelessness in this group (Garrett and Bahr 1976). In Martha Burt's (2001) national survey of service-utilizing homeless people, only 15 percent of women who were homeless with children were currently married; 39 percent were divorced and 46 percent had never married. Among single women, 52 percent were widowed, divorced, or separated, and 45 percent were never married. In our Orlando data, as intimated earlier, nearly 15 percent of the women (with or without children) are currently married and homeless with their husbands; 42 percent have never married; the remainder (43 percent) are victims of marital dissolution, almost always divorce or separation (although 7 percent report being widows).

The concept of the failure of romantic relationships as a cause of homelessness among women has morphed more recently into a concern with the very high rates of domestic violence perpetrated on homeless women. One study in Massachusetts of homeless and very poor but housed women found that 60 percent had experienced violence at the hands of a domestic partner (Browne, and Bassuk 1997). As we just pointed out, numerous studies in a variety of samples of homeless women have shown that about one in four is currently homeless as a direct result of domestic violence. Thus, abandonment and violence are two prominent ways that men make women homeless, not just in the U.S., but pretty much everywhere in the so-called "civilized world." (For evidence on the British case, see Hatty 1996; for Australia see Radley, Hodgetts and Cullen 2006.)

Numerous studies have also identified the risk factors for violence in general and intimate partner violence in particular against poor and homeless women (Jasinski et al. 2010). These include low self-esteem, childhood physical and sexual abuse, and the partner's work history and substance abuse. Most homeless women who have experienced domestic violence as adults (either before or during their homeless spells) also experienced abuse as children. There is also a well-developed qualitative literature confirming many of the same themes and perspectives, a literature that documents the abuse homeless women experience in vivid and shocking detail (See, e.g., Padgett, Hawkins, Abrams and Davis 2006).

The same is generally true of homeless women in Orlando. Sixty-three percent of the women in the Orlando survey self-identified as "a victim of violence," and of those self-identified victims, 40 percent said that having been a victim of violence had interfered with their ability "to get or keep a job." (Of some interest, only about one woman in four said that being homeless had affected their ability to "get or keep a job.") So the violence these women experience is not only widespread but also consequential.

Data on actual victimization show that well more than the 63 percent who self-identify as victims in fact are. Nearly three quarters reported having been the victim of a physical assault at some time in their adult lives (beaten up, choked, slapped, kicked, shot at, stabbed, and the like); 63 percent had been physically assaulted by an intimate partner. Likewise, more than half had been raped at least once (and often, more than once); half the rapes had been at the hands of an intimate partner.

Jasinski et al. (2010) report details of an interview with a homeless woman from Orlando called Mo, whose long history of violence began in childhood. Punched, kicked, and beaten by her father as a child, Mo tried to tell authorities about the abuse but was ignored. She says, "Since I was a little kid, [my dad] always said I fell down or something." She recalls years of wearing long pants, turtlenecks, and "always sweating but scared to go to school with regular clothes on because of the bruises." As a young teen, she tried to fight back, only to have her father call the police, who charged her with domestic violence against her father! Eventually, Mo's school reported the father's abuse and she was removed from the home by child protective services, which contacted her mother. "They made her come get me and I lived with her for a couple of years but after so many years of taking all my dad's crap, when I got there, I started beating the shit out of her." Mo's mother, a drug addict, is currently in prison for first-degree murder. Mo also violently attacked her stepmother: "We were fighting and I guess after so many years of dealing with so much crap I snapped and took it out on her. So I stabbed her ... I stabbed her repeatedly in the head, neck, arm and then I bit a hunk out of her arm. I was really—I had a lot of pent-up anger." Mo served jail time for this savage attack. For Mo, violence was little more than a strategy of coping with and resisting cumulative victimizations and abuses.

Mo refers to her victimization as years of taking "crap" and having "pent-up anger." But she perpetrates violence as a means of resistance to the violence she fears from others. It turns out that "violent resistance" is a type of intimate partner violence perpetrated almost exclusively by women (see Johnson 2008). Many women, not just homeless women, consider violence as a realistic strategy to fend off abuse and anticipated victimization.

In addition to being abused as a child, Mo was also victimized by a number of boyfriends in adulthood. The father of her child tried to kill her while she was pregnant.

His father beat me up every day for about six and a half months. Choking me. ... He said, "If you tell anyone, I'll kill you and the baby." And the last time was when he set me on fire real bad. Both my eyes swelled up. My nose was like—it was almost to the side. My mouth—my lips were so big from being steadily hit. I had handprints around my neck. I had handprints on my arms from him grabbing me. And you could see the marks on my stomach from where he had been kicking me.

When asked if that was the most recent abusive relationship she ever experienced, Mo responded, "I've been in other relationships, but I tell the guys I date, 'Hey, if I think you're gonna get physical—the moment I think you're gonna get physical or any type of violence toward me, I'll hurt you first before you can hurt me.'"

The Women of the WRCC

At the top of the chapter, we mentioned the Women's Residential and Counseling Center, a transitional living center for homeless women with or without children also operated by the Coalition for the Homeless of Central Florida. Women at the WRCC must be employed and drug-free and are charged a program fee of about ~$200 per month. More than half describe themselves as victims of domestic violence, and one of the WRCC services is a twelve-bed emergency shelter for women experiencing violence. Compared to the CWF, the WRCC is a superior residential environment: much nicer neighborhood, more privacy, nicer accommodations, more facilities for children, and enhanced services all around. Based just on the nicer physical facilities, one might think that the WRCC women "have it made." However, life as a homeless woman is a struggle no matter how nice a facility one happens to live in, as we learned in recent focus groups at the WRCC. The point of the focus groups was to evaluate client satisfaction with available services, but some of the findings were of more general interest, as indicative of the residual concerns of homeless women who are, in some objective sense, on the way to self-sufficiency.

The first session was conducted in the spring of 2009 and involved nine WRCC women. The second session was held on September 14, 2009 and eight women participated. Each session lasted about an hour. Both focus groups were semi-structured. A list of guiding questions was used; however, the conversation was allowed to flow as long as it remained relevant to the study. No demographic information was collected. The sessions were not audio recorded. Instead, note takers were present at both sessions.

Child care, safety (protection from abusive husbands and boyfriends), laundry, shelter, tutoring for children, use of the recreational room, counseling, school scholarships, and food were the necessities and services that the women in the first session expected to find upon arriving at the center. When asked which services they took advantage of, they listed all of these and more. One resident said, "I feel good." The women in the second group were generally pleased with the services they were receiving as well. Their overriding concern was case management and specifically, with how case managers could assist them in finding permanent housing.

While some women in the first group stated, "I think we should be given more privileges" (referring to medical, dental, and vision coverage and the ability to cook in one's room, the latter out of the question for legal, code, and safety reasons, of course), women in the second group did not voice any concerns about additional privileges they felt they should get. While virtually all of the women who participated in the focus groups reported taking part in basic services such as meal service and laundry facilities, many of them also seemed to enjoy the WRCC's non-essentials such as writing and yoga classes.

Gender

Several of the women in the first group seemed almost consumed by a sense of entitlement and enraged by the thought that "society" was somehow taking better care of homeless men (although they were unable to state any reason why this would be the case). One said, "I feel, at the Coalition, that the men get more things than the women get here." The specific comparison is to men who sleep at the Pavilion, the guys we discussed in Chapters Three and Four, who receive practically no services at all other than their plastic mat on the concrete floor. Possibly, these women may have been referring to the fact that Pavilion men have their own drug rehabilitation program on site, along with their own on-site AA meetings, which WRCC women do not. There is also a van that is used to take men in the rehab program to off-site meetings. But in all other ways that we can think of, WRCC services and amenities are definitely superior.

Women in the second focus group felt exactly the opposite. Part of the difference between the two groups was that some of the women in the second group had stayed at the Coalition prior to coming to the WRCC and quickly assured all the women present that they were *much* better off at the WRCC than they would be at the CWF. No one in the second group thought that homeless men received more service or better treatment.

Safety

For women in the first group, physical safety was not much of a concern. Although some voiced worries over the safety of the nearby bus stops, others were quick to point out that things outside the WRCC campus are beyond management's control. The women were all grateful that the front door was constantly locked with any resident or potential visitor having to be rung in. It was noted that residents were forbidden from opening the door even for other residents which, again, the women all favored. The lack of fire drills was the only cause for concern; as soon as the question about safety was posed, one woman mentioned immediately that she was concerned about the absence of fire drills and all others swiftly agreed. Some of the women had been at the WRCC for close to a year, yet not one of them could recall ever having taken part in a fire drill. By far, this issue was the greatest safety concern expressed.

In the second group, safety was a bigger concern. Because the air conditioner was not working in the common areas at the time, people were leaving windows and doors open. Although this was only "allowed" when the rooms were occupied, many of the women stated that they had come into rooms and found doors and windows wide open. Others expressed concerns that it would be very easy for someone to jump over one of the walls surrounding the WRCC. No one could recall an incident where this occurred, but they were fearful that it might in the future.

These concerns are not misplaced. Many of the women at the WRCC are victims of domestic violence and the facility's location is common knowledge. Angry men appear at the facility with some frequency demanding to see "their" women. Staff at the front desk are very cautious about who is "buzzed in," and when angry men are at the front door demanding entry, the usual response is to call the police. So having open windows and doors, especially on first floor rooms easily accessible from the streets, is a serious security breach.

Case Management

Overall, in the first session, the women all seemed pleased with their case managers, saying they were very open and helpful. While two or three women did not feel comfortable talking at length with their case managers, they knew case managers were available if needed. The women in the first group felt that they got what they needed, even if they sometimes had to ask for it. "I ask for a referral, and I get a referral." Yet they felt more services should be offered to them without having to ask. "If you ask, they will help you. But they won't unless you ask."

Case managers play a very important role in the lives and eventual self-sufficiency of the women at the WRCC. It is their responsibility not only to offer referrals to residents for any potential services residents might need, but also to assist them in making the transition back to working individuals capable of supporting themselves and their children. Making sure residents are putting money aside each week toward their ultimate savings objectives, reaffirming the ways in which the WRCC can assist them in their larger goals, helping them find work close to the WRCC (or if the need arises, finding them transitional or permanent housing closer to their place of employment), and offering general advice were all noted as duties of the case managers by the women. While some of the women in the first group admitted feeling hesitant toward their individual case managers initially, the vast majority seemed grateful to have someone specifically dedicated to them and their individual goals.

The women in the second session, in contrast, were very unhappy with the case management they had received. Many said they would not even call it case management. While they all met with their case managers regularly, without exception every woman in this session was discouraged by these meetings. They complained that they were told "what we need to do, but not how to do it." The women said that they were not on any waiting lists for housing and did not know what, if any, housing might be available to them or how to get on the appropriate lists. These women seemed almost desperate to move on and yet described themselves as "clueless" as to how they should go about it. One woman, who was over the age of sixty-five and eligible for subsidized senior housing, did not even know that such places existed. She is not on any list and says her case manger has never discussed this as an option with her.

One woman stated that she had been at the WRCC for several months but still could not figure out how to get a childcare subsidy. She said she was told by her case manager to go to Workforce Central Florida, but when she called WCF for an appointment, she was told that she could not come to their offices with her child. The case managers had not explained to this woman (or any of the women) just what steps she needed to take or where she needed to go to obtain a childcare voucher, nor were any of the women actually assisted in doing so. (The relevant office is about three miles west of the WRCC on Colonial Avenue, a challenging, but manageable, walk. Childcare subsidies can be applied for online, although an email address is a required field and that may be problematic for some of these women.)

Attitudes about Staff and Other Residents

Many residents at the WRCC were hesitant to participate in the first focus group. While trying to encourage participation, it was discovered that many of the residents felt the group would be a waste of time. Some of the women did not see how participating in the focus group could make a difference, especially for them. In the end, nine women chose to take part. Many of these women reported that the staff seemed judgmental and unconcerned about them. Evidently mistaking a transitional program for permanent housing, one woman stated, "You work here, but I live here." Many of the women who participated in the first focus group agreed that some of the staff made them feel like "less of a person" because they were at the WRCC. Moreover, one woman reported overhearing two staff members gossiping about a resident, which was very upsetting to her. These women were concerned, overwhelmingly, with being treated with respect—something that many of them felt they did not get from staff or from other residents. Some women also felt that the staff did not act professionally or compassionately. For instance, many women stated that they had medical problems that required a specific regime of medications, water, or food. However, they felt that some of the staff did not respect their specific needs and that they were treated poorly because they were homeless. We have heard the same complaints before in other focus groups at the WRCC.

In contrast to the first group, which was difficult to fill, participants had to be turned away from the second group (which was held immediately following a resident's meeting) because there was more interest than spots available. These women wanted to discuss their issues with case management with someone and wanted to talk about their anxieties about finding permanent housing. As for their treatment by the staff, it was much less of an issue in the second group than in the first: "They're people just like us. They have good days and bad days." Although some said that staff members were at times harsh or not compassionate, no one in this group was too bothered by it. For these women, things such as staff behavior or other privileges were simply not very important. They did not want to waste their time discussing them no matter how often such items were posed to the group. Case management and housing dominated the discussion.

A few common themes surfaced during the two focus groups. In both groups, at least some complaints were voiced about everything from inconsistent enforcement of campus rules to the availability of services, but complaints were voiced mostly about staff, who were either rude and insensitive (group 1) or not working aggressively enough to address the women's housing issues (group 2). Perhaps this is due to the natural tendency of people to complain. At the same time, we have personally witnessed staff being judgmental and insensitive to the women (both at the WRCC and on the main campus) and we have often expressed our concerns that the Coalition's case managers do not pay sufficient attention to housing issues. The participants also admitted that new staff members were generally more sensitive to their needs and that more tenured staff had become somewhat desensitized to the delicacy of many clients' circumstances, suggesting a possible burn-out effect that may compromise the quality of services.

In regard to case management, no one expects case managers to do everything for these women while the women do nothing for themselves, so it is always a delicate balance between fostering dependency and truly helping those in need. Clearly, it is the job of case managers to point these women in the right direction and to provide them with the necessary resources. Just being told that "you need to find housing" or "you should get a job" is not sufficient without strategizing ways these things might be accomplished. At the same time, as comments below will clarify, too much "direction" runs the risk of infantilizing these women.

When both focus groups were coming to a close, participants expressed disappointment that our sessions would not become weekly events. The women truly seemed to enjoy being able to express their opinions and to network with each other. Why it would require a focus group to do this is a mystery. These women live, eat, and attend recreational activities and resident meetings together. They know one another by name and frequently share intimate details of each others' lives. That they appeared to need external stimulation to form support or discussion groups around problems and issues of common concern is perhaps indicative of the degree to which the experience of homelessness itself degrades social skills and fragments women's natural networking capabilities. In any case, just as the best job readiness program is often a cousin who has a job, so too is the best case manager sometimes a roommate who has "been there, done that." We have watched homeless people successfully "case manage" one another in other contexts and perhaps something similar needs to happen at the WRCC as well.

A more subtle and perhaps more serious concern, as intimated earlier, is with inadvertent infantilization of homeless women, a process that has been discussed in many studies of people experiencing homelessness. (One particularly revealing and important study is Hoffman and Coffey 2008.) Labeling theory (Becker 1963) states that if you tell kids they are stupid long enough and insistently enough, they will eventually become stupid. Infantilization is likewise the process of treating adults as if they were children until they come to behave as children and become dependent upon their authority figures. In the Hoffman-Coffey study referenced earlier, comments made by homeless people about their interactions with service providers "often revolved around the notion that they were 'treated like a child,' and 'are like a piece of shit to them.' The attitude that providers know better is what we term the infantilization of people experiencing homelessness" and is certain to promote dependency more than it fosters self-sufficiency. Interactions between staff and clients at the WRCC and the CWF literally drip with staff sentiment that "we know better than you." At the same time, leading these women by the hand through every process, form, and bureaucracy they need to master is hardly empowering either. So staff and case managers at these kinds of facilities must steer, often with great uncertainty, between being "helpful" but not overly directive, aiding but not "enabling," insistent but not infantilizing. Finding the proper mix can be quite a challenge.

Quite obviously, homeless people of all sorts, male and female, with or without children, are expected to live by more, and more rigid, rules than most adults must live by. Adults don't have curfews, but homeless people do. Adults eat dinner pretty much whenever they please; homeless people eat dinner when dinner is served. When adults get home from a long, hard day, they put their feet up and pour a glass of wine. A WRCC resident who did likewise would be discharged from the facility at once. When an adult woman decides she wants to sleep with a man, she invites him over for a night of seduction. Such choices are denied to women living in shelters. In all these ways and thousands more, homeless women (and to much the same degree, homeless men) are treated more as children than adults.

If we expect to make inroads toward solving homelessness it is important that homeless individuals feel it is possible to become a part of mainstream society. This can only be accomplished when they are consistently treated with respect in a variety of settings, and are able to retain a sense of dignity. This issue certainly does not eliminate the need for diverse solutions, particularly when faced with the lack of a living wage, high housing costs, and continued cuts in funding for services. Yet we argue it deserves greater emphasis in the fight against homelessness given the potential benefits that might be derived from such a shift by service providers, who are themselves also subject to bureaucratic forms of authority and experiences of disrespect.

The suggestion, both powerful and disturbing, is that "the perpetuation of homelessness is not internal to the homeless individual as many claim, but rather may be embedded in the service industry itself, which subjects *both* clients and providers to bureaucratic forms of authority and experiences of disrespect."

Conclusions

Women's and family homelessness began to be noticed by research-ers in the 1980s. The first studies mainly focused on comparing the differences between homeless men and women in the problems they face and in the utilization of services. Burt's early study using a nation-wide sampling method comparing homeless men, women, and women with children found that homeless women had the lowest rates of prior institutionalization. A separate study comparing service needs found that both men and women need certain services at similar rates (such as emergency shelter, case management, counseling, and transitional liv-ing), but women need services such as long-term counseling at higher rates than men do, and other services, such as alcohol treatment, at lower rates than men do.

Homeless families with children are now among the fastest growing segments of the homeless population. In its 2004 report on Homelessness and Hunger in America, the U.S. Conference of Mayors reported that in the twenty-seven cities studied, families with children accounted for 40 percent of the total homeless population. In the fiscal year of 2008-09, women, children, and families accounted for 54 percent of the Coalition's total clients served. A National Coalition for the Homeless Fact Sheet points out that "homelessness is a devastating experience for families. It disrupts virtually every aspect of family life, damaging the physical and emotional health of family members, interfering with children's education and development, and frequently resulting in the separation of family members."

Families are often broken apart by homelessness. One issue nation-wide is shelter policies that prevent fathers and older boys from staying in the same facilities as mothers and younger siblings. The Coalition for the Homeless of Central Florida is in fact the only provider in the region that allows whole families to remain intact.

Sadly, the only way to end homelessness among women and children is the same as what would be required to end homelessness among men: more affordable housing, jobs that pay living wages and provide benefits such as health insurance, child care subsidies for working parents, and on through the list. As the National Coalition for the Homeless concludes, "Only concerted efforts to meet all of these needs will end the tragedy of homelessness for America's families and children."

Special considerations must be made for the children of homeless parents. Many programs to help homeless people are targeted towards those who abuse substances or are mentally ill. Homeless women, and especially homeless families, do not have these problems to the same degree as single men. Rather, the homelessness of women is more likely to stem from poor intimate relationships, financial dependence on untrustworthy men, domestic violence, or simple poverty. Rather little can be found in national, state, or local homeless assistance statutes, policies, or procedures that decisively address any of these important factors.

Notes

1. This chapter was co-authored by Hilary M. Dotson and Jana L. Jasinski. Portions are liberally adapted from Dotson's MA thesis, "Homeless Women in the Orlando Shelter System: A Comparison of Single Women, Families, and Women Separated from Their Children." Other portions are adapted from *Hard Lives, Means Streets*, of which Jasinski was the senior author.
2. Although apparently not well-known, many "foster-care" placements (nationwide, about one in four) are to the homes of relatives, not with strangers who have registered as foster care families, mainly because it is simpler for family members to be designated as a child's custodian than for non-relatives to be "qualified" as foster parents.
3. The "we" in this case clearly referred to women, like Amanda, who are in the CWF as single women but who have one or more children somewhere else. As noted, this amounts to about a third of all of the CWF's "single" women.
4. In fact, in some and possibly many of these cases, the children are not allowed to visit their mothers under the terms of their foster-care arrangements. This would be the case, for example, when a woman's parental rights had been terminated. So any effort by the Coalition to *encourage* these visits could potentially open up the proverbial "can of worms."
5. Also possibly relevant is that if the children are formally in the care of the Department of Children and Families (i.e., if they are "officially" in foster care, whether relative care or not), then their mothers have a DCF case manager, a DCF-appointed attorney, and a reunification "case plan."

6

Shelter Life: Risk or Respite?

As we know, homelessness has become a major social issue and one near-universal response to the crisis has been the provision of emergency overnight shelter to people with nowhere else to go. One would be hard-pressed to find a city of any appreciable size that does not have a homeless shelter to provide indoor places where homeless people can sleep and often have a meal, take a shower, and tend to life's other most basic necessities. The shelters are not considered a solution to homelessness, but rather a means of responding to the most immediate needs that homeless people have: shelter from the elements and sustenance for the body. In Maslow's terms, the emergency shelters exist to tend to level one and level two needs.

Homeless shelters are often viewed as dangerous places. Potential health problems ranging from knife wounds to tuberculosis are often associated with homeless shelters. Indeed, if one were looking to design a system that was optimal for the transmission of communicable diseases, the homeless shelter would be it. In most shelters, debilitated men (and women) sleep in close, poorly ventilated quarters. What more could an aggressive bacterium want?

In addition to infectious and communicable diseases, the shelters are also often depicted as hotbeds of drug use, crime, and various other social pathologies. Indeed, when citizens band together to prevent the siting of homeless shelters in their neighborhoods, the frequent rationale is that the shelters are full of rapists, pedophiles, murderers, thieves, and other treacherous sorts. As a result, homeless shelters usually end up being located in the poorest, most rundown areas of major cities, where local residents lack the political clout to do anything about it, and these often unsavory locations make the shelters seem all the more treacherous. Although they are often unpleasant places and clearly do not address the root causes of homelessness, they at least make it possible for homeless people to get off the streets for the night. And that, after all, is the point.

Or in any case, that used to be the point. The advent of Housing First as an intervention philosophy and the development of the "shelterization" thesis (see Chapter Four) have caused many to question the wisdom of the shelter system altogether and to seek alternatives. The shelters, it is argued, can only accommodate a small fraction of the homeless, are unable to provide intensive long-term assistance to help people and families stabilize their lives, fail to address homeless peoples' real needs, are unable to help families overcome the many barriers they face in housing and employment, and only address the symptoms of the homelessness crisis, not the root causes. Far better, the argument continues, to get homeless people and families into housing *first*, and then begin to address their other issues and problems. Strongly supporting this concept is the substantial evidence that people are more receptive to interventions, social services, or mental health and addictions treatment *after* their housing situations have been stabilized rather than while they are living in emergency shelter.

On the other hand, even the most extensive and aggressive Housing First programs accommodate only small fractions of the total homeless population. In Miami (see Chapter Twelve), the total capacity of the Housing First programs amounts to 154 units, in contrast to the thousands of homeless individuals in need. Indicative of the shortfall in capacity relative to need, waiting lists are long for Housing First programs everywhere, so much so that "Housing First" is a misnomer—as we said earlier, it is really Waiting List First, Housing Later. Where, then, do homeless people sleep while they wait to move up on the Housing First waiting lists? The answer, of course, is an emergency shelter, which will doubtlessly remain an important element in the system of care for homeless people for the foreseeable future. The alternative would be hundreds of thousands of homeless people sleeping on the streets, parks, and alleyways each night, and that is politically unpalatable.

This chapter explores life as it is lived and experienced in the Men's Pavilion and in the Coalition's women's shelter, the Center for Women and Families. A small group of Pavilion and CWF clients participated in a series of focus groups to discuss why some choose to use the shelter while others do not. The realities of crime, disease, friendship, and camaraderie in the shelter are also explored. Our goal is to present an accurate portrayal of what life in a homeless shelter entails and to determine whether, on balance, the shelters are places of risk or islands of respite for their inhabitants.

The American history of emergency shelter for homeless people dates to the 1800s (see DePastino 2003). Since that time, the emergency shelter system has grown exponentially, especially since the early 1980s and the apparent explosion of homelessness that began at that time. Recently, as indicated above, the focus has shifted from emergency shelter to more long-term solutions such as transitional programs and permanent housing. Nevertheless, emergency shelters remain an integral part of the homeless service network throughout America and continue to respond to an important need.

A 2000 report from the Urban Institute concluded that while homeless shelter beds increased 220 percent from 1988 to 1996, and have increased even further since, three-quarters of the increased capacity were beds in transitional or permanent housing programs, not in emergency shelters (Burt and Aron 2000). Since 1996, the total inventory of emergency, transitional, and permanent housing beds increased by another 6 percent, but the apparent growth masks a 35 percent *decrease* in the number of emergency beds. All the recent increase, in short, has been in transitional and permanent supportive housing beds (HUD 2007). These trends reflect HUD's emerging emphasis on transitional and permanent housing and the influence of Housing First strategies. Still, according to the 2006 U.S. Conference of Mayors report on hunger and homelessness in America, requests for emergency shelter beds increased an average of 8 percent between 2004 and 2005 in the twenty-three cities that were surveyed. (Overall, 36 percent of the surveyed cities reported an increase in emergency shelter requests.) So despite the declining number of shelter beds, demand continues to increase, partly because of the new focus on long-term solutions and partly because the average stay in emergency shelters appears to have increased over time (National Coalition for the Homeless 2006).

Asking why the demand for emergency shelter has increased is the same as asking why homelessness has increased, and the answers form a familiar litany: the loss of affordable housing, the near-total disappearance of single room occupancy (SRO) hotels (in the 2006 Conference of Mayors report, no increases in available SRO housing were reported in any of the surveyed cities), the general run-up in housing costs nation-wide, and the high rent burdens now borne by many low income families (see Chapter Two).

While there are emergency shelters everywhere that target specialized groups such as women, women with children, the mentally ill, and the addicted, most emergency overnight shelters serve a general population, and one such shelter, the Coalition's Men's Pavilion, provides most of the data for this chapter. Single males have always been, and continue to be, the majority of the homeless population in America. Although the population of homeless women and children has certainly increased, adult men still comprise the larger share of the homeless population in almost all locales. According to HUD's 2007 report to Congress, summarizing point-in-time counts from all cities that applied for HUD "continuum of care" funds in 2006, 47 percent of all sheltered homeless people in America are single adult men. This can be compared to only 20 percent of poor people in the U.S. who are adult men living alone. Therefore, single adult men are highly overrepresented among the sheltered homeless population.

As is widely known, minorities are also overrepresented in the poverty population, and because poverty is a well-established risk factor for homelessness, people of color are also disproportionately represented among the homeless. Burt's National Survey of Homeless Assistance Providers and Clients and practically all other studies (e.g., U.S. Conference of Mayors 2006) show that homeless people are far more likely to be African American than poor but housed people.

Despite the long history of emergency overnight shelter in the U.S., the large number of emergency shelters that can be found in American cities, and the large number of homeless people within them, very few ethnographic studies of shelter life have been published. One or two studies have looked at how youth experience life in youth shelters, at least one study has examined the effects of shelter life on the family relations of women, and a few studies have looked at what shelter life is like for women and children (Arrighi 1997). However, we have found only one study that examines shelter life specifically among homeless men, a participant observation study done in the notorious New York City Armory, which focused largely on the sexual relationships that develop among the men who stay at this shelter (Dordick 1996). And while countless surveys of shelter denizens have been conducted, most of these surveys focus on the demographic characteristics of shelter users, their social service needs, psychiatric functioning, or physical well-being. Surprisingly few inquire about the conditions of shelter life itself.

To understand more about what shelter life entails for both men and women, focus groups were conducted at the Men's Pavilion and at the

Center for Women and Families. As we have already suggested, the Pavilion is a rough shelter that provides virtually no case management or other services to the men. The men sleep on plastic mats on a concrete floor and there are no separate areas for the handicapped, the ill, or the elderly. Emergency shelters are often derided as being just "three hots and a cot." At the Men's Pavilion, it is one "hot" (dinner) and a mat on a concrete floor. "Three hots and a cot" would be a pretty substantial *improvement* in living conditions for these men. Life at the Pavilion, in short, is a Spartan existence, and we expected the men who sleep and eat there to reflect that fact in their focus group comments. (Conditions at the women's shelter, the Center for Women and Families, are considerably better, and we expected that reality to be reflected in the focus groups with the women, which it was.)

The Men

In all, four focus groups were conducted with Pavilion men beginning on April 2, 2007, and concluding on April 9, 2007. Each session consisted of six to seven participants for a total sample of twenty-four men. Sessions were held in a private conference room in an adjacent building. Sessions generally ran for an hour and a half and focused on the perceptions of the men about life in a homeless shelter. Participants were fed breakfast or lunch depending on the time of day and paid $5 for their time.

Participants, although recruited through informal means, were carefully selected. Participants generally had contact with one another at the shelter but were not co-workers, relatives, or close friends. During the day there are approximately fifty men on the premises for various reasons, and each day when the focus group facilitator (Donley) arrived, she and the Pavilion manager would simply approach different men and ask them if they wanted to participate in a focus group. No one declined to do so. Although this sampling technique is one of convenience, it is different from snowballing, as men were not asked to recruit their friends. This was done on purpose to avoid recruiting people who knew each other too well.

We have conducted numerous studies at the Pavilion and at other programs on the same site over the years, employing several different methodologies including interviews, surveys, and focus groups. Experience has shown that this population is particularly receptive to the focus group format (especially if the general topical focus is not threatening or embarrassing). Homeless men and women always seem to enjoy discussing the topics we present and are flattered that researchers from the University have taken an interest in their opinions and views.

Although the focus group format has always been successful for us and is the primary method used here, we have also found it convenient to obtain standard background and demographic information on focus group participants via a short survey filled out at the end of the session. Naturally, assistance in filling out this questionnaire is provided by the research team.

In addition to the focus groups, we also interviewed the manager of the Men's Pavilion to ascertain any potential differences between client and staff perceptions of life in the shelter. The interview with the manager took place on March 15, 2007, and lasted approximately an hour and a half. The interview contains questions very similar to those asked in the focus groups, but the manager's answers were not shared with focus group participants. We did use the manager's information to assist in probing and clarifying as needed.

In all, of the twenty-six men who participated, 90 percent were African American, 5 percent were white, and 5 percent were Hispanic or Latino. The average age was 38.2 years. Approximately half had been homeless several times while the other half was experiencing their first homeless episode. The majority had substance abuse and alcohol problems and approximately half had previously been incarcerated in jails and prisons around the country, most having served time in Florida.

Most also had children; however the vast majority did not have much, if any, contact with their children. Some had many children, one had nine, and most of those with children had children by more than one woman. Many of the men eagerly pulled out pictures of their kids, clearly with love and pride. One mentioned proudly that one of his five children played the violin (he is a musician himself). Another spoke about how his three children were doing so well in school in Virginia, an accomplishment he attributes to their mother being a schoolteacher. So despite evident estrangement and lack of regular contact, those with children spoke lovingly of them, with sentiments that were unquestionably sincere. The minimal (or non-existent) presence of their children in the lives of these men is but one of many tragedies in the biographies of homeless men.

Community

The men were split on the question of whether there is a true "community" within the shelter walls. Some men stated specifically that they did feel strong connections to other men. Some had found father figures in the Pavilion that they looked up to and many found "brothers" that they would hang out with. More commonly, the men said that they had met men on the property that they had come to consider friends. They talked about looking out for one another and having people who would watch their stuff if needed or share food if they were hungry.

Others, however, felt as if they were alone in the shelter, that the 300 or so other people present on any given night did not represent a community, "just a lot of men together in a room." Many intentionally kept to themselves because they did not trust those around them. Some would socialize with other residents, but referred to them as "acquaintances" or "associates," not friends. As one explained, "… associates are fine to hang out with … but they would back stab you or slit your throat and put their own personal needs above yours in an instant."

Many participants pointed out that virtually all of the men at the shelter know one another, at least by face. Newcomers, they say, are easy to spot: they look lost, stay to themselves, and have conspicuously more belongings than men who have been in the shelter for longer periods. One of the men said, "They have a terrified look on their face and a lot of nice new luggage with them. And I did too when I first came here." Even though new men are easy to spot, the men in the sessions said they are not targeted for violence, although they can be targets of theft, mainly because they have so much more "stuff" with them.

Unlike other shelter studies that have reported racial strife and strict racial segregation, racial division is not apparent at the Pavilion. The men are primarily African American (about two thirds), with a sizable minority of whites and Hispanics. When it is time to sleep, the men grab mats and find spots regardless of their racial identity. One man explained that although some people harbor racist views, they are not outwardly expressed on site. Men often hang out with other men of the same racial background, but this is by no means the invariable pattern. None of the men in any of the groups spoke of any racial tension on site. The manager expressed the same sentiment. Thus, however surprising it seems, there are no obvious race issues at this facility.

There is, however, self-segregation based on gender and sexual identity, with the homosexual and transvestite clients (called "punks" by most of the heterosexual men) generally keeping to themselves. This segregation is utterly obvious when sleeping and eating, but there is no outward display of violence towards "punks" by the larger population. As one heterosexual client put it, "Hey, it's 2007. You can be a punk if you want, but I'm not sleeping next to you!" We have also observed that during the day, homosexual and transvestite clients often spend more time with the women on site than with the men.[1] The only homosexual man who participated in the focus groups explained that he earned money by styling both men's hair and women's hair on the premises. He also advised the others in the group "to always have a drag queen in your corner," a remark that was not taken well by the other men. The heterosexual men try to maintain distance from the homosexual clients, apparently because of their own prejudicial stereotypes as well as their fear of being incorrectly identified as "gay" by other men.

Crime

The public perception of the homeless shelters is that they are riddled with crime (see Chapter Ten), and to a certain extent this appears to be true. All of the men we interviewed stated that theft in the shelter was a definite problem. They spoke of sleeping on their shoes to prevent them from being stolen. They also counseled against acquiring a lot of "stuff" since their possessions, they felt, would eventually be stolen. Surprisingly, the men were exceedingly calm in their response to these thefts. Many expressed sentiments such as: anyone who would steal food from homeless men "must have really been hungry," or that a man who would steal their shoes "must have needed them more than me." There was no evident anger or even mild agitation about these crimes. They seemed, rather, to be accepted as an inevitable part of shelter life.

One man recounted an incident when another man tried to steal his shoes while he was sleeping. The man told us that these shoes were torn, old, and ready to be thrown away. When the other man tried to take them, our participant said to him, "If you need them that bad, then just take 'em." None of the men indicated that they had retaliated (or would retaliate) in response to these petty thefts, or resort to violence, even when they would see the perpetrator wearing the stolen clothing.

While the theft of clothing and shoes elicited no serious response, the taking of one's money was seen as far more serious. The week before the focus groups took place, an incident had occurred that involved an old white man having his wallet stolen by a younger black man. One recounts, "You should've seen it! There were like fifteen black guys tackling this black guy to get this white guy's wallet back." In another session, a man recounted how proud he was to see all of the men attacking the perpetrator in order to get the old man's wallet back. "There are a lot of good people [here] and they know the difference between right and wrong."

Elijah Anderson (2000) has written about "The Code of the Street." There is, likewise, a "code of the shelter," or at least a code at this particular shelter, that says theft is acceptable when one is desperate and takes things one really needs to survive, but theft is not to be tolerated when one steals simply to steal or because the person whose stuff one takes is in no position to prevent it (i.e., an easy target).

Despite the prevalence of theft and other property crimes, and even the occasional violent crime at the shelter, most of the men think they are safer in the shelter than they would be living on the streets or in the various homeless "camps" that dot the Orlando metro area (see the next chapter). All of the men expressed a firm belief that homeless people were "easy targets" out on the streets and practically all were familiar with assaults on homeless people in the Central Florida area. Some men said that they avoided being downtown just to reduce the odds of being assaulted. Some said they would try to "not look homeless" by wearing their best clothes and by not carrying belongings with them when they were on the streets. Some of the men expressed a belief that only specific types of homeless people are targeted, i.e., those that are high, look as if they have drugs, or are not mentally stable. Most men knew someone who had been assaulted while on the streets and several had been assaulted themselves.

Hate crimes against homeless people have burgeoned in recent years and have become a nation-wide problem. Since 1999, the National Coalition for the Homeless (NCH) has issued an annual report on these trends, entitled *Hate, Violence, and Death on Main Street USA*. According to the most recent of these reports, "over the past seven years (1999-2005), advocates and homeless shelter workers from around the country have seen an alarming, nationwide epidemic in reports of homeless men, women and even children being killed, beaten, and harassed." A total of 472 violent hate-crime attacks against the homeless were documented in the report, resulting in 169 deaths. In 2005, Florida led the list of states in the total number of attacks.

One of our participants was among the Florida victims of these unprovoked assaults. By this man's account, he was asleep on a park bench in the middle of the day when he was set upon by a group of teenagers who beat him across the chest with a chain. They did not attempt to rob him. "They just beat me up real good, laughed, and left." We asked if he had called the police. He had not. "It would be pointless." Similar stories were related by many of the other participants.

Interestingly, the reaction of the other men in the focus group to hearing this man's story was to ask him what he was doing "out there" by himself. Most expressed some sentiment to the effect, "You should know you cannot do such a thing, it is simply too dangerous." Among other things, this is a useful, even poignant, reminder that "risk versus respite" is very much a relative thing, in this case, relative to the risks inherent in the alternative. Homeless men who sleep in the Pavilion run the risk of getting their shoes stolen. Homeless men who avoid the Pavilion and sleep, literally, in the streets run the risk of being beaten senseless by urban toughs for no apparent reason. And when the choice is minor inconvenience versus senseless savagery, a modicum of inconvenience seems the better bargain by far.

In a parallel focus group study that our team conducted of men living in Orange County's homeless camps (see the next chapter), physical safety was also an issue. (Living in these camps is one alternative to shelter life; living on the downtown streets is another.) In contrast to the rather laid-back attitude that our sheltered homeless men expressed, physical safety was a constant concern to many of the homeless campers, both safety from predators and, somewhat more commonly, safety from the threat of being hit or run over by cars. Many of the campers took pain to reduce their risks of predation: they kept dogs or weapons in their camps; took turns keeping watch; stayed alert to intruders and strangers. But many felt completely vulnerable to the reckless, often aggressive, in-a-hurry, red-light-running motorists who have made Orlando among the least safe cities in America for pedestrians and bicyclists. Significantly, such concerns were never expressed in the focus groups with the sheltered homeless.

Again, we see clearly that "risk" and "respite" are relative to the available alternatives. The sheltered homeless at the Pavilion are much safer in their own minds than the homeless men who live on the streets or in the camps. And yet, remarkably, when we asked our homeless campers why they lived in the woods rather than going downtown where they could find shelter and other services, the most common answer was that downtown Orlando was a dangerous and unfriendly place. Many specifically mentioned the crime rate, the recent upturn in murders, and the thugs and "druggies" as their principal reasons for avoiding downtown. Thus, virtually all of our campers told us they felt much safer in the East Orlando woods than they would ever feel downtown, and a like number of the sheltered downtown homeless felt much safer in the shelter than they would ever feel living out in the woods. Obviously, homeless people, no less than people in general, self-select into the available living options based on what makes them feel the most comfortable and secure.

Disease

Like theft and assault, the fear of disease, particularly tuberculosis, is a very real concern for the men. Hepatitis and "crabs" (pubic lice) were also mentioned as primary health concerns. As we indicated earlier, shelter life presents optimal conditions for the transmission of infectious and contagious disease, and men who live in the shelter are acutely aware of that fact.

Shelter men have evolved various adaptive strategies to help reduce their risks. For example, if a client is coughing excessively or hacking up suspicious sputum, the other clients ask him to leave the shelter for the night. Another example: at night, there is a cooler with ice water in it available to the men. There is a firmly enforced, if unwritten, rule that once this cooler is out of water, scooping out ice with one's hands is not allowed. Those who violate this rule are quickly sanctioned. The men explained that this simply cannot be tolerated; the potential for disease transmission is too high.

Many of the men also expressed displeasure with the level of sanitation at the shelter, although the building is cleaned daily. As one explained, "They let everyone in here—sick, crazy, high and lazy. Then we all sleep in the same damned room together and all use the same damned shower. It's not healthy." The Pavilion manager explained the facility's cleaning and sanitation procedures and boasted that the level of sanitation was in fact pretty good, but acknowledged that there was room for concern. Some men come in drunk and urinate on themselves during the night, not bothering or not able to use the facilities.[2] The bathroom and floors are cleaned daily with bleach, but there has been an outbreak of staph infection in recent months and once a staphylococcus infection becomes established, "it is a nightmare to get rid of," as the manager put it. Other health issues that have plagued the facility in the past year include infestations (mice, roaches), mold, and the usual upper respiratory and skin infections.

Violence

When we asked about violence at the shelter, many responded that "it happens every day. It's a way of life!" But further discussion revealed that the vast majority of this so-called "violence" is nothing more serious or threatening than verbal altercations that rarely turn physical. Granted, verbal altercations are a constant feature of shelter life. The men there are constantly "getting in one another's face" about all matters large and small. Mostly, these seem to be issues of "respect," such as stepping on someone's foot and not saying "excuse me" or making disparaging comments about another's aroma or physical appearance. Minor "dissing" often escalates quickly to a verbal altercation, a shouting match as it were, but these only rarely become truly violent. Many shelter men are far too broken down and debilitated to represent a real physical threat.

This is not to say that truly violent episodes never happen. Men in every focus group took pains to mention a fatal stabbing that happened the previous year, which resulted from a dispute over a donut. This incident clearly scared (many of) these men, although they were not comfortable saying so in so many words. It is a telling observation that none of the men in the focus groups were present during the incident, but all without exception knew about it in detail.

The donut killing, incidentally, is only the most infamous of a number of violent altercations to occur over the past few years. Indeed, the police are frequently called (mainly by staff, rarely if ever by clients) to the Pavilion to break up fights or to intervene in altercations before they escalate into serious incidents. Police or other emergency presence at the site averages approximately one visit a day, but this count is inflated by a large number of medical emergency calls. Many of the incidents that result in a call for police service involve the dealers and hangers-on who frequent the shelter premises despite the best efforts of management to keep them away. Violence is a threat and in extreme cases a very serious one. On the other hand, men who mind their manners, respect the rights and space of other men, and stay out of peoples' faces are at no serious risk. Like many of life's risks, this risk can be managed, and most residents do so successfully.

Substance Abuse

Most men in the focus groups and in the Pavilion at large have or have had an addiction to drugs or alcohol. Drugs are readily available in the surrounding area and many of the men spoke of seeing drug use, sales, and paraphernalia on shelter grounds. Those who are actively involved in drug use did not see this to be a problem. Others—those who have never used or are now in recovery—find the drug presence in and around the shelter to be very detrimental.

Crack cocaine is the drug of choice (not including alcohol) and crack deals are the most visible drug transactions. The manager spoke of "neighborhood drug-dealing thugs" coming on to the shelter property to sell crack to what he considered to be a vulnerable population. He stated, "Periodically, once I know that a guy is a drug dealer, I'll say, 'Hey, man, you know you can't do that here on the property.' A lot of times I don't see them exchanging anything, but after awhile when you are in an area you can pretty much tell who is who, based on how our guys gravitate to this one person. You can tell what's going on." When the manager witnesses drug transactions he takes them very seriously, but explains, "I can't run up on a drug dealer. I don't have a weapon. I can't just grab some guy so I have to be very mindful of what I say or do when there is no police presence. It's more outside, though, than on the property. And a lot of them [the dealers] don't even live here."

The public perception of the Pavilion in Orlando is that it is drug-infested and that drug deals are openly done along the adjacent streets. To a certain extent, this is true. At all hours of the day and night, there are suspicious looking men just hanging out across the street from the Pavilion's main gate, and they are certainly not there doing ethnographies of shelter life. The tell-tale sign of drug activity—a pair of sneakers draped over the utility wires—is always present. Oddly, there is an Orlando Police Department substation less than two blocks away, and yet the police rarely come through to shake down the dealers, make arrests, or tell these men to move on. As the manager took pains to stress, these dealers are not homeless men and they are not Pavilion residents. They are there to prey on the Pavilion population and do so successfully. Therefore, exposure to drugs is definitely one of the risks of Pavilion life or, of course, a source of respite if access to drugs is something one is looking for!

Motivation

Some of the men expressed concerns that the shelter could be a deterrent for homeless people to change their lives for the better. This was generally spoken about in the third person, with only a handful of men saying that they themselves were unmotivated because they know the Pavilion, its staff, and volunteers will provide for them. More commonly, the men spoke about feeling "lazy" at times but quickly getting over it. Some stayed motivated by reading the Bible and by believing that God has a plan for them. (In general, outwardly professed religious sentiment is common among these men.) Others get motivation from other homeless men around them. One stated that he was feeling lazy, not wanting to get up, get out, and find work. He then recalled seeing another resident, an elderly man, heading off to work. He said, "So here goes this elderly man to work and I'm laying here on the floor. If he can get up, so can I!" (As we reported in Chapter Three, about two thirds of the men who sleep there spend their days working or looking for work, most commonly in the nearby day labor outlets.)

Dordick (1996) identifies several ways that shelter life can "discourage or forestall the efforts of individuals to leave." First, the sheer effort required to "get by" within the shelter leaves little time or energy to be invested in getting out. Secondly, relationships and commitments that develop within the shelter represent resources that can be hard to walk away from. Both of these are surely issues for Pavilion men as well.

Some of the men complained about having to pay the dollar-a-day fee to sleep and eat at the Pavilion; others thought the fee should be higher to motivate clients and improve services. (For the record, the funds obtained through the dollar-a-day fee are set aside for Pavilion maintenance.) There is an explicit fear, verbalized by many participants, that the shelter breeds complacency by charging only a dollar, although many quickly added that the individual person must be strong enough to rise above the environment, and that the motivation for self sufficiency must come from within, not from without.

Many of the men expressed a desire for case management, which is not generally available to them at the Pavilion (this issue is broached at some length in Chapter Three). Some said bluntly that they needed help to make a positive change in their lives and that change was not something they would be able to accomplish on their own. As one said, "We are going uphill and need a push." (The Sisyphus metaphor, while evidently not intended, is likewise not inapt. Sisyphus was the ancient Greek king condemned to an eternity of rolling a boulder uphill and then watching it roll back down again.) While many take advantage of services available to them in the area, many add that they are simply not patient or motivated enough to work around the inevitable scheduling issues or give up a chance at a day's work to attend self-improvement classes. The case management that many desire would be on site and available in the evenings when they are at the shelter anyway.

The Women (and Fathers)

Three additional focus groups were also done in 2010 with Coalition women living in the Center for Women and Families, and one group was done with six fathers living in the same facility. The Center for Women and Families is on the same property as the Pavilion, but the two programs are housed in separate buildings. One large dorm houses single women, that is to say, women who are homeless by themselves with no dependent children in their care. As we saw in the previous chapter, of course, many of these women do have children. Another large dorm houses women with smaller children, and there are also family rooms that house women with older children (or lots of children), husbands and wives with children, and even a few single fathers with children. All of these subgroups are represented in the material that follows.

Eight women participated in the first session. Six were at the Coalition as single women. Two had their children with them at the shelter. Another woman had children who lived with their grandmother and still another had grown children who were out on their own. All of the women save one said they were homeless for financial reasons; the remaining woman, Susie, was homeless because she was fleeing a violent relationship. She wouldn't tell us where she was from (nor did we press the issue), only that she had purchased a bus ticket that would get her as far away from her previous relationship as she could afford to get. Susie was a bright, articulate woman but obviously fearful and cautious about revealing too much.

Keya is a homeless woman from the Orlando area. She has a long history of drug use and says that while she had seen the shelter many times before, she would never come on site. We got the impression that despite her own extensive drug history, Keya looked down on the shelter and believed the people who lived there to be losers. Many shelter men had been Keya's drug customers at one time or another, and despite her long drug history, she had always had some place to live (crashing with friends or family members who were also using, if nothing else). So she was somewhat contemptuous of users whose addictions rendered them homeless.

Keya's own drug use has put her in jail and prison numerous times. During one interlude between jail terms, she decided to come to the shelter to visit a friend who was in the Coalition's drug treatment program for women. Keya talked with a case manager and decided she wanted to join the program too—the very next day, if possible! The case manager said that would not be possible. If she wanted to be in the drug treatment program, she would need to get off the streets and into the shelter where she could be assessed and stabilized. So what began as a visit with a friend became Keya's first stay in a homeless shelter. As soon as she was eligible for a slot in the treatment program, she took it, has since graduated, and is now in "a really good place."

Keya mentioned that she wanted to get a cosmetology license and do hair and nails for a living. When we asked if she had thought about how her felony record might negatively impact her ability to get a license or secure employment, she seemed unconcerned, so it fell to the other women in the group to explain to her that this would be a huge roadblock—as it had been for many of them. Said one, "These mistakes stay with you for the rest of your life."

"Shelter life" for the women in this focus group is busy during the week and "boring" on the weekend. Weekdays are filled with appointments with counselors, demands of work or job training and educational programs, chores in the shelter, meetings with case managers and a range of other activities both on site and off. All residents have required daily chores and women who are not working are also required to commit to a certain number of volunteer hours each week. On the weekend, however, there is little or nothing to do. All the women said they needed more things to do on the weekends. One woman suggested yoga classes—"something to clear your mind"—and this was greeted with enthusiasm all around. Most of the women seemed to share Keya's sentiment that "this is a nice place to be. Just do your work. It's a clean place." She added, "I squandered a lot of money on hotels to avoid being at a shelter. I regret it because this is a nice place."

Although many of these women have family, even family in the immediate area in some cases, living with family is not an option for most of them. Olivia stated, "I lived with one of my brothers for a year and slept on his couch until he told me I had to go. He has addictions and tried to sabotage my sobriety by putting alcohol in my drinks. It wasn't good." She says that now, her only family is the other shelter residents. Keya is of like mind. Although she has a sister living just a few blocks away who wants Keya to move in with her, "I refuse because I'm afraid if I leave the shelter and go back into the neighborhood, I'll start using again."

Family estrangement is a common thread in the tapestry of homeless lives, both male and female. We often assume, perhaps stereotypically, that homeless people have simply "burned too many bridges" and would be unable to return to their families even if they wanted to. But as we have learned elsewhere, familial estrangement can be, and often is, a two-way street (Wright and Devine 1993). Sometimes it is true that homeless people would not be welcomed by their families no matter what. However, in many cases, as Keya and Olivia have realized, the families of homeless people are themselves so dysfunctional that returning to live with them would be a huge step backwards.

We convened the focus groups on shelter life among homeless women long after we had started putting this book together, and so it occurred to us to ask the homeless women of "theme-park nation" if they had ever been to Disney World. Our expectation was that for most, Disney would be like El Dorado, the unattainable Lost City of Gold, a fantasy or a mirage more than a lived experience. Much to our surprise, all but one of the eight women in this group had "done Disney" at least once, and one woman, Celeste, who is at the shelter with her two young sons, said she used to go to Disney for family vacations every year. Wondering about the life journey that leads from annual Disney outings to the Center for Women and Families, we pressed Celeste for details, only to learn that she grew up in a trailer park in rural Osceola County (near Disney) and that one of her parents worked at Disney and received free park passes as a fringe benefit of the job. She and her sons are living at the Coalition because she feels that she needs to be in the city to get into a GED program and thereby "make something" of herself.

Another "shelter life" focus group at the CWF consisted of five women, all with children at the shelter and three with husbands *and* children. The differences between these women and the women in the first group (both those with children and those without) were striking. None of the women in this second group complained about being bored, not even on the weekends. All of them were stressed out, nearly to the limit.

Consider the case of Courtney, a fairly young woman staying at the shelter with her husband and their *five* children (the seven of them living in a single room approximately ten feet by ten feet—"wall to wall bunk beds" is the only apt description). The three younger children attend the same public elementary school that all the other elementary-aged kids at the Coalition attend, but the two teenagers—both girls—attend a private school on full-ride scholarships. Private school educations represent outstanding opportunities for the girls, but are huge stressors for Courtney and her husband. While kids in public school get to and from school on the public school busses, Courtney's two girls must take public transportation and the two weekly bus passes are ten bucks apiece. Coming up with the necessary twenty dollars each week is something Courtney worries about every day. The older girls also struggle with being homeless and living in a shelter and Courtney shoulders full responsibility for this. "I know they are angry. I wish they didn't have to be here too. Sure, I understand that they have to get their anger out somewhere. It's not their fault." But understanding the source of her daughters' anger does not make it any less of a burden.

Courtney's husband does what he can. He is a daily regular at the labor pool—some mornings he is successful in securing work, but most mornings he is not. Courtney aspires to a job in customer service and actively pursues every job lead—so far, to no avail. There are weeks, she says, when she has to choose between doing the laundry and buying bus passes for her girls. (There are no laundry facilities on the CWF premises, so laundry implies a trip to the nearby laundromat.) The bus passes win every time. "I just feel so bad," she says. Later in the session, Courtney confesses that she has headaches "all the time" and has lost a lot of weight. She looks and sounds like a woman at the end of her rope.

Shelter life is a struggle for all women and certainly for all women with children, whether there are husbands in the picture or not. But the majority of the mothers in this shelter are single moms who tend to share babysitting responsibilities and support one another in countless ways—large and small. Contrary to what one might expect, these women's lives seem *less* stressful than those of the women with both husbands and children in tow. The single moms seem to comprise a large support and resource-sharing network from which the women with husbands are apparently excluded. Thus, the coupled women seem to take on all of their family members' stress—not just their own, which can be considerable, but their husbands' and children's as well.

Homelessness is clearly a strain on a marriage and the family rooms at the CWF are cramped to say the least. Two of the five participants in the group seemed to be near the breaking point—Courtney (with her constant headaches and weight loss) and Brooke, who is depressed and, she says, "overwhelmed." Brooke came to the shelter pregnant and she now lives there with her baby's father and the new baby—a two-month-old boy born with cystic fibrosis. Brooke's day is consumed with medical appointments, insurance meetings (she has had to switch insurance programs because in Florida, pregnant indigent women receive health care from one program and new-born infants receive care from another), and taking proper care of her ill child. Brooke has a felony record (drugs) and therefore, as she bluntly puts it, "employment is not an option." Her boyfriend (the baby's father) receives unemployment compensation and that is the sum total of their income. She longs to live in a "nice neighborhood." In her mind, this means "a place where the kids can play outside in their own yard. If they are outside in a yard, then you know it is nice and safe." Barring an unforeseen stroke of good fortune, she might as well yearn to live on a yacht.

Marcie is at the shelter with no husband and her youngest son. She has grown children who send her money periodically and that seems to be her main source of support. She says she has been homeless many, many times, usually as a result of domestic violence. She has a strong work ethic and says that all she wants (or needs) is a job. She is currently taking classes to be a security guard. Marcie says that she likes to stay busy and that cleaning helps clear her mind. She often does chores assigned to other women. (Brooke says that Marcie "will clean all day long!") Marcie's son is ashamed to be at the shelter and gets teased at school about being one of the "CoCo Kids" (the pejorative term used by many Orlando schoolchildren to refer to classmates who live at the Coalition). Like the vast majority of the kids at the Coalition, the son likes the Boys and Girls Club (the only Boys and Girls Club we know of anywhere in the country located on the premises of a homeless shelter). The Boys and Girls Club provides a refuge where the children get to have fun, get help with homework if they need it, and get to be with other kids that are in the same situation and understand what being homeless means.

Maria is from Puerto Rico and living at the shelter with her three teenagers. She had been laid off and unable to find work on the Island, so she left Puerto Rico for what was described to her as a "job opportunity" in Florida. When she got to Orlando, she was told that there was a six month waiting list for positions. She is still without work but now she is also homeless. During the week, she fills her days getting her kids off to school, working on her resume, and searching for jobs. She realizes that she needs more education and a certificate to do here what she did in Puerto Rico (work as a pharmacy aide). Her aspiration is to go back to school and be trained to work as a lab tech. In the meantime, she will stay at the CWF as long as she is allowed to. Moving back to Puerto Rico is not an option—"I sold everything before I left. I can't go back."

A third "shelter life" focus group consisted of four women: Denise, a single mother living at the shelter with her twelve-year-old son; Raina, homeless for the first time with her husband of fourteen years; Pam, now pregnant with her seventh child, with none of the other six in her custody or care; and Amiya, homeless for the first time and at the shelter with her husband and their two teenage children.

Amiya's marriage suffered dearly in the process of becoming homeless. She and her husband separated when their impending homelessness became obvious. The husband refused to go to a shelter since doing so equated in his mind to being a failure as a husband and as a man, so he left Amiya and either crashed with friends or slept in his car. Amiya and the kids also couch-surfed for a while, first with her sister and then with other family members, but "it was just too crowded," so she decided that her only option was the shelter. Her husband continued to sleep in his car for another two weeks but then relented and joined Amiya and the children in the shelter. Interestingly and rather surprisingly, she now says that things are "better than they have been in a long time." Despite the obvious downsides, which are numerous, the shelter is a stable place to stay and the stability has helped everyone. The children, she says, "are doing so much better. They are really doing great." They attend family counseling weekly, which has been "truly wonderful." Exercising rights guaranteed under the federal McKinney-Vento Act, Amiya's children stayed in their own schools after the family became homeless and moved to the Coalition. Many staff members at their school know the family's situation, have given the children gift-cards on several occasions, and are being supportive and understanding. Between these acts of kindness at school, the stability afforded by the CWF, and the weekly counseling, the family seems to be doing pretty well.

Denise says that the experience of being homeless for the first time has "been humbling. When I used to see a guy on the side of a road with a sign asking for money, I used to think 'what a loser' and now I know better." Unlike Amiya's children, Denise's son is not doing well. Along with many other Coalition children, the son is being "tormented" and bullied at his middle school, where people know that he is homeless. Denise came to Orlando from elsewhere, so her son is also a newcomer to the school as well as a "CoCo Kid." The son and Denise would very much like to change schools, but doing so would make Denise responsible for the son's transportation to and from school and that is not a responsibility she can presently assume.

Pam is certainly the most challenging, and pitiable, woman in this group. As noted, she is pregnant with her seventh child. None of the previous six are in her custody or care. Evidently, repeated incidents of domestic violence—perpetrated by the father of four of the six kids—have left her with permanent brain damage that makes her unable to concentrate or focus on tasks. Thus employment is not feasible for her and, frankly, neither is parenting. What she wants more than anything else in the world is to be a mother, which to her means keeping the baby she is currently carrying. The Florida Department of Children and Families (DCF) has already told her this is not likely to happen.

So Pam spends her days at the shelter baby-sitting other women's children. Our participant Denise says that her son loves Pam and that Pam is the only person at the shelter she would trust with her child. To repeat, all Pam wants to be is a mom. "I'm a really good mom," she says. "I don't beat my kids like some of these women but they still won't let me keep my baby." Her other children, by the way, are *not* in foster care. Four are with their abusive father and the other two are "back home" living with relatives. The father of the baby she is presently carrying will not even come on the shelter grounds. "He says he won't associate with 'those people.' What he doesn't get is that I am 'those people'."

As for shelter life, all the women agreed, "We get everything we need." Amiya mentioned a group of women who had arranged to pick up the Coalition's teenage girls in limos and take them shopping for prom dresses. "That was really special." All the women spoke very highly of their case managers. "My case manager even got my husband his glasses" (through the Gift of Sight program). By their own testimony, the women appreciate that shelter life is highly structured and that there are rules they and others must abide by. "Some women just want to complain all the time." All the women in the groups stated that they had found friends in the shelter but most also said that they did what they could to "avoid the drama." Pam spoke for most of these women by saying, "We live in the Cuckoo Hotel!"—apparently a reference, unwitting or not, to Ken Kesey's Cuckoo's Nest, i.e., a bunch of crazy people—the advice being to stay away from the crazies and pick your friends wisely. The facility is crowded and Spartan, but also clean and orderly. There is a day-care facility on the premises and a Boys and Girls Club across the parking lot. Three warm, nutritious meals are served every day. It says a great deal about life (in this particular shelter at least) that the biggest complaint our participants voiced was that some women who stay in the shelter don't want to do anything to help themselves. "They even complain about cleaning up after themselves!"

As for the immediate future, Pam is waiting on her disability claim to be processed and then hopes for a Section 8 housing voucher, but with a closed list and a five year wait for Section 8 units, this is not particularly feasible. Denise is not sure where she will go next. Her main priority right now is getting SSI for her son. The two married women in the group. Amiya and Raina, have solid plans to obtain housing. They are both enrolled in the Coalition's "scattered site" program, which assists families in locating scattered-site rental units once they have accumulated $1000 in savings and at least one adult in the family has held onto a job for ninety days. Both women have the requisite amount of money saved. Raina, who has $2,000 stashed away in the bank, says that "some people leave here when they get a tax refund. When the money runs out, they come right back. When I leave, I don't want to come back."

As is obvious from the foregoing account, fathers also live at the CWF, either with their wives and kids or in some cases as single fathers. The CWF is one of the few facilities in the country to allow related men, women, and children to live as intact family groups and also one of a very few who admit single fathers with children in their care. The growing number of men in the facility made us naturally curious about what shelter life meant to them. In March of 2010, there were ten fathers in residence at the CWF, five of them single dads and the other five living with their wives and children. Six of the ten fathers participated in a "dads-only" focus group. (The other four were at work and therefore unavailable.)

Predictably, the experiences of the dads are very different from those of the mothers. One of the dads in the group is Juan, who is at the CWF with his wife and two young sons. (The two sons were with him in the group meeting while his wife was at work.) The family has been homeless for four months. Within a span of four days, Juan and his wife were both laid off from their jobs. Eviction from their apartment followed closely. Juan has a felony record resulting from (his words) "stupid decisions as a nineteen-year-old," which makes finding a job difficult. His wife has found employment, which leaves him as the full time caregiver for the two little boys, at least for the foreseeable future. He is a doting father who managed to entertain his three-year-old, cuddle his one-year-old, and participate in the focus group simultaneously. He is the only man in the group with preschool children.

A common theme among the dads (voiced at least four times by one participant and quickly agreed to by all) was, "I'm a man. I can take it!" And yet, when asked about life in the shelter, all the men discussed their struggles in detail. The dad vocalizing the "I'm a man" theme most insistently is a father of three. For most of his shelter stay, he has been a single dad—caring for three kids, looking for work, and living in a shelter without direct support. His wife simply could not face the reality of living in a homeless shelter and decided to stay with a friend instead. Just recently, she rejoined the family by becoming a client in the CWF drug treatment program to deal with her alcohol addiction. But since she is in the early stages of the program, she must stay in the treatment dorm, away from the father and their children. The father finds this incredibly frustrating and resents that the treatment program is structured in this way. Frankly, he could use some help with the kids.

The dads stick together. They have to: they are the ultimate minority group! Altogether, they are ten men living in a facility with more than two hundred women. In the session, the discussion quickly turned to a perceived "double standard" for dads, one felt most acutely by the single dads, who (they say) must deal constantly with unsolicited advice about how to raise and care for their children from the women in the facility—women with children, women who have never had children, and even women whose children have been taken away from them. Juan sums up: "Like I'm going to listen to some mom whose kids have been taken away from her—just because she's a chick." The chorus of assent made us believe that child-rearing advice pours over these dads as a torrent of hectoring—unwanted, unsolicited, unheeded, relentless. It was easy to understand their annoyance. Adding to the problem was that many of the women seemed to be suspicious of the dads, as if they were all rapists, child molesters, or worse.

Group discussion turned to the recent increase of husbands and single fathers at the Center and in this discussion, the men's relationships with their own fathers surfaced. One of the men, Bob, was at the shelter with his twelve-year-old daughter and said, "My dad wasn't in my life. Just wasn't there. I won't do that to my own daughter." The other men quickly agreed. Most had also grown up without a father, many averred that they were not even sure who their fathers were, and nearly all said that they would not do the same thing to their own kids. Will, a single father living at the shelter with his ten-year-old son, said, "Oh, I knew the bastard all right. Wish I didn't." We asked for a show of hands: "How many of you had a good relationship with your father?" Not one hand went up. "How about an 'acceptable' relationship?" Still no hands.

Juan illustrates the commitment these men feel towards their children. When Juan's wife was pregnant with their first son, they were not getting along very well and they decided to separate. So Juan found someplace else to live. But he showed up the next day to "see my baby" (who had yet to be born)—and again the next day, and the next, and everyday thereafter. His wife explained that it made no sense for him to come "see the baby," particularly because she was still pregnant "and the baby isn't even here yet!" Juan explained that this did not matter: "That is my child in your belly and I will see him and check on his mother every day! I am not going to be in my son's life every other weekend. I'm going to be a dad. Every day. So don't be surprised if I become your next door neighbor." Juan's persistence apparently paid off: he and his wife reconciled and they have since had another child. Despite the obvious challenges of shelter life for a father, mother, and two children struggling against long odds to maintain themselves as a family, Juan is resolute: "I won't be like my dad—if you can call him that. I will raise my boys and be a real dad. I will."

Clearly, homeless men, with or without wives, raising their children in a shelter environment is a pretty recent phenomenon and not one that any shelter we know of is well-equipped to handle. Facilities for homeless women with kids have long grown accustomed to treating Mother's Day as a special event complete with cake, ice cream, and makeovers for the moms. But Father's Day? Who knew?

Conclusion

To ask if shelter life for homeless men is "risk or respite" is to pose false opposites, of course. Yes, clearly, life in a homeless shelter involves risks—risks of criminal victimization, theft, disease, assault, exposure to drugs, etc. However, there is also respite. Although conditions are far short of ideal, the shelter provides a place for these men to eat, sleep, socialize, and enjoy a modicum of protection from the elements, both natural and human. By being indoors or "on property," they are not at risk for being arrested for trespassing or loitering, something that many have encountered while off property in the immediate area. And while many of the men want more services, particularly case management, to be made available to them, they acknowledge the need for shelter, simply because so many of them truly have no other place to go. The manager of the Pavilion, the management of the larger facility where the Pavilion is located, the facility's Board of Directors, and the community at large all see the same need for case management and other services for these men. But funds are limited and go preferentially to the women and children's programs.

Shelter life for women is not nearly the Hobbesian scenario that the men face. The women have case managers, access to programs, child care if they need it, and other amenities that the men generally do not enjoy. Yet even in the cleanest, nicest, best-run, most services-laden facilities, sheltered homeless women rarely forget their homelessness or the "otherness" that comes with being homeless.

One participant—we'll call him Donte—believes that within the homeless world, "there are three classes of people: women and kids, people in the programs, and then us. The men. We are at the bottom of the ladder." The women and kids have been discussed at some length. The "program" that Donte refers to is First Steps, the on-site alcohol and drug treatment program available to Pavilion men (see Chapter Eight). There are thirty-six slots in this program and a long waiting list. Men in First Steps receive case management and individualized treatment plans, sleep in bunk beds rather than on mats on the floor, are quartered in a walled-off room that affords considerably more privacy than other men enjoy, are given more responsibilities in the facility, are also given more slack, and more attention is paid to them. For example, unlike other men, they are not required to leave during the day and are not expected to work at least for their first month or two in the program. To Pavilion regulars, being in First Steps is a privileged status into which only a select few are invited. And indeed, a few of the men in the sessions had been through First Steps, two were currently in the program, and several were considering it. But it is very much a minority experience.

Our focus groups make it clear that there is a "shelter life" with its own norms, culture, and structure of expectations, and that this is true for both men and women. Although individual experiences differ, the Pavilion culture is one that all of the men could, and did, speak to. New arrivals are obvious and they quickly learn the ways of the shelter, often with help or guidance from other men. All of the men know to "watch their backs," but many also say there are men at the Pavilion they can trust. The majority of men speak of their situation as temporary and no one professes to like it at the shelter, but at the same time, they do not openly complain. Most seem grateful that the shelter is there, although they are quick to point out areas of possible improvement. Virtually all of this can be said of the women at the CWF as well.

It is perhaps ironic that many of these men (and women) see their situation as temporary, seem to recognize that they are out of options, and yet at the same time make precious little effort to secure more favorable living circumstances. In part, this is simple dissonance reduction—to define oneself as a victim of outside forces rather than as directly responsible for one's plight, and to rely on future and more favorable chance factors rather than personal initiative to effect positive change.

For so many of the men, the Pavilion is quite literally the only place they have left to go. All other options were abandoned, burned up, or simply exhausted long ago. Pavilion men exhibit all the trials and tribulations of humanity: drug and alcohol addiction, poverty, mental illness, physical disability, irregular employment, prison records, minimal human capital, and a lack of family to fall back on. As Donte put it, "no one would ever choose to be here. It's rough." So much for the theory that people are homeless "by choice." But most of these men are out of options. As one stated, "It [the Pavilion] is needed. We may not love it but we need it." Most of the men explained that while they did not choose to be homeless, they had made "bad choices" that led to being homeless. Usually, this was getting involved in drugs, but for some it was becoming involved in crime or even moving to Florida with an expectation for a good job that simply never materialized. And again, a good share of the above applies equally to the women at the CWF, many of whom are also out of options.

No matter what brought them to the shelter or why they continue to stay, it is clear that they all share a very similar situation—men and women alike. One Pavilion staffer referred to the Coalition as "the last house on the block," the last place people can come—man or woman, drunk or sober, young or old. All aspire at some level to leave shelter life and the condition of homelessness. And some surely will. But for now, the Coalition is home and home is both risk and respite to us all.

Notes

1. The Men's Pavilion is adjacent to the Center for Women and Families, so during the day, men and women inter-mingle despite rules that try to discourage such behavior.
2. Here it needs to be mentioned that by design, the Pavilion is a "low demand" shelter with a "come one, come all" policy. The only men who are denied admission are those that represent an active threat to self or others. So on any given night, some men are drunk, some are high on drugs, and some are actively hallucinating or floridly psychotic, etc. "Sick, crazy, high and lazy" (a phrase residents often use to describe other residents) is a poetic and not inapt description.

7

Lovely, Dark, and Deep:
Central Florida's Woods People[1]

According to reasonable guesses by the outreach team that works with the unsheltered homeless in the region, there are some fifty to sixty homeless "camps" in East Orange County and perhaps a couple hundred throughout the three counties of Central Florida (Orange, Osceola, and Seminole). In East Orange alone, this population of homeless people numbers some several hundred (as many as 800 by some estimates). Most or all of these camps are along U.S. Highway 50 (Colonial Avenue) and are often located near restaurants, gas stations, and other commercial outlets. There is a fair amount of undeveloped (or in some cases, de-developed and now abandoned) property along stretches of Highway 50 that provides relative seclusion, privacy, and a modicum of security for Orlando's woods people.

In February of 2007, partly in response to increasing complaints from concerned citizens about derelicts and vagabonds sleeping on their porches and peeing on the shrubbery, we were contracted by the Orange County government to study the demography, life circumstances, and needs of the unsheltered homeless in East Orange County. We undertook a series of five focus groups with a total of thirty-nine homeless people who lived in the East Orange camps. All participants were recruited for the study by the Orlando Health Care Center for the Homeless HOPE Outreach Team and transported by them to and from the focus group site, the Union Park Neighborhood Center for Families, a community center right on Highway 50 near the camps, whose assistance we gladly acknowledge.

Focus groups began on February 15, 2007, and concluded on February 26. Each group session lasted about two hours and had the customary consent features and refreshments. Contrary to the expectations of many people who have heard us present the results of this study, getting our participants to open up and talk about themselves was not difficult. As a group, they were exceedingly easy to engage. They seemed flattered that people from the University had taken an interest in them and clearly enjoyed talking about themselves and their situations. Within the limitations imposed by their addictions and mental illnesses, they seemed, almost without exception, to give open, honest answers to everything we asked them. Some were clearly bemused by the absurdity of the situations in which they found themselves and made wry, insightful comments that were at once humorous, informative, and heart-breaking.

Results

Participants in the focus groups were comprised of eleven women (28 percent) and twenty-eight men (72 percent). Most were white; 18 percent were Hispanic; only one was African American. The average age was forty-six years. According to the Hope Team, these results are generally characteristic of the unsheltered homeless in East Orange County with whom they work. Assuming this to be the case, the woods people of East Orange are a bit older and dramatically whiter than the homeless people downtown, a point to which we return later.

On average, our participants had been living in the woods for a bit more than five years (5.2 years, to be precise). For most, clearly, life in the woods has not been a short-term arrangement. The most common prior living arrangement was to have been living in their own rented room or apartment (47 percent), followed by living in a house they owned (16 percent). About one in ten had been living with a family member, 8 percent were in jail or prison, and another 8 percent were sleeping in various outdoor locations before they began living in the East Orange woods. No other response was mentioned by more than one person each.

Although most of these homeless people came to Orlando from somewhere else (about one in five was born in Florida), they are relatively long-term residents, having lived in Orlando an average of 16.5 years. In terms of geographic origins, these are about the same numbers as we get for sheltered homeless people living downtown.

One of the ten women (who answered a question on veteran's status) was a veteran of the U.S. Armed Forces; among men (who answered the question), the figure was 30 percent (seven of twenty-three). These figures are comparable to the figures reported by HUD (2007) for the general U.S. homeless population and are definitely higher than the rate for adult U.S. men in general, of whom only 13 percent are veterans (U.S. Census Bureau 2003). The percentage of vets among the men in the woods is about the same as among sheltered men (see Chapter Three).

About four in five of our participants lived in the woods alone, with the other fifth paired up with another adult (usually but not invariably a legal spouse). None of our participants reported having minor children living in the woods with them, although one had an adult son who also lives in the woods of Orlando.

We asked participants if they had ever been told by a doctor, social worker, case manager or other professional person that they had a mental health problem, an alcohol problem, a drug problem, or a physical disability. Just under half (45 percent) reported a previous mental health diagnosis; 56 percent said they had a drinking problem; 37 percent told us about a previous drug problem; and 42 percent reported being physically disabled. Based on our observations in the focus groups, all of these, particularly the first three, are underestimates. All together, over 70 percent admitted to one or more of these disabilities.

Finally, the survey part[2] of the study asked, "What is the number one reason why you are homeless right now?" Issues of jobs and money were most frequently mentioned, cited by 41 percent, followed by medical and disability issues, noted by 18 percent. No other response was chosen by more than two or three people. So despite rather widespread mental illness, alcohol abuse, and drug addiction in this population, very few see these disorders as a primary reason for their homelessness.

Focus Group Observations

Demographics

Educational attainments were predictably modest, with most not having progressed beyond high school and with a sizable minority lacking even a high school diploma or GED certificate. Virtually all have had some labor force experience ranging from professional work to unskilled labor, including at least one each of the following occupations: land surveying engineer, real estate business owner, cook, mason, furniture mover, newspaper deliverer, restoration worker, construction worker, waitress, certified nursing assistant (C.N.A), and general laborer. Likewise, virtually all are now disabled, either mentally, physically, or because of addictions to the point where regular, sustained labor force involvement (i.e., a "real job," as in the frequent response to panhandlers, "Why don't you go get a *real* job?") is not a realistic alternative.

Most were loosely attached, at best, to their primary and extended families—with the exception of a few married couples who participated and a few other paired-up couples who comprised unmarried homeless family units. In fact, the overwhelmingly most common response to our guiding question about having "family or friends you can count on if you really needed to" was, "These people are my family," with some gesture to the other group participants, indicating relatively close bonds among homeless people who live in the woods, an impression sustained by the obvious camaraderie in each group. Still, most did indicate that they had family living somewhere in the area or state, although contact was minimal at best.

Participants offered various reasons for their loose or non-existent family ties. The most common reason was their perception of having been rejected by their families. Typical comments in this connection included, "they're snobs," "I can't put up with them," or "I don't get along well with my dad [kids, brother, etc.]" Other reasons given for strained family relationships included keeping away from loved ones so they "won't worry about me"; the death of the family patriarch or matriarch, or illness of a key family member (who, more often than not, was also the primary source of financial support or the housing provider for the participant); and divorce or separation (i.e., male abandonment). Interestingly, none mentioned distance as an impediment to sustaining close family ties although, as indicated earlier, most of our participants originated in other states.

The majority had been homeless for quite some time and many had experienced numerous bouts of homelessness throughout their lives. In these respects, they seemed to us more chronically homeless than the men in the Pavilion. However, one young couple had been homeless for only a few months (living for most of the time in their car) and had been living in the camps for only a few weeks.

The Camps

The focus groups averaged about eight participants each and on average, those eight people came to us from either two or three distinct camp sites. Boundaries between camps are not necessarily well-defined, but most of our participants had a definite sense of who they lived with and who lived in other camps. Information is shared across camps mainly at a nearby day labor outlet, probably the key node in the socio-matrix that connects all the woods people of East Orange.

The largest camp contained five or six members. Most camps were even smaller, averaging two to three members each. Camp members generally first met at the labor pool; one camp member would meet a new person at the labor pool and ask if the new person wanted to join their camp. The smaller camps were usually married or paired-up couples.

Most participants lived in tents or lean-to shacks built from scavenged scrap materials. (Many who lived in tents were given their tents by nearby churches.) A few couples lived in their cars, while still others lived in abandoned RVs or vacant buildings. One couple had built a whole house out of scrap. One woman in one of the larger camps (she was clearly the leader of this particular group) took evident pride in running a drug-free camp (even though one of the members of this camp admitted to a previous drug problem). Several participants kept dogs for security, companionship, and on the chillier nights, warmth. Indeed, these dogs are definite barriers to the utilization of existing resources and services for homeless people.

The various homeless camps and people in East Orange County are connected by a "grapevine" through which pertinent information travels quickly—information about food availability, what's happening at the day labor outlet, law and code enforcement activities, and the presence of new people in the woods. (To be sure, the quality of the information degrades the further down the grapevine it travels.) Another interesting finding was the degree of informal social control that exists within the camps. As with all other human groupings, social structure quickly emerges in these camps, with someone in charge, a division of labor (daily "chores"), group rules (e.g., about drugs, camp security, newcomers, and the like), and informal social sanctions for rule violations. Many camps have specific "no drugs allowed" policies; many others exist precisely for the purpose of acquiring and using drugs. All have rules against theft from one another and insist on mutual respect for one another's security and things. Drifters, rule-breakers, and other troublemakers are known throughout the population and are often "blacklisted" specifically to encourage them to move on from Orlando.

It needs also to be mentioned that not every participant was associated with a camp or a specific group; some chose to live alone, all by themselves, out in the woods. Without exception, however, even the "loners" said they enjoyed close and regular interaction with one another, either as individuals or as members of a specific camp group. One gentleman who lives by himself nevertheless told us, "Food is less important to me than interaction with fellow campers."

Residential backgrounds

As reported, most participants, although born elsewhere, are long-term residents of the state, having lived in Florida for an average of more than sixteen years. A few, of course, are recent arrivals, some having come to Florida in the previous few months. The reasons given for moving to Florida were diverse: some came to reconnect with a long-lost family member; some came with predetermined plans to stay with a relative; many came to seek employment or get "a fresh start"; quite a number of the veterans came to Florida once they had mustered out of the service; and some were drifters who just "seemed to end up here" after a period of wandering, more or less aimlessly, from place to place.

How People Became Homeless

As in virtually all other homeless populations ever studied, by far the most common theme that emerged as the catalyst for homelessness among people living in the woods was **unexpected adverse life events** from which they were never able to recover. For those whose homelessness resulted from a traumatic life event, the onset of homelessness was literally within a few months.

Commonly reported adverse life events that led to homelessness included moving to Florida, often with no safety net or even a definite plan in place, hoping to find employment that never materialized ("We heard Disney was hiring"); loss of personal identification, often through theft, which in turn made it impossible for them to secure a job, housing, or access to social services; the sudden death of or severe financial reversal suffered by a loved one on whom they were dependent for housing or financial support; the loss of a job; arrest or other law enforcement action, such as a driver's license suspension; and disabling injuries. One couple lost their home to hurricane damage and moved with their two children into the mobile home of the wife's parents, only to discover that the mobile home was far too cramped for six. So, the couple left their children with the grandparents and began living in the woods. We were struck in particular by how often the loss of the ability to prove who one was surfaced as a precipitating event that led to someone becoming homeless. For many others, of course, the downward drift into homelessness was the result of alcohol or drug addiction, or the effects of being impaired by major mental illness—primarily bipolar disorder, as we discuss more fully below.

Daily Routines

The daily lives of woods people are consumed by the struggle to find food, income, and a measure of physical security. In Maslow's hierarchy of needs, they occupy levels one and two: tending to physiological needs such as food, water, sleep, and excretion; and worrying about physical security and safety. Few have the time, energy, or inclination to pursue esteem and self-actualization goals, although most express a degree of pride in their cleverness and survival skills and most seem very sociable, even jovial, in their interactions with others. Although some just "hang around" their camps for the day (often to secure the camp from intruders), daily routines for most are dominated by efforts to secure food and income by various means, both legal and illegal.

Securing Money. All the woods people, men and women alike, engage in one or more of the following types of economic activity to varying degrees:

One type of activity is "scrapping," which involves selling scavenged scrap metal and other "junk" to scrap yards, recycling centers, or junk buyers. From all accounts, this activity is potentially the most lucrative "job" available, with several participants reporting earnings of up to $100 a day or more. We are not accustomed to thinking of homeless people living in the woods as being in the recycling business, but they perform an important public service in helping to keep the roadsides clean.

One woman we interviewed "scraps" every day. She has a device she calls her "scrapper" that has been manufactured from an old shopping cart. She has rigged the scrapper so it can be towed behind her bicycle. And that is how she transports her scrap to a scrap yard in Casselberry, an hour and a half bike ride in each direction. (The only other option is a scrap yard in Bithlo, which is closer than the Casselberry site but pays lower prices for scrap.)

Day labor, principally out of the large day labor pool near the homeless camps on Colonial, is the least popular source of income because of the long hours and comparably low hourly wages. Problems in the day labor industry are well-described elsewhere (Valenzuela et al. 2006). Several of our participants were banned from the day labor pool because of lack of identification and there were many other issues our participants wanted to discuss, among them these:

1. One needs to get to the day labor outlet by 5:00 a.m. to have a chance at obtaining the best assignments, a routine difficulty for people without alarm clocks.
2. Costs of transportation to and from the work site, and often lunch, are deducted from the daily pay, further reducing effective wages.
3. Payment is by check. Our participants do not have bank accounts and must therefore cash these checks at various check-cashing services in the area, usually for a fee of 10 percent, again reducing the effective wage rate.
4. Dispatchers at the day labor outlet are frequently described as indifferent at best and abusive at worst. Between the low wage, various deductions, and the check cashing fee, eight or ten hours of day labor might net a person $35 or $40 in income, barely enough for much other than beer and cigarettes.

Notwithstanding, it is apparent that work in the day labor outlet is as close as our participants usually get to a "normal" job situation; day labor is a principal source of income to the group; and the day labor outlet is a key node in the informal social network that ties the East Orange homeless into a loosely-knit "clan" that shares information and resources.

Panhandling is also a notable activity. Most of the people we interviewed—though not all—panhandle at least occasionally, and a sizably large fraction do so regularly (i.e., daily). In this respect, the woods people differ significantly from the homeless men who live downtown and reside in the Pavilion (see Chapter Three). Panhandling takes two forms: normal panhandling, where people are approached as they enter or exit various business establishments or in other public places and are asked for spare change or a few dollars; and "flying a sign," where people stand or sit by the sides of the roads or in the medians displaying signs ("Will work for food," "Homeless veteran," "Please help") in the hopes that passersby will toss them some cash.

It is hard to say just how lucrative the panhandling business can be for the woods people. There were at least two participants who claimed with great braggadocio to be "the best panhandler in Orange County" and who claimed daily profits in excess of a hundred dollars. We found it impossible to take these claims seriously. The woman with the scrapper fashioned from a shopping cart was rather more believable. She said she panhandled only rarely, only when she was "really desperate" or on days when she was too sore or sick to scrap, because she always made better money scavenging trash metal than begging. Her usual panhandling take was "twenty or twenty-five bucks." Several who panhandled more frequently than this woman seemed to indicate that thirty or forty bucks would be a pretty good day for them too, which is, ironically, about what these same people would earn in day labor (if a day labor assignment were available). Certainly, the average panhandler in this population takes home well less than $50 a day, not several hundred as sometimes claimed.

The downsides of panhandling are obvious and were quickly expressed by our participants: People treat them with scorn and sometimes violence (a few participants recounted tales of physical assault because of their beggary), and there is always the possibility of being arrested for "soliciting without a permit," "obstructing traffic on a public right of way," etc. As we discuss later, these arrests are often very costly. It can also be noted in passing that the participants most heavily involved in panhandling were also much more alcohol and drug abusive than others.

Odd jobs are also an option for the homeless. Construction contractors and others with needs for temporary workers sometimes cruise up and down the areas of Colonial frequented by our participants offering odd jobs for the day or week. One contractor heard about our study and called us to comment favorably on the quality of the work his recruits did, "when you can get them to work." Many, he noted, have experience in the construction trades and reasonably well-developed skills, but lack discipline and a "work ethic." His chief complaint was their tendency to resist authority and to dislike being told what to do. Several people that we interviewed also supplemented their income by selling blood products at every opportunity.

With the exception of day labor, which requires working a full 8-hour shift or longer, the length of time spent in each of the above revenue-generating activities would typically range from one to four hours per day. Most seemed to set daily income goals and would end their "workday" when those goals were achieved; a few sought to maximize income by "working" each day as long as they could. It needs also to be mentioned that at least one of our respondents had a conventional job working as a maid in a nearby motel and that a very small number survived on Social Security Disability Income.

Securing Food. Rather to our surprise, food was not difficult to come by for most of our participants, although most reported only eating one or at most two meals a day and a few recounted instances where they had gone two or three days with no food at all.

By a wide margin, the primary means of acquiring food was "dumpster diving," a term our participants themselves use to describe the practice of scavenging edibles from dumpsters used by restaurants and supermarkets to discard their leftover or date-expired food items. Typically, those who share a camp space also share the responsibility for acquiring food for those in their group—a responsibility that requires the responsible party to arrive at the local restaurant and supermarket dumpsters by 5:00 or 5:30 in the morning, before the night's discards have begun to rot. Everything edible is removed from the dumpsters and stored in what amounts to a communal pantry to be shared by everyone in the group.

As we listened to the tales of dumpster diving, it became entirely obvious that the "best pickings" were those provided by certain workers at the fast food restaurants and convenience stores who would carefully wrap food about to be discarded in clean paper and place it off to the side in the cleaner parts of the dumpster, knowing full well that homeless people would be coming through later for their daily "harvest." It was also obvious that each dumpster diver had his or her favorites: discarded fried chicken, for example, or "expired" Subway sandwiches. None of the people we interviewed seemed the least bit squeamish about any of this, although they freely admitted that in the hot, humid months, the entire food-scavenging process could be a little dicey.

Next to the dumpsters, various local churches were the most common source of food. Several area churches dispense canned goods to needy people and some offer hot breakfasts or lunches at occasional times during the month. A few churches even deliver food to nearby camp areas. In addition to food, the churches also provide blankets, bedding, camp supplies, tents, clothes, and personal items such as soap, shampoo, or laundry detergent. Among our participants, expressions of gratitude for the assistance provided by area churches were common and, as far as we could tell, entirely sincere. "They're good people." "I don't know what we'd do without them." And so on.

Only two of the people we interviewed reported receiving Food Stamps. One couple, the young couple new to the woods, responded to the question by asking, "What are food stamps?" and when told what they were, followed up with the question, "How do we get them?" Ironically, the focus group site is one of the community resource centers where needy people could apply for this benefit, which they did as soon as the session ended.

Gender

One might guess that living in the woods would pose special dangers or challenges for the women, but this did not seem to be the case. In fact, the women seemed to feel very safe either because of the protection offered by their group or because most were coupled up in committed relationships that apparently mitigated their personal safety concerns. Females also seemed more inclined to resist the negative stereotypes associated with being homeless. The males often seemed to accept themselves as 'losers' who were homeless "by choice" or personal failings. The women, in contrast, tended to see their homelessness as resulting from circumstances over which they had no control—an accident that left them unable to work, a foreclosure, male abandonment, and like situations.

Utilization of Downtown Services for the Homeless

While many of our participants reported having been downtown once or twice either to eat at Daily Bread or the Coalition or to seek shelter at one of the downtown facilities, all of them, without exception, described their experiences with downtown homeless services and the downtown area itself in negative terms and said they would not venture back downtown for any conceivable reason, no matter how many services might be available there.

First, our participants perceived downtown Orlando as a dangerous and unfriendly place. Many mentioned the crime rate, the then-recent and much-discussed upturn in murders, and the thugs and "druggies" as their principal reasons for avoiding downtown. As mostly white people, "[they] stick out like a sore thumb" in the historically African American neighborhood of Parramore, where most homeless services are located. As one young guy put it, "there ain't no woods downtown—I'd have no place to hide." Virtually all of our respondents told us they felt much safer in the East Orlando woods than they would ever feel downtown.

Adding to the hesitance, most of our participants would be accurately described as "country people," people who grew up mostly in small towns and rural areas and who feel uncomfortable, even intimidated, in urban settings. When we asked a member of the Hope Team (himself a black man) whether, in his opinion, racism had anything important to do with their avoidance of downtown, he said, "They don't hate blacks, they hate cities." At the same time, the near-total absence of African Americans in the camps and the heavy preponderance of African Americans in the downtown shelters make it hard to deny some degree of racial self-segregation as a partial explanatory factor for the pattern.

Other reasons cited for avoiding downtown included difficulties getting downtown on public transportation; fear of being harassed by law enforcement in the downtown neighborhoods; prior experiences of being victimized by theft or assault when downtown; desire to avoid the temptations of drugs and alcohol that are ubiquitous in many downtown neighborhoods; and fear of violence.

Many participants also recounted numerous previous negative experiences at the Coalition for the Homeless, the Union Rescue Mission, and the Salvation Army as additional reasons to avoid downtown. Here the complaints focused on the costs incurred in staying at these facilities, particularly the Rescue Mission and the Salvation Army; the rules and regulations enforced in these facilities and the consequent loss of independence or "freedom"; the widespread perception, correct or not, that these facilities are dangerous and drug-infested hellholes; filth in the bathrooms; the general "chaos"; and being robbed or victimized while staying in these facilities. Others avoided the downtown agencies simply because living in the woods was (to their minds) more quiet, peaceful, or comfortable. Nearly all of the couples we interviewed said they would not use the downtown facilities because they would be separated into different sleeping and living quarters. Finally and not insignificantly, many of our participants would not go downtown because doing so would force them to abandon their pets, which they would understandably refuse to do under any circumstance.

Some of the concerns expressed about the downtown shelters are real, and some are entirely mythical. Many of the male participants in the focus groups recounted a story about staying at the Coalition that we have heard told literally dozens of times, nearly always in exactly the same terms, and that is the story about having one's pocket slit open with a knife and the contents removed while sleeping. "I woke up and all my money was gone." Hearing this exact same story told for the umpteenth time by several of our East Orange woods people, we made a point of speaking with Mr. Jesse Dixon, manager of the Coalition's Men's Pavilion, where these artful thefts allegedly occur. In the several years that Mr. Dixon had been in charge of the Pavilion, not one such theft had ever been reported to him, this in a population that is prone to complain to management about nearly everything from the quality of the spaghetti to the filth in the showers.

Getting one's pocket slit open while sleeping in the Men's Pavilion and having one's cash removed is almost certainly an urban legend rife among the homeless people in the Central Florida region. And yet, as W. I. Thomas so insightfully stated nearly a century ago, "If men define situations as real, they are real in their consequences," and the consequence of this definition is that the woods people avoid homeless services down-town like the plague. (The original expression of what is now known as the Thomas Theorem was in Thomas and Thomas 1928).

Transportation Issues

As intimated earlier, distance is one barrier to using downtown ser-vices and this point illustrates that transportation issues play a large role in the mobility patterns of our participants. For the most part, they get around on foot or ride bikes, taking the bus only when necessary. A few of our participants had working automobiles and gave rides to others who needed them; another few had friends or family members who could help in this respect. A surprisingly large number use bicycles as their customary form of transportation, the theft of which was also commonly reported. (On ownership and theft of bikes of homeless people, see also Jocoy and Del Casino 2008.)

Personal Safety

Physical safety was a constant concern to many of our participants, both safety from predators and, somewhat more commonly expressed, safety from the threat of being hit or run over by cars. Many take mea-sures to reduce their risks of predation: they keep dogs or weapons (clubs, machetes, but only rarely firearms) in their camps; take turns keeping watch; stay alert to intruders and strangers. However, many feel completely vulnerable to the reckless, often aggressive, red-light-running motorists who have made Colonial Drive the most dangerous stretch of roadway in Florida. We mentioned in Chapter One that in most years, Orlando is found to be among the most dangerous cities in America for pedestrians and bicyclists, a point our woods people grimly confirmed. Indeed, virtually all knew of fellow homeless people who had been injured or killed in encounters with cars and many had their own horror stories to relate. It is an interesting, if somewhat disturbing, finding that errant drivers seem to pose a greater risk to life and limb of these homeless people than the thugs, druggies, and thieves, but such, apparently, is life in Orlando's sprawling metropolitan area.

Exposure to the elements is another personal safety issue, although extreme hot or cold weather did not seem to pose an undue hardship. When asked, "What do you do when the weather turns cold?" they replied with some humor, "Build a bigger fire!" Other cold weather strategies included dressing in layers, "snuggling up," or sleeping with their dogs. One couple said they enjoyed the colder weather because they could build a fire and roast hot dogs and marshmallows, "just like Girl Scout camping!" Some sought abandoned vehicles or buildings for cold-weather shelter.

As indicated earlier, most of our participants slept in tents or in crude structures that kept them dry in rainy weather. Several also reported with evident pride that they had simply "rode out" the hurricanes that had swept through the region in 2004, although one stated adamantly that he "would not stay in the camps" during a hurricane threat. A few reported going to a shelter or hotel to wait out a passing hurricane, and a few others reported being taken in by friends. One man spent Hurricane Charlie in what he thought was the comparative safety of a motel, but when he went outside to check on his truck, he was blown back through a plate glass window and had his right arm severed at the elbow. He is now more than two years into his wait for a disability declaration and showed up at the focus group in a T-shirt that read, "Do I look like a fucking people person?" And yet, he proved a surprisingly articulate and jovial informant.

Law Enforcement

While one focus group was fairly positive about their interactions with law enforcement, the other groups voiced strongly negative re-actions to these interactions. One officer in particular was mentioned repeatedly as "hating homeless people" and taking every opportunity to harass and intimidate them. Most complained of arrests on what they felt were comparatively trivial grounds: "molesting a dumpster," "impeding the flow of foot traffic on a public sidewalk," or "solicitation of funds without a permit."[3] Some described city police as "vicious" in comparison to county law enforcement and cited this as a reason they avoided going downtown if at all possible. Virtually all our participants reported numerous arrests, averaging as many as one arrest a month in many cases.

While not everyone objected to the occasional night in jail (jail is comparatively safe and has hot showers and decent food), most looked on their arrests and re-arrests as one of the causes of their continu-ing homelessness. Said one, "We wouldn't be on the streets if the police stopped putting [us] in jail." First, these arrests generate police records that surface in police background checks; this then becomes a barrier to both employment and housing. Felony arrests linger on one's record even longer than misdemeanors and a federal felony (a federal "number") stays on the record forever. Several men believed ardently that their federal "number" would keep them homeless and unemployed for the rest of their lives and many others looked on their criminal records as formidable barriers to successful reintegration with society and economy.

More significantly, these arrests typically net one a night or two in jail and assessed court costs of about $250. If the fine is not paid within a certain number of days, a bench warrant is issued, the offender is re-arrested, and another fine is assessed. In this manner, many of our respondents have managed to run up debts to the county amounting to thousands of dollars, debts that they can only repay by more panhandling, which is often what gets them arrested in the first place. More than a few expressed despair at ever getting out of this cycle.

Housing Needs

Although many respondents adamantly expressed their preference for continuing to live in the camps because of their sense of camaraderie and their satisfaction in living with, supporting, and depending on one another for survival, there was also an undertone of ambivalence about their perceived shelter needs. When we asked what they saw as the alternative to their current life circumstances, most seemed taken aback by the question. It was not, we felt, a question that they had given any thought to, for the simple reason that many literally could not conceive of living in any other way—perhaps the deepest in a wide range of tragedies that mark these broken lives.

Virtually everyone we spoke with considered themselves to be a "survivalist," fiercely self-sufficient and independent, but most nevertheless expressed some desire to get off the streets if the conditions were right. Said one, "Yeah, it's OK, but I know I can't keep this up forever. I'm tired." Many were quick to add that life in the woods was "hard," much harder than a conventional existence. "It's a real job just trying to survive." Throughout these discussions, there was an undertone of fatalism that is characteristic of people with untreated mental illness.

When we asked what would be necessary to get them out of the woods and into some sort of sheltered existence, the common themes were these:

- Within convenient range of the geographic areas they currently occupy
- Must be safe
- If not emergency shelter, but "real housing," then it has to be very affordable, without a first month's rent and security requirement
- There must be accommodations for married or co-habiting couples and dogs or other pets
- Most importantly, there should be no limits placed on their freedom to come and go as they please

On the whole, less interest was expressed in emergency overnight shelter than in a drop-in center with facilities for showering and laundering, and hot meal service, a policy alternative now being actively discussed by elected officials, faith groups, and local homeless advocates and service providers in East Orange County.

Alcohol, Drug, and Mental Health Needs and Issues

Drug and particularly alcohol dependency is an ongoing struggle for the large majority of our respondents. Most bore the visible *externalia* of a lifetime of heavy drinking and, indeed, freely admitted their alcoholism to us. Among the drinkers, beer is the drink of choice and with food itself readily available in the dumpsters, it is one of the principal reasons why they need cash (cigarettes being the other). In addition to alcohol, whose daily use is nearly universal in this population, most also said they smoked marijuana occasionally, when it was available. A few admitted to current hard drug use (cocaine, heroin) and several more admitted to having had drug issues in the past. One focus group consisted of four men from the same camp, three of whom were active heroin abusers—the only concentrated hard drug use we found in any of the groups. (Interestingly, this group of heroin users was primarily Latino and reported less police harassment, more reliance on the labor pool for income, and less panhandling than any other group.) Overall, the consequences of their addictions have been severe; some have had their drivers licenses suspended, others have lost close friends to drug-induced deaths, and still others attribute their homelessness to their alcohol or drug dependency.

Yet in spite of it all, there was very little interest in alcohol or drug treatment programs. For most, alcohol was the *solution*, not the problem. A few stated that they had recently completed some sort of treatment program, had been clean for a year or more, and only needed to avoid downtown and its many temptations to remain "successful." Others said candidly that treatment would be useless to them because they had no desire to stop their addictive behavior. A few said they had been in treatment before and it never really "took." "Drug and alcohol treatment programs don't do you any good if you don't want to stop." Added another, "I enjoy it. I don't want to stop." We could not escape the overwhelming sense that most of the enjoyment these people got from their lives was found at the bottom of a bottle. It was also obvious that many drank to self-medicate the symptoms of their untreated psychiatric illnesses.

Like the addictions, which were freely admitted, mental health difficulties were also widespread and readily discussed. About half were able to report to us a specific mental health diagnosis, the most common of which were bipolar disorders, schizophrenia, depression, and post-traumatic stress disorder (PTSD). In every group, there were also some participants whose demeanor and behavior were strongly suggestive of undiagnosed or undisclosed mental illnesses.

The ease and terminology with which these participants discussed their mental health diagnoses is evidence that most had been under the observation or care of a mental health worker at some time in the past, but were no longer. Many flatly stated that their drinking and drug use was self-medication of their psychiatric illnesses. Many had been prescribed psychotropic or neuroleptic medications but could not afford to fill their prescriptions. One man stated that if he took all the medication that had been prescribed for him, it would cost him $1200 a month. "Beer don't cost me nearly that much …"

Physical Disabilities

In addition to widespread addictions and mental health disorders, we were struck by the general ill health of this population. This is perhaps to be expected in a population that drinks and smokes heavily and eats leftovers scavenged from garbage cans. Still, two of our participants were amputees, several were suffering from major traumatic injuries, several more were suffering from advanced emphysema or chronic asthma, and still others reported being disabled by diabetes, bone cancer, brain tumors, heart disease, liver disease, impaired vision, advanced hearing loss, etc. Virtually without exception, the only health care any of our respondents received was what was made available to them through the Hope Team and the Health Care Center for the Homeless. A total of 42 percent of the participants reported having been told by a medical professional that they were physically disabled and that number is entirely consistent with what we were able to observe.

Another Note on Veterans

Nearly a third of the men said they were veterans of the U.S. Armed Forces and those that were expressed unanimous and at times bitter frustration over their dealings with the Veterans Administration, who, they said, would routinely deny them health care, pension, or domiciliary benefits and who treated them with indifference bordering on contempt. As best as we could tell, only one of the veterans had a dishonorable discharge, although this was not a question that we specifically asked. Some saw their past military service as a direct cause of their current situation. One vet stated that after living in the jungles of Vietnam, surviving on "bugs and roots," he could no longer function in "normal" society. Many of the veterans also have serious independence issues. Having figured out how to survive more or less on their own, without assistance from the VA or anyone else, they have difficultly adapting to a structured system of rules and regulations as would be the case in any sort of formal "program," most certainly in any VA program to assist homeless vets.

Concluding Thoughts

At present, most of the homeless services and facilities in the Orlando metro area are concentrated in downtown Orlando, and yet the homeless population is widely dispersed across the region; among the people we studied, there is an unmistakable aversion to going downtown. While it is probably unreasonable to expect a network of full-blown homeless shelters and service centers equally dispersed around the region, a system of decentralized day shelters or drop-in centers that provide meals, showers, laundry facilities, and critically, access to a case manager or a social worker for those homeless people who are ready to accept services seems within the boundaries of the feasible. Certainly there is a need for such a facility somewhere in East Orange and in other areas of the region where homeless people camp.

We were struck most of all by the large number of dually diagnosed people in this study, those disabled both by addiction and by poor mental health, which would describe at least half and possibly more than half of our participants. Granted, many will be resistant to treatment, but some will not be. And others who are resistant now may be "ready" in the near future.

We stated earlier that most of the people we studied were homeless mainly because of some adverse life event from which they were unable to recover. In the long run, one hopes that much homelessness could be prevented, but prevention means financial, social, and medical safety nets to help people when they hit the rough spots in life's road. Absent these safety nets, adverse life events turn into financial and health disasters that will continue to propel the weak and vulnerable into homelessness.

Most of our participants say they do not want or need alcohol or drug treatment programs, deny any wish to quit drinking, insist that they are either homeless "by choice" or because of their own personal failings, and profess an overarching desire mainly to be left alone. Given the substantial numbers with diagnosed or evident but untreated psychiatric illnesses, however, it would be short-sighted to take everything they have told us at face value. A common feature of untreated bipolar disorder is to believe in the manic phase that nothing is wrong and to believe in the depressive phase that nothing can be done to help. The chronic mental illness so evident and widespread in this population often leads to a fatalism that is easily mistaken for a carefree, nonchalant, or even happy disposition. Likewise, there is every reason to believe that at least some portion of the widespread alcohol abuse (and to a lesser extent, drug abuse) found among our participants may only reflect efforts to relieve psychiatric symptoms through self-medication, a common feature in co-morbid homeless populations.

Current scientific thinking about substance abuse among the dually-diagnosed concurs that traditional substance abuse treatment programs (e.g., Twelve Step or therapeutic community approaches) are ineffective for those whose addictions are driven by efforts to self-medicate their mental illness, a form of addictive behavior observed most frequently among persons suffering from bipolar disorder (a diagnosis strongly overrepresented among our participants). The widespread denial of any need for substance abuse treatment in this group is best seen as an attestation that these traditional interventions have failed them in the past and will do so in the future. Effective treatment will require far more than just opening additional detox beds for this population.

A great deal of what might be called the "world view" of the homeless people we studied cannot be adequately understood in isolation from their untreated mental illnesses. The survivalist views espoused by many; the extreme sensitivity to perceived police injustices; the fatalistic resignation to the cards one has been dealt; the evident need to form close, family-like attachments to other "outsiders"—all this is highly suggestive of the characteristic thought processes of mentally ill people and illustrates the need for sustained and timely access to mental health care as a critical component of any overall intervention.

We were also struck by the similarities between many of our participants' world views and what Hoffman and Coffey refer to as the process of "opting out," whereby some homeless people avoid conventional services and service providers in part to avoid the excessive rules and regulations that come with accepting services, but also "because to consume services and to interact with providers leads to a deterioration of self-esteem and dignity" (Hoffman and Coffey 2008, p. 217). Those who have opted out "tend to live on the street [or, presumably, the woods] rather than in shelters and tend to ignore other services available to them. They value this sense of independence and often expressed disdain for people who have not opted out. Rejection of the system [of services] is how they hold onto their dignity …" Clearly, these passages described many of our woods people.

We close this chapter with a passage from and an homage to the work of Robert Frost. The first is a line from his poem *Notes for the Hired Hand,* the source of the famous quote, "Home is that place where, when you have to go there, they have to take you in." Homeless people, by definition, lack such a place. Imagine what that must be like! The second is an homage to Frost' poem, *Stopping by Woods on a Snowy Evening,* which gave us the title for this chapter. We have altered Frost's classic poem to tell more of the story of homeless people living in the woods:

> Whose woods these are I think I know.
> His house is in Miami though;
> Perhaps he won't see me stopping here
> To watch his woods and snort some blow.
>
> My little friend must think it queer
> To stop without a shelter near
> Between the woods and flooded lake
> on the darkest evening of the year.
>
> He gives his head a little shake
> As if there's been a big mistake.
> The only other sound's the pierce
> Of sirens, an arrest to make.
>
> The woods are lovely, dark and deep.
> But I have premises to sweep,
> And miles to go before I sleep,
> And miles to go before I sleep.

To conclude on a more academic note, homelessness researchers have been arguing for some time that we need to pay more attention to rural homelessness (see Robertson, Harris, and Fritz 2007). What we have discussed in this chapter is a large population (numbering in the hundreds) of homeless people who are literally camped out—sleeping in tents and makeshift structures, living off the land, forging an existence, or a reasonable facsimile of one, from the waste spaces and products of modern society—right in the middle of the nation's twenty-seventh largest metropolitan area. Rather than continuing to debate how to define "rural" and whether the very definition of homelessness needs to be modified in rural areas, perhaps we should pause to wonder about the real differences between "urban" and "rural" homeless people, which probably have very little to do with the geography of residence.

Notes

1. We gratefully acknowledge the assistance of Delores Edelen, Andrew Freeland, and Christian Bolden in conducting the focus groups on which this chapter is based. An earlier version of this chapter was presented at the Second Annual Florida Homeless and Supportive Housing Conference at the Royal Plaza Hotel in Orlando, Florida, October 6, 2008.
2. To be clear, in almost all of our focus groups, we distribute a short questionnaire either at the beginning or at the end to obtain standard demographic information. This spares us the need to burn up focus group time asking and recording answers to these kinds of questions (age, race, education, time in Florida, time in the woods, etc.)
3. As we discuss in Chapter Twelve, one of Orlando's many anti-panhandling ordinances requires panhandlers to obtain a permit, so being arrested for "soliciting without a permit" is entirely plausible.

8

The Drunk, the Addicted, and the Just Plain Shiftless?[1]

Newsweek magazine ran a "My Turn" essay in 1986 by Stuart Bykofsky, a writer for the Philadelphia Inquirer, entitled "No heart for the homeless." One memorable passage in the essay referred to the homeless as "the drunk, the addicted, and the just plain shiftless." Certainly, the alcohol-impaired "Skid Row bum" probably represents the most common stereotype of homelessness in America today. Like all stereotypes, this one has a substantial basis in fact in that every study ever done of any homeless population reports high levels of alcohol and drug abuse, ranging upwards of 50 percent or more in many studies. And clearly, Central Florida's homeless are not exempt from these—excuse the euphemism—"behavioral disabilities."

While images of bums, drunks, and junkies spring quickly to mind when thinking about the homeless, it is also the case that alcoholism, substance abuse, and homelessness are complex topics that are strongly intertwined and difficult to separate. Astonishingly, contrary to the common stereotype and despite the hopelessness and stigma often attached to addicted homeless people, some homeless addicts in fact manage to "pull themselves up by the bootstraps," recover from their addictions, and go on to lead reasonably independent and productive lives (Rayburn and Wright 2009; Wong and Mason 2001). Even more astonishing, perhaps, is that many homeless addicts manage to recover all on their own, without the assistance of a formal recovery program of any kind, and do so even as they live in the streets and shelters. Many cycle in and out of treatment programs and despite long histories of addiction and relapse, somehow finally manage to get and stay clean and sober. How is this accomplished? Who has told the true "success stories" of homeless addicts who manage to recover, whether on their own or in a treatment program? What are the conditions for success in an Alcoholics Anonymous or Twelve Step treatment setting, the most common form of treatment usually available to homeless men?

When homeless individuals seek treatment for substance abuse, they usually need more medical attention than housed individuals, but have fewer resources of every sort (e.g., Daiski 2007). They are usually dirt-poor, often disheveled and filthy, physically debilitated and mentally ill, and frequently saddled with long, troubled, and unsuccessful treatment histories. In brief, although they need the most help, they are generally the least attractive clients a treatment facility can expect to encounter. Since individuals experiencing homelessness often receive inadequate care in most treatment settings, the literature on recovery among homeless populations is generally a literature of failure, inadequacy, and relapse. But what of those who have successfully overcome barriers and found ways of getting and staying sober? About the successes, little has been written.

Here, we "tell the story" of recovering homeless men in a Twelve Step program developed specifically for clients of the Men's Pavilion in Orlando. Our goal is to illustrate the problems and barriers that recovering homeless men have managed to overcome and show how this is accomplished. If nothing else, examining the problems and exposing the barriers to sobriety that homeless individuals in recovery face can at least shed light on the nature and depth of their struggles. In what ways do recovery programs for the homeless help or hinder their recovery? Just how do people with no homes get and stay sober?

There is, of course, much variability across treatment programs, even programs that are formally similar. One "therapeutic community" program (TC) may bear little or no relationship to another TC on the other side of town. And this is especially true of Twelve Step or Alcoholics Anonymous (AA) programs of the sort normally available to homeless men. All such programs claim to be based on the Twelve Steps, but vary dramatically in how faithfully AA principles are followed and how the steps get "worked." This variability across programs has long been recognized as a barrier to empirical generalizations about the efficacy of AA interventions (see, e.g., Morgenstern et al. 1996; French 2001). This chapter is no different. In fact, one important finding is how the clients we studied, and their program as a whole, adapted elements of Alcoholics Anonymous, Narcotics Anonymous, and conventional Christian religiosity into an amalgam of recovery strategies and principles that were appropriate for the unique recovery circumstances faced by homeless men, but that would be hard to characterize as a "pure" Twelve Step program or, indeed, difficult to place into any known recovery typology.

Twelve-Stepping

Originating in the 1930s, Alcoholics Anonymous has provided the grist for a large body of empirical research. The small group dynamics of AA have fascinated sociologists for decades and pertinent studies must number in the hundreds or even thousands. To narrow the topic to something manageable, we focus here on prior studies dealing with the process of how homeless men become AA members. Clearly, recovery from addiction is a hard enough struggle when family and home are present as support and as motivation. What happens when those most basic features of human existence are absent?

Homelessness complicates the process of recovery in many ways. Homeless people have weak social networks in comparison to those in housing, especially homeless people with addictions (Hawkins and Abrams 2007). To the extent that recovery programs are available to the homeless at all, they are usually Twelve Step groups, yet surprisingly little is known about the efficacy of such programs among homeless populations (e.g., Aase, Jason and Robinson 2008). Without friends or family to turn to for support, the road to recovery may be lonelier or more difficult in other ways too.

Generally, the prevailing opinion among alcohol and drug professionals is that the key to successful treatment is to provide social (and physical) environments where sobriety is positively valued. This, needless to say, is not the environment one expects to encounter on the streets or in the shelters. Indeed, even acknowledging that many people are homeless precisely because of a pattern of chronic alcohol and drug abuse, it is worth emphasizing that some only start drinking and drugging heavily after they have become homeless (Koegel and Burnham 1987; Koegel, Burnham and Farr 1990), and that drunkenness provides many positive benefits for a homeless person. High rates of alcohol and drug abuse will continue to prevail among the homeless so long as this remains true. Getting and staying drunk or high (or both) provides momentary relief from the "slings and arrows of outrageous fortune," may function as self-treatment for various psychological disorders, and help one forget or repress the miseries of existence. Surely, the occasional *illusion* of well-being must be preferable to the reality of daily life for homeless substance abusers. Treatment programs that attempt to address the alcohol or drug issue without also addressing the more basic problems for which alcohol or drug abuse is the client's solution are doomed or, at best, ineffectual. To emphasize, homeless people have many good reasons for getting and staying drunk or high. The key to successful intervention is to provide good reasons for them to get and stay sober. Homelessness offers few such reasons.

Prevailing models of alcohol and drug treatment have come and gone. (The history of substance abuse interventions is recounted in Gerstein and Harwood 1990.) At one time, the so-called "therapeutic community" approach was all the rage. Somewhat later, behavioral modification models rose to prominence. Recent innovations include "recovery coaching" (not unlike traditional AA "sponsorship," about which we have more to say later), "sober housing," or "damp housing" (where homeless men and women are housed on the condition that they remain clean and sober at least most of the time, but where occasional relapse and even "social drinking" are tolerated), and other innovations (see, e.g., White 2006; Nueser, Noordsy and Drake 2003). Unfortunately, many of these more innovative recovery models are only open to clients with a fee source and very few objective evaluations of them have been published. Even today, most treatment options available to homeless substance abusers are traditional Twelve Step AA programs similar to the program discussed here. The reason for this is partly that these programs are relatively inexpensive: hire a counselor who is experienced with "step work," staple up a few Twelve Step posters, obtain the requisite AA reading material, and you are in the alcohol recovery business.

The difficulties a homeless person faces in trying to stay sober can be as simple as not having a place to sleep for the night and as complicated as not being able to fill a prescription for a psychiatric condition.[2] The hurdles to becoming and remaining sober are complex, overlapping, convoluted, and difficult to separate and treat. The day-to-day activities and amenities of which sober housed individuals can avail themselves may be completely nonexistent for the homeless: access to food, transportation, clothing, social networks, and shelter. Since Alcoholics Anonymous is generally tolerant of these dissolute circumstances, AA becomes a prime treatment option for homeless alcoholics. Surveys of homeless substance abusers show that among those who report having ever been in treatment, nearly all say that their treatment program was some sort of AA or Twelve Step program (Zerger 2002).

Some studies have shown more success in AA when meeting locations are accessible and clients have telephones, conditions that may also be compromised when the person in recovery has no home (Campbell and Kelley 2006). More to the point, perhaps, is that "the AA philosophy of stressing alcoholism … above all other problems may lead to significant difficulties in extending and adapting social model [AA] programs to address the broader needs of populations [such as the homeless] who require, among other things, affordable housing and stable employment." This passage is from a study by Bazemore and Cruise (1993), one of a comparative few that examine Alcoholics Anonymous in a homeless context. Replicating this study was a primary initial motivation for the research reported in this chapter. Two key points for further exploration emerged from their study. First, the wide disparities in social status among clients in "mixed" AA groups (i.e., AA groups with both homeless and non-homeless members) may create very distinct and mutually antagonistic subgroups, a process that we also observed in the Orlando study. Secondly, AA philosophy emphasizes recovery from alcohol above everything else, which may present a problem to homeless individuals who are facing pressures to find jobs, housing, and other elements of self-sufficiency. This, too, is confirmed in our research.

AA employs several slogans to remind members that their alcohol problem is the first problem they should deal with and the root cause of all their other problems. One such slogan is the saying, "First things first," the "first thing" being one's alcoholism. Another is the acronym SLIP, which stands for "sobriety loses its priority." When an AA member "slips" up, the implication is that the member has allowed some other problem to assume top priority.[3] No matter how an AA member chooses to say it or which slogan is employed, the understanding is that sobriety must be the most important thing in a recovering alcoholic's life. And yet, for individuals living in homeless shelters, priorities may be different, indeed, necessarily so. Many shelters, just to cite one example, have strict length-of-stay limitations. When one's time in the shelter is about to expire, finding alternative shelter may temporarily become far more pressing than "working the program." Likewise, a person who has not had a decent meal in days may place greater emphasis on finding a soup kitchen than admitting his or her powerlessness over alcohol.[4] Do AA groups that meet regularly in homeless shelters and that exist to serve homeless alcoholics still emphasize the same ideas and priorities as more conventional AA programs? Do program directors of Twelve Step based homeless recovery programs place the same emphasis on alcohol as the "first problem?" With program directors usually having personal experiences with recovery themselves, how do they influence client decisions about which of a client's many problems gets top priority?

We explore these issues in a qualitative study of homeless men in First Steps, a Twelve Step recovery program that operates out of the Men's Pavilion at the Coalition for the Homeless of Central Florida. We asked a convenience sample of First Steps participants about their perceptions of the program, themselves, their needs and ambitions, and their recovery.

The life trajectories of homeless persons are inadequately understood, yet very important in trying to reduce the consequences of homelessness (O'Toole et al. 2007). Although some argue, consistent with the AA model, that homeless alcoholics should make sobriety the top priority, others put emphasis on housing first, employment second, and sobriety third. With a life full of serious risks of every description and where no aspect of a "normal" life can be taken for granted, it is an open question how homeless alcoholics should best begin their quest to regain self-sufficiency. Some research even suggests that economic and housing stability are near-prerequisites to maintaining sobriety, yet getting and staying sober, finding a job, and securing a place to live all at the same time would seem to be a very tall order for nearly anyone (see, e.g., Argeriou and McCarty 1990; Wright, Devine and Brody 1997).

Research on the incidence of addiction disorders among the homeless reports percentages ranging from about a third on the low end to upwards of 70 percent on the high end (Wright, Rubin and Devine 1998). Whatever the "true" number, it is significantly higher than the estimated rate of 5-10 percent of alcohol abuse in the general population. In whatever setting studied, alcohol issues are the most frequently noted health problem of homeless people, and that would be as true of the homeless of Central Florida as it is anywhere else.

Here we seek to identify common problems and barriers in the experiences of homeless AA members in the First Steps program.[5] First Steps participants live in a section of the Pavilion that is walled off from the rest and that is accessed through a single door. Behind the door are eighteen bunk beds, thirty-six foot lockers, and a space for socializing and watching television. First Steps accommodations are unquestionably superior to a mat on the Pavilion floor and First Steps men enjoy more privacy and other privileges than Pavilion men in general. So, there is always a waiting list for the program; in fact, as men move towards the top of the waiting list, they get assigned to floor spaces in the Pavilion adjacent to the First Steps wall, a coveted signification of enhanced status. Along with increased amenities, privacy, and privileges come increased expectations and responsibilities, e.g., to help clean up after the evening meal service, help out in the adjacent CWF kitchen and cafeteria, step up for volunteer jobs, and so on.

Ten men participated in this study; an eleventh potential participant refused. They ranged in age from mid-forties to late-fifties. About half had completed high school; the remaining men were high school dropouts. All were born in the United States except one Jamaican. Most had lived in the Southeast their entire lives. Almost all had once been married, but were currently estranged from spouses, other women, and any children they may have sired. Eight were black, one was Hispanic, and one was white. Virtually all had criminal records.

First Steps was created in 2002. During the study, First Steps was only available to adult men, but a similar program to address the treatment needs of substance-abusive homeless women has since been added. First Steps is similar in design to other alcohol treatment programs available to homeless substance abusers nationally; indeed, it may very well be the modal type.

Each man was interviewed for one to two hours. Participants were encouraged to talk for as long as they liked about whatever aspects of their AA membership or recovery they wanted to talk about. Although there were some prepared "guiding questions," participants were intentionally not led in any particular direction nor were they encouraged to focus on any particular topic. Participants were identified and recruited by asking First Steps members (obvious in the Pavilion because of their distinctive identification badges) if they would be willing to participate in the study and tell their AA story for research purposes. Most were eager to do so. Our data are based mostly on the in-depth interviews, leavened slightly by some participant observation during the AA (and NA) meetings participants regularly attend.

Results

First Steps men collectively experienced four major problems in achieving and maintaining sobriety through their membership in AA. First, they had difficulty identifying themselves as alcoholics and thus had problems becoming full members of an AA group as that term is normally understood in AA. Second, clients' sponsorship relationships were weak or nonexistent. Third, "working the steps" took on different meanings for these men than for domiciled AA members, creating a very non-traditional Twelve Step recovery program. Finally, and somewhat surprisingly, homeless men in AA programs faced unanticipated time constraints that interfered with their recovery.

Identification as Alcoholics

AA emphasizes identification with the fellowship of AA and the AA recovery community. The first step states, "We admitted we were powerless over alcohol, that our lives had become unmanageable." The emphasis here is on the "we," i.e., participants are expected to align themselves with the larger AA recovery community by using and internalizing the term "we." However, the condition of homelessness obstructs this process. When interviewing First Steps men, it was not uncommon for them to make it clear that they did not feel like they belonged to or were part of any recovery group. Rather, as one client put it in his interview, First Steps men "are loners" and this is generally incompatible with AA recovery principles.

At First Steps and, for that matter, at all AA-style recovery programs, clients are required to attend AA meetings as an essential part of the recovery process. There are two options for these meetings. First, AA meetings are held weekly in the Coalition cafeteria ("on-site" meetings). These meetings are attended both by First Steps clients and by outside (non-First Steps) AA members. This same idea, on-site meetings, is often employed in other institutional settings such as outpatient treatment facilities, rehabilitation centers, and correctional facilities.

A key feature of on-site meetings is that they are attended by AA members from the surrounding area. Some of these "outsiders" have lived at the homeless shelter and attend the on-site meeting because they are comfortable there; others may go because they feel like this is their way of giving back to AA. However, unlike First Step clients, outside AA members get in their cars and go home when the meeting is over. Moreover, First Steps men are acutely aware that outside AA members come to the on-site meeting mainly to do their Twelfth Step, "service work."[6] Thus, some First Steps men resent the presence of "outsiders" at "their" AA meeting, in part because the outsiders are not part of the First Steps "community" and in larger part because First Steps men often feel that they are looked down upon by the outsiders as pitiful and needy wretches. And yet, ironically, it is precisely the outsiders who give the most hope to other First Steps clients:

Interviewer: What about the strength of the meetings here?

Participant: Yeah, that plays a major role in your recovery too. To know that people have been there where you've been. And you know, to know that they stayed clean that long—it gives you hope. It gives you hope, you know what I mean. I love it, I love to sit there and listen to them [the outsiders] talk about things. And then, they still have problems too, and just don't pick up. That's the main thing … that's the main goal of it all … just don't pick up.[7]

Thus, the same meeting feature, the regular presence of outside AA members, produces two extremely different reactions: frustration hearing the outsiders share (and perhaps boast about) their long term sobriety; and hope and enjoyment in the very same sharing. If nothing else, this is clear evidence that certain treatment features do not work the same way for everyone!

The on-site meetings at the shelter are exciting events. The room is filled with cheer, new people, coffee, and friendly faces—certainly a different atmosphere than usually found at the Men's Pavilion. In fact, the room can be so inviting that other non-First Steps homeless clients often come in for the hour-long meeting, i.e., other homeless guys from the Pavilion who will often sit in the back of the meeting space, mostly just sitting quietly and drinking the free coffee. First Steps clients set up the room with chairs and tables for the outside AA members who attend and clean up after the outsiders leave. There is a verbal and physical divide between the two groups (First Steps and outsiders). No matter how much they might agree about alcohol and related issues, there is simply no escaping the fact that their very different housing situations make them two very different types of people. And this clearly interferes with the sense of "we" upon which the AA recovery model depends.

The second meeting option is to attend off-site AA meetings. This, too, is common practice with outpatient recovery, and sometimes in in-patient treatment centers also. There is a van that is usually used to take First Steps clients to these outside meetings. This van seats fifteen; at full capacity, First Steps houses thirty-six. So getting to outside AA meetings becomes a "first come, first serve" affair.

First Steps clients are usually bussed to the same outside meeting, at the same time, on the same day of the week. Therefore, the regular members of this outside meeting quickly become aware that, say, Tuesday is the "homeless AA day," the day that fifteen recovering homeless guys from the shelter come to "their" meeting. And obviously, the regulars at this outside meeting make their decisions about whether to attend the Tuesday meeting based on that awareness. Some of the groups' members make it a priority to attend the meeting that First Steps clients also attend, while others make it a priority *not* to attend. The outside meeting therefore often comes to be focused on "them," that "different type" of alcoholic, i.e., the homeless men of First Steps. Some of these off-site AA meetings, in fairness, are able to adapt easily to the needs of the homeless community and are happy to do so. For example, some groups have larger spaces, with more seats, and abundant free coffee. However, other groups may have trouble keeping their finances in order, are often squeezed into a too-small space, and have little or no budget for extra supplies. These latter groups can get defensive or resentful that their space is being taken over by non-members, by that "different type" of recovering alcoholic, and that, of course, makes it difficult for First Steps men to integrate into the group.

For the reasons just summarized, it therefore proves much more difficult for homeless AA members such as the First Steps men to find what is known in AA as a "home group." "The home group" is a term often used in official Alcoholics Anonymous literature:

> Traditionally, most A.A. members through the years have found it important to belong to one group which they call their "Home Group." This is the group where they accept service responsibilities and try to sustain friendships. And although all A.A. members are usually welcome at all groups and feel at home at any of these meetings, the concept of the "Home Group" has still remained the strongest bond between the A.A. member and the Fellowship.
>
> Over the years, the very essence of A.A. strength has remained with our home group, which, for many members, becomes our extended family. Once isolated by our drinking, we find in the home group a solid, continuing support system, friends and, very often, a sponsor. We also learn firsthand, through the group's workings, how to place "principles before personalities" in the interest of carrying the A.A. message (Alcoholics Anonymous 2005).

The excerpt just quoted emphasizes the communal bond between an AA member and the "fellowship" of Alcoholics Anonymous, citing it as "the strongest bond." A home group is therefore an important (if perhaps not quite essential) component of the AA recovery process. It is thus a cruel irony that homeless men in recovery seem to have as much trouble finding and identifying with a home group as they have finding an actual home, and apparently for the same reasons: social isolation, stigma, the unmistakable "otherness" that comes to men of the street. In our view, this is a leading barrier to the successful adaptation of AA recovery principles in a homeless setting.[8]

Sponsorship

Alcoholics Anonymous defines sponsorship loosely in a pamphlet entitled "Questions and Answers on Sponsorship." "An alcoholic who has made some progress in the recovery program shares that experience on a continuous, individual basis with another alcoholic who is attempting to attain or maintain sobriety through AA." Elsewhere in the pamphlet it states that "constant, close support" is an important component to sponsorship. Most people in and out of AA are aware of the concept of an AA sponsor. In movies featuring recovering alcoholics as a central theme, the sponsor is the person who is called when the recovering alcoholic is about to relapse, the person who talks sense, shows kindness and tough love, and whose intervention (in the movies at least) prevents a relapse from occurring. In the popular understanding of AA, sponsorship is probably the single most important aspect of the AA recovery process, the main reason why AA "works."

In most of our interviews with First Steps clients, sponsorship was a difficult topic to address. Sponsorship, we learned, is uniquely problematic for homeless AA members in recovery. For men in First Steps, and presumably for homeless AA members in general, the two problem words in the AA definition of sponsorship are "continuous" and "individual." First, there is little or no continuity in the life of a homeless individual. Circumstances change from day to day even in regard to the regular activities that most take for granted. One may or may not have a bed to sleep in, a meal to eat, or a place to shower. Depending on needs, the bus to transport First Steps members to meetings may or may not be available. In other words, the daily activities of a recovering homeless AA member are difficult to predict. In more general terms, a homeless life is often disorganized and chaotic. As one client said:

> And I got caught out there this time, to where I ended up homeless. I got a sister and brother here, who do fairly well. I could'a said some good stuff, "I'm tired, I'm gonna change," and went and stayed with either one of them. And I knew that by me being sick, I wasn't gonna do nothing but create bad blood with the only close family that I got. So I said, no I can't go there. I need to go somewhere where I can get my head out of the clouds. And I can begin, I ain't never been homeless, this is my first time on the streets, and boy that's a rough life, man. I'm talking about having nowhere to sleep. In the rain, that's a rough life. So, it took me to hit that point.

The problem with the second term, "individual," arises as the sponsor is expected to spend individual time with the recovering AA member being sponsored. However, the homeless have no individual space and very little private time. For them, individual space and time do not exist. They inhabit *public* space: there are group sleeping conditions, group meals, group showers, and group meetings. And their time is strictly regulated: when they must get up, shower, dress, eat, meet, work, pray, and go to bed—all of this is *scheduled.* Therefore, it proves virtually impossible to have even one private, individual conversation with a sponsor, much less to enter into a "constant, close, supportive" relationship with one's AA mentor.

Aside from physical and temporal difficulties, there are mental barriers to sponsorship as well. Homeless AA men seem to have a strong bias against other men telling them what to do. As one client said:

> Participant: I struggle with a lot of stuff that I hear in recovery, you know, but I keep an open mind, like the big book suggests. And I still go through with it, although I struggle with it.
>
> Interviewer: Could you think of an example?
>
> Participant: The example is like—getting a sponsor. I got one, but I struggle with it. I had a real deep struggle with it, because at first I said, "I'm not getting no sponsor man." For me to get a sponsor, is just like saying, I don't trust in my higher power. And then a sponsor is just a human being, just like me. You know, I'm not gonna have nobody telling me, "No, don't talk to her." Man, I like this lady I just met, and I think we … "You not ready for no relationship." *No.* Cut him. I just wasn't ready for that. The sponsor I got, he cool, you know. By me keeping an open mind and trying it, I found out that it ain't that bad.

The interview with this client, incidentally, was the *only* interview of the ten that indicated a traditional AA relationship with a sponsor. This participant had been sober for a year and described the difficulties he had forming a relationship with a sponsor. All the other men either had sponsors who work at First Steps as counselors or the director or did not have a sponsor at all (and had no intention of getting one).

Trying to work a program of recovery with no sponsor is highly discouraged within Alcoholics Anonymous. Although these men may be stalling or refusing to get a sponsor for a variety of reasons, they are at risk of relapse because they do not have someone to discuss personal problems they may be having with their recovery. Most try to lean on the First Steps program director when they have problems they need to discuss, but with the large number of men in the program (thirty-six most of the time and as many as forty-one during the course of this project), the time that the director has to work individually with clients is obviously very limited. An AA recovery process that does not include a close personal relationship with a sponsor is obviously problematic for many reasons, not the least of which is that the absence of a sponsor can interfere with doing "step work," the next issue on our agenda.

Step Work

Another problem for homeless AA members, exacerbated by the problem of sponsorship, is step work. In the Alcoholics Anonymous pamphlet "Questions and Answers on Sponsorship," there is a section titled "What does a sponsor do?" That segment gives many sponsorship suggestions, one of which is that the sponsor "goes over the meaning of the Twelve Steps and emphasizes their importance." Without the guidance of a sponsor, an AA member might have difficulty interpreting the steps or figuring out how to "work" them. It is not uncommon in AA meetings discussing sponsorship for a member to emphasize the importance of working the steps with a sponsor; it is generally frowned upon for a member to work on them alone. In one interview, when asked about which step he was working on, the client misinterpreted the question.

Interviewer: What step are you working on now?

Participant: Wonderful, wonderful. Ugh, I've ... Right now I'm in the process of getting ready to attend [a program] to become a counselor, a drug and alcohol counselor. I've taken my test, like I said I've been out of school for a while now, and I held my head up above water pretty good.

That answer made it clear that the client had misinterpreted the question about step work, which seemed odd considering how aggressively "working the steps" is stressed in all Twelve Step programs. To find out more, we therefore inquired about his sponsor. At this point, we learned several things about how sponsor relationships form in this type of rehabilitation program. First, the man who approached this participant to persuade him to enroll in First Steps told the participant that he was going to be the participant's sponsor. This reverses the usual process, where the person needing sponsorship asks another recovering member to sponsor him. Although the process of a sponsor appointing himself is not unheard of, it is certainly uncommon. Second, the two individuals had a prior relationship, as friends. This also seems to be an uncommon arrangement in the Twelve Step world, although this topic requires further investigation.

Still trying to understand this participant's sponsor relationship, we probed further.

Interviewer: Is your sponsor here [in First Steps]?

Participant: Yes, he's here. And he tells me ... and my sponsor, I love him to death, but he won't let me get past step three. I go steps one, two, and three, and he says, go do them again.

From this part of the interview, we learned that the sponsoring individual is also a member of the First Steps program, and that the participant being interviewed felt frustrated with the progress of their step work together. Other First Steps clients also expressed a similar frustration at being instructed to not go further than a certain step.

> Interviewer: So what step are you working on now?

> Participant: To be truthful with you, I'm still on one. I study [step] one a lot. I'm going towards two. And, that's pretty much it. I got the type of sponsor, he ain't in no hurry to rush me through the steps. Ok, you just read one, and you call me and we'll talk about one. I said, "Can I go to step two?" and he say "No, read step one again, and call me back, and we'll talk about one." And I'll do that. And even the director said, they only been in the program three months, and they're already on the ninth step.

Although some clients had a working knowledge of the terminology of the AA program, some admitted to working the steps without a sponsor, a practice usually frowned upon. It is again apparent that these men have difficulty opening up and sharing with other men. The recurring theme of using a counselor, rather than a sponsor, to do step work is also apparent.

There may be numerous reasons why First Step clients move slowly, if at all, through all twelve steps, but one reason is clearly their difficulties in identifying sponsors and working the steps with those sponsors, the usual AA arrangement.

Time Constraints

One guiding question of this research was how, exactly, a homeless individual stays sober. Balancing the differing requirements in a recovery program with the rest of life's needs and circumstances must be difficult, and the story of the following participant gives some clarification of this complicated problem. First, there are certain requirements mentioned earlier that the First Steps client must fulfill. One of these requirements is early morning community service after breakfast. The participant whose story we are about to relate had been in the First Steps program six months at the time of the interview. Prior to this, he had been sober another previous six months at another similar program for homeless men. Therefore, he had recently celebrated his one-year sobriety birthday, a very big deal in AA. We assumed that by being in recovery for an entire year he had been through most or all of the steps, so we proceeded to ask him about it.

Interviewer: So are you working on a step right now? You've been through them all, I guess ...

Participant: No, you know ... I just ... I been here like six months, and I just got a sponsor. You know, I just got a sponsor. I just got a step-working guide. And I just worked the first step. Yeah. See, I'm doing other things. See, it's ... Recovery is first. I realize that. But you have to ... I try to balance it. 'Cause there's other things I got to do too. I got to live when I get up out of here. You know, so I got to try to go to school, work, I cook at a restaurant ...

At this juncture, we paused to put things together. Perhaps we had been naive to assume that step work and sobriety would be the top priority in these men's lives, or even that they *could* be, even though AA says they *must* be. It was clear we were unconsciously associating homelessness with unemployment, lack of routine, absence of time constraints, and therefore loads of free time available to invest in recovery work. And as it turns out, nothing could be further from the truth. After eating breakfast at 6:00 a.m. and doing his community service work (picking up trash around the shelter), this participant, and many other participants, had to go to work.

Interviewer: How far away is the restaurant you cook at?

Participant: That's like an hour ride on the bus. Every day, this help me though. *Points to portable CD player.* I listen to the radio and I read, you know, I take books in my little pack, and I be there before I realize it. I got a recovery bible that I read. Then I got a Scofield study bible. And there's other self-help books that I read.

So, after breakfast, community service, and an hour bus ride (every day), this participant works an eight-hour day cooking meals. After the hour ride home, dinner, and a meeting, it's time for "lights out" and sleep. Within his schedule, this client also has to find time to squeeze in studying for his GED, talking to his sponsor, finding a place to live, and working on getting a better paying job. (Even with eight-hour days, he explained, restaurant wages do not support living in an Orlando apartment.)

First Steps men must structure their schedules carefully to balance all their responsibilities. Most have felony convictions or other legal troubles that interfere with their ability to work or return to school. Therefore, it seems doubtful that many will ever get a job that pays much more than this participant's job as a short order cook. Homeless men recovering from addictions who also have criminal histories and, in many cases, co-occurring mental health problems, as well as other disabilities and barriers, are not usually seen as outstanding prospects for high-paying jobs. Further contributing to the problem is that these men are in their mid-forties to early fifties. In a society that is increasingly moving towards technological advancements, these men find their manual skills and work experiences less and less needed.

Creative Adaptations?

So far, we have discussed the barriers to traditional AA participation and recovery faced by First Steps men. We also observed interesting adaptations that these men used to overcome their barriers and facilitate recovery. These adaptations assume three forms: excessive twelfth-stepping, aggregated religious and recovery ideologies, and unrealistic ideals.

Taking the Twelfth Step Too Far?

Time and time again, First Steps clients mentioned behaviors associated with giving back to society as part of their "program." Helping is not uncommon among AA members; in fact, the twelfth step instructs members to carry the message to alcoholics and to practice AA principles in all their affairs. AA members commonly refer to this as "twelve-stepping" and it generally means that one AA member will try to "give back" by helping a new AA member in the beginning stages of sobriety. However, the men in First Steps took this concept to another level.

Instead of just helping other alcoholics, these men tried to help everyone around them. They stated a strong desire to give back to society, to do their part, to give instead of take, and to become useful—not sentiments that would be stereotypically associated with homeless alcoholic men. Ideas about and declarations of contribution were strong during the interviews. They often revealed desires to help other homeless individuals, and to help other alcoholics. One client described his hopes for the future:

> I wanna be able to help somebody. I wanna be able to start something. If I wanna go to the grocery story, and out of my pocket, buy lunchmeat, cheese, and a couple of cases of soda, go out on a Saturday, where people at, and just hand out food—I wanna be able to do that. Without, "Oh man I don't know what I'm gonna eat tomorrow. I spent that money feeding them homeless people." I don't wanna live like that. I don't wanna live like that.

Many of the men in the program felt this need to "start something," to create a new recovery program or a new way to help homeless individuals. First Steps clients' strong desire to give back to society is reminiscent of Brown's 1991 study of the professional "ex." In this study, the professional "ex" from a deviant career becomes a counselor. The clients of First Steps, in a way, legitimize past deviance by using it to transform themselves into roles that are of a helping nature.

A Hodgepodge Heaven

First Steps members used the terms Alcoholics Anonymous and Narcotics Anonymous (NA) interchangeably, showing little knowledge of any difference between the two programs. Culturally and historically, however, the AA program and the NA program are very different. But whereas the differences between the two programs would generally be more distinguishable to an AA or NA member, First Steps men recognize few or no differences. They also heavily incorporated the Christian bible into their recovery programs, sometimes using a recovery bible. One participant described this mixture of different program components:

> Participant: I attend meetings, I got a sponsor, I done work the first step, but I don't put everything in one area. That ain't this kind of program. Like I hear in the rooms, what worked for one, don't work for all. So what I had to do is find out what works for me. Some people, some guys, they be like brainwashed with this thing. They wake up with it, they go to sleep with it. I ain't saying nothing bad about it. That might work for them, it won't work for me. My mind is other places too. Like how I'm gonna live.

First Steps realizes that each individual may have different circumstances and may need a different form of treatment. This style is a bit different than the typical "one size fits all" program that usually exists in low-income treatment arenas. This is a general goal of the First Steps program as outlined in their brochure:

> Recognizing the uniqueness, dignity and value of every individual, case managers work closely with each man to develop detailed plans and goals to address his specific needs. The plan is designed to help the client achieve success through inspiration, encouragement and moral support. The rehabilitation includes group sessions, educational and employment training, recreational activities and 12-Step recovery strategies.

One way they are able to achieve this plan is to simply figure out the comfort level of the individual participant with the three treatment ideologies in play. While one client may feel very comfortable with Alcoholics Anonymous and Christianity, they may have some internal bias against Narcotics Anonymous program practices. Therefore, First Steps is able to customize and tailor a program with little or no financial cost.

Going Broke on Perfection

The main text *Alcoholics Anonymous* has a passage that sums up a great deal about the alcoholic according to the program. Perhaps it is even truer of the homeless alcoholic.

> ... we learn that alcoholism is a complex malady; that abnormal drinking is but a symptom of personal maladjustment to life; that, as a class, we, alcoholics are apt to be sensitive, emotionally immature, grandiose in *our demands upon ourselves and others; that we have usually "gone broke" on some dream ideal of perfection; that, failing to realize the dream, we sensitive folk escape cold reality by taking to the bottle* ... (Emphasis added)

Almost all of the interviews we conducted showed evidence of this grandiosity. For example, one man answered that he would like to be able to go on a cruise whenever he felt like it, and purchase an entirely new wardrobe when he felt tired of the one that he had:

> Hell if I wanna go and just up and go and take me a cruise, I wanna be able to do that. If I wanna decide one day, that stuff look kinda old, I'm tired of wearing that stuff, just clear my closet out, and come down here and donate it to some people and start all over with it except what I got on. If I wanna just do that one day, I just wanna do that kind of stuff without it being strain, or without it being stressful.

Other individuals in the First Steps program embraced equally unattainable aspirations even though they were living in a homeless shelter. They had difficulty admitting to their circumstances, and often tried to suggest that they were not as low on life's ladder as they seemed. One client originally said that he chose to come to the homeless shelter.

> I decided to come here. I still have my house. Just walked away from my house. Left my kids. Something I wanted to do. Left everything and I came here. I been here like three weeks. It's ok so far.

However, later in the interview, he admitted that he no longer had a house, that he had lost his residence.

In a similar manner, on several occasions the clients of First Steps referred to other homeless individuals as "the homeless," with the word spoken in such a way as to suggest that they were not "really" homeless themselves. In one situation, as we drove to a meeting in the van, one of the First Steps clients made fun of a homeless man who was pushing his belongings down the street in a shopping cart. The insult revealed a bias against the homeless man with the shopping cart because he did not have enough money or resources to have another homeless person watch his belongings while he traveled. This evidently put him in a lower social class than the First Steps participant responsible for the insult.

We are uncertain if these grandiose ideas the men hold give them hope, or prevent them from getting out of homelessness and alcoholism. The balance between making demands on oneself and the desire to protect oneself is an interesting dichotomy. Throughout the interviews, questions were posed such as: "what are you currently working on?" or "what are your plans after leaving the program?" Most of the men in the First Steps program revealed goals of some "dream ideal of perfection" as the AA text puts it. Perhaps in some situations, these dreams keep the members going, keep them sober. However, it might also be true that just as often, they "fail to realize" the dream, and start using again. If pressed for a definite answer, the interviews point towards the latter.

Thus we learn that these homeless men adapted Twelve Step program concepts to fit their needs in part through exaggeration: an exaggerated sense of "giving back," an undifferentiated, thus exaggerated, sense of recovery theory, and grandiose (exaggerated) aspirations for the future. Perhaps the absurdly exaggerated conditions of their existence—being poor, homeless, addicted ex-cons—promote equally absurd exaggerations in their strategies of recovery.

Concluding Thoughts

We have seen some of the ways homeless men achieve and maintain sobriety despite their homelessness. In some ways, the answer for homeless addicts is the same as it is for everyone else: sobriety is a daily struggle. Yet one by one, the men of First Steps have accumulated days of sobriety that have, in some cases, turned into years—despite the fact that they are still calling the Pavilion home.

Addiction recovery in the face of the adaptations and barriers we have identified is all the more remarkable because sobriety does not seem to "pay off" very handsomely for these men. Alcohol abusers whose recovery allows them to salvage a marriage, hold onto a home, or keep a job have powerful external motivations to get and stay sober. The clean and sober homeless men of First Steps, in contrast, do not face any realistic prospects of reconciliation with spouses or significant others, generally do not find or keep decent jobs, and in the large majority, remain homeless. That they find *something* that justifies the struggle to get and remain sober despite limited to non-existent pay-offs is, in the end, the great mystery that further research will have to address.

Many people have a simple cure for homelessness: sober up, take a shower, and get a job. The data recounted in this chapter have shown the difficulty of that prescription. Issues of identification, sponsorship, step work, and time management greatly complicate even the first requirement of sobering up. When considering all the barriers to recovery that homeless addicts face, the surprise is not that so few succeed in their sobriety, but that any do. And yet, based on First Steps follow-up data, more than half the participants do manage to complete the program and maintain sobriety for at least six months.

A popular saying within AA tells members to put "first things first"; that is, sobriety should be the first priority over all other things in life. It is this same ideology that First Steps has incorporated into its treatment program. First Steps believes that alcohol and drug problems should be taken care of first, and housing, employment, and the like will follow. This implies, first, that alcohol abuse is responsible for these men's homelessness, and second, that if they can get and stay sober, their housing problems will somehow resolve themselves. And yet First Steps clients continue to get and stay sober, but very few are successful in finding affordable housing. If there are no places where these men can afford to live, then sooner or later, they must ask themselves, "What's the point?" Is being clean, sober, but still homeless really an improvement? Although First Steps can apparently produce sober homeless men, it cannot produce affordable housing for the larger community of homeless persons. More to the point, perhaps, if there is little or no housing available that these men could afford, and very little prospect of finding decent jobs that would let them afford better, then why should we be surprised when homeless individuals refuse to sober up?

In an ideal world, there would be no tradeoffs or hard choices: homeless men with addiction issues would sober up, conquer their addictions, and then, as a result, find a place to live (or perhaps a good job and then a place to live). But decent, low-cost housing does not just fall into one's lap, and if recovery work, mandatory meetings, educational activities, and employment take up the lion's share of one's time, then the hours, days, and weeks required to seek out acceptable and affordable housing may simply not be available. Reviewers of an earlier version of this material objected to what they saw as a "false choice" between treatment and housing, but for many of the men in First Steps, this is in fact the choice they are given. Regardless of their own priorities, they are initially required and subsequently encouraged to get their minds off of housing and stay focused on their sobriety. The net result: clean and sober but still *homeless* people.

The appeal of alcohol and drugs to homeless people is, sad to say, easy to appreciate. For those without an attainable future to which they can reasonably aspire, for those with little sense of hope or the opportunity for something better, alcohol and drugs are temporary expedients, momentary highs that offer escape and pleasure in an otherwise dismal life. Why *should* people without a realistic future be expected to defer their momentary pleasures or forego some sense of escape from otherwise harsh and hopeless conditions? Is there really a "free will" choice to be made between momentary euphoria and endless misery? Is it any better to be homeless and sober than homeless and drunk?

The rate of alcohol and drug abuse among the homeless is very high, but it is misleading to conclude from this fact that homelessness is therefore mainly the result of alcohol and drug abuse, as Stuart Bykofsky has evidently done. The better conclusion is that alcohol and drug abusive poor people have great difficulties in maintaining their hold on acceptable housing and therefore become homeless in disproportionate numbers, and that excessive drinking and drugging are often adaptations to becoming homeless. Likewise, the solution to the alcohol and drug problems of homeless people is to be found less in treatment for their addictions than in providing jobs, incomes, and housing that make sobriety more appealing than intoxication. Efforts to address the many problems of the homeless, including their alcohol and drug problems, are bound to be largely fruitless if they do not provide a route to improved material circumstances. Life in the streets and shelters is a very powerful incentive to get high or drunk and stay that way. In the end, then, the solution to the problems of alcoholic and drug-addicted homeless people will be found in the Department of Housing and Urban Development more than in the Center for Substance Abuse Treatment.

Notes

1. This chapter was co-authored by Rachel Rayburn and is loosely adapted from Rayburn and Wright (2009).
2. We have interviewed homeless people who drink heavily as nighttime approaches so they can fall and stay asleep outdoors; and likewise, as we saw in Chapter Seven, a great deal of alcoholism and addiction among the homeless is self-treatment for various psychiatric conditions.
3. Forming and developing new intimate relationships provide many obvious opportunities to "slip," and such behavior is therefore highly discouraged in AA settings.
4. For readers unfamiliar with the Twelve Steps, the First Step is, "We admitted we were powerless over alcohol—that our lives had become unmanageable."

5. It will avoid confusion to emphasize that the program is called "First Steps" *not* because it focuses on the first of the twelve steps of the AA program but because it is conceptualized as the "first step" up off the floor of the Pavilion and into more functional living circumstances.
6. The Twelfth Step: "Having had a spiritual awakening as the result of these Steps, we tried to carry this message to alcoholics, and to practice these principles in all our affairs."
7. "Picking up" is a common term used to mean picking up a drink or a drug, i.e., a relapse.
8. Clearly, the "on-site" meeting becomes the *de facto* "home group" for most First Steps men, but this is at best a short term solution since First Steps (and the Pavilion more generally) is intended as emergency shelter, not as permanent housing. Thus, the membership of the on-site meeting is transient. Recovery, one hopes, lasts a lifetime, whereas time at the Pavilion should only last for a matter of months.

9

"No Place for Sissies": The Elderly Homeless[1]

"Old age is no place for sissies."
—Bette Davis

As we said in the first chapter, many people have come to think of Florida as a Mecca-like destination for the retired and elderly. Indeed, "retiring to Florida" has become something of a cliché. Escape the cold, spend your days on the golf course, and eat dinner at 3:15 p.m. in all-you-can-eat buffet cafeterias where *everything* comes with a senior discount. The Villages, the immense elderly community northwest of Orlando that we mentioned in Chapter One, is the literal incarnation of this cliché. But as we showed in Chapter Two, the cliché does not describe the reality for large numbers of Florida's seniors, many of whom struggle to make ends meet on pitiful incomes. Some, of course, fall all the way into homelessness, and that is the topic of this chapter. Although at present the elderly comprise only a small portion of the total poor and homeless populations, their numbers are destined to grow as the overall population continues to age (Wright, Donley and Dietz 2009).

This chapter culls insights from focus groups and interviews that we have conducted with poor and homeless elderly Floridians over the past four years. Most participants are from Central Florida, but a few are from Miami-Dade County. Data were collected in emergency and transitional homeless shelters, subsidized housing complexes for seniors, permanent housing complexes for the formerly homeless, and at feeding programs. These stories highlight and dramatize the many issues that poor and homeless elderly people across the nation face in their daily lives.

Where appropriate, we have supplemented our qualitative data with more quantitative studies dealing with the changing demography of the aged in American society and with the elderly homeless. Although the elderly homeless are not an especially numerous subgroup within the larger homeless population, they are a matter of concern because they are frail and vulnerable, and because if people are elderly *and* homeless, their very existence signals some failure in the system of elder care. Owing to their compromised physical and mental health, being without a home and securing the basic necessities of daily living must be special challenges to the elderly homeless. Many elders in normal life circumstances contemplate the end of existence with anxiety bordering on despair. Imagine what it must be like to be at the end of one's life cycle and to find oneself sleeping on park benches or in homeless shelters and scavenging an existence from the gutters and trash cans.

Definition of Elderly

When discussing the elderly poor and homeless, it is important to be clear about definitions. In the vernacular, elderly means those sixty-five or older (i.e., eligible for Medicare) or sometimes those sixty-two or older (i.e., eligible for Social Security). But many definitions "kick in" at much younger ages. Denny's offers senior citizen meals to anyone over the age of fifty-five and AARP admits members any time after age fifty. As a rule of thumb, we follow the AARP convention in this chapter. Indeed, more and more researchers use the age fifty as their starting point because by age fifty, many homeless people already exhibit the signs and symptoms of advancing age and yet are years away from eligibility for programs of assistance such as Medicare. Also, the early fifties are when homeless people begin dying off in large numbers. Many programs for the poor and housed elderly also serve people under age sixty-five; some programs begin at age fifty-five, others at age sixty-two—an explicit recognition that social and economic conditions can strongly influence the aging process.

Numbers

Considering the many stereotypes of broken-down *old* homeless men and women, and the concerns about the elderly homeless that sometimes surface in both the scholarly and popular literature, the most surprising fact about the group is not that there are so many of them, but that there are so *few*, a demographic anomaly first noted two decades ago (Wright and Weber 1987). In Burt's (2001) survey, homeless individuals age sixty-five or greater comprised only 2 percent of the total sample; in the 2000 Census, the percentage of the U.S. population age sixty-five or greater was 12 percent. Thus, individuals over sixty-five are underrepresented among the homeless by an apparent factor of five or six to one.

What accounts for the deficit? Two hypotheses have been suggested. First, a range of benefit programs become available to people once they turn sixty-five (among which Social Security, Medicare, and various housing subsidies are the most important). These programs may be sufficient in many instances to get otherwise homeless people off the streets or to allow aging poor people to avoid homelessness. On the other hand, people with sporadic work histories and lesser access to resources (e.g., women, ethnic minorities, the addicted or mentally ill, undocumented workers, and the like) may find that they are not eligible for these programs of assistance or that the benefits are not adequate to keep them housed.

A second and more troubling hypothesis is that homeless people rarely survive to old age. Roughly a dozen studies of mortality among the homeless have been published and the common finding is that the average age at death for various samples of homeless men is somewhere in the early fifties (O'Connell 2005; Morrison 2009). Morrison (2009) asks whether homelessness is itself a factor in premature death or whether the common finding results entirely from risk factors that happen to be associated with homelessness, e.g., excessive alcohol, drug and tobacco use, lack of access to health care, environmental exposures, and the like. These correlated factors, Morrison finds, do indeed account for a portion of the excess mortality, "but homelessness itself confers additional risk."

Elderly homeless were far more numerous in the Skid Row studies of the 1960s and 1970s than they are today. These days, most studies report that the homeless are relatively young, with an average age in the late thirties or early forties, a substantial decline from three decades ago when the average age of the homeless was perhaps fifteen or twenty years higher.

Whatever the current deficit, there is concern that the number of older homeless will increase, perhaps precipitously, in the coming decades as the general population ages and as the demand for affordable housing increases faster than the supply. The "graying of America" has become a cliché but expresses a profoundly important point, namely, that the elderly portion of the U.S. population will grow dramatically in the next half century. The basic demography is well-known. Today, about 12 to 13 percent of the national population is over age sixty-five and 6 percent are over age seventy-five. By 2045, 22 percent will be over sixty-five and 12 percent will be over seventy-five. Thus, in the next three to four decades, the number of elderly will nearly double (Population Resource Center 2010). The proportion of individuals who are very old, those over the age of eighty-five, is expected to triple. There is no reason to think that the elderly *poor* or the elderly *homeless* will be exempt from these general demographic trends.

On Becoming Elderly and Homeless

As the stories we recount later show, elderly people can become elderly *homeless* people through two entirely distinct processes. Some homeless people age into the category of elderly, and some elderly people lose their housing and become homeless late in life. No study of which we are aware has reported direct evidence on the relative proportions. Either way, the elderly homeless face all of the problems that all homeless people face (regardless of age) and all the problems that elderly people face (regardless of their housing situations). There are also interactions that make the situation of the elderly homeless uniquely problematic, for example, an evident need for the vigor and alertness that are important survival skills for all homeless people, coupled with the limited physical capacity and mental acuity that inevitably accompany aging. So, one expects the situation of the elderly homeless to be uniquely problematic.

Concerning the proximal causes of homelessness among the elderly, a study of 103 homeless people in Tampa asked about their "reasons for being homeless" (Rich, Rich and Mullins 1995). Inability to pay rent or to pay the required security deposit were the only factors cited by an outright majority. About two-fifths said their homelessness resulted from alcohol abuse. Other commonly mentioned factors include job loss (35 percent), physical illness (28 percent), and familial estrangement (15 percent). A few were evidently fleeing abusive home situations. Factors such as mental illness or drug abuse (other than alcohol) were mentioned by only about 5 percent. In short, elderly homeless people become homeless for largely the same reasons as all other homeless people: poverty, lack of affordable housing, and problems in accessing services that, if available, might otherwise keep them housed, along with the usual behavioral health issues.

Many older adults become homeless for the first time after the death of a spouse or caregiver who formerly provided instrumental or financial support, as our stories below also illustrate. Factors such as inadequate incomes, substance abuse, or mental or physical health problems may become precursors to homelessness only after the loss of a caregiver. Older women and minorities with less experience obtaining formal support as well as older adults who suffer from mental or physical impairment may not only be more vulnerable to homelessness because they have fewer resources, they may also be unable or unwilling to secure appropriate formal support services that would enable them to avoid homelessness.

Lives and Times of Older Homeless Persons in America

What are the living circumstances of the elderly homeless in America today? The only survey focused specifically on elderly homeless persons, the Tampa survey, showed that the single largest group (46 percent) were "living rough," that is, lived literally on the streets, in parks, abandoned buildings, vehicles, or in other outdoor locations. Less than a third (30 percent) lived in homeless shelters, about a tenth lived in transitional housing, and the rest lived in their own rooms or with family and friends.[2] Many elderly homeless say they avoid the large overnight shelters because the shelters are unsafe, as, indeed, they can be (see Chapter Six), most of all for older homeless people with compromised mental or physical health (who are much more likely to be victimized or injured than other homeless people), or elderly homeless dealing with other issues of aging such as deteriorating eyesight, hearing, and mobility.

More recent national data on living circumstances of the elderly homeless are available in the Burt survey, which obtained "last seven days" housing histories for all respondents. Differences between elderly and non-elderly homeless in that survey were generally minor. The large majority of elderly homeless were again found to avoid the emergency shelters, a substantial percentage lived in transitional programs, and there were sizable numbers who lived rough, spending their nights in outdoor locations, abandoned buildings, transportation terminals, and vehicles. Among the elderly homeless, "living rough" apparently describes the living circumstance of at least one in three.[3]

O'Connell and associates (2004) have provided a recent account of elderly homeless in Boston who avoid the shelters and live literally in the streets. O'Connell's team identified thirty Boston street homeless aged sixty or more in 2000 (twenty-two men and eight women) and followed them via street outreach for four years. Ages at the beginning of the study ranged from sixty to eighty-two years. After four years, nine of the original thirty were dead, six were in nursing homes, seven were still living on the streets, and three were lost to follow-up. Despite intensive efforts by the outreach team, only five, or 17 percent, had been placed in regular housing. In general, elderly rough sleepers suffer exceptional rates of morbidity and mortality and "pose significant challenges to programs seeking to provide housing and supportive health care services" to this vulnerable street population. In particular, "issues of competency and guardianship ... were bewilderingly complex. ... We grew concerned about the ability of many persons to make reasonable judgments regarding safety. ... With the number of homeless elderly likely to grow ... this ethical dilemma will be increasingly difficult to ignore" (p. 105).

Stories from an Emergency Homeless Shelter

As stated earlier, there are two ways that elderly people come to be homeless: they can be long-time homeless people who age into the category of elderly, or they can be elderly people who first become homeless after they turn elderly. Seven of the nine elderly (over age fifty) participants in a focus group we conducted at an emergency homeless shelter in Orlando were experiencing homelessness for the first time, i.e., were in the middle of their first homeless episode. While their specific reasons for becoming homeless were all somewhat unique, two general themes were present: fallout from a declining economy and the loss of loved ones. Many of the participants had lived their entire lives in precarious housing situations such as living with roommates, with family members, or maintaining an apartment while working two hourly-wage jobs. Many had *never* been in a stable residential or financial situation. Once the economy faltered, friends or relatives that were willing to take them in and provide housing could no longer afford to do so (or chose for some reason not to allow the situation to continue). In addition, economic decline wiped out many of the hourly wage jobs that our participants relied upon. In still other cases, participants had spent their adult lives caring for family members who then died and whose deaths eliminated a former income source (e.g., a pension), with homelessness as the near immediate result.

The death of loved ones is a common pathway to homelessness among elderly people. Although people may have always been poor, had a mental illness, or abused substances, there was a support system (and income) in place that allowed them to remain housed. When that support system crumbled, there were no other viable alternatives remaining. People in this situation often have no experience reaching out for support from agencies or government programs, may be unaware of how to do so, and may be resistant to asking for help (or appearing to be "welfare dependent"). Other conditions may also be present that prevent them from doing so effectively, e.g., low literacy, lack of mobility or other transportation issues, lack of access to computers, etc. The result: another elderly homeless person.

Theresa (all names are pseudonyms, of course), is a fifty-five-year-old woman who had been homeless only two weeks when she participated in one of our focus groups. She had been living with a friend for several years. She went on a vacation trip to visit her son and when she returned, she was told to get out of the house. Theresa stated she does not know why she was told to leave and at the point of her interview did not care to know. She said she won't even try to work it out with her former room-mate because the situation will never "feel stable." That is, she realized that she could be put out again at any time even if she reconciled with the former roommate, and therefore decided to come to the homeless shelter and try to make her own way.

Another of our participants, Michelle, worked as a nurse's assistant for many years at a local hospital before being laid off unexpectedly. She lost her apartment two months later. She managed to earn enough money from odd jobs to live in a motel for nine months, but was never able to find permanent employment and eventually became homeless. Michelle has had a hard time facing her homelessness. When she ran out of money, she did not immediately go to the homeless shelter; instead, she went to the emergency room at the hospital where she once worked. She stayed in the waiting room for three days. "I knew I could blend in there. There are always people that are there for a few days."[4] She blended in all right, but had no plan for what would come next. Finally she ran into a former co-worker to whom she confided her situation. The former co-worker advised her to go to the shelter where we met her (the Coalition). While grateful for shelter, food, and other services offered at the Coalition, Michelle had yet to come to terms with her situation. As an adult she had always worked and had her own place to live. Now, in her late fifties, she had joined the ranks of the homeless. This was a discomfiting, indeed horrifying, realization.

In September of 2009, the Bureau of Labor Statistics reported that the unemployment rate for people aged forty-five to fifty-four was 8.0 percent, which compares to a rate of 4.5 percent in September of 2008. For those aged fifty-five or more, the unemployment rate in September 2009 was 6.8, compared to 4.2 a year previously. Across all age groups, the unemployment rate in September 2009 was 9.8 percent. Even though the rates for seniors are lower than the overall rate, they have still increased dramatically, and for at least some in this age group, the loss of employment is the cause of their homelessness.

Our participant Gladys also went to a local hospital when she first became homeless at age sixty-one. She had moved to Florida from California to live with her sister-in-law. She received Social Security benefits and used her monthly Social Security check to help the sister-in-law out with expenses, a satisfactory arrangement all around—until she lost her benefits "because of a glitch." (Gladys never did explain just what the glitch was or where it originated.) Ten days after not receiving her monthly check, she was told she had a half hour to get out of the house. "I'd never been homeless before." She had a little bit of money, so after walking around for hours and getting sunburned, she called a cab. She spent the night in the hospital's waiting room. In the morning, she asked people she saw there if they knew of any resources that would help her. She was told to go to the Coalition and did so later that day. Her Social Security pension had been straightened out by the time of the focus group, but returning to her sister-in-law's home was not an option. She had also learned that there are very few housing options available in the Orlando metro area for someone whose only income is a Social Security pension check. At age sixty-one, she is at least a year away from being eligible for *any* locally available subsidized apartment units of which we are aware, and four years away from eligibility for most of them.

Experiencing homelessness for the first time in her early sixties, Gladys' outlook on life is somewhat surprising. She says, "I feel I'm just in a transition and that things are going to get better. I have a plan, but I've accepted that it's going to take time. I know I will be happy. I am satisfied here because this is where I have to be. I don't have a lot of negative things to say. It's a drag, but it's workable. I know things are going to be fine."

Janice is one of a large number of Central Floridians who have lost their homes to foreclosure. Once she was forced to leave her home, she rented a motel room for a year.[5] She had been at the homeless shelter for a month when we interviewed her. "At that time I was from job to job and I didn't keep my job and I couldn't pay the hotel any longer so they asked me to leave. My daughter pulled up things on the internet and this place [the Coalition] came up. One of the case managers asked me to come in for a cold night. The next day she did bring me in. I'm out of work and I'm out looking for jobs on a daily basis. I plan to move on. I've got a couple of good thing in the works, so, knock on wood. I'd never been homeless before. My mother and daughter live here [in Orlando]. But they've got their own thing going on. My mother is eighty, my daughter has her own thing going on. I'm fifty-five."

Using data from one of the major credit bureaus, the American Association of Retired Persons (AARP) Public Policy Institute conducted a study focusing on foreclosures for people aged fifty and older. They found that people in this group accounted for 28 percent of all 2007 foreclosures. While many might think that people over fifty would have already paid off their mortgages, the study found that 41 percent of all first-time mortgages are held by people over the age of fifty. Foreclosures impact not just homeowners, but people renting homes from landlords that default. The latter is the more common scenario among people that are now homeless due to foreclosure. In a 2009 survey of homeless assistance providers, the median estimate of the percentage of homeless clients who are homeless because of foreclosure is about 10 percent (National Coalition for the Homeless 2009).

Rosa is a quiet woman who sat in our group looking somewhat overwhelmed at what was going on around her. Her story was very similar to Janice's. "I lost my apartment. I was in Northern Florida. A close friend of my family … they called [the Coalition] and tried to get me in here. I've been here almost a month. I'd never been homeless before. I'm fifty-five." It was apparent that she had yet to fully come to terms with her situation. While Janice is outgoing and spent her days looking for work, Rosa seemed confused and unsure about what her next step should be.

The only man in the group, Robert, was at the shelter with his five-year-old son. He explained that his son's mother was addicted to crack and was physically abusive to both him and his son. He decided he had to leave the wife but had nowhere to go. He ended up at the shelter and had been there for just a week. A former big-rig truck driver, he can no longer work in his field because he has sole custody of a preschool child. He receives unemployment compensation, but was only going to receive one more check before his eligibility expired. He said, "We're here to better ourselves. We're hoping to reincarnate ourselves and we're waiting on the economy. It's just him and I."

This was their second time at the homeless shelter. The first time, they stayed at the shelter for a few weeks, but returned to live with the wife and mother when she assured them that things would be better.

They were not—in fact, they rapidly got much worse. While Robert stated that his wife "used to" hit and punch him before they left the first time, once they came back, she "graduated" to trying to stab him with a butcher knife. Robert said that he would rather be homeless, even with his young son, than subject himself and his son to the abuse they endured at home.

Linda had been at the shelter for ten months, a longer-than-average length of stay. "I took care of my dad for ten years," she said. "I wasn't working. When he passed away, the landlady wanted her rent. I didn't have the rent because I didn't have my father's income." She bounced around, living with a boyfriend for a time and then living with different friends. None of these situations was stable or, in her assessment, even safe. She spent some time with a friend "who was a heroin addict. I would wake up with all sorts of men there. I was accused of interfering with her relationship. I was thrown out at 2 a.m. I walked the streets that night and the next night. I stayed at [the friend's] ex-boyfriend's house and slept there and he brought me here the next day and I've been here ever since. I've just started getting disability and I'm hoping to move out in April. They [the disability payments] are retroactive. I'm fifty-five. I've never been homeless before. I lived with my parents because they needed my help."

Linda's story of becoming homeless after her father died is a common one. Throughout the shelter are middle-aged and older people who had a place to live until the parent or relative that they had spent their lives with died. In these situations, we've learned, there is typically no money to speak of in a savings account (see Chapter Two), often the home is a rental unit, and the deceased have provided no safety nets for loved ones left behind. Everyone contributed to what economists call the "household welfare function" in their own way, and so long as things remained stable, everyone stayed housed. But when one family member dies, particularly the one who was receiving Social Security or disability payments or some other form of income, the survivors suddenly find that they are unable to continue paying the bills and soon find themselves homeless. Most, interestingly, do not appear to *think* of themselves as homeless until someone tells them to go to the homeless shelter for assistance.

Three of the women in the Coalition focus group had very obvious psychiatric conditions. Throughout the discussion, all three admitted to their diagnoses (although one believes that hers is an inaccurate diagnosis resulting from her former husband paying off the psychiatrists). All three women receive monthly disability checks but cannot live on their own. They discussed in vivid detail such things as the poison running through the water system, the government workers that come on Coalition property to steal their identification, and the acid that the sheets are soaked in. These women are not receiving ongoing medical or psychiatric treatment for their conditions, have no business living at the shelter, yet cannot live independently and have nowhere else to go. Their very existence bespeaks an immense hole in the social safety net for mentally disabled elderly people.

One of these women is sixty-five years old although she looks much older. She is frail and coughed continually throughout the session. She explained, "I was declared mentally disabled in 1991. The stories have been so blown up. My mom destroyed our lives because she was mentally ill." Her story intersperses biographical fact with what can only be described as extreme paranoia and sadness, and it was difficult to tell which was which. Evidently, she has spent most of her adult life in and out of hospitals and in and out of homeless shelters. She is the only "chronically homeless" person in the group. She says she has no family to rely on and adds, "I'm ready for my grave. I now consider myself deceased because I'm so sick." We could not shake off the thought that she would probably take her own life were she strong enough to do so. What is so tragic about her situation is that she needs to be in a facility that can care for her—frankly, she needs a total care environment—but these are scarce and expensive. It was impossible to listen to her story and not realize that her situation is literally hopeless. In all likelihood, she will die in the very shelter where we met her.

We were surprised to learn that some of our participants had family members they could call on for help but chose not to do so. Some said that they did not want to burden their families. This was particularly true when the relative that could potentially provide help was a child or parent. Others had family that, although they lived in the Orlando area, could not provide support because they had to deal with their own issues, be it mental illness, substance abuse, or something else. One participant had two adult children that she said would take her in if they knew she were homeless. However, they both live out of state and "have their own families—their own lives." In her assessment, asking them for help would be a sign of her failure as a mother. She stated she has a cell phone and talks periodically to her adult children, but she will not tell them that she is homeless or that she needs their help.

Although no one in the group had a concrete plan for escaping homelessness, many were optimistic about the future. Many participants thought that the economy would soon improve and that they would be able to secure work and, soon thereafter, housing. When asked if their age might be a negative factor in their search for work, overall the group thought their age was actually an asset. While this may not be realistic, the group thought that their years of experience in their respective fields would help them find jobs once organizations were hiring again.

Most participants in the group were too young to qualify for low-income senior housing. In and around Orlando are a few subsidized housing programs that kick in at age sixty-two, but most are reserved for low-income people over age sixty-five. Like many other homeless people in late middle age, most of our participants are too young to be eligible for programs for older people. In this group, only one participant had a child in his care. Many programs focus on housing parents and children. (In fact, many of these are only for women with children, which will, of course, not help Robert or other men in like situations.)

The women in the group were all single women without children in their care (although, as we have noted, many do in fact have children) and there are few housing programs targeted specifically to them. Several people in the group explicitly stated that they are not looking for government assistance. What they want is employment that will allow them to be self sufficient. Others, however, are desperate for housing. "I feel like now it's all for the older people." Many despair of being in demographic circumstances that prevent them from accessing any of the resources that might be available to other homeless people.

Homeless Stories from Miami

Many stories similar to those recounted above were also heard in focus groups and interviews with the elderly homeless in Miami. Some, however, were different, highlighting other relevant issues, and so are discussed here.

In a focus group we conducted at an emergency shelter in Miami, Shirley discussed her life of drug abuse and the many episodes of homelessness that she has experienced throughout her life. Shirley has been addicted to drugs for decades. She has gone through treatment twice before, but her sobriety has not lasted. She was at an emergency shelter with her daughter and granddaughter. They all lived together, but had recently been evicted and so became a three-generation homeless family living together in a single emergency shelter. Her daughter has had it with her mother's drug abuse and so, it seems, has Shirley. "I'm just tired," she said. Shirley was waiting to be transferred to a residential drug treatment facility in two days. She had been clean for the three weeks that the family had been at the shelter.

Drug and alcohol abuse are common pathways to homelessness among the elderly, just as they are for younger people. As noted, in the Tampa survey of 103 elderly homeless people, about 40 percent cited alcohol abuse as a reason for their homelessness and a small number cited drug abuse as the main reason.

Katarina is a sixty-seven-year-old German-born woman. She spent her adult life traveling around America, working different jobs and finding friends to live with. This worked well for her until about three years ago. She had wanted to come to Miami because of the climate so she could "retire by the beach." However, when she got to Miami she could not find work and realized that the cost of living is very high there. She lived on the beach for approximately a year and a half when she got a thyroid infection and had to go to a shelter. "I stayed on the streets so long because I always heard from people not to go to a shelter. I had to go though." She spent several months in the emergency shelter before being transferred to a transitional housing program for women. Katarina is not like most elderly homeless people. She looks much younger than she is and is very concerned about her appearance. She was fashionably dressed and would never be considered homeless if someone were to look at her. For Katarina, her life has been about freedom, travel, and independence. But now at sixty-seven she finds herself homeless and having to abide by others' rules. "I had a very fascinating life until three years ago." There was, it seems, nothing fascinating or adventuresome about living in a homeless shelter in Miami.

We met Laura at the same shelter. Laura was experiencing homelessness for the first time, but had a lengthy history of alcohol abuse. She had just fled a violent relationship. Laura is fifty-two years old and stated that she had been an alcoholic for over twenty years. She began drinking as a way to cope with her boyfriend's violent outbursts. Although she left that relationship, her subsequent relationships were also filled with violence. One year ago, she became ill and was admitted to a local hospital. Upon her release, she made the decision to quit drinking and to go to a homeless shelter instead of returning to the apartment she shared with her abusive boyfriend. When we spoke, she had been sober for over a year. She was busy taking courses in understanding domestic violence and was participating in counseling sessions to come to terms with her past.

In a study of homeless Florida women, 24.1 percent of women aged fifty and older said that violence done by an adult partner was one of, or was the main, reason for their homelessness (see Chapter Five). For many homeless women, like Laura, domestic violence has been a part of their lives for years and even decades. All too many of these women are homeless as a result of violence. Laura could have returned home, but she chose to go to a homeless shelter instead of returning to a violent and abusive home situation.

Elderly Poverty

For many elderly homeless, homelessness comes after years of living in or very near poverty. Like the rates of homelessness, the poverty rate among older Americans is low in comparison to other subgroups, at least if the conventional federal poverty standard is used (but see the discussion of poverty rates and definitions in Chapter Two). Still, while the overall numbers may be small, for elderly people who are experiencing poverty and homelessness, this is scarcely any consolation.

Many characteristics can put an elder person at greater risk of living in poverty. Over the past twenty-five years, about 40 percent of America's elderly population experienced at least one year of living below the poverty line at some time between the ages of sixty and ninety (Rank and Hirsch 1999). This implies that many of the elderly may not live in poverty in a given year but are living precipitously close. While point-in-time counts show an apparently low number of elderly poor, the lifetime rates of experiencing poverty are much more telling. Those who were black or unmarried demonstrated the highest likelihood of living in poverty.

Bill, an African American male in his sixties, is not, and never has been, homeless. He is retired and owns outright his modest home in Sanford (a small town north of Orlando). He raised his three children in that home with his wife, who is now deceased. He now lives alone and collects Social Security. We met Bill at the free weekly dinner service hosted in a local community center. The majority of the people at this meal service are homeless people. Some, though, are not, and they come to the dinner service as a way to make ends meet. "I'm not homeless and I don't want to be." Bill talked about the impact of rising costs such as property tax and utility increases. He could account for every dollar he receives from Social Security. Even a five dollar increase on a monthly bill has a major impact on his finances. Being able to eat a good meal for free makes a definite difference, and he is a regular at this feeding program as a result. Bill has struggled, but has managed to stay in his home—so far. For many others, this proves not to be possible. In the

Tampa study, the majority cited not being able to pay the rent or to pay the security and beginning costs of a rental unit as a major cause of their homelessness.

Another important consideration in elderly poverty is the way that poverty is calculated, as discussed in Chapter Two. The current federal poverty formula is driven entirely by the cost of food. Although adjusted annually for inflation, the poverty formula does not take into account such things as medical costs, which have increased much more rapidly than the overall cost of living. A revised formula that *does* more adequately reflect the true cost of living nearly doubles the poverty rate among the aged while the rate drops in other age groups.

This highlights the problem of elderly people living near the economic edge. Since they do not quite meet the current definition of poverty, they do not qualify for many assistance programs. Not that it would matter that much if they did. The current maximum monthly Supplemental Security Income payment for a single person is $623 (which is well beneath the poverty threshold for a single individual). Using the common guidelines for acceptable housing costs, an individual living on SSI could only afford to pay $187 a month in rent. Housing at this rate is nearly impossible to find—in Orlando or anywhere else. An extremely affordable subsidized housing high-rise for seniors in downtown Orlando still charges nearly $500 per month to rent a small one-bedroom unit and the waiting list for these units is about one year.

The Lucky Ones

A final focus group was conducted with seven people over age sixty-two residing at Osceola Villas, a low income housing complex for seniors in Osceola County, the most rural county in the Orlando metro area. The original complex contains thirty-six subsidized units for seniors. Recently a second phase was completed that adds fifty additional subsidized apartments, all for low income seniors. Both complexes are full and have long waiting lists which are now closed. Those who do reside there are very grateful. They enthusiastically discussed all of the services that they take advantage of, including Meals on Wheels (which serves 1,500 meals a day in this area), transportation, the local health clinic, and the mobile clinic. "Of all of these services that are offered, we all take advantage of the housing. One of the reasons is the rent is so reasonable. We could not live the way we live with the incomes we have."

They also discussed the services they were *not* getting. One woman explained that she needs information on transportation "because I need to go to the beauty shop." Many of their unmet needs seemed trivial in comparison to the other needs that have been discussed elsewhere in this chapter. But being provided with affordable housing frees them from concerns about where to live and thus allows them to have these other, seemingly frivolous needs. This is not to say that no one in this complex struggles. Many do. One woman explained that she has no health insurance but is not yet old enough to qualify for Medicare. She relies on the mobile health clinic. "It has been a lifesaver for me. It really has."

Everyone in the complex has some income source since this is a precondition for living there. (These are, after all, subsidized units, not free housing—everyone must have some income and be willing to devote 30 percent of that income to their housing costs.) For most, the income source is Social Security or disability pensions. Carol discussed her own financial struggles. "My husband worked for years at Ford, and you know how much he gets a month? Ninety-seven dollars." They also collect Social Security, but have difficulty making ends meet. They rely on every service available: free food, transportation, medical care, and medication. Without these free services, they would have to make very difficult choices.

All our participants discussed people they knew who were not living in the complex and who therefore had to make those very choices. "My friend just told me that she and her husband couldn't take their insulin for two weeks because they didn't have the money. So now he's in the hospital—dying." This story understandably upset everyone in the group. "When you're old and have health issues and have lost it all, it's hard to find a place to live." They talked about other seniors they know that live in "places infested with rats and roaches. We're very fortunate." They do know how lucky they are and know that the need is immense. Near the end of the conversation, one of the residents made an interesting remark about waiting lists for subsidized housing: "Unless you're homeless, you have to wait."

Elizabeth would certainly have to disagree with this sentiment. She is a sixty-seven-year-old woman who was residing in a transitional shelter for women in Orlando when we interviewed her. This was her second time being homeless. She is not disabled, physically or mentally, and has no substance abuse issues. Still, living in the transitional shelter, she was overwhelmed and confused. She did not articulate any options other than remaining in the shelter and she had no idea what the future might bring. She had been living in the shelter for several months and had no prospects for permanent housing. Her homelessness did not move her up on anybody's waiting list, and in fact, Elizabeth was not even aware that there were programs whose waiting lists she needed to be on.

The idea that homeless people receive all of the benefits and that those who are working or have managed to maintain housing receive no assistance is not uncommon, at least not among the elders at Osceola Villas. At sixty-seven years old and receiving Social Security, Elizabeth certainly qualifies for subsidized housing, but so do so many others. There is simply more demand than supply. Many of the residents at Osceola Villas were on a waiting list for years before they were offered housing in the complex (and none of them was homeless while they were waiting). Many eligible elderly homeless people, like Elizabeth, are evidently unaware of programs that might assist them, a failure of case management if not society at large.

Concluding Thoughts

Although the elderly homeless comprise a small portion of the homeless population, they are still a major concern. America is growing older and the proportion of homeless that are elderly is expected to rise. If the poverty definition were to be changed to reflect the true costs of modern living, then the number of elderly people in poverty would nearly double overnight. While the foreclosure crisis will by all accounts abate, many of the other reasons for poverty and homelessness among the elderly will persist. Moreover, America is aging. While for the last several decades the rates of the elderly poor and homeless have been relatively low, this has already begun to change. Although there has been political discourse on redefining the poverty rate, the issue of the elderly homeless has gotten little attention to date among researchers and policy makers. While the elderly often become homeless for the same reasons as younger homeless people do, their needs may be very different, and likewise the solution: while job training may make sense for a twenty-five-year-old, it may not be realistic for someone who is nearing or past sixty. Policies that address the unique needs of the elderly homeless, and programs that can prevent the elderly from becoming homeless in the first place, need to be developed sooner rather than later.

This, to be sure, is a daunting task. In 1998, the National Symposium on Homeless Research concluded that the "elder homeless need a complex and coordinated system of care that includes: specialized outreach, help in meeting basic needs and sometimes routine activities of daily living, 24-hour crisis assistance, health and mental health care, transportation services, assistance with the development of social relationships and social ties, and a range of housing options with easy access to services." In the decade since, it is clear that these recommendations have become more urgent, not less, and yet further from political reality, not nearer.

Notes

1. Portions of this chapter are liberally adapted from Donley (2010).
2. Since the sheltered homeless are much easier to enumerate and survey than the unsheltered homeless, the relatively small percentage of elderly homeless living in shelters, as revealed in the Tampa survey, may also be partly responsible for the elderly "deficit."
3. It bears mention that the Burt survey only covers service-utilizing homeless people, those who sleep in homeless shelters, eat in soup kitchens, or who are otherwise accessible through the organizations that serve homeless people. If, as seems likely, "rough sleepers" are more likely to be non-users of homeless services, then their numbers must be underrepresented in Burt's data.
4. Medical overutilization of emergency rooms by the homeless is well documented and widely discussed. Less well known is that homeless people also frequently use emergency room (ER) waiting areas as temporary overnight shelter. With four and five hour waits for medical attention now the norm in many urban ERs, it is a place where homeless people can get in from the weather and sit in relatively safe, comfortable chairs for many hours without fear of being challenged as to why they are there. On overutilization of ERs by homeless people, see Pearson, Bruggman and Haukoos 2007. On use of ERs as shelter, see Zane 2009.
5. There are many inexpensive extended stay motels in and around Orlando that cater to the economically marginal and even social service programs that cater to the "motel homeless."

10

Mean as a Snake, Crazy as a Shithouse Rat:
Public Perceptions of the Homeless[1]

To this point, our focus has been largely on Central Florida's poor, near-poor, and homeless populations. In this and the next two chapters, we shift our attention to larger factions relevant to the general drift of our arguments: to the public at large and its views of the homeless (the present chapter); to those who volunteer their time, talent, and treasure to the homeless (Chapter 11); and finally, to public policy-makers (Chapter 12). To the extent that a common theme can be discerned in these chapters, it is that perceptions influence behaviors; and when the perception is that poor and homeless people are unworthy, undeserving, or morally backward, the result is regressive and generally unhelpful social policies.

For example, in the popular mind, homelessness and crime are closely interwoven. Homeless shelters and other locales frequented by homeless people are routinely avoided because they are perceived as crime hot spots, and homeless people themselves are routinely avoided because of their real or imagined criminal potential, their sometimes unsavory appearance and odor, their inebriation, or their mental illness. (In any case, *apparently* homeless people are routinely avoided for these reasons, although we hasten to add that many homeless people are women and children, and that many homeless men go out of their way not to look homeless.) While it is obviously true that some homeless people do commit crimes, one of the few real studies of the topic showed that the typical arrest of a homeless person is for a minor offense such as vagrancy or shoplifting (Snow, Anderson and Baker 1989). And yet, consider the following from the Cambridge, Massachusetts, police department:

The Crime Analysis Unit understands that the most common complaint of the average citizen or business involves "visible" problems such as public intoxication, aggressive panhandling, and sleeping on public benches—not necessarily harmful or malicious incidents. However, we suspect that if the average Cambridge citizen or business comprehended the extent of crimes committed by homeless individuals—particularly in the Central Square area—their priorities regarding homeless crime would rapidly shift. (http://www.cambridgema.gov/CPD/reports/2003/ annual/adobe/homeless.pdf)

One is struck by the undocumented innuendo in the quoted passage. And yet police departments across the country routinely promulgate the view that people experiencing homelessness are dangerous and should be approached with caution. In Orlando, city police often visit senior centers located near homeless facilities and gathering spots to warn elders of the potential danger. Indeed, the perception that homeless people commit, and the facilities that serve them attract, both property theft and violent crime is one major reason why citizens and local associations so often oppose the siting of homeless facilities in their neighborhoods.

People may be perceived as homeless when in fact they are not. This is most relevant in the case of panhandlers. As we see later, many in the general public think of "panhandler" and "homeless person" as virtually synonymous. In reality, most panhandlers are not homeless and most homeless people do not panhandle, as Chapter Three took pains to document, but it is not clear that any aspect of this reality is reflected in the outlooks of the average citizen. Thus, someone could have an unpleasant—indeed, threatening—experience with a panhandler, assume that the panhandler was homeless, and let the experience influence his or her views of the homeless as a class, however unfair, misguided, or bigoted that might be.

In general, homeless people are viewed in one of two ways. The first is that they have chosen their lifestyle and have no one but themselves to blame. The second sees the homeless as victims of macro-level forces: a shortage of affordable housing, extreme poverty, mental and physical disabilities, and a lack of social service assistance. Doubtlessly, there is some truth in both perspectives. When thinking about homelessness and crime, however, viewpoints become less polarized; people want the homeless to be helped in some abstract way, but often view them as dangerous simultaneously. Thus, public perception frequently seems to equate homelessness and crime, whether this belief is empirically supported or not.

Many people are afraid of the homeless or (better) are afraid of what they perceive the homeless to be. The most visibly homeless are often recognizable because they are dirty, reek of alcohol, or cart around their belongings. Lacking a place to go during the day when the shelters are closed, they might sit for hours on a bench, in a public library, or in a park, all alone, apparently lost in psychosis, and potentially menacing. Their visibility, appearance, and demeanor make many people nervous. And nervous people easily assume the worst.

This negative view of the homeless leads to NIMBYism (Not in My Back Yard), a phenomenon often apparent in a community's opposition to a proposed shelter siting in their neighborhood. In one city (see Snow et al. 1989), residents opposed the building of a shelter because of their fears that the homeless would commit crimes, including raping neighborhood women. Who wants a gang of rapists moving in across the street? Efforts to relocate Orlando's largest homeless facility in an area near a local high school were opposed on the grounds that the men utilizing the facility contained child molesters, pedophiles, drug dealers, and other unsavory types who would pose a serious danger to students. (Interestingly, homeless men also opposed this site because of their fear that gangs of high-school teens would threaten their physical safety!)

Online sources also reveal peoples' fears of the homeless. One aptly named site, BumFinder.com, "enables anybody to locate and discover areas frequented by Homeless People, Vagrants, and Bums so they can avoid those areas to feel more safe and secure." The text on the site states "major cities around the country aren't doing enough to keep their citizens safe from Homeless People, Vagrants and Bums." The site includes the ability to click on a city name and obtain a satellite map with all known concentrations of homeless individuals shown. These data are apparently compiled by "tips" sent in from people who visit the site and weigh in with reports of homeless hot spots in their own cities.

One video available on YouTube.com, a preview for a supposed upcoming short film on damage done by homeless people, includes the following text posted by the creator: "I am sick and tired of the false notion that most bums are war heroes. Most of them are dangerous criminals that have never served in our armed forces. ... We need to bus them out of the country" (http://www.youtube.com/watch?v=nIeIOxFo9sQ)—as if the federal government had some right to deport unsavory U.S. citizens to Mexico or Canada. Elsewhere in the video, homeless people are referred to as "trash," "beasts," and "monsters." Although sites such as these do not show the number of people that fear the homeless, they do illustrate a common perception that homeless people are dangerous and should be avoided.

As evidenced by numerous studies (e.g., Metraux and Culhane 2004, 2006; Greenberg and Rosenheck 2008), it is true that many homeless people, especially younger homeless men with lots of accumulated street time and frequent contacts with the mental health system, have incarceration histories, sometimes quite extensive ones; and many incarcerated people were homeless at the point of their incarceration. But these same studies also show that most of the crimes homeless people commit are non-violent offenses such as loitering, public intoxication, theft, or shoplifting, not rape, pedophilia, armed robbery, or assault. Many cities, among them Miami and Orlando, have recognized that their local criminal justice institutions are in fact the largest mental health treatment facilities in the area. If proper, effective treatment for mentally ill homeless offenders could be found, large chunks of the local "crime problem" would disappear.

One assumes that the media must play some role in shaping popular perceptions of the homeless and other indigent groups. Surely there are more people who read about homelessness in the papers or hear stories on television than have day-to-day encounters with homeless people. Such, in any case, are the conclusions of two recent studies of media influences on popular perceptions. One of them, *Framing Class* (Kendall 2005), discusses how the media represent members of various classes in very different ways. She argues that television news programs, particularly the "info-tainment" programs and newspaper stories, promote and celebrate higher class people while propagating negative stereotypes about people in the lower classes. A major part of this is "media framing," the way in which media of all genres frame a story before it is aired or printed. In the process of framing, the tone that will be conveyed, the images that will be shown, and the terms that will be used are all determined. It is in this process that the presentation of stories about people from different classes is shaped.

By analyzing *New York Times* articles, Kendall showed how homeless people are presented. She determined that while those in the upper classes are discussed in great detail, the poor or homeless are often presented as numbers, not as people; and as problems, not as members of a community. Her analysis showed that poor people are typically portrayed as "losers, welfare dependents, mentally ill persons or criminals" (p. 94) and that poverty was frequently linked with both crime and suicide.

Another recent study (Borchard 2005) also examined media representations of the homeless via content analysis. This study focused solely on the homeless, was confined to Las Vegas, and used both newspaper articles and homeless service providers' mailings and other documents. The study revealed three main themes in press coverage: first, homeless men should be feared; second, they should be given sympathy; and third, they should be both feared and pitied. There is obviously some synergy between these media themes and popular perceptions of the homeless.

There is limited national data available on perceptions of the homeless, most of it contained in a survey from the early 1990s, the so-called Link survey (Link et al. 1995) that has been reanalyzed by numerous investigators (Donley 2008; Lee, Link and Toro 1991; Toro and McDonell 1992). This survey showed that domiciled respondents recognize multiple causes of homelessness but tend to emphasize structural forces and bad luck over individual deficits, a more nuanced understanding of homelessness than of poverty in general (usually attributed to personal failings). The public also perceives the characteristics of homeless people in reasonably accurate terms and holds mostly favorable views towards them (Lee, Tyler and Wright 2010). Further analysis shows that whites, males, and political conservatives are more likely to believe in individual causes, hold negative opinions, and endorse restrictive measures to address the problem than non-whites, females, and liberals. Virtually any kind of direct exposure to homelessness erodes stereotypes and promotes more positive attitudes.

As already indicated, most people must get the bulk of their information about homelessness from the news media. In addition to what we have already reported about media coverage, it has also been shown that the volume of coverage follows an annual cycle, cresting during the holiday season as ritualized concern for the unfortunate; over the long term, coverage has declined markedly since the peak year of 1987, although it remains higher than it was prior to 1980 (Buck, Toro, and Ramos 2004). There has also been an apparent trend in the content of coverage. Stories during the early 1980s portrayed the homeless sympathetically, as challenged by circumstances beyond anyone's control and hence deserving of aid. In the past two decades, in contrast, coverage of homeless issues has been noticeably harsher, with more emphasis on deviance and disorder created by the homeless. These peculiarities of coverage often appear to be at odds with the public's more sympathetic and sophisticated views.

As indicated, the Link survey is just about the only national data available that deal with the public's views on the homeless. While those data are now nearly twenty years old, they remain useful for several reasons. First, the Link survey focuses on the homeless as a threat or potential threat. Second, most surveys of opinions about the homeless ask about the reasons behind homelessness or the causes of homelessness rather than perceptions of the homeless themselves. Third, despite a fairly large secondary literature, much of the data has not previously been analyzed. Fourth, the survey contains questions about media consumption that allow us to analyze the media's affects on popular perceptions. The simple fact that the Link survey continues to generate secondary literature is itself proof that to date, nothing superior has been produced.

These points made, a large chunk of what follows is our own reanalysis of the Link data, with one emphasis on racial differences in perceptions of the homeless and a second emphasis on media effects. Following this reanalysis, we then present an analysis of a survey we conducted in 2009 in the Orlando metropolitan area that was designed specifically as a local replication of the Link survey.

Black-White Differences in Perceptions

All of the papers Link and his associates produced out of the survey, and nearly all of the secondary analyses, have been based exclusively on the white subsample. However, the black sub-sample represents 10 percent of the total sample, and black-white differences in perceptions of the homeless turn out to be quite interesting. The original study found that whites' estimate of the percentage of the homeless population that is black was positively correlated with the belief that homeless people are dangerous. An obvious question: Do blacks feel the same way? If not, what variables are significant in blacks' beliefs that homeless people are dangerous?

One series of questions asked respondents to estimate what percentage of the homeless are black, Hispanic, male, etc. Among whites, mean responses were 42 percent black, 32 percent Hispanic, and 59 percent male. This question reflects what people believe the percentages to be, not what they actually are, but as a matter of fact, all these would qualify as pretty good guesses. The same is true in the Orlando survey, as we see later.

The outcome variable of interest is the "perceived dangerousness" of homeless people, a simple summated scale composed of six component statements with responses ranging from definitely true to definitely false. The components:

1. it is important to remember that homeless may be dangerous,
2. homeless are more likely to commit violent crimes than other people,

3. homeless people are no more dangerous than other people,
4. it is natural to be afraid of a street person,
5. in the interest of public safety, homeless people should not be allowed to gather in public places, and
6. if I knew a person had been homeless I would be less likely to trust him or her.

The resulting scale was normed for the number of components answered and thus ranges from one to six where higher numbers mean higher perceived dangerousness.

There are some noteworthy patterns evident in the individual items. Over half of the respondents agreed (said it was true) that it is natural to be afraid of a street person (62 percent). At the same time, majorities did **not** feel that "the homeless may be dangerous" (52 percent false) or that they "are more likely to commit more violent crimes" than others (73 percent false). Moreover, while 69 percent stated that the homeless are no more dangerous than others, 41 percent stated that they would be less likely to trust someone if they knew that they had been homeless. Across the six items, then, the percentage giving a response indicative of a perception that the homeless are dangerous varied from 27 percent (more likely to commit violent crimes) to 62 percent (natural to be afraid of street people).

In the original analysis of the white subsample, the perceived percentage of blacks in the homeless population was a significant predictor of perceived dangerousness in every model tested. That is, the higher the perceived percentage of blacks among the homeless, the more dangerous the homeless were perceived to be. Gender (females more fearful) and age (elderly more fearful) were also significant in all models. Political orientation (liberal to conservative), a belief in structural versus individual causes of homelessness, and a measure of social desirability were all negatively correlated with the belief that homeless people are dangerous. The consistently strong effect in all models for a social desirability measure implies that the response that homeless people are **not** dangerous reflects both social desirability bias and true attitudes.

When we replicated the above analyses on the black sub-sample, we discovered interesting differences. First, the general demographic profile of the black subsample was similar to that of whites. But there were some differences in the perceptions of homeless demography. Among blacks, the mean perceived percentage of blacks in the homeless population was about 10 percentage points higher (52 percent) than it was for whites, while the perceived Hispanic (29 percent) and male percentages (56 percent) were both slightly lower. Black respondents also reported slightly higher scores on structural causes, social desirability, and perceived dangerousness measures, although these differences too were not large.

We then ran the exact same regressions as in the original study but just on the black subsample. Among blacks, the perceived percentage of blacks among the homeless was *not* significantly related to the perception of homeless people as dangerous. Indeed, the only variable that was positively and significantly correlated with the perception of homeless as dangerous was the perceived percentage of the homeless who were *men*. (As with whites, education, political orientation, and social desirability were all negatively associated with perceived dangerousness.)

The general result, then, is quite interesting: Whites fear the homeless because they perceive the homeless to be black. Blacks fear the homeless because they perceive the homeless to be men. Does that not say a great deal about race and gender in contemporary America?

Media Effects

Over 90 percent of the Link sample reported at least some exposure to homelessness through newspaper articles or TV shows. A follow-up asked, "How important has the media been in the formation of your opinions on homelessness?" Over half (52 percent) said the media had been very or somewhat important and only 12 percent said the media was not important in the formation of their views.

We examined the effect of newspaper and TV exposure on perceived dangerousness first by simple two-variable crosstabs with all six items in the perceived dangerousness scale. We found consistent and significant, although relatively small, differences. In all six cases, the greater the exposure to newspaper articles, the less likely were the homeless to be perceived as dangerous, exactly the opposite to what one would expect given the generally negative coverage of homeless issues in the media in recent years. Effects for TV exposure were generally weaker and in the opposite direction. And when we looked at the self-assessed importance of the media in forming one's views, we found that the higher the rated importance, the less likely were the homeless to be perceived as dangerous.

Although no clear and consistent pattern dominated these results, some weak trends were evident. Overall, greater exposure to homelessness through newspaper articles was positively correlated with the belief that the homeless are not dangerous. For television, the pattern was weaker but generally in the opposite direction; greater television exposure was related to a higher perceived dangerousness. But when we dumped everything into a multiple regression equation, the media variables completely wiped out. Perceptions of homeless demography were significant; the respondent's race was also significant; and political liberalism, belief in structural causes, and social desirability were significant. But none of the media exposure variables showed statistically significant effects in either direction. Exposure to media coverage of homelessness does not appear to affect people's opinions of the homeless as dangerous, net of all other factors.

Why not? When social scientists first started investigating the effects of mass media back in the forties and fifties, it quickly became obvious that people were selectively attentive to media in the first place—paying more attention to outlets and content that were consistent with their *a priori* opinions and less attention to media that contradicted those opinions. "Reinforcement, not conversion" was the consensus finding, i.e., because of selective attention, the principal effect of the media was to reinforce pre-existing outlooks, not to convert people from one outlook to its opposite. Likewise, we suspect, with opinions about the homeless. People with generally progressive views will seek out media consistent with those outlooks; those with negative, punitive, or fearful opinions will find no shortage of media content that sustains and reinforces such beliefs.

The Rights of Homeless People

A final line of analysis that can be pursued with the Link data is the perceived rights of homeless people to occupy and use public space. There are three questions of interest in the survey: whether the homeless have a right to panhandle, a right to sleep in public places, and a right to set up tents in public parks.

General public loathing of beggary is evident in that most people in the survey (69 percent) agreed that the homeless do *not* have the right to panhandle. Only eight percent thought that they definitely had the right to do so, an opinion shared, incidentally, by the Supreme Court. Opinions regarding the right to sleep in public places were markedly different, with half the sample affirming this right and half denying it. But this did not extend to the right to set up tents in public places, with about two-thirds saying the homeless definitely or probably did *not* have this right.

As would be anticipated, people who perceived the homeless as dangerous were significantly less likely to affirm any of these rights than people whose views of the homeless were more benign. This was apparent in simple crosstabs and also held up in multivariate analyses. Indeed, the perception of the homeless as dangerous was a consistently strong predictor of peoples' opinions about the rights of the homeless in every model we tested; in most cases, this was the strongest predictor. In general, the patterns of association between predictor variables and acknowledging homeless peoples' rights were quite similar to those reported earlier for perceived dangerousness.

Update: The 2009 Orlando Area Survey

In July-August 2009, we surveyed 483 adult residents of Orange, Osceola, and Seminole Counties to determine current public perceptions of the homeless in Central Florida and opinions about regional agencies that serve this population. Much of the survey content was taken directly from the Link survey so that meaningful comparisons would be possible; other questions were taken from a Miami survey done earlier in 2009; and several questions were developed specifically for this survey.

It needs to be emphasized that while this survey was being done, the national and regional economies were in turmoil and the local media were running near-daily stories on home foreclosures, food banks being overrun by formerly middle class people, and people being forced into homelessness because of job loss, eviction, layoffs, down-sizing, and related misfortunes. Media coverage of homeless issues and media depictions of homeless people were generally quite sympathetic (much like the media coverage of people rendered homeless by the hurricanes that periodically sweep through Florida) and this must have surely had some effect on public outlooks about homeless issues.

Seriousness of the Problem

One question we pursued was whether or not homelessness was considered to be a significant problem in central Florida. Unambiguously, our Central Florida respondents confirmed that homelessness is a serious regional issue. A majority (55 percent) described homelessness as a "major problem" in Central Florida, 34 percent described it as a minor problem, and the remainder either said it was not a problem (6 percent) or had no opinion (5 percent). An overwhelming 90 percent agreed that, nationally, the homeless problem is getting worse (of those, 59 percent said the problem had gotten "a lot worse").

Correlational analysis showed that women and the better educated were more likely to perceive homelessness as a serious regional issue than men and those with less education. The more people said they had seen, read, or heard stories about homelessness in the media, the more likely they were to regard the problem as serious. Those who personally knew someone who had been or was homeless (40 percent of the sample, incidentally) were also more likely to see homelessness as a serious problem. Interestingly, no measure of perceived dangerousness was correlated with the measure of problem seriousness—people think the problem is serious whether they believe the homeless are dangerous or not. The more serious the problem was perceived to be, the more likely respondents were to agree that the region's municipal and county governments should do more to address the issue.

Homeless Demography and Perceived Dangerousness

One of the more interesting sequences in the Link survey was the series of questions asking people to estimate demographic characteristics of the homeless. We expanded the series a bit and got these results (these are the mean percentages as estimated by our respondents): men, 65 percent; married, 35 percent; Hispanic, 25 percent; black, 38 percent; and with a criminal background, about 40 percent. Depending on how "criminal background" is defined, all of these median perceptions are close to the correct percentages. The only minor exception is that the percentage of males is probably somewhat overstated.

In the national sample of whites, the perceived racial composition of the homeless was significantly related to the perception of dangerousness; among non-whites, the critical variable was the perceived male percentage. Neither of these patterns was found in the Central Florida data. Rather, significant correlations with perceived dangerousness were observed only for the question about the estimated percent that are *married*, and then only for whites. On two of three measures of perceived dangerousness, as the estimated married percentage increased, white perceptions of the homeless as dangerous decreased. Also, in the total sample, the perceived percentage of men among the homeless was positively and significantly correlated with one of the three measures of perceived dangerousness, but the correlation was weak ($r = .13$).

Several possible explanations for the differences between our results and Link's original findings come to mind. First, our sample sizes are smaller, so it is harder for the Central Florida correlations to achieve statistical significance. In favor of this hypothesis, the *signs* of the coefficients in our data and in Link's are broadly comparable. Second, it is possible that Central Florida is just different from the rest of the nation. Third, it is possible that in the past twenty years, opinions about the dangerousness of the homeless have improved to the point that correlations that were once significant no longer are. Fourth, Link's survey was done in the early 1990s, a time of prosperity; our survey was done in the middle of the worst economic downturn since the Great Depression. Peoples' opinions about the dangerousness of the homeless may be different today simply because they have a different image of "the homeless" in mind.

Table 10.1 shows the comparison on the three comparable items, and while it is clear that attitudes are different now, the differences are not all of a piece. Specifically, more of our respondents thought it is "important to remember that the homeless may be dangerous" than Link's respondents did (60 percent to 48 percent). On the other hand, more of his respondents thought it was "natural" to fear street people than our respondents did (62 percent to 40 percent). Finally, opinions that the homeless are more likely to commit violent crime seem to be about equal in both groups (27 percent and 21 percent). So change is evident, but it is not all change in one direction.

We included additional questions about what things were true of "most homeless people." Except for the 60 percent who felt it was "important to remember that the homeless may be dangerous," these items revealed a generally sympathetic Central Florida public (much to the surprise of many local opinion leaders, among whom there is a perception that most of their constituents despise the homeless). Specifically, there was a very strong consensus that "it is hard for homeless people to be safe and

Table 10.1
Perceptions of the Homeless as Dangerous:
Link's Results Compared to the Central Florida Results

	Percent Definitely or Probably True	
	Link Survey	UCF Survey
Even when homeless people seem all right, it is important to remember that they may be dangerous.	48	60
It is "natural" to fear homeless street people	62	40
The homeless are more likely than others to commit violent crime	27	21

free from harm" (79 percent thought this was definitely or probably true of most homeless people)—clearly, a perception that homeless people live dangerous lives whether they are themselves dangerous or not. And interestingly, a like percentage (79 percent) felt that "most homeless people could take care of a home." There was also majority sentiment that most of the homeless have "good job skills" (59 percent). Majorities on the order of 60 percent also *rejected* the ideas that most homeless people can be identified by appearance alone (61 percent false or probably false) and, as already noted, that it is somehow "natural" to fear homeless people (62 percent false or probably false). Finally, very large majorities *rejected* the idea that homeless programs are too expensive (20 percent definitely or probably true) and that "it is hard to understand how anyone becomes homeless" (19 percent definitely or probably true). The current economic downturn, it seems, has made it very easy for people to understand how other people can become homeless.

Correlational analyses of these perceptions of the homeless did not reveal much of interest. Unsurprisingly, "more positive" attitudes about the homeless (they have good job skills, could take care of a home, etc.) tend to be significantly and negatively related to "less positive" attitudes (the homeless may be dangerous, homeless programs are too expensive, etc.). We thought that personal knowledge of a homeless person would be positively related to more positive attitudes and negatively related to less positive attitudes, but no. Apparently, just knowing someone who is or has been homeless matters less than just what homeless person you've known. There was a weak tendency for better educated respondents to embrace more positive opinions and reject more negative ones, but this was not always true, and the correlations were only rarely significant. Gender made an occasional difference (women more positive), but religion, age, and other demographic variables were insignificant in all comparisons.

We also asked our respondents whether their opinions of the homeless had changed "in the last year." About one in three (35 percent) said yes. Of those whose opinions changed, 95 percent said they had become more sympathetic. The declining economy and its effects in making people homeless was the most significant reason given for changing attitudes (61 percent). No other reason was cited by more than 5 percent. As economic times worsen, people find it easy to understand that people can become homeless through no fault of their own, and this recognition makes many people more sympathetic.

Portrayal of Homelessness in the Media

As in the Link data, Central Floridians see, read, or hear stories in the media related to homelessness quite regularly: 15 percent daily, 30 percent at least weekly, 28 percent monthly, and the remainder less often. Overwhelmingly, these media accounts are seen as showing homeless people in a negative light (73 percent). But in fact, heavier consumers of homelessness content in the media were more likely to describe homelessness as a major problem in Florida and more likely to believe that nationally, the problem was getting worse. On the other hand, consistent with our analysis of the Link data, media consumption was not significantly related to peoples' opinions about the homeless (whether positive or negative) or their perceptions of homeless demographics. (The one exception: heavier media consumers estimated lower Hispanic percentages than lighter consumers.)

Panhandling

For all the political and media attention panhandling in Central Florida has received in recent years, only 48 percent of our respondents say that panhandling is a problem in the region; 43 percent say it is not a problem; the remainder had no opinion. More than half (58 percent) believe that most panhandlers are also homeless; 42 percent disagree. A total of 87 percent also agree that "most homeless people panhandle at least from time to time." Opinion was about evenly divided between the view that people panhandle because they are poor and have no alternative (39 percent) versus the opinion that panhandling is "an easy way to pick up cash" (45 percent), with 15 percent saying they didn't know or giving some other answer.

These perceptions of panhandling are strongly at odds with studies of panhandling both locally and nationally. Michael Scott, former Chief of Police in Lauderhill, FL, prepared a report on panhandling, titled *Panhandling*, for the U.S. Department of Justice in 2002, a study whose results we discussed in Chapter Three. Contrary to the beliefs of a substantial majority of Central Floridians, "only a small percentage of homeless people panhandle, and only a small percentage of panhandlers are homeless."

We also asked respondents how frequently, if ever, they gave money directly to people on the street. Almost half (46 percent) said never, whereas one in ten gives once or more per week. Those who said they gave were asked how much money they gave "each time you give." The median response was about two dollars.

Multiplying the frequency of giving times the median amount given times the number of adults in the three counties surveyed times the number of workdays in the year yields an estimate of the total amount of money given to panhandlers in the region annually. The resulting estimates are 12,700,000 annual gifts to regional panhandlers, and with a median gift of $2.06, that generates an estimate of $26,000,000 given to panhandlers annually. It is hard to take this estimate very seriously, and in fact, when we announced the result, no one did. Obviously, the estimate is fraught with uncertainties. The "how often" question almost certainly generates socially desirable responses rather than completely accurate ones, and there may also be a tendency to exaggerate. For example, it is easy to see how someone who is panhandled a couple of times each week, week after week, might respond, "Every damned day!" And once every third or fourth week might easily be remembered as "once a week." There is no corresponding reason why people would understate the frequency (or amount) of giving, so all the measurement error would be in the same direction (overstatement). Another uncertainty lies in converting the categories of "how often" into numbers of gifts per year; still another arises from possible exaggerations in how much people give when they do give. Certainly, few if any people keep systematic track of how often and how much they give to panhandlers, so the questions can only elicit crude guesses at best.

Twenty-six million a year breaks down to about $70,000 per day. Based on our studies of Orlando's "woods people" (Chapter Seven), who are apparently the most frequent panhandlers within the local homeless population, a daily take of, say, $50 would be a pretty good day. To make the numbers add up, this would require 1,400 panhandlers a day somewhere in the three counties, and that too seems like an unreasonably large number. On the other hand, no one has ever tried to count the region's panhandlers, so who can really say?

Obviously, data of this sort are useful, at best, in suggesting an order of magnitude for the total dollars given to panhandlers in the region each year. If all the measurement bias and exaggeration are in the direction of overstatement, which seems certain, and we therefore reduce the estimate by half, we still get a figure near $10 million annually. If a reduction by half does not seem enough and we reduce the result by half again, the annual order of magnitude is still somewhere in the millions. Given these data, it is a pretty safe conclusion that the annual panhandling total is at least as large as (or somewhere respectably near) the annual operating budget of the Coalition for the Homeless of Central Florida (about $3.5 million).

As a point of comparison, an identical series of questions in a Miami survey earlier in 2009 generated an annual estimate there of a total nearer to $40 million a year in gifts to panhandlers. The biggest difference between the Miami and Orlando area data is the much lower percentage in Miami who said they never gave to panhandlers: 22 percent versus our 46 percent. Otherwise, the data are very similar.

In 2004, the Orlando Mayor's Working Committee on the Homeless recommended that "The City should create a public awareness campaign to educate the community regarding the issue of panhandling, as has been done successfully in cities such as Memphis; Columbia; and Savannah. The results of this campaign would be to discourage panhandling and encourage meaningful community contributions to established care providers." No action was ever taken on this recommendation, which seems unfortunate since established care providers may be missing out on millions of dollars of potential annual revenue. The story of the Mayor's Working Committee and its report is recounted in Chapter Twelve.

Respondents who said they gave to panhandlers were asked why. One in three said they "felt sorry" for panhandlers, and one in four said "I think it is the right thing to do." No other single reason was given by more than one or two percent. Another question asked whether people ever gave food directly to people on the street: 62 percent said no, never; the remainder said this was something they did at least occasionally, with positive responses clustering in the "once a month" to "once or twice a year" range.

What Does the Community Need to Do?

The survey asked, "In what ways can the community improve home-less assistance programs?" This was an open-ended question and multiple responses were allowed. About 42 percent of the answers we received fell into five broad categories. In rank order of frequency of mention, citizens of the region said: provide more shelter (28 percent); do a better job of communicating ways in which the public can donate or volunteer (14 percent); provide more food banks (8 percent); provide more afford-able housing (7 percent); and provide places to drop change to be used for homeless assistance (2 percent). The remaining 58 percent of the answers to the question fell into a large number of "other" categories that were, predictably, all over the map, from "chase them out of town" to "improve outreach and communication with those who need services" to "change the attitude that all homeless people are mentally ill or have drug problems" to "be kinder to panhandlers." However, these "other" responses did tend to cluster around a few central themes: greater involvement of the churches and the faith community; greater community involvement and awareness; counseling programs; expanded treatment options for the substance-involved and the mentally ill; and perhaps the leading response, more attention to job training, education, employment opportunities, and income needs.

A later question asked, "In your opinion, is enough being done to address the issue of homelessness in our community?" A substantial majority, 73 percent, said no, and another 14 percent simply didn't know. Only 13 percent—about one Central Floridian in seven or eight—thought that enough was being done to address the issue. We also asked, "Should Central Florida's municipal and county governments do more to fund programs that address homelessness?" The resounding majority, 83 percent, said yes—a result that generated a few upturned eyebrows when it was presented to Central Florida's municipal and county leaders.

Agencies that Serve the Homeless

The survey contained numerous questions on public awareness of and opinions about the Coalition for the Homeless of Central Florida, the Central Florida Commission on Homelessness, and the Homeless Services Network.[2] Most questions referred to the Coalition since it is the largest provider of homeless services in the region. It is also the only entity of the three that a majority of respondents had ever heard of (75 percent, versus 16 percent for the Commission and 4 percent for HSN). (Questions about the Commission and HSN were included largely because both contributed resources to conduct the survey.)

Among those who had heard of each organization, the run of opinion was generally positive (or at worst, neutral). About three quarters (of those who had at least heard of the Coalition) had mostly or entirely positive impressions; ditto for 46 percent of those who had heard of the Commission (with the plurality, 48 percent, "neutral"), and for 62 percent of the (very small number of) people who had heard of HSN. In all three cases, media coverage (television and newspaper combined) was how most people had first become aware of these organizations, followed by family and friends, with large percentages in all cases mentioning some "other" source. Predictably, there was nothing systematic or even particularly noteworthy about the "other" responses to these questions. Churches were mentioned with some frequency as a source of information, as was propinquity ("I work [live] near there") and volunteer activity.

Concerning the Coalition specifically, 6 percent of respondents who had ever heard of the Coalition (n = 358) said they had visited the Coalition's blog, Twitter, Facebook, or YouTube sites; 94 percent had not. We also asked, "To the best of your knowledge, what does the Coalition do?" Four answers plus "other" were offered. In rank order, the responses were: helps families (82 percent), helps women (79 percent), feeds and shelters homeless men (74 percent), and offers education and job skills training (46 percent). In every case, most of those not saying "yes" to each of these said "don't know." Quite clearly, the Coalition's multi-year campaign to raise awareness of "the changing face of homelessness in our community" has been successful at least to the point of convincing very large majorities that it is women, children, and families, not just homeless men, who benefit from the services that the Coalition offers.

About a quarter of respondents (who answered the question) gave an "other" response. Many people (correctly) noted that the Coalition also feeds the homeless and many also made reference to the Coalition's job training, job placement, education, and GED programs. Many of the "others" made reference to medical assistance (which is handled by the Health Care Clinic for the Homeless, not the Coalition). Several people were aware of the Coalition's transitional and permanent housing programs ("they help with transitional housing and they have a women's shelter and provide day care …") and a substantial number mentioned lobbying and advocacy efforts on behalf of the homeless. On the whole, the "other" responses struck us as a fairly accurate depiction of what the coalition does.

Conclusions

The perception that homeless people are potentially dangerous—that they are addicted, mentally ill, prone to violence, sexually perverted, or in some other way threatening to the social order—clearly undergirds repressive political measures to deal with them, chiefly the various efforts mounted in many cities to criminalize the behaviors of homeless people or the condition of homelessness itself. The increasing numbers and visibility of homeless people in the streets of our cities has proven to be a source of great aggravation to downtown business people, residents, and urban politicians, especially in areas that are being revitalized or "gentrified." Those seeking "new urban lifestyles" rarely include encounters with homeless people among the urban diversities they wish to experience. The result in cities everywhere has been a great deal of political pressure to "do something" about the homeless hordes, to "clean up the streets," or in short, to be rid of homeless people by whatever means necessary. In rare instances, this has meant some effort to address the larger issues of poverty and low income housing from whence homelessness springs. Far more commonly, the effort is focused on criminalizing the behaviors that annoy us. We are resolved, it seems, to dealing with the homeless problem by making homeless behaviors illegal, as evidenced by the increasing number of cities attempting to enact ordinances to prohibit such things as panhandling, loitering, public intoxication, or public feedings. What this lacks in cleverness or compassion it makes up in sheer spite.

A 2006 joint report by the National Coalition for the Homeless and the National Law Center on Homelessness and Poverty reported that criminalization initiatives are on the rise. Comparing the most recent report with a similar one conducted in 2002, the study found a 3 percent increase in laws that prohibit loitering, loafing, or vagrancy; a 14 percent increase in laws that prohibit sitting or lying down in specific public spaces; and an 18 percent increase in laws prohibiting aggressive panhandling.

Another facet of criminalization involves the violence that homeless people endure on the streets of American cities. Assaults against homeless individuals are apparently also on the rise. A report issued by the National Coalition for the Homeless (NCH) compiled all of the known cases of homeless victimization. The NCH reports 142 violent acts against homeless persons occurring in 2006, including twenty deaths. Many homeless advocates believe that the attacks against homeless people demonstrate the effects of the homeless being despised, feared, and unwanted. So we deal with the perceived dangers and criminality of the homeless by criminalizing them and their behaviors, even when study after study has shown that people experiencing homelessness are far more likely to be the victims of crime and violence than the perpetrators. From the perspective of public policy, this is madness.

Data on public perceptions of the homeless reveal both sympathetic and hostile views. Judging from the marginal frequencies reviewed in this chapter, many people harbor both positive and negative views simultaneously—i.e., are sympathetic towards homeless people in some respects and hostile towards them in others. But even this simple observation buttresses an important point, namely, that public opinion on this issue is not "of a piece." And likewise, the views of people who show up at public hearings to protest the proposed location of a new homeless shelter or those who appear at City Council meetings to demand that "something be done" about the panhandlers downtown, or those that write angry letters to the editor of the local paper are not necessarily representative of the views of the larger public.

Consider: No one would think of Central Florida as a "haven" for the homeless or accuse local citizens of being "soft-hearted" on poverty and homelessness issues. And yet, most people in Central Florida believe that homelessness is a major problem in our community, that too little is currently being done to address the problem, and that Central Florida's municipal and county governments should be doing more to fund programs that can help, and overwhelmingly reject the view that programs of assistance to the homeless are "too expensive." With few exceptions, most people in Central Florida hold sympathetic views towards homeless people. There is a lingering perception that homeless people are possibly dangerous and a strong misperception of the link between homelessness and panhandling, but for the most part, public impressions are demographically accurate and generally sympathetic to people who are suffering from circumstances largely beyond their control. Most people whose views about the homeless have recently changed say that they have become more sympathetic to homeless people, not less.

In contrast to the generally sympathetic views of the general public that the data presented in this chapter document, there is a strong consensus that the media portray the homeless in a generally negative light, both locally and nationally. Perhaps it is media portraiture more than public opinion that drives social policy on this issue. We and others have not found much evidence that the media have any effect on popular outlooks, but perhaps they do influence the thinking of public officials. And almost certainly, most policy makers would have a much firmer grasp of local media opinions on homelessness than they would understand the views of the average Joe. To this extent, the media would be far more influential on public policy than public thinking would be.

We conclude with a point made in the title of a book by the Rumanian author, Dmitry Sokolov (2002): "You cannot drive tramps off the street with a club!" Regardless of the beliefs of the media, political elites, or the general public, evidence shows that many homeless people respond positively to services, outreach, health care, or anything else that seems to represent an alternative way of living. But there is practically no evidence anywhere to suggest that they respond positively to threats, intimidation, or enforcement of laws that attempt to prohibit or criminalize their behaviors, or that anything useful is to be gained by stigmatizing them as violent, lazy, shiftless, crazy, or otherwise hazardous to the well-being of the public at large.

Notes

1. Coauthored with Jana L. Jasinski. Major portions of this chapter are adapted from Donley 2008.
2. The Central Florida Commission on Homelessness was established in June 2007 in response to a succession of calls for some sort of regional entity to examine the area-wide homeless problem. The Homeless Services Network is the regional lead agency for the Continuum of Care. For more details on both entities, see Chapter Twelve.

11

The Kindness of Strangers:
Volunteers, Volunteerism, and the Homeless

Nationally, about three-quarters of the total effort on behalf of home-less people comes from the private sector, principally churches and other faith-based organizations, and not from public programs at the federal, state, or local level (e.g., Aron and Sharkey 2002). Much of this assis-tance comes in the form of volunteers who go to the shelters and soup kitchens to prepare and serve meals, donate clothing, and otherwise pursue the social ministry of their faith. Many are clearly motivated by the well-known passage in the Gospel according to St. Matthew 25:35-36: "For I was hungry, and you gave me something to eat; I was thirsty, and you gave me something to drink; I was a stranger, and you invited me in; I was naked, and you clothed me; I was sick, and you visited me; I was in prison, and you came to me." A great deal of Christian ministry to the poor, the homeless, and the oppressed can be traced to these famous passages.

In their reliance on volunteers, homeless service agencies in Central Florida are no different than homeless facilities everywhere. In the calendar year 2008, to illustrate, over 15,000 volunteers donated time and talent to the Coalition for the Homeless of Central Florida. These 15,000 kind souls contributed 66,000 hours of labor to pursue 372 dis-tinct volunteer projects, not including food service, to which we return momentarily. Indeed, the Coalition was founded in 1987 by a group of church-based volunteers who recognized that homelessness was becom-ing a major problem in Central Florida and organized the Coalition as a response. (The Coalition's history is recounted in the next chapter.) All the other major Central Florida facilities for the homeless (the Christian Service Center, Salvation Army, and Orlando Union Rescue Mission) have similar roots in religiously-motivated volunteerism, outreach, and ministry, and the same is true in most other cities and regions.

As an organization founded by volunteers, the Coalition has always depended on the generosity of volunteers—the kindness of strangers—in executing its mission. One of the most visible and important volunteer programs at the Coalition is the nightly feeding of clients. Altogether, the Coalition operates three feeding programs—one for homeless men and members of the general community in the Men's Pavilion (which serves as many as 400 meals each night), one for the women and children who live in the Center for Women and Families (about 200-250 meals), and one at the Women's Residential and Counseling Center (about 100-125 meals). Altogether, in calendar year 2008, the Coalition provided almost 300,000 hot meals to thousands of homeless and destitute people, all this on a cash budget of about $40,000, most of which is spent making sure that the Coalition is in compliance with applicable state laws and regulations regarding the feeding of children, such as serving fresh milk.

In conjunction with a local service club, we buy, prepare, and serve the evening meal at the WRCC about twice a year. Recently, we prepared food for 90-100 people at a total cost of $300, and while our meal was probably somewhat "fancier" than usual, $3 per meal served is probably a pretty indicative price of the meals served by volunteers. It is therefore easy to see why the Coalition's auditors put the value of the volunteer feeding effort alone at nearly $1 million per year, a dramatic illustration of the dependence of organizations like the Coalition on volunteer efforts.

There are many other programs at the Coalition that depend entirely on volunteers. One of these is a children's art program called ABCs (Art by Coalition Children). Professional artists in the community come to the Coalition to teach children who live there about the artists' media and their craft; over the years, practically every artistic medium imaginable has been featured in these 6-8 week modules: photography, sculpture, drawing, painting, ceramics, vocal and instrumental music, drama, even puppetry and videography. There are also yoga and running programs in place for the men in First Steps (the Coalition's drug and alcohol treatment program), conceived of and staffed by volunteers and an important part of the overall re-socialization program. Law student and faculty volunteers from the nearby Florida A&M University School of Law offer free legal clinics once a week. In the past year, volunteers have come to the Coalition's facilities to provide Halloween and birthday parties for the children, free hairdos and cosmetology for the women, and messages of faith and spirituality to the men. Volunteers have rehabilitated restrooms, refurnished living spaces, done yard maintenance and landscape work, and repainted the interior and exterior walls. None of these programs, and hundreds of other volunteer projects that are financially subsidized or underwritten by the Coalition, would exist but for the efforts and talents of the extensive volunteer cadre.

Thus, volunteers are not just an asset, they are a necessity. Were it not for the dedication of volunteers, the Coalition would not be able to feed or shelter the thousands that they currently do. There would be no enrichment programs for the residents, no art programs or after-school tutoring for the children, no "dress for success" efforts on behalf of the women. Absent volunteers, the entire environment of the facility would be immeasurably poorer. And, of course, much the same can be said for almost every other homeless facility (Harrison 1995; Cloke, Johnsen and May 2007).

The Coalition recognizes the importance of volunteers and the need for proper motivation and management. When the budget allows, there is a full-time Director of Volunteer Services and a full-time assistant volunteer coordinator. Volunteers are recognized on the Coalition website and on the walls of the facility. Staff works side by side with the volunteers because they know they could not fulfill their mission without them.

Within the volunteer program, there are three different categories of volunteers. The first are the meal service volunteers. These are generally church groups or other organizations that have committed to one feeding (sometimes two) per month. These volunteers are responsible for feeding the men, women, and children that reside at the Coalition's facilities as well as many of the people that live in the surrounding community. Our surveys of the evening soup kitchen line at the Pavilion show that about 20-25 percent are not homeless people but rather low-income people who live in the nearby neighborhoods. (Burt's national survey of homeless service providers shows approximately the same result. Again, the Coalition is by no means unique in this regard.) The ability to eat free meals at the Coalition is what allows many in the community to stretch their incomes around their expenses and thus avoid becoming homeless themselves; we often refer to the community feeding as the Coalition's homeless prevention program. Meal service volunteers account for the majority of volunteers at the Coalition, about two out of three.

The second category is "group volunteers," which account for most of the remainder. These are people affiliated with organizations that volunteer, but not in meal service. Examples include a group from Hands On Orlando that holds monthly birthday parties for the children and weekly Bingo nights for the adults, a group from the UCF sociology department that sponsors a weekly movie night for the children, large groups from Disney (Volunt-EARS) who come for various projects, and numerous others.

The third and smallest category consists of individual volunteers who often come to the Coalition seeking a volunteer opportunity or a chance to do something meaningful in the community. Because they are not affiliated with any known group, these individuals, unlike the other volunteers, go through background checks and an orientation process before being assigned to a specific staff member or department.

The Director of Volunteer Services oversees all three categories of volunteers and reports directly to the Coalition's Executive Director. Thus, the position is on the same level as the Director of Program Services, the comptroller, the Director of Development, etc.—indicative of the importance of volunteers to the organization.

New volunteer orientation sessions are held as necessary. Often, people with very good intentions believe they want to help the homeless, but are grossly unprepared for the conditions they will confront. This is explained to potential recruits and often the outcome is a mutual decision that the person will be happier elsewhere. Without proper management of the volunteers, the Coalition would quickly disintegrate.

As stated, volunteers are categorized into one of three groups: meal service, group volunteers, and individual volunteers. Meal service and group volunteers are treated quite differently from individual volunteers. This is because only individual volunteers have prolonged contact with clients. Meal service and group volunteers come to the Coalition to fulfill specific tasks but do not work one-on-one with clients. Thus, there is no special recruitment process in place for the meal service or group volunteers. Meal service groups, as we have already indicated, consist primarily of church groups that have been serving meals at the Coalition on a set day every month for years. Because of this, there is no need to actively recruit—volunteers are "recruited" by the group from whence they come. Occasionally, a scheduled meal service group will fail to make their scheduled date, but this is rare. The meal service groups are almost eerily reliable.

Group volunteers are also not actively recruited. Generally, these groups approach the Coalition with some volunteer activity in mind and request permission to do it. They generally do not provide essential services, but rather provide the "extras" for residents—monthly birthday parties for the children, installation of a new volleyball net and court, painting of walls, etc. The activities of group volunteers are obviously not essential, but do contribute to the quality of life for all residents.

For meal service and group volunteers, there is no orientation, application procedure, or background check. From time to time, the Director of Volunteer Services attends the meal service and other volunteer activities to thank volunteers for their efforts and to encourage retention by asking if anything can be done to make their work easier.

Individual volunteers do provide direct services, for example, in the nursery school working with kids on their reading skills, in the life-long learning classroom helping to administer examinations or helping clients prepare for their GEDs, etc. Often, these individuals come to the Coalition seeking a volunteer opportunity, but can also be recruited through advertisements on the Coalition website. When potential individual volunteers are located, they are initially screened via telephone, e-mail, or in person by the Director of Volunteer Services. Often, the initial screening conversation indicates that the Coalition may not provide a good fit for the potential volunteer's desires, talents, or needs. The majority of individual volunteers come to the Coalition because they want to work with children and as a result, the children's programs are frequently overrun with volunteers. So most individual volunteers have to be persuaded to work with adults despite their wishes, and if they are uncomfortable with this, they are often referred to other agencies.

If the initial conversation seems to indicate a good fit, the volunteer fills out a formal application, provides references, and attends an orientation session. At this time a background check is also done. If the background check and references are good and orientation is completed, then the volunteer is assigned to a manager, department, or task. While there is no "official" probationary period for volunteers, any problems with the volunteer or the placement become quickly apparent. In most cases, the volunteer and the Coalition part ways amicably. However, this is rare; screening and orientation usually generate a good fit.

A major part of volunteer management is retention. For meal service volunteers, the retention strategies are simple. The Director of Volunteer Services attends meal service, asks the volunteers if they need anything, tries to fill whatever requests they may have, and most importantly, thanks them for the work they do. Recognition is understood as an important retention strategy and can be informal or formal as well as private or public. At the Coalition, recognition tends to be informal and private. Expressions of gratitude are inexpensive, but flashy "volunteer recognition" events are not. Coalition management and staff believe the volunteers would not be overly receptive to such things in any case. The volunteers know and believe in the work of the Coalition and do not want scarce resources wasted on events that do not benefit clients directly. Later in this chapter, we present survey data that indicate that these management viewpoints on volunteer attitudes are generally valid.

Many of the group volunteers are "episodic" volunteers who come to the Coalition to perform one assignment or help with one fundraiser and do not have a long-standing commitment. Other group volunteers are members of a host volunteer organization. Retention strategies for these group volunteers are generally left to the host organization.

The individual volunteers have a more structured retention program in place. Because individual volunteers work regularly to provide specific services, their work is evaluated just as if they were paid employees and their evaluations are kept in the volunteer's personnel file. Periodically, the Director of Volunteer Services will discuss a volunteer's performance with the relevant manager as well as with the volunteer. The evaluation process is a way for each side to better achieve what they want: fulfilling and meaningful experiences for the volunteer, quality services for the Coalition's clients. The Director of Volunteer Services will also talk to staff if there seems to be a problem and, on rare occasions, individual volunteers are let go.

While the Coalition cannot afford elaborate shows of gratitude for the thousands of volunteers who work at the Coalition every year, the Director of Volunteer Services, Coalition management and other staff, and the Board of Directors are all aware of the impact of volunteers on the ability of the Coalition to serve thousands of homeless and low-income people. As we see in the survey data presented later, volunteers do not come to the Coalition looking for recognition. They come to do what they believe is right and, in most cases, that is enough.

It needs also to be mentioned that donors are equally as important to the Coalition, and to most homeless service providers, as volunteers. Private donations and annual fundraiser events account for about a third of the overall operating budget. At each meeting of the Coalition's Board of Directors, a list of $500+ contributors is distributed (this always runs to several pages of listings) and the Board is asked to send thank you notes and emails to donors whom they know.

Survey Data on Volunteers

Most of our homelessness research these past several years has focused on homeless people, but in 2003, we surveyed 123 food service volunteers who worked an evening meal line at the Coalition. The purpose of the survey was to obtain information from volunteers on their backgrounds and demographics, their reasons for and experiences with volunteering, and their potential willingness to volunteer in other, non-food-service capacities. The brief survey took about 5-10 minutes to complete and was implemented by service-learning students in an urban sociology course.

The survey was done at the request of the Coalition's Director of Volunteer Services and attempted to follow up on her frequent observation that food service volunteers seemed to be interested only in serving food and not in becoming involved with any of the numerous other volunteer opportunities at the Coalition. The hope was that the survey would shed some light on why this was the case and perhaps suggest some strategies to get these volunteers interested in other Coalition activities. As indicated, food service volunteers represent about two-thirds of the volunteer total and thus represent a huge potential labor pool for other important volunteer tasks, if only they could be interested in something besides serving food.

Students were instructed to do surveys with volunteers in both the Pavilion and CWF food lines. (For various reasons, WRCC volunteers were not surveyed.) On a typical evening, there are more meals served and more people serving them at the Pavilion line than in the Center for Women and Families. This notwithstanding, two-thirds of all surveys were done with CWF volunteers, evidently because the CWF feeding operation is more orderly and more conducive to surveying than the Pavilion feeding operation (where some 400 or more meals are served nightly). Interviewers also reported that CWF volunteers seemed more amenable to being surveyed. Pavilion volunteers, in contrast, were typically interested in heading home as soon as the evening food service was completed. (All interviews were done *after* the food service was completed so as not to disrupt people trying to serve food under generally trying circumstances.)

Consistent with studies of volunteers in other contexts (Hiatt et al. 2000; Hiatt and Jones 2000; Thoits and Hewitt 2001), the typical Coalition food service volunteer is a well-educated white female over age forty-five. Overall, 60 percent of the volunteers were women and their median age was 46.7 years. The very large majority, 84 percent, were white, with a sprinkling of other races and ethnicities (10 percent African American; 3 percent Hispanic; 3 percent Asian). Just over 60 percent had college degrees and a mere 14 percent had no education beyond high school.

Among the volunteers we surveyed, only 11 percent were first-time Coalition volunteers; the very large majority (the remaining 89 percent) had volunteered at the Coalition previously. Half (51 percent) volunteered at the Coalition at least once a month; about a tenth (9.2 percent) volunteered even more frequently than that; most of the remainder (33 percent) volunteered "several times a year."[1] More than three-fifths (63 percent) said they had been Coalition volunteers for "several years." Consistent with the observation of the Director of Volunteer Services, the very large majority, 86 percent, are at the Coalition "just to serve food," and only a small fraction (14 percent) had tried to involve themselves with other Coalition activities.[2] Interestingly, the substantial majority (66 percent) said they also volunteered at other agencies; only a third "specialized" in volunteering at the Coalition.

Like bananas, Coalition volunteers come in bunches. Of the volunteers we surveyed, nearly all (92 percent) were at the Coalition with a group. Most of these groups (63 percent) were church groups, a few were business groups (15 percent) or civic and professional organizations (12 percent), and the remainder were semi-organized groups of family and friends.

We asked volunteers what they liked most and least about volunteering at the Coalition. These were open-ended questions that people could answer however they pleased. Concerning things they liked, a quarter spontaneously mentioned "helping people in need," and another quarter said simply that they "enjoyed the people" they served. Other fairly common responses: "It makes me feel good" to volunteer (12 percent), "I enjoy preparing and serving food" (9 percent), and "This gives me a chance to give something back" (6 percent). Remaining responses were strewn over a wide range of categories.

Concerning dislikes, a substantial plurality (43 percent) said there was nothing about the experience they disliked, an encouraging response and one that perhaps explains why the majority of Coalition volunteers have been doing it for such a long time. The remaining respondents noted a wide variety of dislikes: the inherent sadness of dealing with people who have no place to live (16 percent); the occasional rudeness or lack of manners of some clients (8 percent); living conditions at the Coalition (especially the Pavilion, where a number of people noted their dislike of the fact that Pavilion men sleep on pads on the concrete floor); the heat (5 percent); and (of all things!) preparing onions (3 percent). The remaining complaints were scattered over a wide variety of categories (running out of food, problems with staff, the noise, feeling scared, having to clean up, etc.).

We also tried to get at volunteer motivations with a close-ended series of items. Survey respondents were read a list of eight reasons "people have given for volunteering here at the Coalition" and were asked whether each reason was very, somewhat, or not really an important reason to them. Results are shown in Table 11.1. Most of the offered reasons were "very important" to substantial majorities. The three items scored as "very important" by 90 percent or larger majorities were: (1) "I believe in the work that the Coalition does"; (2) "Volunteering is my way of giving back"; and (3) "I like helping homeless people." Items rated as very important by at least 80 percent included: (4) "It makes me feel good about myself"; and (5) "I have friends and family who volunteer here." Of decidedly lesser importance are that volunteering "is part of my church's outreach" (very important to 68 percent), "I enjoy working in food service" (very important to only 36 percent and not at all important to 30 percent), and at the very bottom of the list, "I am required to volunteer," dismissed as unimportant by 92 percent.

Of the survey findings concerning volunteer motivations, the only one that seems to bear additional comment is that relatively few cited the intrinsic enjoyment of "working in food service" as a "very important" reason why they volunteered; likewise, only about one in ten spontaneously mentioned the enjoyment of "preparing and serving food" as something they liked about volunteering. That the very large majority

Table 11.1
Reasons Given for Volunteering at the Coalition (in percentages)

Reason	Very Important	Some-what Important	Not Imp't	DK
I believe in the work that the Coalition does	95.9	4.1	0	0
Volunteering is my way of giving back	91.9	8.1	0	0
I like helping homeless people	90.2	8.9	.8	0
It makes me feel good about myself	84.6	13.0	1.6	.8
I have friends, family, etc. who volunteer here	82.1	9.8	8.1	0
It is part of my church's outreach	68.3	4.1	27.6	0
I enjoy working in food service	35.8	34.1	30.1	0
I am required to volunteer	6.5	1.6	91.9	0

of volunteers are at the Coalition only to serve food is therefore not a function of the intrinsic enjoyment to be derived from the activity *per se*, but evidently reflects some other factor or factors. We speculate later on what these "other factors" might be.

As is evident from the large number of volunteers who come to the Coalition as part of a church group, religion is very important in the lives of these volunteers. Indeed, the plurality of volunteers (43 percent) said that religion was "the **most** important thing" in their everyday lives and an additional 36 percent said it was "very important" (if not the single most important thing). By these measures, almost 80 percent have deep religious convictions. We also return to this point later in the discussion.

How interested are the volunteers in the totality of Coalition programs? We asked whether volunteers were "very interested in all the Coalition is doing" or, alternatively, whether they were "here just to help needy people." Of those who answered the question (N = 116), the majority, 54 percent, were at the Coalition "just to help needy people." We also asked how interested volunteers would be in "receiving information from time to time about other opportunities to help here at the Coalition." Only one in three was "very interested." (An additional third were "somewhat interested" and the remaining third were indifferent to the suggestion.) Would volunteers like to be honored from time to time "with some sort of public recognition?" The large majority, 83 percent, said no, they would prefer to remain anonymous. Continuing the theme, only half (50 percent) were "very interested" in touring the Coalition facilities. Thus, only a minority of the food service volunteers appear to be potential conscripts for other Coalition activities.

A final sequence in the survey asked volunteers about their experiences with homeless people. Only one in four said that they had ever had "a negative personal experience with a homeless person." Of those who had (N = 29), a quarter said this had happened just one time and about two-thirds said it had happened "a few times." Only three people had had "many" negative experiences with homeless persons, about 2 percent of the total sample.

How do the Coalition's "regulars" differ from less active or less committed volunteers? For purposes of this brief analysis, we defined a regular as someone who volunteered at the Coalition at least once a month (or more frequently) *and* who had done so for at least a year (or more). By this definition, 44 percent of the 123 volunteers surveyed qualify as Coalition regulars (50 percent of those volunteers who answered both component questions). Table 2 shows some of the differences between the regulars and the others. These differences are generally small. Compared to the others, the regulars are *more* likely to say they are there just to serve food (91 percent to 81 percent), *more* likely to be "very interested" in receiving information about other volunteer opportunities at the Coalition (35 percent to 28 percent), *less* likely to be "very interested" in a tour of the facility (42 percent to 57 percent), *more* likely to say that religion is the single most important thing in their lives (52 percent to 41 percent), and slightly *less* likely to report having had a negative personal experience with a homeless person. None of these differences is categorical and, given the small sample sizes, none are statistically significant. But they do form an interesting pattern.

Clearly, the substantial majority of food service volunteers only serve food while they are at the Coalition and most do not seem, in general, to be very interested in doing anything else. So in the first instance, these results confirm the initial observations of the Director of Volunteer Services that motivated this survey. Still, it needs to be emphasized that there are sizable minorities of volunteers who *are* interested in other volunteer opportunities and who *are* interested in knowing more about the Coalition. So there is clearly a subgroup of food service volunteers who are candidates for recruitment into other volunteer activities.

Obviously, the data only show patterns and at best give some hints about possible explanations. Two lines of explanatory speculation seem worthy of consideration:

One, volunteers in general seem more interested in direct, hands-on contact with clients than in doing other important tasks (such as sorting

Table 11.2
"Regular" Volunteers Compared to Other Volunteers

	Regulars (n = 54)	All Others (n = 54)
Percent here "just to serve food"	91	81
Percent who volunteer just at Coalition	33	30
Percent "here with a group"	100	96
Percent here "just to help the needy"	52	48
Percent very interested in other volunteer opportunities	35	28
Percent who want public recognition	20	17
Percent very interested in a tour	42	57
Percent saying "religion is the **most** important thing"	52	41
Percent who have had a negative experience with homeless	20	26

rummage) that do not involve direct contact. Food service provides ample opportunity for one-to-one interaction. In the Pavilion feeding line, for example, a volunteer has several hundred chances each night to be told "thank you" by a grateful fellow human, and our experience is that many homeless clients *do* express their thanks to the servers, sometimes quite effusively. At the CWF and the WRCC, most of those grateful fellow humans are women and children, groups society has traditionally obligated itself to nurture and protect. Thus, the gratifications to be had from serving food to homeless people are immediate and direct, unlike the gratifications to be had from other possible volunteer activities, which may be more indirect or even non-existent. Relatively few people, for example, will derive any warm, fuzzy feelings from sorting a pile of donated shirts, blouses, and slacks according to size. Serving food also responds tangibly and immediately to the most basic human need. In contrast, the effects of, say, after-school tutoring or working in the ABCs program often may not be apparent for months or even years.

Two, at a somewhat deeper level, there is an intimate symbolic connection between serving food and the Christian sense of grace. "Protestants connect grace with social responsibility to feed the hungry, clothe the poor, and help the downtrodden" (Sack 2000), as in the famous passage from Matthew with which we began. Surely, this connection is one reason why soup kitchens are essential outreach programs in many churches. Indeed, from the unleavened manna that Jehovah rained down upon the starving Israelites in their diaspora through the desert to the New Testament parable of fishes and loaves to the symbolic re-enactment of the Last Supper in weekly Communion, food symbolism is rampant throughout Christian eschatology. The argument is that on some symbolic level, the Coalition's food service volunteers experience the nightly food service as a religious "calling," as an effort to nurture souls by providing nourishment for the body. (On religious motivations among volunteers, see also Becker and Dhingra 2001.)

Further evidence on the religious motivation to volunteer is available in the "perceptions" survey discussed at length in Chapter Ten. In the sequence of questions about the Coalition, we asked people if they had ever donated money to the Coalition or volunteered there. About a third (36 percent) said they had donated money to the Coalition at least once in their lives (fewer, incidentally, than the percentage who said they give to panhandlers) and one in six (17 percent) said they had volunteered there.

With a current *adult* population of about 1.3 million in the three-county area, a 17 percent volunteering rate would yield an estimate of ~221,000 coalition volunteers, which seems implausibly high. On the other hand, the Coalition was founded in 1987 and has been in existence for more than two decades. (The question asked about *ever* volunteering or *ever* donating; the average respondent in the "perceptions" survey was 48 years old and had therefore been an adult for thirty years.) If we spread 221,000 volunteers over the 22 years of the Coalition's existence (as of the time of the survey), that yields ~10,000 volunteers per year. And as we have already pointed out, nearly 15,000 volunteers donated their time and talents to the Coalition last year. Even granting the possibility of some social desirability bias in responses to questions about things like donating and volunteering, the survey at least yields an estimate that is apparently accurate to the nearest order of magnitude.

What are the correlates of knowing about, volunteering for, and contributing to the Coalition? Pertinent data are in Table 11.3. The effects of county of residence are predictable and significant. In terms of awareness and volunteering, Orange County (where Orlando and the Coalition are located) leads the way, with suburban Seminole County in a close second, and more rural Osceola County a distant third. In volunteering, Orange and Seminole are effectively tied, with Osceola, again, a distant third.

Contrary to expectation, personally knowing someone who is or was homeless has no apparent effect on awareness or volunteering, but personal knowledge has a small and marginally significant effect on giving: 41 percent of those who have personal knowledge of a homeless person have donated to the Coalition versus 32 percent of those who do not.

Whites and blacks are about equally likely to be aware of the Coalition, Hispanics significantly less so. But given awareness, both blacks and Hispanics are more likely to donate and volunteer than whites.

Knowing about the Coalition increases with education, but giving and volunteering are not significantly different across educational groups. In direct contrast, being a member of a faith organization (church, synagogue, and the like) has no significant effect on awareness but does sharply increase both donations and volunteerism. Indeed, members of faith-based organizations are nearly twice as likely to have given to the Coalition (43 percent to 26 percent) and are almost three times as likely to have volunteered (23 percent to 8 percent) as non-members. Finally, gender and age were insignificant variables, with one prominent exception: young people were significantly less likely to know about the Coalition (57 percent) than either the middle aged (83 percent) or the old (77 percent). Given awareness, however, patterns of donating and volunteering were about the same across ages and genders.

Table 11.3
Social and Demographic Correlates of Knowing About, Giving to, and
Volunteering at the Coalition for the Homeless of Central Florida

Percent who Have:

	Heard of	Donated*	Volunteered*
County			
Orange	81	39	18
Seminole	72	35	20
Osceola	50	20	3
Know a homeless person?			
Yes	77	41	18
No	73	32	15
Race**			
White	79	33	15
Black	76	42	26
Hispanic	63	39	24
Education			
High School or Less	57	40	12
Some College, AA	74	31	17
BA or higher	81	37	17
Member of a Church, Synagogue, Mosque***			
Yes	77	43	23
No	72	26	8
Gender			
Female	77	38	19
Male	72	34	14
Age			
18-35	57	34	18
36-64	83	35	16
65+	77	42	17

*Questions about donating and volunteering were only asked of those who said they had heard of the Coalition.

**All other races omitted from the table.

***The question reads: Are you a **member** of a local church, synagogue, mosque, or other religious or spiritual community?

The survey contained several additional measures of religiosity. Concerning religious preference (whether Protestant, Catholic, Jewish, other, or none), Protestants were more likely than any other group to know about the Coalition (89 percent versus 77 percent of Catholics and 69 percent of Jewish respondents), but given awareness, there were no differences in donating or volunteering. A question about the importance of religion in one's life (very important to not important at all) was not significantly related to awareness, but given awareness, was positively related to donating and to volunteering (i.e., those for whom religion was more important were also more likely to give and to volunteer). The same was generally true of church attendance, which was unrelated to awareness, but given awareness, was significantly associated with donating and volunteering. To illustrate, weekly or nearly-weekly church attendees volunteered at the rate of 21 percent, whereas the rate among those who only attend a few times a year or less was only 8 percent; for donations, the two rates were 42 percent and 21 percent. These and earlier findings underscore the need for and potential value of outreach to the faith community by facilities like the Coalition and the obviously strong religious motivation that underlies much service on behalf of homeless people.

Some other results of interest were that donating and volunteering were negatively related to the measures of perceived dangerousness discussed in Chapter Ten (although not as strongly as one might expect—none of the correlations reached statistical significance). Donating and volunteering were unrelated to the opinions that "not enough is being done to address the issue of homelessness in our community" and that Central Florida's local governments "should do more to fund programs to address homelessness." Evidently, people do not compensate for the perceived need for or lack of policy action on the issue by stepping up personally, a somewhat discouraging result. People who give to panhandlers were marginally more likely to give to the Coalition as well, but no more likely to volunteer. Of all factors examined, propinquity (living in the county where a facility is located) and religiosity seem to be the only strong and consistent predictors of "the kindness of strangers."

A final source of data on volunteering and homelessness are "debriefing" interviews done with people, mostly students, who help us out with the annual Point in Time (PIT) count done by the Homeless Services Network in cooperation with our shop. Each year, we and our volunteers do the PIT face-to-face surveys at the Salvation Army's soup kitchen and men's shelter, the Daily Bread (which serves lunch), and the Coalition's

Men's Pavilion, along with covering other facilities on an as-needed basis. To accomplish this, we solicit 10-12 volunteers each year from the staff at our survey lab and from our current students. Most are motivated more by curiosity or coursework than by religious beliefs.

To explore a different kind of volunteering that involves different kinds of volunteers and volunteer experiences, we recently asked a handful of our annual "regulars" to reflect on the impact of their volunteer experiences on their perceptions of homeless people, i.e., to tell us about what they thought of homelessness before the PIT count and how those views changed (if at all). Although far short of a pretest-posttest experiment, their responses shed light on how one-on-one contact with homeless people can alter people's a priori assumptions.

Amber, who has participated in two PIT counts to date, stated

> Prior to volunteering, I held a somewhat detached view of the homeless: a kind of out-of-sight, out-of-mind mentality, mixed with pity. Afterwards, I realized that the homeless situation is very real and closer to home than I thought. I also came to the realization that we have more in common than I thought. Before volunteering, I subconsciously placed them in a separate category from myself.

This theme of the "otherness" of homeless people is a common refrain in the debriefing interviews. We are reminded of the concept of "othering" as developed in the critical analysis of colonialism, whereby the positive identity of the colonizer is maintained by the stigmatization and dehumanization of the "other," the colonized. This psychological process is often identified with Frantz Fanon's famous 1961 book, *The Wretched of the Earth,* where it is rendered as the essential psychopathology of the imperialistic mind. The notion of "othering" is also common in contemporary discussions of popular opinions about the homeless (e.g., Cloke et al. 2000). A consistent experience reported by our volunteers is an initial sense of "otherness" that melted away as their personal contacts with homeless people increased.

We asked our volunteers if they remembered specific experiences or encounters that stuck out in their minds. Amber remarked

> I realized that the categories [of homelessness] that I had created in my head were wrong when I told one homeless man that we were administering these surveys in an attempt to create "increased funding for you guys." He responded, "Who is 'you guys'?" This comment made me come to my senses, it made me aware of my incorrect view towards the homeless.

To Amber, at least in the beginning, "the homeless" were an undifferentiated mass of lost souls needing assistance. The homeless themselves, she realized, recognized numerous internal differentiations and lines of distinction that often assume far more importance than "outsides" appreciate.

Lacey, a first time volunteer, stated

> Prior to volunteering I wasn't too involved in the problem of the homeless nor did I spend too much time contemplating the issues with them. After volunteering I have such a better understanding of the problem in Central Florida, and have found that I am very interested in further volunteering or possibly pursuing more research opportunities to garner funding and support for them.

Note, again, the undifferentiated "them." For Lacey, the most memorable incident of her volunteer experience came when speaking to a veteran.

> When I was speaking to a war veteran, I was deeply moved by hearing his story, but more impressed by the tenacity and optimism he had about the "temporary inconvenience" he was experiencing. It was really humbling to see how positive he could be in such a tough situation.

Another first time volunteer, Alexis, explained that at first, "I was intimidated because I had never been around anyone who was homeless." Alexis had emailed us prior to the count to inquire about the exact logistics, expressing a fear that she might be alone in the Parramore area in the evening. She also stayed very close to her supervisors in the beginning. But as the night unfolded, we watched her slowly relax and even begin to enjoy her experiences. She said that after volunteering, "aside from the few crazies that I encountered, they seemed like regular people whose circumstances led them to becoming homeless. They are just like the rest of society—some were polite, others weren't. They didn't seem so different from us." At one point, Alexis was attempting to conduct an interview with a resident at the Salvation Army when her respondent asked if he could interview *her*. She agreed and they proceeded to interview each other.

> He was very outgoing and seemed like someone who would get along with most anyone. He wasn't the kind of person I had perceived as being homeless. I had assumed that anyone who was homeless must have terrible social skills and very little going for them, however he seemed quite normal to me.

One of volunteers had been with us for four consecutive years and surprised us with her comments. Nicole was always an eager employee at our lab and we felt nearly certain that she was equally eager about her first opportunity to participate in the PIT count. We were surprised to learn that she had not been. To the contrary, she explained that her first time out, "I was weary and uncomfortable being around them, because I didn't know anything about the homeless. I thought they were dirty, uneducated, and lazy, most were drug addicts and many of them didn't want to try to get out of their situations, they just wanted the free handouts. This sounds ignorant, I know, but that's how I felt." After volunteering, she realized that

> Although some are drug addicts, most aren't. Many of the homeless have just recently lost jobs, homes, are victims of abuse and have had to leave situations that caused them to become homeless. Many are well educated and were successful before losing their jobs. Many of the homeless I interviewed were trying to find work from labor pools every morning just to stay somewhere where they aren't sleeping outside and where they can get a hot meal.

After four years of volunteer experience, her most vivid memories are of the men and women who were homeless with their children. "It just broke my heart to think about children, let alone anyone, sleeping outside, especially when it gets as cold as it does here in Central Florida." (The PIT count is done in January, which is often very cold by Florida standards.)

One of our Spanish-speaking surveyors was a graduate student when she volunteered with us. She was very educated about homeless issues long before she volunteered and her views were not impacted by her volunteering because she had done this type of work before. However, her language skills brought her insights about some commonly misunderstood or overlooked issues that homeless Latinos often face. Her most vivid recollections involved "talking to homeless Latinos who are even worse off because they are stuck in the political chaos that is our immigration law. They are homeless and have no resources, they face language barriers, and they fear anyone who might be an authority figure. This type of situation is one that I had not thought about until I encountered it on several occasions. The experience of talking to these men completely stuck out."

Not all volunteer experiences are positive or enlightening and it would be irresponsible to suggest otherwise. One first-timer, Kendall, said that her belief that people are homeless because "they are people who are the product of unfortunate circumstances or predisposed disposition" did not change after volunteer experience. What she remembers most is "how verbally hostile a young black man was towards me because I am white." Kendall and other volunteers have reported, and we too have observed, that while the African American men are almost unfailingly polite and respectful towards our (mostly) white volunteer crew, the men of Caribbean origin are sometimes aggressively unpleasant and resentful. We have no ready explanation for the difference, although we are by no means the first investigators to point out that African American individuals and Caribbean American individuals are often quite different (e.g., Chatters et al. 2008; Lincoln et al. 2008; Broman et al. 2008).

Over the years, our most perceptive PIT volunteer has been Blanche, a PhD student who has since completed her degree and moved on. Blanche had considerable contact with homeless people long before her PIT experiences and also worked for several years as an advocate for domestic violence victims. So her initial pre-PIT views were pretty sophisticated: "Largely based on information received from homelessness experts, I viewed the homeless population as predominantly 'between homes,' with a relatively minor portion chronically homeless. I am sure I have been guilty of judging the homeless in the distant past before becoming educated on social inequalities, but fortunately, these attitudes were long gone by the time of my involvement in the PIT count." Her reflections on her volunteer experiences are an eloquent summary of many of the themes of this chapter, and indeed of the book:

Blanche: My participation affirmed for me what I had learned in an academic setting about the homeless, but added a level of humanity that I could not have gotten from a textbook, or even from hearing of the first-hand experiences from homelessness experts. My experience in the PIT count and other projects with the homeless gave me a sense of responsibility to this population in terms of using my skills and knowledge to work for this population at any chance I get. It also put into perspective for me how similar the homeless really are to the "housed" in terms of how easily it can happen without resources, particularly in difficult economic times.

Interviewer: Any certain experiences that stick out in your mind?

Blanche: The *people* are what stick out in my mind: the little girl who looked just like my own daughter who, on a night so cold we were wearing several layers (jeans, sweatshirts, gloves) and still were cold, was wearing what appeared to be a men's XL t-shirt and sandals as she entered the coalition; the chronically homeless and HIV infected man in line who hugged me and thanked me for caring about what he had to say after he answered my questions; the woman who gave up her job to care for her ailing mother and grandmother, only to be rejected by her family when they died and she had nowhere to go; the man who lost his job, his family, and his home, when he suffered a ruptured colon and could not afford the medical bills; the countless veterans who were either middle-aged and chronically homeless, or the twenty-six-year-old who had been more recently discharged and had nowhere to go, etc., etc., etc.

Interviewer: Please tell me anything else you think would be pertinent for me to know regarding the effect of participating in a PIT count on your views/perceptions on homelessness and homeless people.

Blanche: I think homelessness is one of the social problems that can only truly be appreciated by seeing it. It has the ability to instill a sense of genuine empathy that cannot be achieved in any other way, and also gives participants the opportunity to see how pervasive the problem is (i.e., it is quite shocking to see how many people are at each of the facilities). You also get a good sense of the political corruption associated with serving this population, which inspired me to become more politically active and aware of social policy pertaining to the homeless and other disadvantaged groups.

Notes

1. Over the years, the various church and other meal service groups have come to "own" specific nights, e.g., the first Wednesday of the month, the second Tuesday, and so on. Thus, most volunteer groups have a standing monthly commitment to serve, which accounts for the large percentage that volunteer monthly and have done so for years.
2. Of the small number who had done something other than serve food, the most common "other task" performed was assisting in organizing and sorting donations. Other items mentioned included giving parties, raising money, and one-on-one ministry.
3. It is likely the case that many people interpreted these questions more broadly than we intended them, i.e., as questions about donating to or volunteering at homeless service agencies in general, not just at the Coalition. For present purposes, this scarcely matters.

12

A Tale of Two Cities:
Homeless Politics and Services in
Miami and Orlando

What to do with, for, or about the homeless has bedeviled American cities[1] since the current outbreak of homelessness began in the late 1970s and early 1980s. In this, Florida cities are no exception. In the early 1980s, vast segments of the city of Miami, Florida's largest metro area, approximated Third World homelessness conditions, with immense homeless camps under many of the bridges and overpasses, thousands of street people wandering about the city, and a quasi-official policy of dispersal, indifference, and repression. Street sweeps, demolition of homeless camps, and the confiscation and destruction of homeless peoples' belongings were near-daily occurrences. Much of this went on with the tacit consent of local government and the implicit approval of many downtown business and development interests. And with good reason: the uncontrolled growth of homelessness in downtown Miami was threatening to destroy the quality of urban life.

Homelessness wasn't doing much for the quality of life in Orlando in those years either. Articles in the local paper, the Orlando *Sentinel,* circa late-1980s, routinely referred to the "flood of homeless people" in the city's streets and public places.[2] By 1987, the homeless situation in Orlando was sufficiently alarming to the city's Downtown Development Board that they coughed up $350,000 to help a group of concerned citizens, mostly people of faith, open a shelter to get homeless men off the streets at night. (This shelter eventually became the Coalition's Pavilion, which has been featured in many previous chapters.) An article in the New Orleans *Times-Picayune* compared the homeless situation in Orlando before the shelter opened with the then-current situation in New Orleans and remarked on the "hundreds [of homeless people] that Orlando police say once roamed the business district, almost taking over public spaces after sundown" (Charles 1996). Lake Eola Park, the very lovely centerpiece of the City Beautiful, "was once so rife with homeless people that visitors feared to use it." (The presence of homeless people in the park is still a point of contention some two decade later.) In the late 1980s and early 1990s, homeless encampments in and around Orlando were so common that the City Council enacted an anti-camping ordinance as a homeless containment measure. Orlando police, following the lead of Miami, routinely arrested hundreds of homeless people each year for violating various municipal ordinances involving camping, loitering, panhandling, or public intoxication. A 1997 document discussing these efforts stated, "In the past three years, Orlando police have taken more than 2,400 people to jail for camping, panhandling or loitering, according to jail records. And the frequency of the filings continues to grow" (Budd 1997).

In sum, by the early 1990s, homelessness had become a serious problem in both Miami and Orlando. In both cities, it seemed, homeless people were *everywhere*, and alarmed citizens were loudly demanding that something be done. From these shared beginnings, however, local policies and politics towards the homeless took divergent paths. The result, some twenty years later, is that Miami is a nationally recognized center of excellence in the provision of homeless services whereas Orlando struggles to fund even its rudimentary feeding and shelter programs.

The Miami-Dade County Homeless Trust, the principal entity in Miami that oversees the provision of homeless services, is widely perceived as a model that other cities visit and try to emulate (Donley and Wright 2010). Indeed, officials from Orlando have site-visited the various Miami homeless facilities on numerous occasions to try to figure out what makes Miami so successful. (As we see later, the answer turns out to be pretty obvious, but no one wants to hear it.) Miami's Homeless Trust was among the first in the nation to adopt Housing First as an intervention model for the city's chronically homeless population; has won prizes for the deployment and creative use of its Homeless Management Information System; has worked with the Miami-Dade County school board to develop and implement a public school homelessness awareness curriculum; has forged alliances with many dozens of community partners, and with its private-sector partner, the Community Partnership for the

Homeless, has built two state-of-the-art homeless shelters (Miami-Dade's famous Homeless Assistance Centers, or HACs) that are widely regarded as among the best emergency shelter facilities in the nation.

Orlando, on the other hand, waged a decade-long battle with the Coalition for the Homeless of Central Florida over the very *location* of the city's principal service center for homeless people (a battle that has finally been resolved), has only recently developed (and has yet to meaningfully fund or implement) its ten-year plan to end chronic homelessness (in this regard, Orlando lags behind some 350 other U.S. cities), continues to land in the national media for its efforts to criminalize homelessness, and was identified in a 2009 joint report from the National Law Center on Poverty and Homelessness and the National Coalition for the Homeless as the third "meanest" city in America in terms of policies towards the homeless (out of 224 cities covered in the report). How the two cities started where they did and got to where they are is an interesting story recounted in some detail in the following pages.

Miami

Our Miami story begins with a homeless man named Michael Pottinger. In 1988, Pottinger, along with two other homeless men named Peter Carter and Berry Young, in conjunction with the local chapter of the ACLU, filed a class-action lawsuit alleging that

> The City of Miami has a policy of harassing homeless people for sleeping, eating, and performing life sustaining activities in public places. In addition ... the city routinely seizes and destroys [homeless persons'] property and fails to follow its inventory procedures when confiscating personal property. Pursuant to 42 U.S.C. Sec. 1983, the class asserts that the city's activities constitute cruel and unusual punishment, malicious abuse of process, and unlawful searches and seizures, in violation of due process, the right to privacy, and the Equal Protection Clause.[3]

In relief, the suit demanded "declaratory judgment, compensatory damages, and reasonable attorney's fees. Additionally, the class sought to stop the city from arresting homeless people for conducting necessary life sustaining activities and from destroying their personal property."

Advocacy groups in many other cities, Orlando included, tried to pursue similar legal strategies at about the same time or shortly thereafter (and for that matter, ever since), but none had the outcome or dramatic effect of *Pottinger*. The Court's decision in this now-famous case was the game-changer, the initial impetus for a fundamental transformation in how Miami's movers and shakers looked upon their homeless population. A second major factor, not discussed at length here but not to be dismissed, was Hurricane Andrew, the devastating 1992 Category 5 hurricane that leveled the better part of South Florida and rendered thousands of its victims homeless. Andrew was the object lesson, there for anyone to see, that innocent people could become homeless for reasons beyond their control, and that being homeless was not necessarily the homeless person's fault.

The *Pottinger* suit bubbled through the legal system for four years before it was decided in favor of the plaintiffs in the U.S. District Court for the Southern District of Florida in November 1992. Ironically, and perhaps not coincidentally, this was just three months after Hurricane Andrew had destroyed an estimated 25,500 homes and inflicted serious damage on an additional 100,000—no time to be insensitive to the needs of the homeless! The ruling was a slam-dunk. The court found that Miami's practice of arresting people for "harmless life sustaining activities that they are forced to perform in public" was in violation of the Eighth Amendment (these arrests were found to constitute cruel and unusual punishment), the due process clause of the Fourteenth Amendment, and also "burdened the fundamental right to travel in violation of the Equal Protection Clause." Police seizure and destruction of homeless persons' property was found to be in violation of the Fourth Amendment guarantee against unreasonable search and seizure. For relief, the court ordered the City of Miami to comply with the plaintiffs' requests for declaratory and injunctive relief. The City was required to establish safe zones where homeless people could stay without being arrested for "life-sustaining activities." The injunction defined eleven specific "life-sustaining misdemeanors," e.g., being in a park after curfew hours; eating, sleeping, sitting, congregating, or camping in public places; public nudity, urination or defecation; living or sleeping in a vehicle; and the like, for which homeless persons could not be arrested (or even warned about). The police were also ordered to stop arresting homeless people for these activities and to stop confiscating and destroying their property. Numerous other provisions to protect Miami's homeless population from official abuse, harassment, and discrimination were also made.

The City, of course, immediately appealed the court's decision, challenging the basis and scope of the injunction. The appeal was heard two years later, in December 1994, was remanded to the District Court for clarification, and was reheard in April 1995, at which point the original findings and injunction were basically upheld. In February 1996, the entire matter was referred to mediation and a mediation agreement was reached in December 1997, nearly a decade after the original suit was filed. (In the interim, Pottinger himself had died—where, when, or how, no one seems to know.) The agreement provided for law enforcement training, policy, and protocols to prevent the arrests, harassment, or destruction of the property of homeless people; for an advisory committee to monitor compliance and investigate complaints; for a compensation fund of $600,000 to be disbursed in $1,500 lots via pre-loaded debit cards to homeless persons who had been injured by the unconstitutional conduct of the Miami police; and for "reasonable" attorney's and expert witness fees, a small chunk of which went to the senior author of this book for his testimony on behalf of the plaintiffs.[4]

Despite the decision to appeal the Court's ruling, the City was under no illusions about the likely outcome. In an off-the-record conversation with the plaintiff's expert witness, the city attorney defending the case admitted, "We really don't have a leg to stand on." Even before the appeal was heard, Miami-Dade County took two dramatically positive and significant steps forward. First, a systematic 1992 assessment of the regional homeless problem determined that the problem was far too large to be solved by the private sector alone and that some sort of dedicated, ongoing source of public funding for homeless services would be necessary. The Florida State Legislature, supported by then-Governor Lawton Chiles and acting on the request of the Miami-Dade County Commission, passed legislation enabling a 1 percent "add-on" sales tax on food and beverages sold by establishments with gross annual revenues exceeding $400,000. This tax was implemented in Miami-Dade County in 1993 without significant opposition and now provides about $14 million per year in dedicated funding for homeless services (with 15 percent of the revenue dedicated to domestic violence shelters). Affluent people in Miami who run up a hundred-dollar bar bill get dinged for one extra buck, and the result is eight figures of dedicated annual revenue to fund homeless services. How many site visits does it take to figure out that this must be a significant element in the Miami success story?

In addition to the food and beverage tax, on May 18, 1993, the Miami-Dade County Commission appointed a Task Force on Homelessness to determine what services Miami should be trying to provide to its homeless people with the new revenues. The Task Force was charged with developing a plan to comply with *Pottinger*, but went beyond mere compliance to create a truly comprehensive approach to dealing with the region's homelessness problem. A central part of the plan, the *Dade County Community Homelessness Plan*, was to create the Miami-Dade County Homeless Trust "to oversee that portion of the Food and Beverage tax dedicated to homeless programs and to ensure that the proceeds are used in a manner which will provide the greatest benefit to homeless persons and the community as a whole" (Task Force on Homelessness 1994: 21).

Significantly, the co-chairs of the Task Force on Homelessness that created the Community Homeless Plan were then-Commissioner Alex Penelas and Mr. Alvah H. Chapman, Jr. Penelas was at the time the youngest county commissioner in Dade County history. On October 1, 1996, he became the first Executive Mayor of Miami-Dade County, serving in that capacity until 2004—i.e., throughout the formative period of the Homeless Trust and the Community Homeless Plan. From the Trust's inception in 1994 until the end of his tenure as Mayor, Penelas also served as the Trust's chair. Mayor Penelas was an enormously charismatic and influential figure who was voted "America's sexiest politician" by *People* in 1999. That the Community Homeless Plan was *his* plan made a huge difference in getting Miami's influential citizens to take the plan seriously.

Penelas' co-chair was Alvah Chapman, one-time publisher of *The Miami Herald*, chairman of the Knight Ridder newspaper chain, and by all accounts one of South Florida's most influential philanthropic and civic leaders. Chapman's list of accomplishments includes literally scores of philanthropic and charitable activities. In 1995, he became the founding chairman of the Community Partnership for the Homeless, the private partner of the Miami-Dade County Homeless Trust and the entity that operates the Homeless Assistance Centers. The downtown Homeless Assistance Center is adorned by Chapman's bust. It is doubtlessly a fair assessment that pretty much anyone Penelas could not "deliver" to the service of the homeless plan, Chapman could—and this kind of political leadership was also a decisive factor in Miami's long-term success.

Significantly, Penelas was succeeded as Executive Mayor by the current incumbent, Mayor Carlos Alvarez, a former director of the Miami-Dade Police Department. Alvarez has also embraced the cause of homelessness and sits voluntarily as a member of the Board of Directors of the Homeless Trust. Numerous other influential community members also serve on the Trust's Board of Directors, which is chaired by Ronald L. Book, described in *Newsweek* as "one of the state's most powerful lobbyists." Clearly, Miami's Homeless Trust has never suffered for lack of political clout.

Over time, the Miami-Dade County Homeless Trust became the regional lead agency for the U.S. Department of Housing and Urban

Development's "Continuum of Care" (CoC). Each year, HUD awards an array of program funds to local communities to combat homelessness and requires that all applications from a particular area or jurisdiction be coordinated through a single "Continuum of Care" lead agency. Thus, the Homeless Trust has become the organization responsible not only for overseeing the distribution of proceeds from the Food and Beverage Tax, but also for organizing the entire community-wide Continuum of Care effort, an effort that directly or indirectly involves scores of community agencies and programs. Considering both HUD funds and tax revenues, the Trust has annual revenues of more than $40 million.

Most homeless service providers in the Miami CoC also fund-raise independently of the Homeless Trust and operate homeless programs other than those funded by the Trust, so the Trust's $40 million is only a down-payment on the annual cost of providing direct services to Miami's homeless people. According to David Raymond, Executive Director of the Homeless Trust, the total annual expenditure on direct homeless services in Miami-Dade County is at least *twice* the Trust's $40 million, including leveraged funds—i.e., $75 or $80 million each year and quite possibly more than that. In contrast, the Orlando Mayor's Working Committee on Homelessness (about which we will provide more later) estimated in its 2004 report that the equivalent figure for the Orlando metropolitan area was on the order of $10 million; today's figure, according to Orlando's Homeless Services Network, may be closer to $20 million, but surely not much more than that.[5] Miami-Dade County is about twice as populous as the Orlando metro area but spends four or five times more money each year to feed, clothe, treat, shelter, and house its homeless population.

Equally as impressive is the vision expressed in the original Dade County Community Homelessness Plan and the degree to which that plan has been followed in the decade and a half since. In 1994, the homeless population of Miami-Dade was estimated to be about 6,000 persons (at the time, figures of eight or even ten thousand were also being promulgated, but a count of about 6,000 was cited repeatedly in the *Pottinger* proceedings and no one on either side contested this figure). In contrast, the public emergency housing system in early 1990s Miami consisted of some 230 emergency shelter beds and perhaps 50 transitional beds. Non-profit organizations added about 600 emergency beds to the overall capacity, most of them targeted to single men. Finally, there were perhaps 500 "treatment" beds in mental health and substance abuse programs serving a predominantly homeless clientele.

At the outside, the total capacity in 1994 was adequate to provide shelter and some minimal services to not more than one out of four homeless people in Dade County.

The Task Force's plan to address the shortfall was a three-stage system of services: *temporary care* to "provide immediate short term housing and basic support services to persons now residing in public places"; *primary care* to provide transitional housing with treatment and rehabilitation to homeless persons found in need of substance abuse treatment, vocational training, mental health treatment, or basic education; and *advanced care*, defined in the plan as "supported long term housing such as church assisted housing, supported Single Room Occupancy residence, and assisted apartment or other residential arrangements" (p. 5). In contemporary parlance, these are immediately recognizable as emergency assistance, transitional care, and permanent housing—i.e., what we now know as the HUD Continuum of Care. So in its thinking about a comprehensive continuum of services, the original Community Homeless Plan was quite forward-thinking.

To support and promote the three-stage services system, the plan envisioned aggressive outreach whereby professionals and volunteers from the emergency shelters would "visit homeless people to urge them to enter into the centers." This outreach function was expected to be a "formal networking system between provider agencies and law enforcement personnel to ensure a humane and sensitive approach to dealing with homeless persons" (p. 9). These observations led directly to the Miami-Dade County outreach program, a network of more than fifty paid outreach workers, many of them formerly homeless people, who work out of the Miami police department's Neighborhood Enhancement Centers to reach out to street people and bring them into the Continuum of Care. And while this outreach function is not without problems, it would be nearly impossible for a homeless person to be on the streets of Miami or Dade County for more than forty-eight hours without being approached by an outreach worker and referred to a treatment center or emergency shelter, depending on apparent need.

The Task Force was clear that the first priority would be emergency shelter through the Homeless Assistance Centers. The original plan was for 1000-1500 new emergency beds, but as they evolved, the two centers came to serve approximately 750 homeless people and families nightly (with other providers making up the difference). The first center opened in downtown Miami in October 1995; the second began operations in October 1998 at the former Homestead Air Force Base in South

Miami-Dade County (ground zero, incidentally, for Hurricane Andrew in Florida). Construction of the first HAC, then, was well underway before the City's *Pottinger* appeal was even heard. In fact, the appellate court noted favorably that since the 1992 order, the City and its private partners had begun construction of homeless shelters that would address some of the problems that undergirded the district court's ruling. Rather than endless hemming and hawing about where to locate a shelter, the Community Partnership for the Homeless (CPH) found a suitable site, negotiated a "good neighbor" agreement with the surrounding community, and stuck a shovel in the dirt. This is indicative of what can be accomplished with the kind of political leadership and funding CPH and the Homeless Trust have enjoyed over the years.

CPH now provides daily food, shelter, and case management services to about 750 homeless men, women, and children on two separate physical campuses. The annual budget for the overall CPH operation is about $12 million. The Coalition for the Homeless of Central Florida also provides daily food, shelter, and case management services to about 750 homeless men, women, and children on two separate physical campuses. And the annual budget for their operation is about $3.5 million. Is it any surprise that the HACs seem to realize better outcomes?

In addition to 1000-1500 new emergency shelter beds, the plan also envisioned 750 new "primary care" beds within three years. There was no stated goal for stage-three permanent supported housing, only the recognition that such would be the "final stage" in the continuum of care and that "during the next five years, considerable attention must be placed on expanding advanced care facilities for homeless adults and families" (p. 14). As indicated, the plan also anticipated the need for an extensive program of outreach and likewise a need "to coordinate interagency prevention efforts."

The Homeless Trust as it exists today bears a striking resemblance to what the Task Force on Homelessness envisioned fifteen years ago. The outreach system has already been described. As of 2008-09, the Homeless Trust and its Continuum of Care had developed the following capacity:[6]

- 1,402 emergency shelter beds, 786 beds for single individuals and 616 set aside to shelter families, with another 132 emergency beds currently under development. The total shelter capacity in place or in development amounts to 1,534 beds, compared to the original target of 1000-1500. (In 2009, 54 additional emergency shelter beds were added to the capacity, bringing the total to 1,588.)

- 1,895 transitional treatment beds for homeless people with alcohol, drug, psychiatric, physical or other disabilities (versus the original target of 750).
- Some 2,666 units of permanent supported housing already on-line, with a goal to add a hundred new units per year. All told, the Homeless Trust and its partners command approximately 6,000 units of housing for formerly homeless people, almost half of which is supported housing with wrap-around services and the remainder of which is mainstream affordable housing for very low income people.

Today, including clients seen in the homeless prevention program, the Trust and its many collaborators serve 19,000 people annually. The Continuum of Care consists of some twenty-seven agencies and providers working together in a well-coordinated network along with innumerable other collaborations with various city, county, and regional entities. With a few exceptions, the homeless encampments have been largely eliminated, the number of homeless people living in the streets has declined from an estimated 6,000 at the time of *Pottinger* to somewhere around a thousand today (the "official" number from the most recent count is 1,074), and a very extensive and aggressive system of outreach has been established throughout the county to assure that homeless people are aware of the services available to them.

As one Miami stakeholder explained to us in an interview, the key to the Trust's success is that they took a "visionary plan, implemented it, and have stuck with it from the beginning. They have provided consistency and steadiness of vision, have established coordination among the providers, manage their money well, and bring in lots of it." These are not things that would be said of Orlando, whose leaders have a long, sorry history of indifference to a succession of homelessness plans, recommendations, and reports, up to and including the current "Ten 2 End" plan to eliminate chronic homelessness in the Orlando community.

Miami's initial Community Homeless Plan certainly did not envision the end of homelessness, but in the past decade, Miami, along with about 350 other U.S. cities (now including Orlando), have developed and have begun to implement ten-year plans to end homelessness. With program models developed and promulgated by the Interagency Council on Homelessness and the National Alliance to End Homelessness, and with new funding in the pipeline from HUD, many cities have (more or less) realistic aspirations to be rid of homelessness, or at least chronic homelessness, once and for all.[7]

Miami's paradigm for ending homelessness (the same as in many other cities) is to "close the front door and open the back door," i.e., to be aggressive about preventing people and families from becoming homeless in the first place and even more aggressive about getting them out of shelters and back into housing once they have become homeless. Yet a third piece is to develop housing infrastructure to provide acceptable housing options to low income people.

Miami's Homeless Trust has relatively successful programs focused on homeless prevention through rent assistance and case management, rapid rehousing of persons and families who have fallen into homelessness, and Housing First (an intervention strategy discussed at length in Chapter Four). Of these, homeless prevention has proven the most vexing. A well-worn cliché promises that "an ounce of prevention is worth a pound of cure." However, the number of people on the verge of becoming homeless is so large (see Chapter Two) that trying to prevent a significant fraction of them from becoming homeless may be like trying to bail out a sinking ocean liner with a teaspoon. Most homeless prevention programs find themselves overwhelmed by demand that quickly depletes the resources available, and in this Miami is no exception. Thus, in terms of sheer economic efficiency, it may be necessary to let people become homeless, intercept them as early in the process as possible, then get them back into housing quickly—i.e., rapid rehousing instead of homeless prevention.

As for infrastructure development, Miami's Homeless Trust has advocated aggressively for the "30:30" campaign, an effort to set aside 30 percent of the affordable housing stock for people at or below 30 percent of the area median income. They have also forged dozens of collaborative arrangements with affordable housing developers and providers, some of whom receive Trust funding and many of whom do not. No big city has enough affordable housing to satisfy the need and probably won't anytime soon, and no city will be able to eliminate homelessness completely so long as this remains true. But Miami and its Homeless Trust are at least making the effort.

In their meta-evaluation of CoC evaluations, Burt et al. (2002) conclude that the question about ending homelessness needs to be divided into two distinct questions: (1) Has the system managed to generate more and better exits from homelessness? (2) Has it prevented fewer entries? In Miami, the answer to the first question is a qualified "yes." With 2,666 units of permanent supportive housing to work with, being "fed" by nearly 2,000 transitional treatment beds, little of which existed when the Trust was formed sixteen years ago, homeless people in Miami have vastly better exit chances today than they did before. And clearly, there are many fewer homeless people on the streets. On the other hand, both the treatment programs and the permanent housing programs have waiting lists, and vacancies in the permanent housing programs are rare, so "exit" remains problematic for many.

As for limiting new entries into homelessness, a massive investment of resources in homeless prevention would be required and that is probably not in the cards anywhere, the federal Homelessness Prevention and Rapid Rehousing Program (HPRP) notwithstanding. As Burt et al. explain

> With possibly one or two exceptions, none of the communities we visited appears to have reduced the entry of newly homeless people into the system, or the overall volume of homeless people served by the system. To do so will require addressing the two ends of the CoC, prevention and affordable housing, neither of which can be done without significant involvement of mainstream agencies and strong support from the wider community.

Miami has clearly gone further than most CoCs in bringing "mainstream agencies and the wider community" to the table, so while ending homelessness altogether is an audacious and unattainable goal, it is less improbable in Miami than in most American cities.

Orlando

We began our Miami story in 1988, when the *Pottinger* suit was filed. The Orlando story begins in 1987 with the founding of the Coalition for the Homeless of Central Florida and the opening of the city's first large shelter for homeless men. As in most cities, there were certainly precursor organizations that provided some services to some of the city's homeless population. The Salvation Army had been a presence in Orlando since 1915. The Orlando Rescue Mission was founded in 1948; the Christian Service Center, in 1971. But all three of these programs were focused on homeless individuals with alcohol or other addictions problems and were "high demand" shelters that offered shelter and services only to homeless people who had some weeks or months of sobriety under their belts and who were anxious, or at least willing, to work a program and make some changes. Despite these programs, many of Orlando's growing number of homeless people literally had no place to go. They would spend their days in downtown parks and other public places and their nights sleeping in storefronts, alleyways, or simply out in the open. These very visibly homeless people were increasingly seen as a nuisance and pressure mounted to get them off the streets and into some sort of contained facility.

When the shelter that would eventually become the Pavilion opened in Orlando in 1987, in the former site of the downtown bus station, it was widely hailed as an innovation deserving of emulation elsewhere. Indeed, the Dade County Community Homelessness Plan referred approvingly to the "Orlando Plan" as "one model for the Homeless Assistance Centers." The Orlando model was also cited favorably in the New Orleans *Times-Picayune* article that we quoted earlier (Charles 1996). "With its lenient rules, airy design, and 500-bed capacity, the Pavilion was conceived as a way to attract and consolidate the hard-core homeless men who wandered downtown in Orlando, a city ever sensitive about the image it portrays to tourists, the life blood of its economy." "Attract and consolidate"—a pleasant euphemism for getting homeless people out of sight and out of mind. And that has always been Orlando's basic homeless strategy. Note, too, the inevitable reference to the region's tourists. Speculation about what the tourists might think has driven a great deal of public policy-making in Central Florida for the last four decades.

What made the Pavilion and its bus-station precursor "innovative" and of interest to other cities was simply that it was a low-demand facility: all comers were welcome so long as they were not actively hallucinating, not seriously ill, and not of immediate danger to self or others. "Unlike most shelters for the homeless, the Pavilion admits men still glassy-eyed from alcohol or other drugs. It allows them to hang out all day, under only gentle pressure to devise a plan for their recuperation" (Charles 1996). Over the years, the stay-all-day policy has changed. Today, Pavilion men are rousted at 6:30 or 7:00 in the morning and made to leave unless they are ill, physically handicapped, or work nights and need to sleep in the day.[8] But as the first Director of the Orlando shelter put it in her interview with the *Times-Picayune*, "One of the things we *don't* do is make judgments and select who can get service." This come-one, come-all policy has only recently wavered.

When the shelter first opened, there was an apparently dramatic reduction in the numbers of homeless men hanging out in downtown public spaces, especially at night. But the shelter was located at the western edge of the developed downtown area and the city was rapidly growing in exactly that direction, so there was an almost immediate sense that the shelter needed to be moved elsewhere. Attention focused on Parramore, the city's historically black, mostly low-income neighborhood. Parramore was (and is) characterized by high rates of crime and poverty and a great deal of substandard housing and abandoned property. The shelter was relocated in 1992 to the former studios of WFTE-TV, well inside Parramore and outside what was then the Central Business District (CBD), and was re-opened as the Pavilion, offering pretty much the same services as it offers today.

By the time of the 1992 relocation, the homeless "problem" in downtown Orlando was again worsening and demands to "do something" were again being voiced. One obvious solution—opening additional homeless facilities or expanding the capacity of existing facilities—ran into a stone wall in 1998, when the City Council enacted a 120-day moratorium on adding new beds to any facility for the homeless anywhere in the city limits. A few months later, the city amended its land use policy to include the following clause: "The location of new homeless facilities and social service agencies in the Parramore Heritage area shall be prohibited." Any expansion of existing social service facilities was also banned. What soon came to be called the Parramore moratorium in essence denied the city's poorest neighborhoods any further social services facilities or capacity beyond what had existed as of October 1998. Significantly, virtually all the city's homeless services had by 1998 been relocated into the Parramore neighborhood, so this amounted to an immediate halt to any new, improved or expanded services for Orlando's homeless population, which continued to grow.

Why the moratorium? By the end of the 1990s, Parramore was being looked on as the last remaining chunk of developable real estate in the near-downtown area and the "redevelopment of Parramore" was therefore seen as an integral element in any plan to rejuvenate downtown. Parramore's City Commissioner had long objected to the presence of the Pavilion in particular and homeless services in general in her District because they seemed to attract "undesirables." Thus, from the late 1990s until 2008, there was intense political pressure to relocate the Pavilion yet again. Indeed, the 2004 Orlando Mayor's Parramore Task Force Report specifically recommended—as a "first step" toward the goal of improving the community's "compatibility" with larger development goals—"Relocate the Coalition for the Homeless and other similar facilities ... to achieve goals such as neighborhood preservation" (Mayor's Parramore Task Force 2004: p. 25).[9]

Enforcement of the moratorium frequently bordered on the bizarre. The Christian Service Center tried to pull permits to build locker rooms with showers so its male clients could clean up before job interviews. Denied! The Orlando Union Rescue Mission asked for permission to remodel its façade into something more compatible with the surrounding neighborhood. Denied! The Salvation Army, responding to a growing number of homeless families, acquired property and asked for permission to build low-cost housing units for those very families. Denied! The Coalition for the Homeless rapidly outgrew its facility in the old TV station when it added programs for women, children, and families (all before the 1998 moratorium, of course), but every request to expand or even remodel within the existing footprint was denied. Various advocacy groups threatened legal action from time to time, but it was 2008 before the moratorium was successfully challenged, and then only partly. As of this writing (2010), the legal status of the moratorium is *still* not completely clear.

The Coalition and its Men's Pavilion were at the heart of the moratorium controversy and city officials spent the better part of a decade trying to move the facility somewhere else. Why? First, the Coalition occupies about three acres of land in the very heart of Parramore, and whenever discussions about the redevelopment of the neighborhood would break out, the Coalition's three acres were always an attractive target, even though there are large tracts of re-developable and, in some cases, entirely abandoned land all over the neighborhood, including large vacant lots on two sides of the Coalition site. As a matter of fact, a great deal of redevelopment has already taken place in Parramore despite the Coalition's presence: the Amway Arena (where the Orlando Magic play basketball), a new "events center" (where the Magic *will* play basketball starting in 2011), a new federal court house, the new FAMU Law School, an Orlando Police Department facility, and new national offices for the Hughes Tool Corporation (the latter also featuring several retail outlets and some high-end condos—all literally across the street from the Pavilion).

More important, perhaps, than the Coalition's three acres was its symbolic significance as Orlando's largest facility for the down and out. The poverty, racism, and political indifference that created Parramore and that now create homelessness are realities that Orlando, like most cities, would prefer to regard as things of the past, as last century's problems, not as continuing realities in today's world. The persistence and visibility of homeless people in the very heart of the Parramore community seems symbolically incompatible with revitalization plans and, in a larger sense, with Orlando's self-image as a post-modern city.

In 2004, we initiated a series of focus group studies to bring the voices of homeless people themselves into the relocation debate. What would it mean to the day-to-day existence of Coalition clients if the homeless center were moved out of downtown? About half the people served by the Coalition are women and children. How would the children's lives be impacted? In May of 2004, we conducted focus groups with five homeless women and nine homeless men to broach these topics and establish a baseline of information. Thereafter, each time a new site was proposed, we would load a group of clients into a Coalition van, visit the proposed site, then come back and do another focus group. Between 2004 and 2008, about a half dozen of these little mini-studies were conducted.

The focus groups dealt with issues of time, inconvenience, cost, safety, relative isolation, and the psychological stressors associated with each of these. Some of the things we learned were predictable and had gone into the original development of the Board's relocation criteria, but the homeless participants in our studies also grasped subtleties that had eluded everyone else. Since the current location is within walking distance of the main bus terminal, Coalition residents can get pretty much anywhere downtown in thirty to sixty minutes. They simply walk to the central station and board whatever bus takes them where they need to go. Relocation to a more remote site, they feared, would cause them to miss busses, miss appointments, be late picking their children up from child care, or be late for work. They would need to take one bus to the main terminal then transfer to another bus to get where they needed to go. These problems were compounded by the local bus system's notorious unreliability, the likelihood of missed connections, and the added expense in boarding a new bus once the transfer (good for only ninety minutes) had expired. In one woman's case, moving away from the central location would have added another hour of travel time to and from work and would require her to transfer her daughter to a new school. (This was a problem for several women.) The added travel time would have also made her unable to be home with her daughter before and after school, thus imposing significant child care expenses that she could ill afford.

One proposed location would have required daily treks through an area infested with prostitutes and drug dealers. Many clients, male and female, worried about how this might affect their personal safety, but the women eloquently voiced another concern: the possibility that they would be mistaken for prostitutes. These women already struggle daily with the stigmas of poverty, homelessness, and (for the majority) race. Adding the misperception that they were also hookers was more than they could bear.

Despite their misgivings, Coalition residents were stoic about and resigned to the larger forces in play. One woman said

I know whatever place they intend to move us to would be worse than this place. This area is beginning to clean up a little bit and so now they want to make lots of money off us rather than let us stay here. And, maybe us having helped a little bit to make this section of town a better place than it used to be is part of the problem. But we don't see that credit being given to us. There's 200 of us in this tiny building that want better than what we had when we got here.

In the same vein, another stated, "I know without a shadow of doubt that if they move us, it's going to be in a worse area of town. I know they wouldn't find us a better place." With only a couple of exceptions, the City's proposed sites confirmed the accuracy of these perceptions: an abandoned industrial site with no nearby amenities or services, a drug-infested area far from the city core, a site bordered by active and busy railroad tracks, and so on.

In another investigation, we surveyed the people in line at the Coalition's evening feeding program. We learned that a fifth of those in line were not homeless people, but rather poor people and families from the surrounding neighborhoods. (In our tabulations from Burt's national survey [2001], about a third of persons surveyed in soup kitchens were not currently homeless.) If the Coalition were relocated to a remote site, where would these individuals and families eat? When concerns were expressed about the "bums and beggars" that lived at the Coalition's Men's Pavilion, we undertook a survey of the men about their economic activities (see Chapter Three). Two out of three spent their days working or looking for work (often in the nearby day labor outlets); more than half of the remaining third were disabled and were literally unable to work.

The wrangling about where to locate the region's largest facility for homeless people finally ended in 2008, when the city announced that the Coalition would be allowed to stay where it was indefinitely, to expand and improve its services, and to replace the Pavilion with an all-new Men's Service Center. It is hard to say exactly what "turned the tide," but it was certainly not any of the research we had done. In retrospect, the city had been as frustrated as the Coalition with its inability to locate an acceptable alternative. Part of the frustration, surely, was that every time information about a potential new site was leaked, local residents, businesses, and neighborhood associations would flood City Hall with howls of protestation. In addition, the collapse of the real estate market in 2008 and the ensuing collapse of the local and national economies made Parramore's redevelopment an increasingly unlikely proposition. Why think about new high-rise condo buildings in Parramore when downtown developers were already going bankrupt because the market for high-end downtown condos had suddenly evaporated? A series of plans and drawings prepared by an architect on the Coalition Board made it visually obvious that a new facility would be a vast improvement over the current facility; a planned-for reduction in overall capacity and provisions for a secluded "day center" where homeless men could spend their days further allayed anxieties both in City Hall and in the Parramore neighborhood. Plans for the new facility were jump-started in 2009 when the City and County appropriated more than $5 million in construction funds.

While the City administration was dithering about where to relocate the Coalition for the Homeless, the City Council was finding new and creative ways to criminalize homeless people and their behaviors. Indeed, Orlando has been so relentless in its pursuit of a "legislative solution" to homelessness that it is routinely cited as one of the ten "meanest" cities in America towards homeless people.[10] Panhandling, for example, is commonly, but wrongly, associated with homelessness, as we saw in an earlier chapter, and is usually at the forefront of criminalization efforts. In 1996, Orlando responded to public demands to "do something" about panhandling by enacting an ordinance that required panhandlers to obtain a permit from the municipal police department in order to panhandle legally. Begging without the requisite permit can lead to sixty days in jail and a $500 fine. In 2000, the panhandling ordinance was amended to restrict downtown panhandling to designated areas marked by blue boxes painted on city sidewalks. That same ordinance prohibited "aggressive" panhandling:

> It shall be unlawful for any person to panhandle in any of the following manners: (a) By blocking the path of the person solicited; (b) By using profane or abusive language, either during the solicitation or following a refusal; (c) By panhandling in a group of two or more persons; or (d) By any statement, gesture, or other communication which a reasonable person in the situation of the person solicited would perceive to be a threat.

The city's long-standing anti-camping ordinance was discussed earlier. In 2002, the city code was again amended to prohibit lying or sitting on public sidewalks:

> It is unlawful for any person, after having been notified by a law enforcement officer of the prohibition in this section, to sit or lie down upon a public sidewalk or upon a blanket, chair, stool, or any other object placed upon a public sidewalk, in the Downtown Core District.

Exceptions are made for medical emergencies; age, infirmity, or disability; parades, festivals, and rallies; and when "the sitting or lying is while waiting in an orderly line for entry to any building, including shelters, or awaiting social services such as provision of meals; or outside a box office to purchase tickets to any sporting event, concert, performance, or other special event." Sitting or lying as part of a "planned public protest" is also permitted.

Much of the local agitation to enact these and similar ordinances results from the routine presence of the homeless in Lake Eola Park (and also Heritage Square Park, which is bounded by the Orlando Public Library and the Orange County History Center). A casual stroll around Lake Eola Park reveals "robust palm trees, beds of cheery begonias, a cascading lake fountain [now defunct], clusters of friendly egrets and swans, and an amphitheater named in honor of Walt Disney."[11] On an average day, the same stroll will bring one into contact with a handful of homeless people and also numerous posted signs that sternly summarize the applicable local ordinances. Near the shrubbery and benches are signs warning: "**Do not lie or otherwise be in a horizontal position on a park bench. Do not sleep or remain in any bushes, shrubs or foliage** ... per city code sec. 18A.09 (a) and (o)." Visit the public restroom in the park and you will be reminded: "**Bathing and/or shaving in restroom is prohibited** ... per city code 18A.09 (p) ... **Laundering clothes in Lake Eola Park is not permitted**." Fox News commented, "Since joggers and dog walkers tend not to snooze in flower beds, and because employees at the glittering office towers around Lake Eola don't scrub laundry in park sinks, it's clear at whom the notices are targeted"—the homeless. Indeed, the head of data management for the Orange County Jail once referred to these laws as the "homeless ordinances" and was unable to recall even a single housed person who had ever been arrested for violating any of them.

The latest twist in the Lake Eola Park saga was a July 2006 ordinance banning public feeding of homeless people, an ordinance that generated heaps of national publicity, none of it favorable. Various local groups, notably Food Not Bombs, had established the practice of feeding homeless people on the weekends in Lake Eola Park. This generated hostility among nearby businesses, local residents, and city leaders, and demands for some action to deter or prevent this behavior. Bowing to pressure, the City Council enacted a new law stating that persons or groups cannot feed more than twenty-five people at a time in any Orlando public place without obtaining a permit. This permit can only be obtained twice a year. A week before this ordinance took effect, the city of Las Vegas followed suit by making it illegal to give any food to transients in any city park, even one at a time. Maria Foscarinis of the National Law Center on Poverty and Homelessness was quoted in the Fox News story to the effect that Orlando and Las Vegas had "gone beyond punishing homeless people to punishing those trying to help them."

At first, the Orlando police simply ignored the ordinance as unenforceable, then tried to work with local religious and advocacy organizations to assure that homeless people were being fed in lots of twenty-four or less. But in March of 2007, under pressure from downtown residents and business interests, the Orlando police arrested an activist from Food Not Bombs after he was filmed violating the feeding ordinance by undercover officers. His arrest was the first real effort to enforce this controversial ordinance and, so far as we know, the first time in American history that someone was arrested for feeding homeless people. Feedings, of course, continued despite the arrest and the ACLU has challenged the constitutionality of the feeding ban in a suit that is still percolating through the system. The protestor, Eric Montanez, was later found not guilty. (In fairness, there are numerous feeding programs for homeless people in the downtown Orlando area and most service providers have pleaded with the Food Not Bombs people to work with existing programs as an outlet for their charitable impulses, so far to no avail.)

Snow, Baker and Anderson (1989) have remarked on the "ironic interplay" between the criminalization of homeless survival behaviors and the commission of serious crimes by homeless men. "Perceptions of heightened and threatening criminality ... can readily translate into political resistance to much needed services and facilities" (p. 546). Examples include everything from "criminalizing begging ... to blocking shelter construction," both of which have characterized Orlando's homeless policies. The concern, prescient in its insight, is that as homeless people's options narrow as a result of criminalization, "the option of more serious criminal activity as a survival strategy may become more viable, thus leading to a self-fulfilling prophecy of sorts. Hence, community decision makers may be well-advised to be more circumspect about passing laws that further criminalize life on the streets" (1989: p. 546-47).

Anti-panhandling ordinances clearly do not stop panhandling—not in Orlando or in any of the dozens of other cities that have tried them. Laws against sleeping in the parks do not prevent people from falling asleep wherever fatigue or inebriation overtakes them. Laws against feeding the homeless do not deter well-meaning, often religiously motivated, people from providing food to the hungry. These facts being incontrovertible, one might think that a city that was trying to solve its homeless problem by outlawing camping and loitering, requiring permits to panhandle, and prohibiting concerned citizens from feeding homeless people in public places must be suffering from a near-total absence of good advice on how to approach its homeless problem. But no. Since at least 1999, the city of Orlando has been blessed with a flood of expert reports, task force recommendations, and generally good advice, all of which has essentially been ignored. When Miami's leaders first saw their Task Force's Community Homelessness Plan, the general reaction was, "OK, that's the plan. What do we need to do to make it work?" When policy makers in Orlando receive a new plan, they politely thank the people who produced it, then shove the plan into their back pockets and go on about business as usual.

This story begins with a June 1999 report prepared by the UCF College of Health and Public Affairs and the Florida Institute of Government, *Homelessness as a Regional Problem in Central Florida: Analysis and Recommendations* (Poole, Chepenik and Zugazaga 1999). The very title expresses a problem recognized by nearly all observers of the Orlando scene for at least the last decade: since most homeless services in the region are concentrated in downtown Orlando, most of the region's homeless people are also found in downtown Orlando. However, they come into downtown from everywhere in the region; thus, the regional character of the problem has to be recognized and the associated costs have to be shared. Orlando city government bears a grossly disproportionate share of the cost of providing services to what is clearly a *regional* homeless population.

Alas, the Orlando metropolitan area (by Census definition) consists of four independent county governments and thirty-six independently incorporated municipalities, and when one city (Orlando) starts talking about a "regional" problem, the other thirty-five cities and all four counties slide their hands over their wallets and hang on. A "regional problem" can only mean that the one city has a problem that it wants everyone else to help pay for. So the recommendation of the UCF report to "establish a regional homeless commission" (p. 39) was ignored until the same recommendation was made again in a 2002 report from Mayor Glenda Hood's Community Conference on the Homeless, and then again in a 2004 report from Mayor Buddy Dyer's Working Committee on Homelessness. And even then, another three years passed before a

Regional Commission on the Homeless was finally established in June 2007. By 2010, incidentally, this long-awaited and much-anticipated Commission was hoping to merge with the local Homeless Services Network, but more on this later.

The 1999 UCF report was well-researched and tightly reasoned and the report's recommendations were fundamentally sound. However, all of it was ignored. The report cited the region's predominantly service sector employment as a "critical predictor of homelessness." "Most of the jobs in this sector involve lower-order services at minimum wage with marginal benefits" (pp. 31-32). The region's lack of affordable housing was also noted as a contributing factor, along with an explosive population growth that had brought large numbers of low-skilled people to the region in the hopes of finding economic opportunities that never materialized.

Among the weaknesses the report noted in the Orlando system of care were the reliance on emergency shelters as the point of entry, the concentration of shelters in the downtown area, the scarcity of good jobs and support services, the lack of detoxification and rehabilitation facilities for homeless substance abusers, an absence of efforts to prevent homelessness, and the "lack of comprehensive systems to plan, coordinate, integrate, evaluate and distribute responsibility for services across the full continuum of care throughout the region" (p. 34).

The report issued a series of "Action Recommendations" that went largely unheeded: develop a five-year plan to expand transitional and permanent housing options and shift away from the reliance on emergency shelter; establish comprehensive one-stop service hubs "within counties and across the region"; expand job placement and supported employment services for the homeless; increase treatment options for the addicted; "decentralize homeless facilities in Central Florida"; and expand what was then the Orange County Homeless Services Network (HSN) into a three county regional network. Of these and several other recommendations, only the latter was fully implemented. There has also been some decentralization of homeless services throughout the region, but mainly as a result of efforts by HSN and concerned citizens in the outlying counties, not as an official policy.

The local Homeless Services Network was incorporated in 1993 as an effort to coordinate homeless services across several dozen service-providing programs and agencies in Orlando and Orange County. Two years later, in 1995, HSN was designated as the lead agency for the local Continuum of Care and is thus the Orlando counterpart to the Miami-Dade County Homeless Trust. Then in 2000, following the UCF recommendation, HSN expanded to become a regional body representing Seminole County and Osceola County as well as Orange County. Until the Regional Commission was established in mid-2007, HSN was as close as the local area came to a regional entity focused on homeless issues.

For most of its existence, HSN was governed by a Board of Directors comprised entirely of representatives from the very service agencies that benefited from HUD Continuum of Care grants. In fact, the organization's bylaws *required* that Board members be homeless service providers. Thus, the organization's needs assessments and annual plans were always dominated by the needs and plans of the agencies represented on its Board, a source of considerable contention. This began to change when the current Executive Director of HSN took over the organization in 2006, demanded and received significant bylaw changes, and began expanding the Board to bring a wider range of expertise, contacts, and influence to the Network. Since 2006, HSN has received increasingly larger annual HUD awards and has emerged as a leading voice for the homeless in the Central Florida region, but has struggled to overcome its early history as "just" a little club of self-serving homeless providers.

There has always been, and remains even today, some local sentiment that HSN's functions should be vested in some other entity and the organization disbanded.[12] There was, for example, a much-discussed editorial in the Orlando *Sentinel* on January 7, 2003, which accused HSN of "dropping the ball" on its HUD application and laid the blame squarely on a Board of Directors made up mostly of "heads of small homeless agencies." The HSN Board, the editorial railed, had "failed to reach out to broader segments of the community," noting in particular that the HSN Board contained "no business people, no hospital executives, no high-ranking city, county, or law enforcement official." The editorial concluded with a call for local community leaders to step up and provide HSN with some "desperately needed fresh blood." To a significant extent, this has in fact happened under the organization's new leadership, but the HSN Board is still notably thin on political heavyweights.

HSN's annual Point in Time census of the homeless for 2009 (HSN 2009) counted just fewer than 4,000 homeless people in Central Florida. The 2009 HUD award to HSN was nearly $5.8 million, the largest HUD allocation in the organization's history. Interestingly, the 2009 Point in Time count in Miami showed 4,333 people in shelters, supportive housing, or on the streets. And the HUD award for 2009 to the Miami-Dade County Homeless Trust was $25.6 million. Converting to a *per capita* allocation, the Orlando award amounted to $1,461 for every homeless person; in Miami, to $5,908 per homeless person. This 4:1 differential is not to be understood as a measure of HSN's incompetence, but rather as the price Orlando has paid for decades of indifference to its homeless population and for its failure to adopt a comprehensive long-term homeless plan until the Ten 2 End plan was announced in 2008. As the *Sentinel* editorial from January 2003 concluded, "HUD expects grant applications to be more than pleas for a federal handout. It wants evidence that communities have a grasp of the bigger picture." HUD, we may fairly surmise, has concluded that Miami has a much firmer "grasp of the bigger picture" than Orlando does.

Following the 1999 UCF report, then-Mayor of Orlando Glenda Hood called for a "Community Conference on the Homeless" to take place on December 18-20, 2002. About seventy or eighty local advocates, agency representatives, elected officials, and concerned citizens showed up at the Orlando Expo Center to debate what should be done about "a growing number of chronic homeless in downtown." The conference was not burdened by any formal agenda or even an obvious purpose or goal. The *Book of Proceedings* from the Conference consisted of brief summaries of the twenty-five breakout sessions. There was no effort to compile a comprehensive list of recommendations and the closest the conference came to prioritizing anything was a final-day vote ranking the session reports according to some loose sense of priorities. The "drop-in center" received the most votes, followed by "affordable housing," "health care," and "leadership and coordination." The latter was focused on the regional commission concept, and the action plan called for Mayor Hood to take the lead in getting a commission established. Otherwise, the sessions were "all over the place" and tended to address the animating concerns of the session organizer. Thus, one session was focused on what would be needed to make Orlando friendlier to walkers; another on employment opportunities for ex-offenders; another on spiritual outreach to the homeless; another on affordable housing.

Local media coverage focused mainly on the regional commission, which was dealt a serious setback in January 2003 when Mayor Hood was named by Governor Jeb Bush to be Florida's next Secretary of State, just weeks after the Community Conference had ended. While local advocates promised to move forward with plans for a commission, Hood's departure killed all momentum and the concept lay dormant until Hood's successor, Buddy Dyer, established his own Working Committee on Homelessness later in 2003.

Dyer's Working Committee met almost weekly for more than a year. The Committee was made up of local attorneys and business people, various homeless service providers, a few area academics, and others. In October 2004, the Working Committee issued its report (City of Orlando Mayor 2004). The Report acknowledged that "over the past few years, the City has experienced a growing number of citizen concerns" about homelessness "that led to some significant responses from our City Council." Explicit reference was made to the panhandling ordinances and the prohibition against lying or sitting on public sidewalks. These ordinances, the Report confessed, have "had relatively little impact on the growing numbers of downtown homeless" (p. 5).

The Report articulated five "basic understandings and perspectives," and made twenty-four more or less specific action recommendations. The five "understandings" are relevant to our narrative. The first, again, was that the city should take the lead in establishing a Regional Commission. The second was that nothing of any great significance could or should be implemented until "the Regional Commission is established and commences its work." Third, the report made no effort to "put a cost estimate with each Recommendation," expressing the opinion that "decisions related to the allocation of scarce resources are best made by the elected officials." Fourth, the Mayor's Working Committee explicitly made no "specific recommendation related to the location of the Men's Pavilion," i.e., did *not* recommend relocation of the Coalition as part of the overall homeless plan. Finally, the Committee took no position on the Parramore moratorium, declaring that to be beyond the Committee's scope.

Since other mayoral committees and task forces were recommending at about the same time that the Coalition be relocated, the refusal of the Working Committee on Homelessness to endorse such a recommendation was seen as a fairly significant victory for the Coalition and its allies. At the same time, the Committee's refusal to take a position against the moratorium was seen as something of a setback.

Local homeless advocates and Mayor Dyer's administration differ over how many of the report's twenty-four specific action recommendations were implemented. Spokespeople for the Mayor routinely claim that "more than half" were implemented; advocates scoff at this number. Our own review and analysis of the recommendations and the subsequent history concludes:

- Sixteen of the twenty-four recommendations were ignored, although a few of these are arguable.

- Three were partially implemented via city action.
- Two more were implemented by HSN acting on its own, not through City action.
- Three were fully implemented by City action.

The latter three are of greatest interest, of course. Chief among them was that "the City should support the creation of a regional commission on homelessness." Although nearly three years elapsed between this recommendation and an actual implementation, a Regional Commission on the Homeless was constituted in June 2007. The Working Committee also recommended that the city "should designate a special assistant to the Mayor as a point-person for homeless issues," i.e., a homeless czar. For years, and to some extent even today, the Mayor's "point person" on homelessness had been the City Clerk, who has many duties and responsibilities other than city homelessness policies. In March of 2008, however, the City Council approved the creation of a Homeless Prevention Coordinator and the Mayor eventually filled the position. (Alas, as of this writing, the position is again unfilled.) Finally, the Working Committee recommended that "the City should control/manage public meal distribution/feeding programs throughout Downtown Orlando through educational programs and appropriate ordinances," which was implemented by passing the ordinance forbidding the feeding of homeless people in public places.

The Mayor's Working Committee presented its report to Mayor Dyer at a Friday afternoon meeting at City Hall. The Mayor was there to receive the report and acknowledge his gratitude to the Committee for their long hours and hard work. Then each member was presented with a bag full of City Hall tchotchkes, including an official Buddy Dyer ball point pen, a City of Orlando insulated coffee mug, and a stack of "City of Orlando Office of the Mayor" post-it sticky notes. The more astute among those assembled saw this as indicative of how seriously the report and its recommendations would be taken.

Clearly, many people in Central Florida have long believed some sort of regional body to be an integral element in any comprehensive homelessness plan. To much fanfare, the Central Florida Regional Commission on the Homeless was announced in June 2007, immediately formed itself into four sub-committees, organized an October retreat, site-visited homeless services in Atlanta, and by February of 2008 could boast of two significant accomplishments: (1) The interim Regional Commission on the Homeless had been disbanded in favor of what was conceived as a permanent Central Florida Commission on Homelessness co-chaired by the Orlando and Orange County Mayors, with a prominent civic-minded local banker designated as the managing chair. In addition, (2) the Commission had formulated its Ten 2 End (Ten Years to End Homelessness) plan, the region's first comprehensive, area-wide initiative to "end homelessness in Central Florida."

Inevitably, many of the Ten 2 End strategies were foreshadowed in previous reports and recommendations. On the housing side, one recommendation was to establish a local Housing Trust, something that had also been recommended by the Mayor's Working Committee. The plan called for 800 emergency shelter beds, 1,425 transitional housing beds, and 700 units of permanent supportive housing. The Commission also said it intended to spearhead the development of more affordable housing and reduce housing barriers. There were recommendations to enhance educational and job-training options for the homeless; improve discharge planning from correctional and health care facilities and the foster-care system; create a network of at least four 24/7 drop-in centers throughout the region; develop a comprehensive system of regional outreach; implement Housing First; develop a Homeless Court to divert homeless people out of the criminal justice system; and on through a long list. The Commission also put a price-tag on implementation of the plan: A total of $110 million in capital costs over ten years to build the necessary facilities and infrastructure; and annual expenses on the order of $50 million. Local leaders who didn't gasp, laughed.

It has now been about three years since the Ten 2 End plan was announced and not much has happened. The Commission is nominally chaired by the region's two most powerful politicians and is made up of an A-list of influential Central Floridians. Indeed, including the two mayors, seven of the region's twenty-five most powerful people (as identified in an annual Orlando *Sentinel* listing) sit on the Commission. But the Mayors only rarely show up for meetings and despite the star quality of its membership, the Commission's efforts to raise funds for the plan have not been successful. The annual fundraising goal of $50 million was quickly lowered to $3 million. In the first year, the group raised about $425,000 and in the second year the total raised dropped to less than $100 thousand, barely enough to keep the Commission's office open and its Executive Director paid. To be sure, the Commission is fund-raising at a time when city and county budgets are very tight, but as local columnist Scott Maxwell put it, "This community finds money for the things it truly wants"—e.g., $10 million to put Astroturf in the Citrus Bowl or a cool half *billion* for a new Performing Arts Center.

The problem, evidently, is that many of Central Florida's political and community leaders believe that homelessness is a losing proposition and that the homeless do not command a very significant or legitimate claim to scarce public resources. The heavy hitters on the Commission remain optimistic that they can see things through to some sort of conclusion, but they also tried to merge with HSN and were ultimately rebuffed. Maxwell comments, "Perhaps merging the two groups [would have made] each more effective. Or perhaps the merger would simply be the first step toward allowing this once-celebrated commission to fade away, becoming just another bone in Central Florida's vast graveyard of forgotten task forces." As the local paper editorialized (Orlando *Sentinel* 2009) when the now-defunct merger plan surfaced, "If people could reside in dusty recommendations and abandoned lofty resolutions, Central Florida's homeless crisis would already be a faint memory."

Conclusions: Miami and Orlando Compared

One question we asked nearly everyone we talked to in the evaluation of Miami's Homeless Trust is why the Trust has been so successful, especially in comparison to other CoCs around the country, many of whom have floundered. Outstanding leadership is the most common answer we got. The principal author of the Dade County Community Homeless Plan, Alex Penelas, who was a County Commissioner at the time, went on two years later to become Miami-Dade's first Executive Mayor, and during his entire term as Mayor also sat as the Chairman of the Board of the Miami-Dade County Homeless Trust. The principal authors of the various Orlando homelessness plans were (1) obscure social work professors from the University of Central Florida; (2) a consultant to a Mayor whose term of office ended within weeks of her plan's publication; (3) the co-chairs of Dyer's working committee, attorney Terry Delahunty and the Executive Director of the Christian Service Center, Robert Stuart; and (4) Tracy Schmidt, Chief Financial Officer of CNL, an Orlando-based financial and insurance group, who chaired the original Regional Commission on the Homeless. All of these are talented and well-meaning people, but none commanded the clout in the Orlando region that Penelas and his co-chair Alvah Chapman did in Miami-Dade. Likewise, the current Chairman of the Board of the Miami-Dade Homeless Trust is often described as one of the most powerful political lobbyists in the State of Florida. The Chairman of the Board of the Homeless Services Network is the Executive Director of the Health Care Clinic for the Homeless—a very talented guy, to be sure, but not someone whose very presence causes politicians to tremble. In short, Orlando has suffered because no local Leviathan has stepped forward to champion the homeless cause.

A second obvious difference is Miami's food and beverage tax, a dedicated source of funds that provides $14 million each year for homeless services. Among other things, these funds have allowed Miami-Dade to aggressively pursue grant opportunities that require cash matches, whereas Orlando passes annually on numerous grant opportunities because the requisite cash match cannot be found. Needless to add, losing the *Pottinger* suit was an important impetus for the passage of this tax and for the formation of the Task Force on Homelessness that developed the Community Homelessness Plan.

A third point, perhaps less obvious but doubtlessly important, is that the Miami-Dade County metropolitan region has been administered by a county-wide metropolitan government since 1957 (Mohl 1984). This was the nation's first "metro" government and is routinely cited as one of the most successful examples of consolidated urban government anywhere in the country. Beginning in 1957, Miami-Dade metro government slowly and successfully expanded its powers and usurped many of the functions of the county's (then) twenty-seven independently incorporated municipalities, all of which continue to exist, elect mayors and other officials, and otherwise act like real cities, but each of which is very much in the back seat when it comes to driving metro-wide policies like the homelessness plan. (The original twenty-seven municipalities have since expanded to thirty-five.) This, of course, did not happen without a struggle. The metro government in Miami-Dade has endured vociferous opposition ever since the July 1957 referendum. But the many successes of regionalized government in Miami-Dade—in areas such as expressways, mass transit, modernized law enforcement, region-wide development policies and land use codes, strict pollution controls, regional water management, and numerous others where real progress could only be made with a regional approach—simply overwhelmed localist attacks. So, when a regional plan was presented in 1994 to deal with what was obviously a regional homelessness problem, no one looked askance or worried that their pockets were being picked. The contrast with parochial Orlando and the surrounding county and municipal governments could scarcely be sharper. Clearly, the homelessness issue and many others have suffered as a result.

Fourth, the Miami business community seems to have a more enlightened view of homeless issues than the Orlando business community.

Both cities, of course, have Downtown Development Boards (DDB) or Authorities that are concerned about the effects of homelessness on tourism, the business climate, people's willingness to come downtown, and the overall downtown image. And both Boards have expressed concerns about panhandling, public feedings, and homeless people inhabiting public spaces and sleeping in the streets, and have championed ordinances to deal with these issues. But in Orlando, the Downtown Development Board seems to regard homelessness as a nuisance that needs to be eliminated whereas Miami's Downtown Development Authority (DDA) looks on homelessness as a problem that needs to be solved.

The Orlando DDB was represented on the Mayor's Working Committee on Homelessness and provided numerous memos and documents outlining the concerns of the business community. Quoting from one of these, "The Downtown Development Board fields numerous complaints related to panhandling, public urination and a wide variety of loitering from people using our downtown. In particular, panhandling throughout downtown, mass feeding programs and congregations in Heritage Square top the list of complaints." A later passage added, "Many people are uncomfortable and feel threatened by their exposure to this activity," meaning exposure to the alleged activities of the homeless: panhandling, public urination, etc. And finally, "It is common to receive reports that businesses are hesitant to entertain clients because of the concern related to a large downtown homeless population. A good number of potential visitors and customers are also hesitant to venture downtown due to the concentration of homeless individuals in the Central Business District (CBD). In addition, there has been widespread acknowledgement of the devastating impact of concentrated homeless care providers within the Parramore neighborhood."[13] The policy recommendations from the Board to the Committee were a public awareness campaign to discourage people from giving to panhandlers (a recommendation that the Committee accepted), a code amendment to "prohibit public meal distribution/feeding programs throughout downtown" (this was also done, as discussed previously), prohibition of "impromptu worship services for the homeless in Lake Eola Park" and elsewhere in the CBD, greater outreach to street people, and an extension of the Parramore moratorium to the entire downtown core.

Like its Orlando equivalent, the Miami Downtown Development Authority says that it receives three main complaints from residents, visitors, and business owners in the downtown area: "too little parking, too much litter and filth, and too many homeless people." There is a "persistent homeless problem here in downtown" and over half of all emergency shelter beds are within the DDA district boundaries (i.e., downtown Miami). Also like Orlando, the Miami DDA supported a "no-panhandling zone" ordinance that was eventually enacted. But our contact at the Miami DDA was also quick to distinguish between panhandlers and homeless people and to stress that most of the panhandlers in downtown Miami are *not* homeless. Many, we were assured, are out-and-out criminals that try to appear homeless but have places to live. These people also prey on homeless people in the downtown core (a point later confirmed to us by the Miami Police Department). The Miami DDA was also more than willing to sit down with the Homeless Trust and other advocacy groups to "soften" the ordinance so that the rights and interests of homeless people would be protected to the maximum extent possible.

Miami's DDA staff is even encouraged to volunteer at the Homeless Assistance Center. "We want staff to understand the issue." For a business-oriented group, the DDA is engaged in homeless issues in a relatively progressive way. That is, they seem genuinely concerned about the welfare of homeless people, not just with keeping the streets "clean." "We are not taking proper care of our homeless population—if they are mentally ill and such and we are just leaving them out on the street to be subjected to crime and so forth, it's inhumane" (Donley and Wright 2010).

One of the organized activities that grew out of the Mayor's Working Committee on Homelessness was a "fact-finding" trip to Miami by a group from Orlando—people from the Mayor's Office, from the Working Committee, various service providers, a columnist from the local newspaper, etc. Shortly after their return, the Orlando *Sentinel* ran an editorial "call to arms" urging Orlando's civic and political leaders to follow Miami's lead in providing world-class facilities for Orlando's needy, destitute, and homeless. Alas, neither the fact-finding group nor the *Sentinel* editorial mentioned any of the following salient points of difference between the two cities and their respective situations:

(1) The editorial remarked on the outpouring of concern, civic virtue, and re-sources that led to the creation of Miami's outstanding Homeless Assistance Centers, but failed to mention that all of this resulted (at least to some extent) from a court decision against the city in the *Pottinger* case. It is certainly possible that the HACs and the larger system of homeless services would have been created regardless of the *Pottinger* decision, but there can be no denying that *Pottinger* put some urgency into the process. At one point, the

appellate judge became so exasperated by the City's foot-dragging that he threatened to put Miami into receivership unless something significant was done. The Community Homelessness Plan, the Miami-Dade County Homeless Trust, and the food and beverage tax were the "significant somethings" the court was looking for.

(2) Miami's downtown HAC is right in the middle of a historically African American, economically depressed, but obviously redeveloping area called Overtown. The shelter is literally within blocks of schools, churches, commercial establishments, and relatively pleasant residential neighborhoods. Here the important lesson—not mentioned in the *Sentinel* editorial—would seem to be that a large, well-designed, and capably managed facility for homeless people is not incompatible with neighborhood revitalization—not in Miami's Overtown and not in Orlando's Parramore either. Yet the struggle to relocate the Coalition and its Men's Pavilion out of Parramore continued for another five years.

(3) As pointed out earlier, the budget for Miami's HAC facilities is more than $12 million per year, about three to four times the operating budget for the Coalition. The Coalition serves about the same number and mix of homeless people with a third of the HAC's budget and well less than half the number of staff. Exhortations to provide better services to homeless people are gratuitous unless there is a plan to provide the necessary staff and other resources and invidious when the vast differences in existing resources are not acknowledged.

(4) As we have seen, much of the money Miami spends on the HACs and other homeless services comes from its dedicated funding source, the 1 percent food and beverage tax. Every observer of the Miami scene agrees that a dedicated funding stream makes all the difference. Yet nothing in the *Sentinel* editorial spoke to the issue of where the money for improved services was going to come from. People in Central Florida are notoriously tax-aversive. A recent referendum to add one cent to the local sales tax to fund transportation improvements was resoundingly defeated despite consistent poll results identifying traffic congestion as the number one threat to the quality of life. More taxes to pay for homeless services? Not a chance!

The *Sentinel* editorial concluded that "Central Florida won't bloom into a world-class community until there is a broad and effective plan to address homelessness." Agreed! Yet, as we have shown in this chapter, Central Florida's leaders have largely ignored a succession of "broad and effective plans" stretching back to at least 1999 and continuing to the present day. Central Florida may well boast world-class theme parks, a beckoning climate, a shiny new Performing Arts Center, a new Events Center, and perhaps one day soon, an NBA championship. But we will not become a world-class *community* until we realize that effectively addressing homelessness in Central Florida entails more than finding creative ways to keep our homeless citizens out of Lake Eola Park.

Notes

1. And cities elsewhere. Homelessness is not uniquely an American problem. See Toro et al. 2007.

2. Never light on rhetorical flourish, a *Sentinel* writer (Kassab 2003) once opened a story on the decay of a former tourist area in downtown Orlando with the observation that it had become infested with "homeless people, termites, and rats the size of small dogs," all of these equally undesirable vermin in the eyes of the *Sentinel*, it seems.

3. Quotations retrieved from http://law.jrank.org/pages/13212/Pottinger-v-City-Miami.html (retrieved August 25, 2009).

4. During the period 1991-1992, Wright consulted extensively with the ACLU attorneys who pressed the case, was deposed by the city attorney, testified at trial, and his opinions and conclusions were heavily cited in the Court's opinion and findings. A key element in the City's defense was that homeless people were "homeless by choice." In response, the Court opined that "as was established at trial, the City does not have enough shelter to house Miami's homeless residents. Consequently, the City cannot argue persuasively that the homeless have made a deliberate choice to live in public places or that their decision to sleep in the park as opposed to some other exposed place is a volitional act. As Professor Wright testified, the lack of reasonable alternatives should not be mistaken for choice."

5. How much money a city spends on "homelessness" cannot be known precisely, since local emergency rooms, police and corrections, community mental health centers, alcohol detox and rehab centers, etc. all spend money on providing services to homeless people, but rarely tabulate their expenditures in such a way that the sums going to the homeless can be separately counted.

6. All the following figures are taken from the Trust's "Ten Year Plan, 2008 Update" and from the associated spreadsheets.

7. Most ten-year plans focus on the chronically and episodically homeless because transitional homelessness—short spells of homelessness occasioned by all manner of personal, social, and economic crisis—is the sort of thing that cannot be realistically eliminated.

8. The Coalition is in the process of replacing the Pavilion with a new Men's Service Center, and part of the plan for the new facility is to have courtyard space where homeless men *can* "hang out," i.e., a resurrection of the original plan to get them and keep them off the city's streets both day and night.

9. Discussions about relocation began about the time the moratorium was enacted (1998) and were only resolved in 2008, so the struggle consumed a decade's worth of energy and political attention, and when it was all over, the Coalition stayed where it was after all.

10. In truth, this designation is largely undeserved in that it is based mostly on the symbolism of City Council decisions, not on some official Orlando policy of harassment or physical intimidation of homeless people. Orlando officials often seem indifferent to the needs of the homeless and clueless about how to respond to them, but they are rarely mean-spirited. And while local law enforcement makes more nuisance arrests of homeless people than seem necessary, it has been years since anyone accused the local police of brutality towards the homeless, which is more than many cities can say.

11. Taken from a Fox News story, "Debate ranges in Florida over law against feeding homeless." Retrieved at http://www.foxnews.com/story/0,2933,250141,00.html

12. In fact, many of the calls over the years for a regional commission were motivated by frustration with HSN and by the hope that a regional entity would take over the

HSN role as lead agency for the Continuum of Care. It is thus ironic that within three years of its founding, the Central Florida Commission on Homelessness had announced its intention to merge with HSN (an intention that eventually came to naught).

13. Despite the quantitative language—*numerous* complaints, *many* people, a *good number*, and the like—the DDB never did produce real data on how many complaints, how many people, etc.

13

What Have We Learned?

Ronald Reagan, fortieth President of the United States and no friend to the homeless (although he did sign into law the Stuart B. McKinney Homeless Assistance Act in 1987, the single most important piece of federal homelessness legislation ever enacted), remarked during the course of the 1988 election campaign, "You know, if I listened to him [Michael Dukakis] long enough, I would be convinced we're in an economic downturn and people are homeless and going without food and medical attention and that we've got to do something about it." Reagan was convinced that poverty, hunger, and homelessness had been largely eradicated in America and that the small pockets of homelessness that remained were comprised mostly of people whose miseries were self-inflicted. As the Great Communicator himself put it on *Good Morning America* (January 31, 1984), defending his administration against charges of callousness, "You can't help those who simply will not be helped. One problem that we've had, even in the best of times, is people who are sleeping on the grates, the homeless who are homeless, you might say, by choice."

That people were mostly "homeless by choice" was a key element in the City of Miami's defense against the *Pottinger* suit. The logic was this: If people were homeless by choice, then behaviors such as camping under the interstates or urinating in public were also choices—illegal choices at that—and in that case, the City was perfectly within its rights to arrest homeless people for these voluntary but illegal behaviors. The simple fact that there were many more homeless people than shelter beds was sufficient to persuade the judge that homelessness was not a matter of choice, but an involuntary status inflicted on people by extreme poverty, addictions, mental illness, and a severe shortage of affordable housing;

and that it was unconstitutional to punish people for things over which they had little or no control.

Many people in Central Florida would also like to believe that homelessness is a voluntarily assumed status. In fact, one local effort to overturn the anti-camping ordinance was dismissed by the courts when the City produced evidence that the local shelters were rarely full to capacity, the implication being that homeless people were not compelled to sleep in public places: there was shelter they could utilize instead. The same logic is used by county law and code enforcement in their periodic efforts to dislodge homeless people living in the woods. The woods people, they argue, *could* go downtown, *could* present for services at various homeless facilities, *could* spend their nights at the Pavilion. Yet, despite these options, which are well-known to the people who live in the woods, they continue to trespass on private property and otherwise violate county laws and codes. Since this is allegedly a matter of choice, the police and code enforcement officers have no qualms about arresting people for it. That the woods people have very good reasons as to why they live where they do and avoid downtown is of no consequence (Chapter Seven).

The principal evidence in favor of the "homeless by choice" theory is that upon interview, many homeless people will say they are happy enough with their lives and circumstances; in these interviews, some will even stress the positive features of being homeless—the freedom, the adventure of living on the edge, and the like. Some of the woods people in our focus groups were positively flamboyant in their enthusiasms for their life style. However, there is every difference between accommodating the cards life has dealt you and being happy with the hand. When homeless people say they are "satisfied" with being homeless, what they usually mean is that they are unable to conceive of an attainable alternative, not that a life of homelessness is positively preferable to such alternatives that may exist.

We have interviewed numerous homeless people in and around Central Florida who told us that they were "happy" being homeless or that they were homeless "by choice." In most of these cases, one or more of the following things has been true:

- Respondents are so mentally incapacitated (whether by psychiatric illness, addictions, or other disabilities) that they would not be legally entitled to receive their own disability checks. Their claims of choice are sheer bombast.

- They are trying to save face (and retain some sense of pride) by declaring that they choose to live this way rather than confessing that they are victims of larger social, psychological, economic, or interpersonal forces that are beyond their control.
- They have in fact "chosen" to be homeless (i.e., drop out of sight, disappear into the streets, shelters, or woods) to spare their friends and families the need to deal with them in their cracked-out, inebriated, psychotic, or otherwise dissolute state.

None of these represent true "choices" in the usual sense of the word.

Consider what a homeless person would choose by "choosing" to be homeless. The rate of AIDS infection among the homeless exceeds that among the general population by roughly a factor of five to ten (Robertson et al. 2004), the rate of sexual assault on homeless women exceeds that on women in general by a factor of ten or twenty (Jasinski et al. 2010), the rate of tuberculosis among the homeless exceeds that among the general population by a factor of perhaps a hundred (Moss et al. 2000), and the average age of death for homeless men is around fifty-three years versus a "normal" life expectancy of more than seventy (see Chapter Nine). One does not "choose" to sleep in the gutters (or, for that matter, in the shelters), scavenge food from dumpsters, or forgo twenty years of life expectancy, however directly that existence may have followed from other choices and decisions one may have made.

We often refer to "homeless by choice" as the "Let's Make a Deal" theory. "Let's Make a Deal" is a popular game show. At the end of the show, the most successful contestants are asked to choose one of three doors, with each of them winning the prize behind whichever door they choose. Behind one of the doors might be a new luxury car; behind another is a trip to some exotic destination; behind the third resides something worthless and silly, such as a can of pork and beans. Suppose, now, that a contestant chooses the first door and "wins" the can of pork and beans. Would we then say that this contestant actually chose the can of beans in preference to the car or the vacation? Of course not. If the contestant had been able to foresee the consequences of his or her choice, a different decision would certainly have been made.

All things considered, "Let's Make a Deal" is not a bad metaphor for life. All people, day in and day out, confront choices that have to be made but whose consequences cannot be anticipated, and it is a mistake to confuse the choice with the unforeseen consequences of the choice. So too with homelessness. All homeless people have faced critical turning points, or decisions, that went the wrong way and whose unforeseen, unintended, and unchosen consequence was an episode or even a life of homelessness. This is not to say that people choose to be homeless, but rather that homelessness is often the result of choices whose consequences could not be predicted. Saying that people are "homeless by choice" is a pretty obvious case of blaming the victim.

Not that the victims do not deserve to share the burden of blame, at least from time to time. It is very difficult to watch the same homeless man show up at the Pavilion night after night, reeking of alcohol, glassy-eyed from smoking crack, and not want to grab him by the shoulders and shake some sense into him—or the young homeless woman, all of twenty-three, who has three kids already and is pregnant with her fourth. Thus, as a social problem and a political issue, homelessness is most discomfiting. Most people seem to regard the homeless as unfortunate souls, down on their luck, deserving of compassion and assistance (Chapter Ten). Certainly, most people who do research on the homeless embrace this viewpoint, most assuredly including us. However, more mean-spirited, hard-bitten outlooks also exist and are voiced with what seems to be increasing frequency: that the homeless choose to live as they do and are thus responsible for their own miseries; that they are just a bunch of broken-down alcoholics for whom little can be done in any case; that they are dangerous people who should be avoided; or that they are social parasites deserving of contempt. In response to a question asking what he would do about homelessness, Newt Gingrich quipped, "Give the park police more ammo." Most researchers, again including us, spend a lot of time and effort trying to disabuse students, lay people, and policy makers of such punitive notions. At the same time, no capable researcher could possibly fail to notice that there is a grain of truth in many of them.

A genuine solution to the problem of homelessness—locally, regionally, or nationally—seems as elusive today as it did when the homeless were "rediscovered" on the streets of U.S. cities in the early 1980s, now some thirty years ago. To be sure, there are many cities, Orlando among them, that have formulated plans to end chronic homelessness within the decade, and there are promising new strategies available to achieve this end such as homeless prevention programs, rapid rehousing programs, and Housing First. When the good folks from the National Alliance to End Homelessness show up to talk about strategies for ending homelessness altogether, most people pay attention and the NAEH speakers are rarely laughed out of the room. At the same time, the poverty rate is going up, not down, and while the housing bust has lowered housing prices in most markets, very little of that has trickled down to rental housing, which is where most low income families live. There is some evidence to suggest that the numbers of chronically homeless street people are declining and that is very good news indeed. But the numbers of episodically and transitionally homeless people seem to be increasing at the same time, which is not good news at all, most of all in an economic climate where episodic and transitional homelessness can easily turn chronic (see Swarns 2008).[1] In Central Florida, the 2009 Point in Time count showed about a 17 percent increase in the number of homeless people over the number counted in 2008. So, if there is in fact a national decline, it hasn't shown up in Central Florida yet.

All investigators seemingly agree that the stereotypical understandings of homelessness that characterized decades past are no longer appropriate. The oft-romanticized hoboes of the Depression era and the grizzled old Skid Row drunks of the 1950s have yielded to new and starkly more disturbing images of shelters filled with battered women and young children; whole families standing by the roadside with signs offering to work for food; muttering old women in disheveled garb pushing shopping carts up and down city streets; and young, scarified "gutter punks" panhandling the passers-by. The new imagery of homelessness illustrates one important lesson, namely, that the homeless in Central Florida and across the nation are a diverse and heterogeneous group: men, women, and children; young, middle-aged, and old; black, white, and Hispanic; the sober and the besotted; the lucid and the insane. Even the very phrase, "the" homeless, implies a unity of kind that is not observed empirically. This diversity of kind is matched, of course, by a diversity of problems, circumstances, and social service needs (Smith 1985).

When all is said and done, homelessness results when people can't afford to house themselves; structurally, homelessness results from a mismatch between incomes and housing costs. As the 1999 UCF study concluded, "the single most critical predictor of homelessness is the proportion of the population employed in the service sector" (p. 32). We argued in Chapter One that the "Disneyfication" of the regional economy has made the service sector by far the largest and fastest growing category of employment in Central Florida. Chapter Two illustrates the result: a disturbingly large segment of our community living perilously close to economic disaster.

In a book full of bad news and disturbing results, two of the most disturbing are that two-thirds of the homeless men who frequent the Pavilion spend their days working or looking for work and that more than a fifth of the people who line up each night for the Pavilion's evening meal are in fact not homeless but rather poor but housed people looking to stretch their monthly incomes around their expenses. Contrary to stereotype, we are not talking about "lazy, shiftless bums" but about *working people* who simply can't make ends meet and end up at the Pavilion for food and shelter. Good grief!

The low-income housing situation in the Central Florida region was analyzed by the Mayor's Working Committee on Homelessness in some detail, although relatively few of the findings made their way into the Executive Summary. Updating to the most recent available data:

> By federal definition, an "extremely low-income" household is one earning 30 percent or less of the annual area median income (AMI). The estimated AMI for the Orlando metro area in 2009 is about $60,000 for a family of four; 30 percent of that sum is about $18,000. If one takes the accepted standard that a household can afford to spend only 30 percent of its income on housing, then the rent ceiling for extremely low-income households in metro Orlando would be around $450 per month, the maximum housing burden an extremely low-income family could "afford." It goes without saying that there is virtually no unsubsidized housing in metro Orlando that rents at or below that standard. Thus, most low and very low income families must either overspend on their housing or become homeless. Most opt for the former: according to the 2000 Census, the City of Orlando had 25,809 households (out of 75,817 total households) that were paying more than 30 percent of their income toward housing, which equals 34 percent of all households regardless of income level. (See also the discussion of housing burdens in Chapter Two, where we showed that among Central Florida's low and moderate income households, over half now pay more than 30 percent of their income on housing.) But some, obviously, are unable to overspend on housing and "choose" to be homeless as a result. At least 10,000 people in the three-county Central Florida region will experience one or more episodes of homelessness this year.[2]

The HUD-defined "fair market rent" for a two-bedroom unit in the Orlando metropolitan area now stands (2009) at about $1,019 per month or well more than twice what an extremely low-income family could afford. Indeed, again using the 30 percent standard, that level of rent would require an annual income of $40,776. And that would require an hourly wage of about $20 per hour, versus the actual median wage of area renters, which is about $13-14 per hour. At the current minimum wage ($7.25 per hour), a worker would need to average about 108 hours of labor per week to afford a two-bedroom rental unit at the fair market rent.

Orlando's leading supplier of housing to the very low income population, the Orlando Housing Authority, closed the waiting list for Section 8 housing subsidies in 1999 with more than 4,000 names remaining on the list. The list is still closed today. The waiting list for public housing (housing in units owned and managed by OHA) contains more than 3,000 names, with a wait for families on that list of between three months and one year. OHA generally serves clients within 60-80 percent of AMI rather than the neediest at the bottom of the income distribution. (Elderly clients are a partial exception.) Finally, in order to be eligible for public housing in Orlando, the adult wage earner in the household is required to have worked at least thirty-five hours per week for at least six months and must pass a criminal record check (no convictions in the previous three years) and a drug test. The grim situation for low income families in Orlando's private housing market is not significantly relieved by public housing. The same is true in many cities. Clearly, the inability to find and maintain affordable housing in the lower income and wage groups is a significant cause of homelessness both regionally and nationally.

Although adult men remain the modal type of homeless person in the Orlando region, women, children, and families comprise a very fast-growing subgroup. Concerning the men, perhaps our most significant finding (other than the percentage of labor force participants) is that they consist of two very distinct "ideal types": the "regulars," many of them chronically homeless men who sleep in the shelters most nights, and the "transients," who are in the shelters for brief periods of time and (often) are never seen again. (Empirically, of course, there are men to be found all along this continuum.) Nationally, there is some evidence that the former group can best be served through Housing First models that get them into permanent housing as quickly as possible with minimal conditions and restrictions. To date, Central Florida has not implemented any Housing First programs, although this is one of the major recommendations of the Ten 2 End plan. One important barrier is that the types of chronically homeless men who are often targeted by Housing First are also the least sympathy-engendering subgroup within the homeless population. Housing them in preference to housing women, children, and families is a very tough sell.

Homeless men in Orlando, as is true almost everywhere, are predominantly young, single, and non-white, demographic facts that compound their employment difficulties and thus their housing options. Their demographic similarity to other "problem" populations (for example, the incarcerated, or the drug-abusive) is obvious. The percentage of non-whites among homeless men exceeds not only the percentage in the larger community, but even the percentage in the local poverty population. This, too, is generally true, and is not unique to Central Florida.

On the one hand, an overrepresentation of minorities among the homeless seems "obvious." Why would one expect things to be otherwise? But as Kim Hopper has argued, "the robust legacy of the black extended family" seemingly makes the large number of young, homeless African American men an anomaly. "Kinship," Hopper reminds us, "has historically provided the first line of defense against misfortune and the bedrock of social security" (p. 160), and that, clearly, has changed. Part of the answer here is the matrilineal nature of the African American family and the consequent fact that if anyone has to be turned away, it will tend to be the boys. Factors that "jinx one's welcome at home" will inevitably increase homelessness, and boys seem much more adept at "jinxing" themselves than girls. As Hopper states, "women do the work of kinship; their investment in the social capital of family ties—and thus their expected return—is greater and more durable than that of men ... surely stronger than that of young men, many of whom have yet to secure the foothold in the labor market that would enable them to perform as 'responsible' members of the family" (Hopper 2003: 168).

The relative youth of the homeless population implies, contrary to stereotype, that the elderly would be underrepresented among the homeless, and as we showed in Chapter Nine, they are, at least partly because of the excessive homeless mortality rate. At the same time, the inevitable "graying of America" that is a result of the aging baby boom cohorts implies that there will be more elderly homeless people in the future than has been the case up to now, a fact that will soon pose serious challenges to our system of elder care.

Another element of conventional homeless stereotyping is that most of the homeless are chronically so, i.e., once you become homeless, you are homeless forever. Important research undertaken in the 1990s made it clear that the truly chronic segment of the homeless population amounts to only 10-20 percent of the total; most are episodically or transitionally homeless. Our studies of shelter utilization at the Pavilion (Chapter Four) confirm this result. Overreliance on one-shot, one-night shelter-based surveys seriously misled us for several decades, simply because the chronically homeless are grossly overrepresented in these samples.

The realization that the chronically homeless are a very small portion of the total (annual) homeless population has radically transformed our collective thinking about effective interventions. That a small fraction of the homeless consumes a large fraction of the emergency shelter capacity implies that if permanent housing could be found for that small fraction, the total demand for emergency shelter would drop precipitously. This is the key insight behind the effort to "end chronic homelessness in ten years" via Housing First programs. As for the far larger number who experience short-term, temporary homelessness, they appear to be candidates for prevention or rapid rehousing programs. Either way, the need for emergency shelter would be drastically reduced.

At the same time, Housing First, rapid rehousing, and related interventions do not comprise the panacea that many advocates claim. Culhane's findings and our replication show that the chronically homeless tenth consume about half of the total shelter resources, but that does not mean that they consume half of *everything* we spend on homeless services. Some chronically homeless people who show up each night for shelter are almost pathological in their avoidance of any other service or treatment. Housing programs can be breathtakingly expensive and are thus easiest to justify in cities that already spend a lot on homeless services (New York, Miami), not in cities that don't (Orlando). Then, too, a focus on housing the chronically homeless requires a public commitment to the least attractive, least sympathetic element within the homeless population—the chronically homeless, often addicted, frequently disabled, single homeless man. Finally, in an economy as bad as ours currently is, transitionally homeless people may find themselves "transitioning" in and out of homelessness with sufficient frequency that they soon become episodically homeless; sooner or later, the interlude between episodes may become sufficiently short that chronic homelessness results. Housing First is an interesting and innovative way to think about what homeless people need and how they can best be served, but contrary to the enthusiasms of Housing First advocates, it will not "end homelessness as we know it." At best, housing programs are one weapon in the policy armory, not the magic bullet that solves everything.

In recent years, somewhat more than half the people receiving services from the Coalition for the Homeless of Central Florida have been women, women with children, men with children, and intact husband-wife homeless families. Study after study in one city after another reports that women, children, and families are the fastest-growing subgroup (Rog and Buckner 2007; Lewis, Anderson and Gelberg 2003; Rosenheck, Bassuk and Solomon 1999). It is of some interest that studies of homeless populations back in the 1950s found very few women. Bogue's 1958 study in Chicago, to illustrate, found that women accounted for no more than 3 percent of that city's skid row population. In the "new homelessness" of today, the women are more than ten times that figure (Rog and Buckner 2007).

As with the homeless generally, homeless women are themselves not a homogeneous group, a fact recognized early in the 1980s and in every study since (the large amount of literature on the point is reviewed in Dotson 2009). They are, of course, differentiated by the usual demographic factors, by their family and fertility statuses, and by the nature, duration, and causes of their homelessness. Concerning family and fertility, one important finding from the studies reported in Chapter Five is that the *current* presence of dependent children in a homeless woman's care is an imperfect indicator of her true lifetime fertility. Among women seen in one year at the Center for Women and Families who entered the facility as "single," one in three in fact had one or more children living in someone else's care. And of the women who entered the facility with kids, about one in four had other kids from whom they were separated. Thus, the line of demarcation between "single" women and "women with children" is not as clear-cut as one might assume; moreover, the loss of one's children is evidently a common experience for homeless women in Central Florida and presumably elsewhere, although this topic deserves more research attention than it has so far received.

As would be expected, homeless women become separated from their children for a variety of reasons. In a few cases, separation is voluntary, as when mothers (and sometimes fathers) see an episode of homelessness on the horizon and try, however fitfully, to protect their child or children from the consequences by seeking temporary alternative living arrangements. Based on very limited data from one focus group with a small group of women in one homeless facility, we'd guess that these voluntary separations account for perhaps one in four of the total. Thus, by far the larger share are involuntary separations occasioned by substance abuse, mental illness, child neglect or abuse, and/or state termination of parental rights. The same focus group also taught us that while virtually all women who had been separated from a child have diffuse desires for reunification, hardly any have concrete plans. Reunification with children was a pleasant thought, almost an abstraction, not something the women we studied were actively working to achieve.

Experiences with domestic violence are another common and unwanted theme in the lives of homeless women everywhere. Male violence, abuse, and abandonment are the direct precipitating causes of homelessness for about one in four and comprise some thread in the fabric of life for perhaps three in four. Half the homeless women in a Central Florida sample had been raped at least once in their lifetime. Thus many women find themselves homeless because they "choose" life in the streets and shelters in preference to daily beatings, psychological terror, and rape. Some choice!

All homeless people, men and women alike, regardless of their circumstances or the nature of their homelessness, also get to "choose" between availing themselves of emergency shelters or living out in the open—in cars or vans, on the streets or in the woods, in abandoned buildings or public spaces (parks, bus stations, subway stops, and the like). This situation fulfills the classic definition of a dilemma: a forced choice between equally unfavorable or unattractive alternatives. No matter which decision you make, the odds are good that the outcome will not be pleasant.

The first option, shelter life, was analyzed in some detail in Chapter Six; one of the second options, living in the woods, was the topic of Chapter Seven. The advantages and disadvantages of each option are easy enough to anticipate. Shelter life is more predictable but more rule-bound and requires that a person be comfortable sharing group quarters with hundreds of others and be willing to sacrifice a degree of personal freedom. Life in the woods is more independent and in some sense more adventurous, but also much less predictable. A hot meal is served every night in the Pavilion and, other than standing in line for a half-hour or so, can be consumed with practically no effort. Equally little effort is required to obtain lunch (available every day at the Christian Service Center just across the street from the Coalition). On the other hand, well-meaning volunteers, not you, decide on the menu options. In contrast, people who live in the woods spend a significant portion of their time and energy scavenging for food and are not always successful, but on the other hand, they can "choose" which dumpsters to dive in. "Um, let's see now: discarded fried chicken or half-eaten cheeseburgers ... what choice will I make?" Clearly, there are advantages and disadvantages on both sides of this equation.

There are also obvious cultural norms that govern behavior in both places and internal systems of social stratification and social control. Both in the shelters and in the woods, there is a very strong norm about sharing resources whenever possible. Indeed, theft is considered to be acceptable if someone is desperate and must take things they need to survive, but stealing simply to steal or because the person whose stuff you are taking is in no position to prevent it is not tolerated. In the camps, there is a very obvious internal division of labor to assure maximum deployment of resources: some assume responsibility for securing the camp, others scavenge for food, still others try to earn or beg for money.

Personal safety is always of concern to homeless people regardless of their living arrangements. In the shelters, the principal concerns are disease, violence, and addictions; in the woods, the primary concern is being run down by an inattentive motorist. Interestingly, most of the men in the shelter reported that they felt much safer in the shelter than they would be living on the streets or in the woods, whereas people living in the woods felt much safer there and cited safety concerns as a major reason why they avoided the shelters. (Downtown Orlando street people also routinely mention the "dangerousness" of the Pavilion as the main reason why they "choose" to sleep in the streets.) Partly, this difference reflects the differing demography of the two groups: the woods people are mainly from small town and rural backgrounds; Pavilion men are overwhelmingly of urban origins. In no small part, the difference reflects that process of accommodating the hand you've been dealt that we mentioned at the top of this chapter.

Many Pavilion men have prior or active drug and alcohol abuse histories, and the same is true, obviously, for the men and women in the camps. Almost all the woods people drink to excess and a few of the camps are known explicitly as "drug camps" where abusers and addicts congregate to shoot heroin or smoke crack. Alcoholism and homelessness, and to a lesser extent drug abuse and homelessness, tend to be closely linked in the public mind. So it is important to recognize that while most homeless men (and many homeless women) indeed have abuse histories and still drink and take drugs from time to time, the majority of the men we interviewed in the Pavilion in 2009 were currently clean and sober, and most of those who were not recognized and readily confessed their need for a treatment program. (This assuredly was *not* true of the woods people, who readily confessed their addictions but indicated little or no interest in treatment.)

Estimates of the rates of alcohol and drug abuse among the homeless vary wildly, in part because terms like "alcoholism" and "addiction" are not very precisely defined. It has been said that an "alcoholic" is anyone who drinks more than his doctor, and that an "addict" is anyone who does more drugs than his attorney! But certainly, chronic alcohol abuse is an important intermediate cause of homelessness in many cases. One study of homeless male alcoholics in Baltimore reported that almost three in five confessed that they were homeless *because* of their drinking; studies in Los Angeles suggest that about one in four drink to excess *because* they have become homeless. Thus, drinking can be an adaptation to the conditions of homelessness, as many studies have shown (Koegel and Burnham 1987). Also, many homeless people drink and do drugs to self-medicate their mental and physical illnesses. In general, the rate of alcohol and drug abuse among homeless men is estimated to fall somewhere around 50 percent, although in some populations, and with expansive definitions of "abuse," this figure can rise to 70-80 percent.

In Chapter Eight, we presented findings from studies of homeless men in recovery in the Pavilion's First Steps program, a traditional Twelve Step addictions recovery program. While the vast majority of the literature on addictions recovery among the homeless is a literature of failure, we decided to focus instead on the successes and raise the question of how homeless, mostly unemployed ex-cons manage to get and stay clean and sober. Part of the answer, we learned, was that they have found ways to overcome numerous barriers, including surmounting barriers to identifying themselves as alcoholics and identifying with a "home group," developing sponsor relationships in an environment where that is a very challenging thing to do, adapting core Twelve Step principles to the unique conditions and circumstances of homelessness, and, ironically, finding the time and energy to "work the program" inside what turns out to be, quite surprisingly, a very busy and structured life.

An important AA adage is "First Things First," which translates into "worry about and focus on your addiction and not on life's other annoyances." This may very well be sound advice to recovering addicts who have jobs and places to live, but homeless men often have neither, and to advise them to ignore their housing and employment needs while they "focus" on their recovery is not always helpful. Homeless men in recovery must carefully structure their days around mandatory breakfast at 6:00 AM, the demands of their jobs (for those who have jobs) or the demands of the job search (for those who don't), meeting with sponsors, looking for an apartment, and "working the steps." Given the obvious constraints, the surprise is not that so many fail, but rather that any succeed. Recovery in the face of many obvious barriers is all the more miraculous when one realizes that sobriety does not seem to confer any great advantages on these men. Since they have long ago burned bridges to kith and kin, they garner no "reunification" points by being sober; are not rewarded for their sobriety with promotions, raises, or advancement into better jobs; and do not suddenly gain access to quality low-cost housing because they have cleaned themselves up. How, if at all, is being clean and sober rather than drunk and addicted, but still unemployed or underemployed and homeless, any real improvement?

Chapters Ten, Eleven, and Twelve shifted the focus away from the poor and the homeless themselves and towards larger populations of interest: the general public, those who volunteer themselves and their money to the cause of homelessness, and the policy-makers who must deal with homelessness as a political issue. A recent review concluded as follows:

> The public's beliefs about the causes of homelessness are important because they can influence behavioral and policy responses to homeless people. Surveys show that domiciled respondents recognize multiple causes but tend to emphasize structural forces and bad luck over individual deficits. These results suggest a more nuanced understanding of homelessness than of poverty in general, which is usually attributed to personal failings. Members of the public also perceive the characteristics of the homeless in reasonably accurate terms and express as many favorable as unfavorable attitudes toward them. On balance, the American public's perspective on homelessness appears sympathetic—albeit to a lesser degree than their European counterparts—and has remained so over time. (Lee, Tyler and Wright 2010: 511).

Data reviewed in Chapter Ten for both the nation and Central Florida are broadly consistent with these conclusions, but reveal both sympathetic and hostile views towards the homeless. Indeed, it seems obvious that many people entertain both positive and negative opinions about the homeless *simultaneously*. This should come as no surprise. As we indicated in the opening of this chapter, a lot of public thinking about the homeless amounts to "blaming the victim," but at the same time, many of the "victims" deserve at least a share of the blame for the condition they are in.

Central Florida is generally regarded as a pretty conservative place and it would come as a great surprise if local residents proved to be "soft-hearted" on poverty and homelessness issues. And yet, most clearly state that homelessness is a major problem in our community, that too little is being done to address the problem, and that local governments should be doing more to help. A region that refuses to tax itself to improve transportation, one where even ballot propositions to improve public schools often go down to defeat, nonetheless overwhelmingly *rejects* the view that programs of assistance to the homeless are "too expensive." And lest it be thought that these findings are anomalous or otherwise untrustworthy, they are virtually identical to results from a 2007 three-county survey undertaken for the Central Florida Commission on Homelessness, which found:

- 62 percent of participants from all three Central Florida counties stated that homelessness was a problem in their county and that more needs to be done to solve the problem.
- When asked whether enough was being done to fight the root cause of homelessness in Central Florida, the numbers were even higher: 73 percent voiced in the negative, saying not enough was being done.
- While recognizing that homelessness is a real problem in Central Florida, participants went even further, with 59 percent saying that establishing programs and solutions to end homelessness should be a high priority for our community and elected officials.

The Commission's survey also found that, overwhelmingly, Central Floridians believe that "the most appropriate source of funding to address the needs of homeless individuals should be some combination of corporate and private donations, local and state governments, and a dedicated source of government funds" (quotation from p. 56 of the Ten 2 End Plan). A "dedicated source of government funds" is the Holy Grail for many local movements and issues (something, for example, that the transportation people have craved for decades) and, as our comparison of Miami and Orlando suggested, the sort of thing that Miami has used to great effect in becoming a recognized center of excellence in the delivery of homeless services.

Aside from the persistent concern that homeless people may be dangerous and, of course, the routine linkage in the public mind between homelessness and panhandling, Central Florida residents' perceptions of the homeless are for the most part both demographically accurate and sympathetic. Most of those whose views have recently changed have become more sympathetic to homeless people, not less, this despite what is perceived to be generally negative press coverage of the issue.

Our local survey data also revealed that 17 percent of adult residents in the three-county area say that they have volunteered at a homeless program or facility. Both general survey data and direct surveys with Coalition volunteers confirm that being a person of faith is the most important predictor of who volunteers (and who donates) to homeless causes. Virtually all homeless programs maintain web pages and links that potential volunteers can follow to find out about program needs, rules and regulations (e.g., whether a background check is or is not required), hours of operation, upcoming special volunteer events, and so on. The mere presence of these web pages attests to the critical role that volunteers play in every homeless organization.

Across the nation, the United Way have branded themselves as *the* place to go to "Give. Advocate. Volunteer." Research on a small number of United Way websites, including the local Heart of Florida United Way site, confirms that once you are at any United Way website, you are only three or four mouse-clicks away from direct links to local homeless agencies looking for volunteer assistance. Also of interest in this connection are the increasing number of high schools, colleges, and universities that require some number of "service hours" for graduation. Many homeless facilities are literally inundated by queries from local students looking for opportunities to amass the requisite number of hours. There is even a Web site and page where students who have done so can go to share their experiences: http://www.43things.com/things/view/186937/volunteer-at-a-homeless-shelter. The National Coalition for the Homeless maintains an online "Directory of Local Homeless Service Organizations" specifically to assist local volunteers in looking for places they can go to help. The listing is woefully outdated and incomplete and yet still runs to nearly a hundred pages.

Finally, there is enormous variation from one city to the next in how they approach issues of poverty, hunger, and homelessness: how much financial support local governments provide to homeless agencies versus how much cities have to rely on HUD grants and private donations, how aggressively local jurisdictions enact and enforce ordinances against homeless behaviors, how local services are structured, how involved the faith community and volunteer groups are, etc. Our comparison of homeless policies and politics in two Florida cities, Miami and Orlando, showed that forward-thinking political leadership, a dedicated source of funding, and a thoughtful plan can make all the difference. And it clearly doesn't hurt if your city has lost a big court case either! At the very least, a successful suit gets a city moving on the issue, as opposed to the seemingly endless dithering that results when elected officials are left to their own devices. There is much more to the Miami-Orlando comparison than *Pottinger*, of course, but there is likewise little doubt that the *Pottinger* case got Miami moving in a generally positive direction while Orlando has done little but hem and haw.

What Is to Be Done?

It is customary, almost *de rigeur* even, to conclude a book such as this with a statement of "policy implications." Alas, these statements are as often an expression of authors' political preferences or ideology as they point to genuine *implications* of the research that was done. The fact is, research of the sort we and most other social scientists do is often very good at *describing* an issue or social problem, but is far less eloquent when it comes to a real solution, a way out. It would be disingenuous to suggest that our research is any different.

Indeed, it would be a pretty straightforward exercise to go through the preceding chapters and write a paragraph or two about the unique needs faced by the group of homeless people being described. The homeless men of Chapter Three need better jobs and income; the homeless women of Chapter Five need lawyers, parenting skills classes, and protection from violent men; the woods people of Chapter Seven need housing, jobs assistance, more and better health care, alcohol and drug treatment, and, above all, mental health assistance in the long run, and all sorts of social work interventions in the short run; the elderly homeless of Chapter Nine need additional subsidized housing options; and so on. All this is true, of course, but not one of these conclusions requires much data, research, or analysis to reveal itself. These are not "policy implications" of research; they are common-sense notions that would occur to practically anyone.

It is also easy to see what things would be required to address the conditions or alleviate the hardships suffered by the poor and near-poor of Chapter Two. Indeed, the report from whence the chapter is derived waxes at great length on this very topic. Among the exhortations to be encountered in that report are prescriptions for a living wage, expansion of the Earned Income Tax Credit, and policy attention to the continuing gender inequity in wages; a national program of day care subsidies to offset the economic penalties faced by working mothers (and fathers); universal, portable health insurance; a policy of full employment, so that there is plenty of work available to anyone who wants to work; and finally, a frontal assault on the low income housing crisis. And there is, of course, very little doubt that if all these measures were enacted as federal policy, the conditions of the poor and near-poor would dramatically improve. What does it matter that with the partial exception of expanded health insurance, none of these things could be said to be on the national political agenda and none are likely to be any time soon. Or that the means to fund them were not addressed or even mentioned? Again, these measures and recommendations derive more from a political ideology that your authors deeply believe in than they are the inevitable conclusions to be drawn from our research.

To conclude, as we have in various passages, that the regional issues of poverty and homelessness ultimately result from "unrestrained growth run amuck," that those issues reflect "structural deformities in American society" and ultimately result from an "urban political economy that is broken and needs to be fixed" may very well be correct (indeed, we are certain that they are correct—this is *a matter of faith*), but none of these conclusions tells us what to do or how to resolve the mess in which we find ourselves. Many decades ago, some decisions were made about Central Florida's regional development that had implications for jobs, incomes, and housing, and those implications have resulted in the poverty and homelessness problems we face today. So what? Those decisions cannot be unmade and the "structural deformities" that ensued are now built into the regional infrastructure—into the highways and suburbs and theme parks that define Central Florida. However much we might like to, we cannot turn back the clock and start over. And it is not at all obvious that anything much would change even if we did.

Rather than closing the book with a detailed statement of largely ad hoc and entirely gratuitous "policy implications," we end instead with the more academic observation that there is increasing interest (among scholars and even some advocates) in bringing more international and historical perspectives to bear on the understanding of homelessness in our place and time. The historical perspective reminds us, critically, that homelessness is not a new problem that somehow shot up out of nowhere in the late 1970s and early 1980s in big American cities. To the contrary, there have been numerous waves of homelessness in the United States since Colonial times (see Depastino 2003; Kusmer 2002). Indeed, we routinely forget that America was *founded* by homeless people, by Europeans who, fleeing religious persecution, eventually washed ashore at Plymouth Rock—America's original "boat people." And likewise, homelessness is not a uniquely American problem either, but rather a problem that to greater and lesser degrees is being confronted by all the advanced industrial and post-industrial societies. Societies throughout history and around the globe have confronted issues of pauperization, destitution, and homelessness, none of them with a great deal of success. Indeed, when we were assembling data on homelessness in Canada, France, Great Britain, Sweden, Australia, and elsewhere for another project, we were inevitably reminded of a remark, possibly apocryphal, by Mohandas Gandhi, who was being interviewed by the Indian press upon returning from his first visit to Great Britain. When a reporter asked what Gandhi thought of Western civilization, the Mahatma allegedly replied, "I think it would be a good idea." If more civilization is not the answer to homelessness, nothing is.

Notes

1. Swarns reports New York City data showing that while the number of (counted) chronically homeless people in that city declined by almost 1,800 from 2005 to 2007, the total number of (counted) homeless people regardless of chronicity *increased* by more than 2,200 in the same time period.
2. The HSN annual "period-prevalence" estimate is produced by multiplying the Point in Time nightly count by 2.5, a very conservative "multiplier." Studies suggest that in most cities, the annual count is 3 to 5 times the nightly count. In the data reported in Chapter Four, a nightly shelter count of 300-350 produced an unduplicated annual count of 3,477, suggesting a multiplier nearer 10 than 2.5. Thus, the number of Central Floridians destined to suffer at least one episode of homelessness this year could be as high as 40,000 and is probably closer to 20,000 than 10,000.

References

Aase, Darrin M., Leonard A. Jason, and LaVome A. Robinson. 2008. "12-Step Participation Among Dually-Diagnosed Individuals: A Review of Individual and Contextual Factors." *Clinical Psychology Review* 28:1235-48.

Acs, Greg. 2009. "Poverty in the United States, 2008." The Urban Institute.

Alcoholics Anonymous World Services, Inc. 2005. *The AA Group.*

Allman, T. D. 2007, "Beyond Disney," *The National Geographic Magazine*, March. Retrieved on September 2, 2010, at http://ngm.nationalgeographic.com/2007/03/orlando/allman-text/

Anderson, Elijah. 2000. *Code of the Street: Decency, Violence and the Moral Life of the Inner City.* New York: W.W. Norton and Co.

Argeriou, Milton and Deniis McCarty (Eds). 1990. "Treating Alcoholism and Drug Abuse among Homeless Men and Women: Nine Community Demonstration Grants." *Special Issue of Alcoholism Treatment Quarterly* 7:1 (entire issue).

Arrighi, Barbara A. 1997. *America's Shame: Women and Children in Shelter and the Degradation of Family Roles.* Westport, CT: Praeger.

Bassuk, Ellen L., and Lenore Rubin, 1987. "Homeless Children: A Neglected Population." *American Journal of Orthopsychiatry* 57:279-286.

Bassuk, Ellen L., Lenore Rubin and Alison S. Lauriat. 1986. "Characteristics of Sheltered Homeless Families." *American Journal of Public Health* 76: 1097-1101.

Bassuk, Ellen L., John C. Buckner, Linda F. Weinreb, Angela Browne, Shari Bassuk, Ree Dawson and Jennifer N. Perloff. 1997. "Homelessness in Female-Headed Families: Childhood and Adult Risk and Protective Factors." *American Journal of Public Health* 87: 241–248.

Bazemore, Gordon and Peter L. Cruise. 1993. "Resident Adaptations in an Alcoholics Anonymous-Based Residential Program for the Urban Homeless." *Social Service Review* 67:599-616.

Beall, Pat. 2004. "Happy days are here again: April 23-29." *Orlando Business Journal.* Available at: http://www.bus.ucf.edu/dpi/PDF%20Files/Happy%20days%20are%20Ohere%20again.pdf

Becker, Howard S. 1963. *Outsiders: Studies in the Sociology of Deviance.* New York: Free Press.

Beeghley, Leonard. 1984. "Illusion and Reality in the Measurement of Poverty." *Social Problems* 31:322-333.

Berg, Joel. "Welfare Reform: The Promise Unfulfilled." *Journal of Gender, Race and Justice* 11:47-66.

Berke, Richard L. 1992. "Clinton: Getting People off Welfare." *New York Times*, September 10.

Binstock, Robert H. 2007. "Is Responsibility Across Generations Politically Feasible?" Pp. 285-308 in *Challenges for an Aging Society: Ethical Dilemmas, Political Issues*, edited by M. Smyer and R. Pruchno. Baltimore, MD: The Johns Hopkins University Press.

Blank, Rebecca. 2008. "Presidential Address: How to Improve Poverty Measurement in the United States." *Journal of Policy Analysis and Management* 27: 233-254.

Blank, Rebecca and Ron Haskins, editors. 2001. *The New World of Welfare*. Washington DC: Brookings Institution Press.

Blechman, Andrew. 2008. *Leisureville: Adventures in America's Retirement Utopias*. New York: Atlantic Monthly Press.

Braveman, Paula A., Catherine Cubbin, Susan Egerter, David R. Williams, and Elsie Pamuk. 2010. "Socioeconomic Disparities in Health in the United States: What the Patterns Tell Us." *American Journal of Public Health* 100: S186-S196.

Browne, Angela and Shari S. Bassuk. 1997. "Intimate Violence in the Lives of Homeless and Poor Housed Women: Prevalence and Patterns in an Ethnically Diverse Sample." *American Journal of Orthopsychiatry 67:* 261-278.

Buckner, John. C. 2008. "Understanding the Impact of Homelessness on Children: Challenges and Future Research Directions." *American Behavioral Scientist* 51: 721-736.

Budd, Lawrence. 1997. "Arresting Orlando's Homeless Policy." *Orlando Weekly.* December 25.

Burt, Martha. 1999. *Homelessness: Programs and the People They Serve.* Washington DC: Urban Institute Press.

Burt, Martha & Laudon Y. Aron. 2000. "America's Homeless II: Populations and Services." Presentation. Urban Institute. Available at: http://www.urban.org/Uploaded-PDF/900344_AmericasHomelessII.pdf

Burt, Martha, Laudon Y. Aron, and Edgar Lee. 2001. *Helping America's Homeless: Emergency Shelter or Affordable Housing?* Urban Institute Press.

Burt, Martha R. and Barbara E. Cohen. 1989. "Differences among Homeless Single Women, Women with Children, and Single Men." *Social Problems* 36: 508-524.

Burt, Martha R., Dave Pollack, Abby Sosland, Kelly S. Mikelson, Elizabeth Drapa, Kristy Greenwalt, and Patrick Sharkey (with Aaron Graham, Martin Abravanel, and Robin Smith). 2002. *Evaluations of Continuums of Care for Homeless People.* Washington DC: U.S. Department of Housing and Urban Development, Office of Policy Development and Research.

Bykofsky, Stuart. 1986. "No Heart for the Homeless." *Newsweek*, December 1.

Campbell, Scott W. and Michael J. Kelley. 2006. "Mobile Phone Use in AA Networks: An Exploratory Study." *Journal of Applied Communication Research* 34: 191-208.

Center for an Accessible Society. 2002. "Disability and the 2000 Census: What Reports Need to Know." Accessed on August 8, 2010 at http://www.accessiblesociety.org/topics/demographics-identity/census2000.htm

Charles, Alfred. 1996. "Homeless in New Orleans: Florida Shelter Might be Inspiration." *New Orleans Times- Picayune.* January 22.

Citro, Constance F. and Robert T. Michael (Editors). 1995. *Measuring Poverty: A New Approach*. Washington, D.C.: National Academy Press.

City of Orlando Mayor, 2004. *Mayor's Working Committee on Homelessness Executive Summary*. Orlando, FL: Office of the Mayor.

Corcoran, Mary, Greg J. Duncan, and Martha S. Hill. 1984. "The Economic Fortunes of Women and Children: Lessons from the Panel Study of Income Dynamics." *Signs* 10: 232-248.

Cowal, Kirsten, Marybeth Shinn, Beth C. Weitzman, Daniela Stojanovic, and Larissa Labay. 2002. "Mother-Child Separations Among Homeless and Housed Families Receiving Public Assistance in New York City." *American Journal of Community Psychology* 30: 711-730.

Culhane, Dennis P., Edmund F. Dejowski, Julie Ibanez, Elizabeth Needham, and Irene Macchia. 1994. "Public Shelter Admission Rates in Philadelphia and New York City: The Implications of Turnover for Sheltered Population Counts. *Housing Policy Debate* 5: 107-139.

Culhane, Dennis P. and Randall Kuhn. 1998. "Patterns and Determinants of Public Shelter Utilization Among Homeless Adults in New York City and Philadelphia." *Journal of Policy Analysis and Management* 17: 23-43.

Culhane, Dennis P., Chang-Moo Lee, and Susan Wachter. 1996. "Where the Homeless Come From: A study of the Prior Address Distribution of Families Admitted to Public Shelters in New York City and Philadelphia. *Housing Policy Debate* 7: 327−366.

Culhane, Dennis P. and Steven Metraux. 1999. One-year Prevalence Rates of Public Shelter Utilization by Race, Sex, Age and Poverty Status for New York City (1990, 1995) and Philadelphia (1995). *Population Research and Policy Review*, 18: 219-236.

Daiski, Isolde. 2007. "Perspectives of Homeless People on Their Health and Health Needs Priorities." *Journal of Advanced Nursing* 58:273-81.

DeNavas-Walt, Carmen, Bernadette D. Proctor and Jessica C. Smith. 2009. U.S. Census Bureau, Current Population Reports, P60-236, Income, Poverty, and Health Insurance Coverage in the United States: 2008, U.S. Government Printing Office, Washington, DC.

Depastino, Todd. 2003. *Citizen Hobo: How a Century of Homelessness Shaped America.* Chicago: University of Chicago Press.

Devine, Joel A. and James D. Wright. 1993. The Greatest of All Evils: Urban Poverty and the American *Underclass*. New York: Aldine de Gruyter.

Donley, Amy M. 2008. "The Perception of Homeless People: Important Factors in Determining Perceptions of the Homeless as Dangerous." Unpublished PhD dissertation, Department of Sociology, University of Central Florida.

Donley, Amy M. 2010. "Sunset Years in Sunny Florida: Experiences of Homelessness among the Elderly," *Journal of Long-term Home Health Care* (forthcoming)

Donley, Amy M. and James D. Wright. 2010. *The Miami-Dade County Homeless Trust Continuum of Care Evaluation Report.* Orlando, FL: UCF Department of Sociology.

Dordick, Gwendolyn. 1996. "More Than a Refuge: The Social World of a Homeless Shelter." *Journal of Contemporary Ethnography* 24: 373-404.

Dotson, Hilary. "Homeless Women in the Orlando Shelter System: A Comparison of Single Women, Families, and Women Separated from Their Children." Unpublished MA Thesis, Department of Sociology, University of Central Florida.

Dougherty, Conor. 2009. "Florida Suffers Rare Population Loss," T*he Wall Street Journal,* August 14.

Duany, Andres, Elizabeth Plater-Zyberk, and Jeff Speck. 2000. *Suburban Nation: The Rise of Sprawl and the Decline of the American Dream*. New York: North Point Press.

Duncan, Greg J. and Saul D. Hoffman. "A Reconsideration of the Economic Consequences of Marital Dissolution." Demography 22: 485-497.

Economic Research Service. 2009. "Food Insecurity in the United States." Washington DC: US Department of Agriculture. Accessed on August 27, 2010 at: http://www.ers.usda.gov/Briefing/FoodSecurity/

Edwards, Kathryn Anne and Alexander Hertel-Fernandez. 2010. "The Kids Aren't Alright—A Labor Market Analysis of Young Workers." Economic Policy Institute Briefing paper # 258.

Ellwood David T. 2000. "Anti-Poverty Policy for Families in the Next Century: From Welfare to Work-- and Worries." *Journal of Economic Perspectives* 14:187-98.

Erickson, W., Lee, C., von Schrader, S. (2010, March 17). Disability Statistics from the 2008 American Community Survey (ACS). Ithaca, NY: Cornell University Rehabilitation Research and Training Center on Disability Demographics and Statistics (StatsRRTC). Retrieved Aug 24, 2010 from www.disabilitystatistics.org

Evans, Robert.1994. "Chapter 1" in *Why are Some People Healthy and Others Not?* In R. Evans, M. Barer, and T. Marmor (Eds.) New York: Aldine De Gruyter.

Fisher, Gordon M. 1997. (revised). "The Development of the Orshansky Poverty Thresholds and Their Subsequent History as the Official U.S. Poverty Measure." U.S. Census Bureau. Poverty Measurement Working Paper series. Available at http://www.census.gov/hhes/www/povmeas/papers/orshansky.html.

Foglesong, Richard E. 2003. *Married to the Mouse: Walt Disney World and Orlando.* New Haven, CT: Yale University Press.

Frantz, Douglas and Catherine Collings. 2000. *Celebration, USA: Living in Disney's Brave New Town.* New York: Holt.

Frencj, Michael T. 2001. "Economic Evaluation of Alcohol Treatment Services." *Recent Developments in Alcoholism* 15: 209-228.

Garrett, Gerald R. and Howard M. Bahr. 1976. "The Family Backgrounds of Skid Row Women." *Journal of Women in Culture and Society* 2: 369-381.

Gerstein, Dean R. and Henrick J. Harwood. 1990. *Treating Drug Problems.* Washington: National Academy Press.

Grunberg, Jeffrey and Paula F. Eagle. 1990. "Shelterization: How the Homeless Adapt to Shelter Living." *Hospital and Community Psychiatry* 41: 521-25.

Gulcur, Leyla, Ana Stefancic, Marybeth Shinn, Sam Tsemberis, and Sean N. Fischer. 2003. "Housing, Hospitalization, and Cost Outcomes for Homeless Individuals with Psychiatric Disabilities Participating in Continuum of Care and Housing First Programs." *Journal of Community and Applied Social Psychology* 13: 171-186.

Hatty, Suzanne. 1996. "The Violence of Displacement: The Problematics of Survival for Homeless Young Women." *Violence Against Women* 2:412-428.

Hawkins, Robert, and Courtney Abrams. 2007. "Disappearing Acts: The Social Networks of Formerly Homeless Individuals with Co-occurring Disorders." *Social Science & Medicine* 65: 2031-2043.

Hays, Sharon. 2004. *Flat Broke with Children: Women in the Age of Welfare Reform.* New York: Oxford University Press.

Hayward, Mark D., Toni P. Miles, Eileen M. Crimmins, and Yu Yang. 2000. "The Significance of Socioeconomic Status in Explaining the Racial Gap in Chronic Health Conditions." *American Sociological Review* 65: 910-930

Hoffman, Lisa and Brian Coffey. 2008. "Dignity and Indignation: How People Experiencing Homelessness View Services and Providers." *The Social Science Journal* 45: 207-222.

Holden, Karen and Pamela J. Smock. 1991. "The Economic Costs of Marital Dissolution: Why Do Women Bear a Disproportionate Cost?" *Annual Review of Sociology* 17:51-78.

Homeless Services Network. 2009. "2009 Point in Time Count of the Homeless Population of Orange, Osceola, and Seminole Counties." Orlando: Homeless Services Network.

Hopper, Kim. 2003. *Reckoning with Homelessness.* Ithaca & London: Cornell University Press.

Hopper, Kim and Jim Baumohl. 1996. "Redefining the Cursed Word: A Historical Interpretation of American Homelessness." Pages 3-14 in J. Baumohl (Ed.), *Homelessness in America.* Phoenix, AZ: Oryx Press.

Iceland, John. 2003. *Poverty in America: A Handbook.* Berkley and Los Angeles, California: University of California Press.

Jasinski, Jana L., Jennifer Wesely, James D. Wright and Elizabeth Mustaine. 2010. *Hard Lives, Means Streets: Violence in the Lives of Homeless Women.* Boston, MA: University Press of New England.

Jocoy, Christine L. and Vincent J. Del Casino Jr. 2008. "The Mobility of Homeless People and Their Use of Public Transit in Long Beach, CA." Final Report.

Johnson, Michael P. 2008. *A Typology of Domestic Violence: Intimate Terrorism, Violent Resistance, and Situational Couple Violence.* Hanover: Northeastern University Press.

Kassab, Beth. 2003. "Decay is Roadblock to Urban Renewal," *Orlando Sentinel,* August 31: B-1.

Katz, Peter. 1993. *The New Urbanism: Toward an Architecture of Community.* New York: McGraw-Hill.

Koegel, Paul, and Audrey Burnam. 1987. "Traditional and Non-Traditional Homeless Alcoholics." *Alcohol Health and Research World* 11: 28-34.

Koegel, Paul, Audrey Burnam, and R. K. Farr, 1990. "Subsistence Adaptation among Homeless Adults in the Inner City of Los Angeles." Journal of Social Issues 46: 83-107.

Koegel, Paul, Greer Sullivan, Audrey Burnam, Sall C. Morton and Suzanne Wenzel.1999. "Utilization of Mental Health and Substance Abuse Services among Homeless Adults in Los Angeles." *Medical Care* 37: 306-317.

Koenig, David. 2007. *Realityland: True-Life Adventures at Walt Disney World.* Irvine, CA: Bonaventure Press.

Krugman, Paul. 2008. "The Poison of Poverty." *Orlando Sentinel.* February 19: A-13

Kuhn, Randall and Dennis P. Culhane. 1998. "Applying Cluster Analysis to Test a Typology of

Homelessness by Pattern of Shelter Utilization: Results from the Analysis of Administrative Data." *American Journal of Community Psychology* 26: 207- 232.

Kusmer, Kenneth. 2002. *Down and Out, On the Road: The Homeless in American History.* New York: Oxford University Press.

Lasser, Karen E., David U. Himmelstein, and Steffie Woolhandler. 2006. "Access to Care, Health Status, and Health Disparities in the United States and Canada: Results of a Cross-National Population-Based Survey." *American Journal of Public Health* 96: 1300-1307.

Lee, Barrett and Chad Farrell. 2003. "Buddy, Can You Spare a Dime? Homelessness, Panhandling, and the Public." *Urban Affairs Review* 38: 299-324.

Lee, Barrett A., Kimberly A. Tyler, and James D. Wright. 2010. "The New Homelessness Revisited." *Annual Review of Sociology* 36: 501- 522.

Lewis, Joy H., Ronald M. Anderson and Lillian Gelberg. 2003. "Health Care for Homeless Women: Unmet Needs and Barriers to Care." *Journal of General Internal Medicine* 18: 921-928.

Lichter, Daniel T. and Rukmalie Jayakody. 2002. "Welfare Reform: How Do We Measure Success?" *Annual Review of Sociology* 28: 117-141.

Loprest, Pamela. 1999. "Families Who Left Welfare: Who Are They and How Are They Doing?" The Urban Institute.

Loewentheil, Nathaniel and Christian E. Weller. 2005. "The Renter Squeeze: Minority and Low Income Renters Feel Pressures From Housing Boom and Weak Labor Market." *Review of Policy Research* 22: 755-769.

Mannheim, Steve. 2003. *Walt Disney and the Question for Community.* Burlington, VT: Ashgate Publishers.

Marmer, Theodore, Morris Barer, and Robert Evans. 1994. *Why Are Some People Healthy and Others Not? The Determinants of Health of Populations*. Hawthorne, NY: Aldine.

Mayor's Parramore Task Force, 2004. Orlando, FL: Office of the Mayor, June 23.

McLean, Diane E., Shawn Bowen, Karen Drezner, Amy Rowe, Peter Sherman, Scott Schroeder, Karen Redlener, Irwin Redlener. 2004. :Asthma among Homeless Children." *Archives of Pediatric and Adolescent Medicine* 158: 244-249.

Mendes, Elizabeth. 2010. "Hawaii Leads in Wellbeing; West Virginia Ranks Last." July 23. Available at: http://www.gallup.com/poll/141539/Hawaii-Leads-Wellbeing-West-Virginia-Ranks-Last.aspx#2

Meyer, Daniel R. and Geoffrey L. Wallace. 2009. Poverty levels and trends in comparative perspective. *Focus*. 1-13. Available at: http://www.ssc.wisc.edu/irpweb/publications/focus/pdfs/foc262b.pdf

Minkler, Meredith and Ann Robertson. 1991. "Generational Equity and Public Health Policy: A Critique of "Age/Race War" Thinking." *Journal of Public Health Policy* 12: 324-344.

Mishel, Lawrence, Jared Bernstein, and Sylvia Allegretto. 2007. *The State of Working America 2006/2007. An Economic Policy Institute Book*. Ithaca, N.Y.: ILR Press, an imprint of Cornell University Press.

Mishel, Lawrence, Jared Bernstein, and Heidi Shierholz. 2009. *The State of Working America 2008/2009*. Ithaca: Economic Policy Institute.

Mohl, Raymond A. 1984. "Miami's Metropolitan Government: Retrospect and Prospect," *The Florida Historical Quarterly* 63: 24-50.

Morgenstern, Jon, Christopher W. Kahler, Ronni M. Frey and Erich Labouvie, 1996. Modeling Therapeutic Response to 12-step Treatment: Optimal Responders, Nonresponders, and Partial Responders." *Journal of Substance Abuse* 8: 45-59.

Morrison, David S. 2009. "Homelessness as an Independent Risk Factor for Mortality: Results from a Retrospective Cohort Study," *International Journal of Epidemiology* 38: 877-883.

Moss, Andrew R., Judith A. Hahn, Jacqueline P. Tulsky, Charles L. Daley, Peter M. Small, and Phillip C. Hopewell. 2000. "Tuberculosis in the Homeless: A Prospective Study." *American Journal of Respiratory and Critical Care Medicine* 162: 460-464.

Mueser, Kim T., Douglas L. Noordsy, and Robert E. Drake. 2003. *Integrated Treatment for Dual Disorders: A Guide to Effective Practice*. New York: Guilford Press.

Mussenden, Sean. 2004. "For Many Disney Jobs, the Future is Part Time." *The Orlando Sentinel*. December 5.

National Coalition for the Homeless. 2006. "Factsheet: Who is Homeless?"

National Coalition for the Homeless (in conjunction with six other homeless advocacy organizations), 2009. Foreclosure to Homelessness 2009: The Forgotten Victims of the Subprime Crisis. Retrieved on August 3, 2010 at http://www.nationalhomeless.org/advocacy/ForeclosuretoHomelessness0609.pdf

Newman, Katherine S. 1999. *No Shame in My Game: The Working Poor in the Inner City*. New York: Alfred A Knopf and Russell Sage Foundation.

Nissen, Bruce, Eric Schultz, and Yue Zhang. 2007. *Walt Disney World's Hidden Costs: The Impact of Disney's Wage Structure on the Greater Orlando Area*. Miami: Center for Labor Research and Studies, Florida International University.

Nock, Steven L. 1998. *Marriage in Men's Lives*. New York: Oxford University Press.

North, Carol S. and Elizabeth M. Smith. 1993. "A Comparison of Homeless Men and Women: Different Populations, Different Needs." *Community Mental Health Journal* 29: 423-431.

O'Connell, James J., Jill S. Roncarati, Eileen C. Riley, Cheryl A. Kane, Sharon K. Morrison, Stacy E. Swain, Joslyn S. Allen & Kendall Jones. 2004. "Old and Sleeping Rough: Elderly Homeless Persons on the Streets of Boston." *Journal of Long-Term Home Health Care* 22: 101-106.

O'Connell, James. 2005. "Premature Mortality in Homeless Populations: A Review of the Literature." Nashville: National Health Care for the Homeless Council, Inc.

Orlando Sentinel. 2009. "Mission Undone," *Orlando Sentinel* November 20.

O'Toole, Thomas P., Alicia Conde-Martel, Jeanette L. Gibbon, Barbara H. Hanusa, Paul J. Freyder, Michael J. Fine. 2007. "Where Do People Go When They First Become Homeless? A Survey of Homeless Adults in the USA." *Health & Social Care in the Community* 15: 446-453.

Orr, Charles. 2006. *Homelessness: A Challenge to African American Males.* Mustang, OK: Tate Publishing.

Padgett, Deborah K., Robert L. Hawkins, Courtney Abrams, and Andrew Davis. 2006. "In Their Own Words: Trauma and Substance Abuse in the Lives of Formerly Homeless Women with Serious Mental Illness." *American Journal of Orthopsychiatry* 76: 461-467.

Pearce, Diane. 1978. "The Feminization of Poverty: Women, Work and Welfare." *Urban and Social Change Review* 11: 28-36.

Pearson, David A., Amanda R. Bruggman, and Jason S. Haukoos. 2007. "Out-of-Hospital and Emergency Department Utilization by Adult Homeless Patients," *Annals of Emergency Medicine* 50: 646-652.

Piliavin, Irving, Michael Sosin, Alex H. Westerfelt and Ross L. Matsueda. 1993. "The Duration of Homeless Careers: An Exploratory Study." *Social Service Review* 67: 576-598.

Poole, Dennis L., Nancy Chepenik, and Carole Zugazaga. 1999. *Homelessness as a Regional Problem in Central Florida: Analysis and Recommendations.* Orlando, FL: Florida Institute of Government and College of Health and Public Affairs, University of Central Florida.

Population Resource Center, 2010. The Aging of America. Retrieved on August 30, 2010 at http://www.prcdc.org/300million/The_Aging_of_America/

Radley, Alan, Darrin Hodgetts and Andrea Cullen. 2006. "Fear, Romance and Transience in the Lives of Homeless Women." *Social & Cultural Geography* 7: 437-461.

Rafferty, Yvonee and Marybeth Shinn. 1991. "The Impact of Homelessness on Children. *American Psychologist*, 46: 1170– 1179.

Rank, Mark. 2007. "Measuring the Economic Racial Divide Across the Course of American Lives." *Race and Social Problems* 1- 57-66.

Rank, Mark R. and Thomas A. Hirschl. 1999. "Estimating the Proportion of Americans Ever Experiencing Poverty During Their Elderly Years." *Journals of Gerontology* 54B: S184-S193.

Rayburn, Rachel and James D. Wright. 2009. "Homeless Men in Alcoholics Anonymous: Barriers to Achieving and Maintaining Sobriety." *Journal of Applied Social Science* 3: 55-70.

Rice, Douglas and Barbara Sard. 2007. "The Effects of the Federal Budget Squeeze on Low-Income Housing Assistance." Center on Budget and Policy Priorities.

Rich, Diane Watt, Thomas A. Rich, and Larry C. Mullins. 1995. *Old and Homeless – Double Jeopardy.* Westport, CT: Auburn House.

Richards, Tara N., Tammy S. Garland, Vic W. Bumphus, and Roger Thompson. 2010. Personal and Political?: Exploring the Feminization of the American Homeless Population. *Journal of Poverty, 14:* 97-115.

Robertson, Marjorie J., Richard A. Clark, Edwin D. Charlebois, Jacqueline Tulsky, Heather L. Long, David R. Bangsberg, and Andrew R. Moss. 2004. "HIV Seroprevalence Among Homeless and Marginally Housed Adults in San Francisco." *American Journal of Public Health* 94: 1207-1217.

Robertson, Marjorie, Natalie Harris, and Nancy Fritz. 2007. "Rural Homelessness." Paper presented at HUD's 2007 National Symposium on Homelessness Research, February.

Rog, Debra J. and John C. Buckner, 2007. "Homeless Families and Children." Chapter Four in D. Dennis, G. Locke and J. Khadduri (eds), *Toward Understanding Homelessness: The 2007 National Symposium on Homelessness Research.* Washington, DC: US Department of Housing and Urban Development and US Department of Health and Human Services.

Rosenheck, Robert, Ellen Bassuk, and Amy Salomon. 1999. Special Populations of Homeless Americans. In L. Fosburg and D. Dennis (Eds.) "Practical Lessons: The 1998 National Symposium on Homelessness Research." U.S. Department of Housing and Urban Development and the U.S. Department of Health and Human Services, August.

Ross, Andrew. 1999. *The Celebration Chronicles: Life, Liberty and the Pursuit of Property Value in Disney's New Town.* New York: Ballatine Books.

Rossi, Peter H. 1991. *Down and Out in America: The Origins of Homelessness.* Chicago: University of Chicago Press.

Rossi, Peter H., James D. Wright, Gene Fisher, and Georgia Willis. 1987. "The Urban Homeless: Estimating Composition and Size." *Science* 235: 1336 - 1341.

Schneider, Mike. 2009. "Orange Co. Joins Ranks of Majority-Minority." Associated Press News Release, May 14.

Schutt, Russell K., Benjamin Weinstein, and Walter E. Penk. 2005. "Housing Preferences of Homeless Veterans with Dual Diagnosis." *Psychiatric Services, 56*: 350-352.

Schwartz, Mary and Ellen Wilson 2008. "Who Can Afford To Live in a Home?: A Look at Data from the 2006 American Community Survey." US Census Bureau.

Scott, Michael S. 2002. *Panhandling.* Washington DC: US Department of Justice, Office of Community-Oriented Policing Services.

Schaffner Goldberg, Gertrude and Eleanor Kremen (Eds). 1990. *The Feminization of Poverty: Only in America?* New York: Greenwood Publishing.

Shapiro, Thomas. 2004. *The Hidden Cost of Being African American: How Wealth Perpetuates Inequality.* New York: Oxford Press.

Shinn, Mary Beth, Debra Rog, and Dennis Culhane. 2005. *Family Homelessness: Background Research Findings and Policy Options.* Washington: Interagency Council on Homelessness.

Shipler, David K. 2005. *The Working Poor: Invisible in America.* New York: Vintage-Random.

Siegel, Paul M. "On the Cost of Being a Negro." *Sociological Inquiry* 35: 41–57.

Smith, Neil, 1985. "Homelessness: Not one Problem but Many." *The Journal of the Institute for Socioeconomic Studies* 10: 53-67.

Smock, Pamela J., Wendy D. Manning, and Sanjiv Gupta. "The Effect of Marriage and Divorce on Women's Economic Well-Being." *American Sociological Review* 64: 794-812.

Snow, David A. Susan G. Baker, and Leon Anderson. 1989. "Criminality and Homeless Men: An Empirical Assessment." *Social Problems* 36: 532-549.

Sosin, Michael R., Piliavin, Irving and Alex H. Westerfelt. 1990. Toward a Longitudinal Analysis of Homelessness. *Journal of Social Issues* 46: 157-174.

Starrels, Marjorie E., Sally Bould and Leon J. Nicholas. 1994."The Feminization of Poverty in the United States: Gender, Race, Ethnicity, and Family Factors." *Journal of Family Issues* 15: 590-607.

Susser, Ezra S., Shang P. Lin, Sarah A. Conover and Elmer L. Struening. 1991. "Childhood Antecedents of Homelessness in Psychiatric Patients." *American Journal of Psychiatry* 148: 1026-1030.

Swarns, Rachel. 2008. "U.S. Reports Drop in Homeless Population," *The New York Times*, July 30.

Task Force on Homelessness, 1994. *Dade County Community Homelessness Plan.* Miami-Dade County, Florida: Dade County Commission.

Thomas, William I. and Dorothy S. Thomas. 1928. *The Child in America: Behavior Problems and Programs.* New York: Knopf.

Toro, Paul A. Carolyn J. Tompsett, Sylvie Lombardo, Pierre Philippot, Hilde Nachtergael, Benoit Galand, Natascha Schlienz, Nadine Stammel, Yanélia Yabar, Marc Blume, Linda MacKay, Kate Harvey. 2007. "Homelessness in Europe and the United States: A Comparison of Prevalence and Public Opinion." *Journal of Social Issues* 63: 505-524.

Treas, Judith. 1987. "The Effect of Women's Labor Force Participation on the Distribution of Income in the United States." *Annual Review of Sociology* 13: 259-88.

US Census Bureau. 2003. *Census 2000 Briefs: Veterans 2000.*

US Census Bureau. 2010. Orange County, Florida. Selected Social Characteristics in the United States: 2008. Data Set: 2008 American Community Survey 1-Year Estimates.

U.S. Department of Health and Human Services. "Temporary Assistance for Needy Families (TANF): Percent of Total U.S. Population, 1960-1999." Accessed online at www.acf.dhhs.gov/news/stats/6097rf.htm

U.S. Department of Housing and Urban Development. 2007. *The Annual Homeless Assessment Report to Congress.*

U.S. Department of Housing and Urban Development Office of Policy Development & Research. 2009. *FY2009 HUD Income Limits Briefing Material.* April 20.

U.S. Department of Labor, Bureau of Labor Statistics. 2009. "The Employment Situation: September 2009."

U.S. Department of Labor, Bureau of Labor Statistics. 2010. "Consumer Expenditures in 2008." Report 1023. March.

Valenzuela, Abel, Nik Theodore, Edwin Melendez and Ana Luz Gonzalez. 2006. *On the Corner: Day Labor in the United States.* UCLA Center for the Study of Urban Poverty.

Van de Water, Paul N. and Arloc Sherman, 2010. "Social Security Keeps 20 Million Americans Out of Poverty: A State by State Analysis." Washington: Center on Budget and Policy Priorities.

Waite, Linda J. and Maggie Gallagher. 2000. *The Case For Marriage: Why Married People Are Happier, Healthier, and Better Off Financially.* New York: Broadway Books.

Weinberg, Daniel H. 2006. *Measuring Poverty in the United States: History and Current Issues.* U.S. Census Bureau, Center for Economic Studies, Working Paper CES 06-11. Washington, DC. Available at www.ces.census.gov/index.php/ces/cespapers?down_key=101751.

White, William L., 2006. "Sponsor, Recovery Coach, Addiction Counselor: The Importance of Role Clarity and Role Integrity. "Philadelphia, PA: Philadelphia Department of Behavioral Health and Mental Retardation Services.

Willis, Jessie. 2000. "How We Measure Poverty: A History and Brief Overview." Available at: http://www.ocpp.org/poverty/how.htm

Wong, John H. and Gene L. Mason. 2001. "Reviled, Rejected but Resilient: Homeless People in Recovery and Life Skills Education." *Georgetown Journal on Poverty Law and Policy* 8: 475-503.

Wong, Yin-Ling Irene. 1997. "Patterns of Homelessness: A Review of Longitudinal Studies." Pages 135-164 in *Understanding Homelessness: New Policy and Research Perspectives*. Washington, DC: Fannie Mae Foundation.

Wright, James D. 1990. "Homelessness is Not Healthy for Children and Other Living Things." *Child and Youth Services* 14: 65-88.

----- 1991. "Poverty, Homelessness, Health, Nutrition, and Children." Pages 71-103 in J. Kryder-Coe, L. Salamon and J. Molnar (eds), *Homeless Children and Youth: A New American Dilemma*. New Brunswick, NJ: Trans-ACTION Books.

----- 2005. "The Graying of America: Implications for Health Professionals." *Journal of Long Term Home Health Care* 23: 178-184.

----- 2010. "Poverty among the U.S. Elderly under 'Old' and 'New' Poverty Definitions." *Care Management Journals* 11:3 (2010), pp. 201- 204. "

Wright, James D., Beth Rubin and Joel Devine. 1998. *Beside the Golden Door: Policy, Politics and the Homeless*. Hawthorne, NY: Aldine de Gruyter.

Wright, James D. and Joel A. Devine. 1993. "Family Backgrounds and the Substance-Abusive Homeless: The New Orleans Experience." *The Community Psychologist* 26: 35-37.

Wright, James D. and Eleanor Weber, 1987. *Homelessness and Health*. Washington, DC: McGraw Hill.

Wright, James D., Joel Devine, and Neil Eddington. 1993. "The New Orleans Homeless Substance Abusers Program," *Alcoholism Treatment Quarterly* 10: 51-64.

Wright, James D., Joel A. Devine and Charles J. Brody. 1997. "Evaluating an Alcohol and Drug Treatment Program for the Homeless: An Econometric Approach." *Evaluation and Program Planning* 20: 205 - 215.

Wright, James D., Amy M. Donley, and Tracy Dietz. 2009. "Elderly Homelessness: A Growing Concern." Chapter 16 in R. McNamara (Ed.), *Homelessness in America*, Volume 1. New York: Greenwood Publishing.

Wright, James D., Amy M. Donley, and Kevin F. Gotham. 2009. "Housing Policy, the Low Income Housing Crisis, and the Problem of Homelessness." Chapter 2 in R. McNamara (ed.), *Homelessness in America*. Volume 2. New York: Greenwood Publishing.

Zane, Richard D. 2009. "Use of EDs for Food and Shelter by Homeless People." *Annals of Emergency Medicine* 52: 598.

Zerger, Suzanne. 2002. *Substance Abuse Treatment: What Works for Homeless People? A Review of the Literature*. Nashville: National Health Care for the Homeless Council.

Zuvekas, Samuel H. and Steven C. Hill. 2000. "Income and Employment Among Homeless People: The Role of Mental Health, Health and Substance Abuse." *The Journal of Mental Health Policy and Economics* 3:153–163.

Index